A

Special Sorrows

SPECIAL SORROWS

The Diasporic Imagination of Irish, Polish, and Jewish Immigrants in the United States

Matthew Frye Jacobson

Harvard University Press
Cambridge, Massachusetts
London, England
1995

This book is printed on acid-free paper, and its binding
materials have been chosen for strength and durability.

Library of Congress Cataloging-in-Publication Data
Jacobson, Matthew Frye.
Special sorrows : the diasporic imagination of Irish, Polish, and
Jewish immigrants in the United States / by Matthew Frye Jacobson.
p.   cm.
Includes index.
ISBN 0-674-83185-3 (acid-free paper)
1. Immigrants—United States—Political activity—History—19th
century.   2. Immigrants—United States—History—19th century.
3. Irish—United States—Politics and government.   4. Poles—United
States—Politics and government.   5. Jews—United States—Politics
and government.   I. Title.
JV6477.J33   1995
304.8′73—dc20
94-31496
CIP

To my family:
Sarah Frye Jacobson and Jerry Jacobson;
Beth Smith and Carol Wright

Acknowledgments

I have incurred more than my share of debts in the years since I first came upon this topic, and they are owed to a wide circle of mentors, friends, and acquaintances.

In the years I worked under his direction, Howard Chudacoff was both an invaluable critic and *zeyer a mentsh*. He was a careful and skeptical yet always encouraging reader. I am also indebted to Mari Jo Buhle and to Robert Lee for their guidance on issues of gender and on theoretical questions of racial formation and reformation. Richard Meckel posed many crucial questions on immigration and immigrant literatures.

My research began in 1985; I trust that Carol Petillo will recognize our late-afternoon conversations as the kernel of this study. My other mentors in the American Studies Program at Boston College included Judith Smith, Christopher Wilson, Andrew Buni, and the late Janet James. My primary language teachers, Sylvia Fuks-Fried and Edmund Ronowicz, made this research possible ultimately; and, perhaps more important, they made it *seem* possible initially.

No one did as much for the overall scope of this work as Lee Kolm. Her expertise in issues of gender and questions of inclusion reframed this project from top to bottom. By her philosophical turn of mind she continually confounded my facile assumptions about power, exploitation, allegiance, enmity, strength, and expression. Joanne Melish spent a great deal of time engaging the historiographic puzzles and worries attached to the research.

David Burner has extended one kindness after another since my arrival at Stony Brook, many of which have helped to see this project into print. Karl Bottigheimer, Paul Gootenberg, and William Taylor each offered valuable advice on portions of the manuscript. The following people also shared their material, ideas, and time with me: Gail Bederman, Teresa Bill, Oscar Campomanes, Jim Cullen, Ann DuCille, Bill Ferraro, Elizabeth Francis, Carol Frost, Kevin Gaines, Todd Gernes, Linda Grasso, Bill Hart, Dagmar Herzog, Amy Kaplan, Margaret Kelleher, Kate Monteiro, Louise Newman, Thomas O'Grady, Laura Santigian, Lyde Cullen Sizer, Nancy Spiegel, and Michael Topp. Ira Livingston, Iona Man-Cheong, Nick Mirzoeff, and Kathleen Wilson engaged me in many fruitful discussions of scholarship and method. I benefited from the useful comments of the anonymous reviewers who read the manuscript for Harvard University Press. Thanks also to Carlo Corea and Amanda Friskin for their good index; Carlo, moreover, put in many hours running down biographical material on some of the figures who appear in these pages.

The work of four scholars has influenced this book decisively. David Noel Doyle and Willard Gatewood first raised the questions which have guided my own research on foreign policy and domestic pluralism; Cynthia Enloe's work on gender and international affairs has reordered my understanding of politics, both nationalist and international; and Kerby Miller's insight on the significance of emigration to the experience of immigration has changed the way I look upon the issue of international migrations.

This project was financed in part by a grant from Brown University's Center for International Studies; the final preparation of the manuscript was aided by a summer grant from the Social Sciences Division of the State University of New York at Stony Brook. The research relied heavily upon the expertise of numerous librarians and staff members, but I especially want to thank the staff of the inter-library loan office at the Rockefeller Library at Brown University, and their counterparts at the National Yiddish Book Center in Amherst, Massachusetts. Aida Donald and Anita Safran of Harvard University Press made this a far better book than the one I submitted.

Francesca Schwartz managed to stay safely out of the path of this project until 1993. (You can run, but you can't hide.) Down the homestretch she gave segments of the manuscript a very tough reading, and she helped to exorcize some of the demons that haunted my prose and my formulations. The lingering demons must be mine for keeps, as I hope I am hers.

Over the years the members of my immediate family—Sarah Frye Jacobson, Jerry Jacobson, Beth Smith, and Carol Wright—have been supportive to an extent which is patently absurd.

Contents

Note on Usage

My use of the words "immigrant" and "migrant" is principally adjectival, not literal. Following Kerby Miller's model of the culture of exile, I include in "migrant cultures" participants who are not necessarily migrants themselves. Humphrey Desmond, for example, the editor of the *Catholic Citizen,* was American-born, yet his writings and assumptions about the "sea-divided Gael" set him very much within the diasporic conventions of a distinctly migrant culture—that is, a culture for which the experience of geographical movement and resettlement was formative.

I have likewise adopted an unorthodox use of "Yiddish": I use the adjective (instead of Jewish) to modify "immigrants" in instances where the distinction between Yiddish-speaking Jews and other American Jews is crucial. In discussing American Zionism, this distinction is often as important as it is tricky: while I have been most interested in Yiddish-speaking East European immigrants, it is impossible to discuss the movement as a whole without reference to non-Yiddish speakers like Rosa Sonneschein and Richard Gottheil, assimilated, Western European Jews who staffed the upper echelons of American Zionist organizations. The adjective "Yiddish," if unusual, has in many instances seemed clearer than "Jewish" and less cumbersome than "East European immigrant Jewish."

Special Sorrows

Introduction:
The Diasporic Imagination

> Here at our sea-washed, sunset gates shall stand
> A mighty woman with a torch, whose flame
> Is the imprisoned lightning, and her name
> Mother of Exiles.
>
> —Emma Lazarus, "The New Colossus"

While the story of immigration in America has been all but dominated by Emma Lazarus's imagery of "huddled masses" of economically motivated migrants, "tempest-tost" and "wretched," a second dimension of that history is nicely captured by her less famous choice of the word "exile." The word conveys those aspects of the immigrant experience most often eclipsed by American mythologies of "golden door" opportunity: the outlook of the migrant who left the old country only reluctantly; the feelings of loss of those who experienced the flight from the Old World as a form of political banishment and whose first and enduring devotion was to the land and the people they left behind. Unlike "immigrant" or even "emigrant," the word "exile" evokes the sensibility of those for whom a lamentable absence from the Old World was among the most salient aspects of life in the New.

Despite the economic basis of most international migrations in the nineteenth century, many of the newcomers experienced emigration as inherently political. The periods of peak migration—the Famine era in Ireland, the decades following the May Laws in Russia—represented times of crisis for the sending countries. Political interpretations of these crises were inescapable among the intelligentsia, and émigré leaders sought in various ways to impress upon the masses the political, structural dimension of their circumstances. Addressing his countrymen and women from exile in Switzerland in 1879, for example, Polish leader Agaton Giller wrote: "It is a fact . . . that almost a half million Poles have gathered in America. This fact cannot be reversed. This situation was created by a fate unkind to the nation—by the miserable and criminal politics of our enemies, who took as their purpose the ruin of the Polish nation, and by means of Poles' weakness in their own land motivated or compelled them to emigrate."[1]

Less politically active migrants may not have shared Giller's sophistication in broadly interpreting the plight of a Poland, an Ireland, or a Russia. But neither could they have been completely unaware of the scale and import of the events taking place in their homelands. Migration addressed the immediate, individual problems posed by changing land-ownership patterns, the upheavals of industrialization, or legal persecutions and pogroms. But the individual solution of departure did not foster the migrant's conviction that theirs were simply isolated, idiosyncratic problems. The greatest waves of migration, by definition, took place within a context of broad social and political crisis; an awareness of this crisis was among the meager bundles which some immigrants hauled ashore with them upon their arrival.

American historians tend to write about immigration as arrival and settlement, but the migrants themselves often experienced the move—and the weight of emigrant cultures perpetually enforced interpretations of the move—as departure and absence.[2] The point is compellingly made in Eva Hoffman's recent memoir of migration from Poland to Canada, *Lost in Translation*. Hoffman recalls her surprise upon first seeing faraway Poland on a world map from the perspective of a Canadian schoolgirl. Until then, she muses, Poland had occupied a place in the imagination "coeval with the dimensions of reality, and all other places on the globe have been measured by their distance from it." But now this onetime home has become "a distant spot, somewhere on the peripheries of the imagination . . . I have been dislocated from my own center of the world, and the world has been shifted away from my center."[3] In her attention to this "internal geography,"[4] Hoffman reminds us that migration entailed departure as well as arrival; that presence in the New World entailed a poignant absence from the Old; that packing off to North America meant taking up residence on the periphery of one's former world, and yet former centers did not necessarily lose their centrality.

In recasting the immigrant experience as largely an emigrant experience, I seek to recover the extent to which the beleaguered peoples left behind—imagined as nations—retained a central position in the migrants' ideological geographies. Collective emigration nourished a political culture based on ideas of injury and displacement. For many of the Irish, Polish, and East European Jewish migrants who came to the United States in the second half of the nineteenth century, allegiance to the old centers of experience translated into an emergent, New World zeal for Old World nationalisms: Irish nationalism, Polish nationalism, Zionism, and various brands of Yiddish labor nationalism. What forms did immigrant nationalisms assume on American soil? How did Irish, Polish, and Zionist national ideologies translate into specific understandings of American citizenship and American state power? To what extent has life in the diaspora communities remained oriented toward the politics of the old center, and what has been the legacy of immigrant nationalism as immigrant politics has gradually become ethnic politics over the course of the twentieth century?

Answers to these questions underlie the structure of the book. In Part I, I examine aspects of nationalism in these three immigrant cultures and trace their nationalist ideologies as they pervaded everyday life in the late nineteenth century. Following an outline of the Old World background of the three movements, the focus turns upon the most overt political manifestations of immigrant nationalism in the United States in organizations like the Polish National Alliance, the Clan na Gael, and the Federation of American Zionists. Going beyond strictly political arenas, Chapter 2 is a discussion of the nationalist fabric of immigrant popular culture: the tenor of the immigrant press, the icons and mythologies of popular religion, the secular calendar of national holidays, and the popular formulas of vernacular theatre. Chapter 3 is devoted to immigrant literary life and the ways in which Old and New World poetry and fiction, popularized in cheap editions and in the penny papers, at once reinforced the sense of collective national destiny among these scattered peoples and advanced their arguments for political self-determination.

This pervasive nationalism constituted a critical dimension of the immigrants' response to their adopted country's "splendid little wars" at the turn of the century. Ongoing nationalist discussion provided the principles which many immigrants used to assess the meaning of American conduct. This is the terrain of Part II (Chapters 4 and 5). Scholars have most often approached immigrant nationalism as a matter of divided loyalty, whose most telling moments, of course, were when the country of origin and the adopted country came into direct conflict—World War I for German-Americans or World War II for Japanese-Americans, for instance.[5] In this book, in contrast, the Spanish-Cuban-American and the Philippine-American wars of 1898–1903—wars in which Ireland, Poland, and Zion were nowhere in the picture—are taken as a sounding board for gauging the salience of national-liberationist motifs in these three immigrant cultures. The unique circumstance of an anticolonial war followed immediately by an imperialist adventure on the part of the United States became the occasion for a great deal of commentary on national rights, international justice, the uses of American power, and the duties of American citizenship. Wartime debates reveal a great deal about the relation between Old World political ideals and emerging, Progressive Era definitions of Americanism, even though loyalties were not strained in precisely the same way as when the immigrants' countries of origin were at war with their adopted country.

The subject of Chapter 4 is the immigrant discussion of the Cuban situation in the period of American intervention in 1898. The Cuban revolution and U.S. intervention on behalf of the revolutionaries was a highly resonant cause. Spanish domination and atrocities in Cuba were reminiscent of British rule in Ireland, the Russification and Prussianization of Poland, and the legal circumscription of Jewish rights in Eastern Europe. As early as 1897 the Polish National Alliance, for instance, passed a resolution of sympathy for "the brave sons of Cuba, who, like the Polish heroes of yore, sacrifice their blood, property, and life for Cuban liberty."[6]

Editorial debate and popular demonstration were laced with Old World referents to national rights and the nearly sacred obligations of national rebellion; the war likewise provided an unexpected outlet for the ideals of militarized masculinity which characterized nationalist culture. The immigrants' engagement in the Cuban cause reflects more than their desire simply to prove themselves as loyal Americans. Interpretations of the Cuban plight, the meanings of soldiery, and the public rituals surrounding the military venture all reflected a complex, enduring interest in the prospects for these groups' three subjugated homelands.

Chapter 5 explores immigrant discussion of the Philippine cause, as the United States sought to put down the Filipino independence movement in the aftermath of Spain's defeat. When Admiral Dewey defeated the Spanish fleet in Manila Bay in May of 1898, the United States took upon itself the decision of what to do with the Philippines. As U.S. imperialist sentiment rose to high tide, and particularly after fighting had broken out between Filipino and American soldiers in February 1899, immigrants found their adopted country suddenly on the conqueror's side of the imperial equation. "How do you like it," asked James Jeffrey Roche of the Boston *Pilot*, "you who thought you were escaping tyranny forever when you became American citizens?"[7]

Not all had shared this faith in American ideals or fancied themselves to have "escaped tyranny forever," but Roche was not alone in identifying U.S. activity in the Philippines as a betrayal of nationalist principles and an ironic breakaway from the initial goal of Cuban liberation.

In the political life of these groups, the war brought New World aspirations into unforeseen collision with Old World sensibilities. As Elizabeth Gurley Flynn later recalled, "My father saw the whole picture clearly way back in 1898. When one understood British imperialism it was an open window to all imperialism."[8] Old World experience provided the venom for a bitter critique of the emergent policy of American imperialism in the Pacific.

Yet even some vociferous nationalists embraced their adopted country's "mission" in the Philippines as their own, and they most often did so on the basis of race. "In regard to civilization," wrote one Milwaukee Pole in defense of imperialism, "the Polish nation stands higher beyond comparison than the Filipinos."[9] While Old World sensibilities broadened the stream of American political discourse, it is equally important to point out the significance of whiteness to the European immigrants' acceptance of (and in) America. True, nationalism lent itself easily to opposing America's "manifest destiny" in the Pacific, but Euro-American racialism provided an alternative logic by which this destiny could be accepted, even applauded. Focus on the Philippine Question thus affords a unique angle of vision on the perceptual history of Irish, Polish, and Jewish migration, as immigrants negotiated the ideological terrain of group allegiance (couched in nationalist terms) on the one hand, and emergent notions of Americanness (couched in racial terms) on the other.

The last chapter offers snapshots of the diasporic imagination at work later in the twentieth century. Immigrant nationalisms did not simply go to the grave with the members of the migrating generation; on the contrary, a cultural thread links the diasporic political vision of the immigrants with the ethnic gestures of their grandchildren and great-grandchildren. Late-twentieth-century debates over the IRA, Solidarity, or Israel among American ethnics flow in part from a longer history of New World engagement in Old World politics. Although this section is more suggestive than conclusive, in it I propose that the ebb and flow of ethnic identification itself may usefully be examined in the transnational context of America's many diaspora communities and the turbulent politics of their overseas homelands. The so-called

Troubles in Ulster, that is, may be part of what keeps the Irish in America Irish.[10]

I came at this topic from many directions at once. First, I have taken a cue from the recent trend in immigration historiography to recover "the inner world" of the immigrants, in Robert Orsi's phrase—not only to recount what immigrants experienced, but further to reconstruct the worldview through which they experienced it.[11] The project is especially indebted to Kerby Miller's work on "the culture of exile" among the Irish in North America.[12] Like Miller, I am interested in the extent to which international migration registered as "exile" on the political-moral consciousness of the migrants and their descendants, and the ways in which this outlook was embedded in immigrant (and later, ethnic) cultures.

I have been equally influenced by literary, cultural, and American Studies approaches, which generally have made but a small impression on immigration historiography proper. In thinking about "the inner world" of immigration, I initially conceived this as an intellectual history, drawing upon David Hollinger's conception of "a social as well as an intellectual activity [which] entails interaction between minds, and ... revolves around something possessed in common." For Hollinger, "the most concrete and functional elements shared" by a community are *questions*.[13] At the heart of this study, then, is a constellation of turn-of-the-century questions concerning peoplehood: questions regarding assimilation; questions regarding the meaning of migration; questions regarding national rights and national destiny; questions regarding Old and New World obligations; and questions regarding patriotism and (in the parlance of the period) "patriotism of race."

Further, I have found literary approaches to the various texts of immigrant culture (whether poems, stories, newspaper editorials, or parades) to be useful in examining the workings of nationalist ideology. Mary Poovey's work on Victorian England, for instance, proved an inspiring model for pursuing the issue not only of the engagement of minds but of the engagement of ideologies.[14] To cite a specific case: conceptions of nation are integrally entwined with certain conceptions of gender, most often some version of a militarized masculinity and an eternal, essentialized, culture-keeping femininity. The "ideological work" (in Poovey's phrase) by which cultural forms articulate, challenge, uphold, or refashion these intersecting ideologies is central to my treatment of these three nations and their diasporas. The interaction between the overarching ideologies of gender and nation, and their power mutually to sustain one another, constitute an important dimension of the engagement of individual minds.

Hence I concentrate far less on questions of economics, class, labor, and mobility than has been customary in immigration historiography, and far more on matters of superstructure: the cultural production of narratives and representations. The phrase "diasporic imagination" itself refers precisely to this realm of ideologies and engagement of minds: both the shared currency of cultural imagery, and the mindset of the individual as he or she navigates the inner geography of international migration.[15] There has been no shortage of scholarly attention to the hegemonic function of nationalism in serving particular class interests within a given national group.[16] But nationalist icons and rhetorics were deployed for quite different purposes and to quite different effect by different factions within each of these groups. The language of Irish nationalism, for instance, was employed to express *both* the middle-class aspirations of the lace-curtain Irish in their quest for American respectability *and* the challenges of the Knights of Labor to the inequities of capitalism.

A cultural approach is useful because Nationalism was not exclusively a hegemonic frame by which elites maintained allegiance and insured their own stewardship of group resources. The nationalist imagery was constantly appropriated, contested, and reappropriated in ways that multiplied its meanings for these transplanted communities. Nationalist idioms functioned to counter New World patterns of ethnic hierarchy, to salve immigrants' sense of having abandoned their compatriots to an unkind fate in the Old World, and to galvanize group members for a number of political or social aims—labor strikes, entrepreneurial cooperation, proto-feminist protest, or turning out the vote on behalf of the local machine.

Concentrating on the realm of representation, of course, is not without its problems. In examining those elements of experience which can be articulated, the historian necessarily casts his or her lot with the articulate. As Brook Thomas comments, "the question of representation turns back on the new historicism itself. How representative is the evidence employed in its analysis? And if it is representative, what does it represent?"[17] A thorny question indeed, and one which unites new historicism with an older, myth-and-symbol paradigm in American Studies to an extent which is currently unfashionable to admit.

I have sought to minimize these problems in two ways. First, I have explored rather broadly the texture of immigrant cultures. While the prolific editorialists of the *Irish World, Zgoda,* the *Abend blatt,* and other journals serve as focal figures in this examination, the study also documents participatory practices like street demonstrations and parades, sermons, the resolutions of voluntary organizations, letters to the editor, and popular ballads, poems, stories, novels, and amateur and professional theatrical productions. This analysis of the popular as well as the "high" cultural artifact, of the participatory as well as the literary, of the sacred as well as the secular, is meant to diminish the problem of relying upon isolated intellectual informants.

Second, I wish to underscore the various internal divisions within each group along lines of class, gender, tactical orientation, and political stripe, even while stressing the common cultural paradigm of the diasporic imagination. James Jeffrey Roche does not represent anyone but James Jeffrey Roche. Rather, the pervasiveness of nationalist icons and mythologies—of which Roche's writing is but one manifestation—helps to plot the field upon which much immigrant discussion took place, however raucously. His work, taken along with a multitude of other articulations and cultural forms, speaks not to the historiographic goblin of consensus, but rather to Hollinger's "concrete and functional elements shared" by the Irish in North America: the shared questions of peoplehood, collective destiny, orientation, and obligation.

None of this does away with Brook Thomas's question of representation; it simply adds to the volume of material whose representativeness the wary reader will question. But the risk has seemed worthwhile. The social emphasis in immigration scholarship threatens to mute the immigrant voice and fully to divorce immigrants, as historical subjects, from the historiographic notion of "intellectual activity [which] entails interaction between minds." The sum of immigrant thought will never be known, it is true; but we need not ignore the accessible fragments simply because they are fragmentary. The traces left by people like Roche, Teofila Samolinska, Leon Kobrin, Katherine Conway, and Private Józef Nowalski have been obscured by language barriers and by the cliometric methods of much social historiography.

Why, out of all of the possibilities, a comparison of Irish, Polish, and Jewish immigrant cultures? The three differ in many important respects, and they offer kaleidoscopic points of contrast; the experience or character of one—in terms of religion, social profile, timing of migration, or linguistic relation to the host culture—will often cast a nice light on certain aspects of the others, and vice versa. Two chief structural differences are especially worth emphasizing at the outset: first, by the 1890s the Irish had achieved political dominance in many of the American cities in which the Poles and Jews were freshly arriving. And second, both before and after the establishment of an independent Poland, Poles returned to the homeland at conspicuously high rates as compared with Irish-American returns to Ireland, or Jewish re-emigration either to Europe, or, after 1948, to Israel. Before and after World War I, for instance, Polish returns were calculated in the tens of thousands, while the corresponding figures for Jewish re-emigration in the years immediately following the establishment of Israel were most often calculated merely in the hundreds.[18]

Nonetheless, success in American urban politics does not seem to have displaced Irish nationalist narratives and symbols in Irish-American culture; and if post–World War I Polish re-emigration rates are high by comparison to other groups, they are considerably *lower* than one might expect on the basis of pre-independence figures. Re-emigration figures for the pre-independence years of 1908–1914, for instance, had run well into the tens of thousands; and the impressive rate for 1921 (42,207) still did not match the figure for 1908 (46,727).[19] The diasporic imagination, in other words, often has more to do with how one sees and thinks about the world than with where one ultimately chooses to live in it. As Marshall Sklare discovered in one survey of Jewish American attitudes, 94 percent of Jewish adults professed to feel positively about Israel, but only 4 percent expressed interest in actually living there.[20] Perhaps similar surveys of Irish-America and Polonia would have turned up similar attitudes.

In any case, despite their many and obvious differences, throughout my research on these three cultures I have consistently been struck by the similarities among them; and, in general, it is similarity which I have stressed. In this respect my work is meant to challenge the trends toward Balkanization and exceptionalism which currently characterize much of the field. Close studies of single ethnic groups in particular locales yield substantial insights into the social processes attending international migration, but the use of the microscopic lens threatens to exclude some important features of the overall picture—the power of migration itself, for example, to leave a similar imprint on peoples and cultures dissimilar in myriad other respects.

I return, finally, to Eva Hoffman's notion of immigration as displacement. Historians have long investigated the place of the Old World—its habits, customs, orientations—in the lives of those now removed to the New. The most fundamental shift in the scholarship is best summed up by the contrast between Oscar Handlin's *Uprooted* (1952) and John Bodnar's *Transplanted* (1985). At issue is a constellation of polar opposites in the rendering of the immigrant experience—alienation or adjustment; change or continuity; loneliness or community; fatalism or agency. This study discovers some elements of both interpretations: transplanting, in that immigrants were not simply launched into a new American cosmos but held tenaciously to earlier attachments and orientations; uprooting, in that nationalist culture at once fed and fed upon a sense of displacement much closer to Handlin's model of alienation than to Bodnar's model of robust adaptation. It is this sense of cherished injury which is so nicely captured in Rosa Luxemburg's description of nationalism as a parcel of "special sorrows."

The Irish, Polish, and Yiddish migrants' enduring psychic engagement with Ireland, Poland, and Zion defies linear models of assimilation or standard formulations of hyphenated identity. As John Boyle O'Reilly described the Irish contribution to America in "The Exile of the Gael,"

> . . . the hearts we bring for Freedom are washed in the surge
> of tears;
> And we claim our right by a people's fight outliving a
> thousand years![21]

Not their willingness to turn away from former allegiances, therefore, but their very commitment to Old World struggle and their hearts cleansed by the special sorrows of national oppression constituted the chief Irish claim to America. Drawing upon the traces left by the many who resettled in the United States in the nineteenth century, this portrait of the diasporic imagination—that sense of undying membership in, and unyielding obligation to, a distant national community—may fruitfully complicate the usual saga of immigrants coming to America and ineluctably becoming American.

I

The Culture of the Diaspora

1

Exiles, Pilgrims, Wanderers: Migration in the Context of National Struggle

All this force and fraud will fail, Mr. Gladstone. You are now, unlike the past, dealing with two Irelands. The Greater Ireland is on this side of the Atlantic. This is the base of operations. We in America furnish the sinews of war. We in America render moral aid.

—Patrick Ford, *Criminal History of the British Empire*

In Ireland, Poland, and the Jewish ghettos of Eastern Europe, the periods of heaviest emigration were also characterized by an intensifying interest in ideals of national liberation. Emigration thus came to hold a special place in the political symbolism of the envisaged "nation," both among Old World political leaders and among the emigrants themselves. Three metaphors emerged to describe the three respective groups of emigrants and to underscore their links to the continuing struggle for liberation: the Irish exile, the Polish pilgrim, and the Jewish wanderer. Not emigrants merely, but living symbols of oppression, these figures poignantly testified to the horrors of misrule and tacitly argued in favor of the nationalist solution to regional woes.

The figure of the exile gained wide currency in popular parlance among the Irish. Folk culture itself offered an array of precedents: as Kerby Miller points out, the Irish lords of song and story had taken flight only under duress, "sighing all the weary day and weeping all the night."[1] Throughout the Famine period and after, the expression surfaced and resurfaced among publicists along every point of the political spectrum. In an open letter to Great Britain (1881), firebrand Patrick Ford accused England's "Great Criminal Class" of having "driven millions into exile beyond the Atlantic waves." When Maud Gonne visited the United States on a speaking tour in 1898, the Irishwomen of New York officially greeted her on behalf of those "who are exiled from our beloved island." The convocation ritual of the Ladies' Auxiliary of the Ancient Order of Hibernians included a supplication to the Lady of Limerick: "we lay at your feet all our anxieties for our Faith and for our dear Fatherland from which we are exiles." And even an assimilationist address by Boston *Pilot* editor John Boyle O'Reilly drew upon the theme of exile in conjuring the image of the American melting-pot: "Exile is God's alchemy!/ Nations He forms like metals."[2] The casually blurred distinction between exile and emigration, between political fate and economic necessity, kept the cause of the homeland current for the overseas community and emphasized that the Irish nation had been dispersed, perhaps, but not dissipated.

The corresponding figure of the Polish pilgrim emerged in the romantic works of Adam Mickiewicz, written in exile following the failed November rising of 1831. In his *Books of the Polish Nation and the Polish Pilgrims* Mickiewicz assigned a singular messianic role to the Polish nation in world history, and he defined a singular role for the emigrant in Polish history. "The Polish Pilgrims are the soul of the Polish nation," he wrote. "No Pole on his pilgrimage is called a wanderer, for a wanderer is a man straying without a goal; nor is he an exile, for an exile is a man exiled by the decree of the government, but his government did not exile the Pole." The pilgrim "hath made a vow to journey to the holy land, the free country."[3] Although never as common in vernacular expression as the Irish use of the word "exile," Mickiewicz's figurative "pilgrim" was widely used by later Polish leaders abroad. Colonization societies, parish priests, and nationalist organizations like the Polish National Alliance all defined their task as insuring that the Poles abroad were neither "denationalized" nor "lost for the Fatherland."

And finally, the age-old figure of the "wanderer" was deployed by Zionist leaders to underscore the fact of massive dislocation among Jewry in the east and to raise the hope of establishing a national "home." In his *Aims of Zionism* (1898) Richard Gottheil cited the flight of East European "unfortunates," combined with the unwillingness of the West to absorb them, as the most salient arguments of all in favor of a Jewish state. "But perhaps I am wrong, and the Jew is destined ever to remain a wanderer?"[4] Diaspora nationalist S. M. Dubnow likewise couched his later discussion of emigration in the political/religious language of the historic Jewish condition: "the new Egyptian oppression," "the land of bondage," "exodus," and "wandering."[5] Like the Irish exiles and the Polish pilgrims, the wanderers themselves tacitly yet eloquently pleaded the nationalist case.

Not only did emigration come to symbolize the political plight of each nation, moreover, but nationalist leaders uniformly assigned the resulting communities-in-exile critical roles in their ongoing national struggles. "No more can the Cromwellian system be applied to Ireland," cried John Boyle O'Reilly. "Why? Because of the expatriated millions, because of the great moral and political force the Irish and their descendants have in many great countries." In Michael Davitt's finer phrase, Irish-America was to be "the avenging wolfhound of Irish nationalism."[6] Agaton Giller similarly argued that, if the Poles abroad maintained their Polishness and their Polish ties, "we will see that the evil designs calculated to ruin Poland will be overturned . . . to her greater power and glory." He and others seized upon America's Polonia as the nation's "fourth partition," an indispensable battalion in the war for liberation.[7] And as early as 1881 Emma Lazarus identified American Jewry as the chosen of The Chosen, uniquely situated to aid in the "repatriation" of the Jews to Zion. "No other Jews in the world," she wrote, "can bring to bear upon the enterprise . . . such long and intimate familiarity with the blessings and delights of liberty."[8]

The political culture of each of these emigrant groups, then, contained an element of compelling obligation: by nationalist lights, the emigrants not only ought to dwell upon the nature of the calamity by which they now found themselves in a state of exile, pilgrimage, or wandering in North America, but they should recognize as well the unique vantage point from which they might now serve the nation they had left behind.

Nationalism and Migration

Nationalism itself requires definition at the outset, partly because the word carries an imprecise meaning in vernacular usage, and partly because its theorists, from Ernest Renan to Rosa Luxemburg to Hans Kohn, have used the term in very different ways. In both common parlance and scholarly discourse the term often becomes confounded with the related phenomena of patriotism, chauvinism, and ethnic consciousness. How does nationalism differ from these other forms of group feeling and expression? How is it related? What is the relation of international migration to these varieties of group feeling?

One theorist has recently offered some especially useful distinctions. James Blaut, Jr., both a Marxist and a Puerto Rican nationalist, emphasizes two critical facets of nationalism. First, unlike various pride movements or a simple love of country, nationalism in his view necessarily involves the question of state power and its uses. No movement is truly nationalist which does not attempt to grasp state power or otherwise affect its disposition. And second, nationalism is not a static or constant "tribal impulse," but has the dynamic quality of a struggle between two contending forces. No nationalist struggle can be properly understood without equal account of whatever counterforce is in opposition to its aims.[9]

Blaut's emphasis on state power has the virtue of sharpening the distinction between nationalism and simple chauvinism; it also lends cohesion to a variety of political situations which are similar but not identical. His definition of nationalism includes struggles of liberation from colonizing states (Irish, Cuban, and Philippine nationalism); the struggle to liberate and reunify a divided state (Polish nationalism); the struggle to create a new state (Zionism); and the struggle for recognition as an autonomous national minority within an envisioned socialist state (Bundism).[10] Each of these movements sought in some way either to seize the reins of state power, or significantly to alter its existing character on the behalf of a specific group. And each movement was influenced by the nature of the opposition it encountered on the part of one or more ruling powers.[11]

Notwithstanding its central aspiration to state power, nationalism does often blur into other, related varieties of group feeling. In galvanizing their followers, nationalist leaders inevitably depend on ethnic consciousness (the sense of being "a people"); they often attempt to fuel patriotism (the love of country); and they sometimes lapse into the flattering rhetoric of chauvinism (the claim of a group's superiority to other groups). These categories are not marked off from one another in every instance by bold, clean lines. A single stanza by Yiddish poet Morris Rosenfeld thoroughly scrambles the categories: "O, no, I cannot go begging with shame for a home in foreign lands— / Old bands of love yet bind me fast to my beloved country."[12] Here the reference to homelessness in a "foreign" land denotes ethnic consciousness; the binding ties to "my beloved country" bespeak patriotism; and in the context of actual Jewish statelessness, these lines seem tacitly to endorse a Zionist political solution.

Blaut's distinction between movements that involve state power and those that do not is critical nonetheless. Ethnic consciousness in itself does not go far enough in accounting for liberationist efforts. An acute awareness of one's Polish ethnicity, for example, could be sustained without ever considering the prospect of reuniting Polish lands as a sovereign nation. Nor do patriotism and simple chauvinism go very far in explaining why many European nationalists responded so sympathetically to the plight of *other* oppressed nations—including Cuba and the Philippines. Jewish chauvinism alone could not have prompted Moishe Zeifert to decry Spain's rule in Cuba as "the Spanish inquisition of the nineteenth century." Likewise, James Jeffrey Roche was expressing something more than mere Irish patriotism when, as the tide of U.S. expansionism rose in 1898, he lamented "the prospect of extending to the Philippines . . . the accursed system of foreign rule which has so long blighted Ireland."[13]

Although frequently intertwined with other forms of group feeling, nationalism itself is thus a very particular concern for issues of state power, domination, liberation, and sovereignty. As the term is used throughout this study, it refers to the activities and debates directly surrounding such political movements, and to the ethos attending these movements—the general outlook by which questions of group identity were infused with political meaning. As Irish leader Michael Davitt announced in 1903, "I have come from a journey through the Jewish Pale, a convinced believer in the remedy of Zionism."[14] This endorsement of the Zionist political solution on the part of an Irish activist nicely illustrates both the programmatic element and the underlying sensibility of nationalism as it is defined here.

While this first qualification distinguishes nationalism from the less politicized phenomenon of ethnic consciousness, Blaut's second major proposition—that nationalism is constituted by the dynamic tension between opposing forces—underscores just how closely the two are related. This second contention is of special import in respect to the politicizing influence of international migration. Blaut's emphasis on "struggle" is no doubt aimed at defending nationalist politics as potentially progressive, and clarifying his own position as committed nationalist and devoted Marxist.[15] But in identifying nationalism as a two-sided struggle, Blaut indirectly discloses the kinship between nationalism proper and what recent sociologists have called "emergent ethnicity."

Like nationalism, ethnic identity is neither fixed nor constant. It is not immutably rooted in a given group's shared heritage, nor does it correspond to any set of biological facts. Rather, it is situational—a fluid cultural construction which shifts over time in response to new social, economic, and political circumstances. Peasants from Silesia or County Cork, for instance, might discover and embrace their "Polishness" or "Irishness" only after arriving in urbanized and culturally diverse settings like Chicago or New York. Further, the ethnic boundaries distinguishing one group from the next may themselves shift over time: discrete groups may merge and redefine themselves as a single group in response to the demographics and social conditions of a given locale. The relatively recent formation of Latino identity is a vivid instance of this fluid ethnicity; the shifting and localized distinction between Polish and Lithuanian identities is another.[16]

If nationalism is a dynamic encounter rather than a static condition, then its relationship to the fluid, situational construct of ethnic identity is clear. Both depend on one group's defining itself *against* another (or others). Polish nationalism as we know it emerged from the long history of invasion, partition, and foreign rule, just as the Polishness of the mass of peasants awaited discovery in a foreign land. The surge in ethnic identity which often accompanied migration and resettlement provided an especially fertile medium for the full bloom of political nationalism.

As early as 1879, Agaton Giller himself recognized the "emergent" Pole abroad as particularly ripe for enlistment in the nationalist cause. The migrant "feels foreign and misunderstood here," he explained, "and so he looks for people who would be able to understand him, and he finds Poles who have arrived from other provinces." The commonality of language and ideas which the migrant found among fellow migrants in the midst of a foreign culture awakened a sense of ethnic distinctiveness, and the migrant began to feel "but a particle" of a larger mass. "After these ideas and his national [ethnic] consciousness have been stirred in him, if he is found by one who is able to explain his national character to him and to make him recognize the obligations which go along with this character—then this simple man, hitherto passive and dim to the national cause, changes into an individual consciously and actively serving the ideas which rest upon nationality."[17]

"Identity is perception," comments sociologist Liah Greenfeld. Where self-definition assumed new shapes in response to newly perceived collectivities, individuals were likewise apt to be moved—if not mobilized—by the novel political language of national destiny. In the context of global migration, emergent ethnicity itself replicated a state of what Eric Hobsbawm has called "popular proto-nationalism"— "feelings of collective belonging . . . which could operate, as it were, potentially on the macro-political scale which could fit with modern states and nations."[18] For Agaton Giller, accordingly, self-redefinition as a Pole among non-Poles was a first step toward an understanding of, and potential involvement in, the political struggle taking place between Poland and its non-Polish national enemies. Irish leader Patrick Ford, too, argued that ethnic enclaves in America broke down the village parochialisms of the Irish countryside, coaxing the Irish out of "the littleness of countyism [and] into the broad feeling of nationalism."[19]

In an effort to codify this connection between migration, ethnic identity, and nationalism, historian Victor Greene has outlined a developmental scheme of three stages: "ethnic naiveté," in which ethnic identity has little or no salience; "cultural nationalism," a state of as yet unpoliticized national awareness (corresponding roughly with what I have called ethnic consciousness); and "nationalism" proper, a state of political awareness and agitation. Although he departs from Giller in the specifics of *how* the process of "ethnicization" occurred, Greene does set these three states along a single continuum.[20] But this general pattern was subject to kaleidoscopic variations, depending, among other things, on the social conditions in the locales of both departure and resettlement, the timing of migration, the nature and strength of ethnic leadership in the New World enclave, and the personal inclinations of individual migrants. A few caveats are therefore in order. First, movement along Greene's continuum from naiveté to nationalism should not be regarded as automatic. Parochial village or county allegiances often kept a tenacious hold on the migrants long after settlement among their "compatriots" in America. The persistence of local or subnational identity was reflected in the sometimes violent intercounty rivalries among the Irish, in the establishment of Yiddish *landsmanshaftn* (village associations), and in regional antagonisms among migrants from the three Polish partitions, which frustrated early attempts at organization along broad, national lines.[21] Moreover, even in those cases where the immigrant did look beyond these parochial ties to discover his or her "national" identity, this discovery in itself was no guarantee that the national idea would take on a political charge. For many, Greene's second and as yet apolitical stage was the final one.

Second, the precise relation between ethnicization and migration varied from group to group, and even from instance to instance within single groups. For example, given the long history of Jewish expulsions and persecutions in Europe, and given, especially, their harsh treatment in nineteenth-century Russia, few Yiddish-speaking migrants could be described as ethnically "naive" on the eve of their departure from the Pale of Settlement. In this instance the process of ethnicization (which included anti-Semitic property laws and increasingly frequent outbreaks of ethnic violence) figured as one of the causes of migration, not one of its effects. Here the genesis of full-blown Zionism depended more upon lingering memories of the Old World than upon a dawning ethnic awareness in the New.[22] A similar case might be made for those Irish and Polish emigrants from regions where "the dominion of the stranger" was most keenly felt.[23]

But despite the many deviations from his three-stage progression, Greene's model remains useful in explaining the development of European nationalisms on American soil. While the particulars varied from group to group and from case to case, much Irish, Polish, and Yiddish discussion in America did flow from this matrix of ethnicization, migration, and nationalism. The period of departure and resettlement was often attended by a flux either in the degree or the nature of ethnic consciousness. Upon arrival, migrants often came into contact with people from different counties, villages, or *shtetls* in a way which allowed for a reinterpretation of Old World experiences in national terms, rather than in simply local ones. Cultural resources such as the immigrant press in America were often controlled by nationalists who had a stake in cultivating national constituencies or in promoting nationalist ideologies. And continued hardship and discrimination in America often fed into a politicized, hopeful view of the cause of the homeland (or, in the case of Jews, the cause of *a* homeland). It was in this social context that organizations like the Lovers of Zion, the Polish National Alliance, and the Clan na Gael took root and flourished.

To argue that nationalist activity and ideology were pervasive within these three groups is not to suggest a real or perceived identity of interests or a unanimity of opinion among diverse individuals. In its rigid conceptions of "us" and "them" nationalist ideology can perhaps disguise the power relations within the imagined nation and may partially cloak the extent of a group's diversity of interests. But it cannot conceal such diversity entirely. Class conflicts, for instance, were never far from the surface within these movements. Labor nationalists were wary of the hegemonic potential couched in the ideal of national unity; and middle-class nationalists worried over each movement's demeanor and respectability.[24]

Likewise, as Cynthia Enloe has argued, the particular brand of liberation sought by nationalist movements often reflects an ethos of "injured masculinity," and hence the experiences of national struggle and the benefits of national liberation differ greatly across the gender line.[25] These movements developed within an ideological context of masculinized politics; "nation," "national duty," and "citizenship" were gendered conceptions. Logistically, too, nationalist agitation was rooted in the homosocial world of the fraternal association and the saloon. As Rosa Sonneschein remarked with some irony after the first Zionist Congress in 1897, "strange to say, with this strong craving for liberty and equality, the Zionists began their proceedings by disfranchising women."[26] Like the blueprints for liberation, nationalist grievances, too, were gendered: the women who fled Ireland in disproportionate numbers in the post-Famine era had been "exiled" as surely by the patriarchal customs of Irish land tenure as by the Saxon villainies so often harped upon by their brothers and fathers. (A Jewish woman recently summed up this issue when, pausing in the mammoth task of preparing a Passover seder, she asked, "for this we came out of Egypt?")[27]

At the same time, however, ethnic violence, religious persecution, and ethnically inscribed legal codes were compelling; women as well as men saw something to gain through national agitation. In Europe women were active in the Irish Land League, the Jewish Bund, and in the Polish resistance to the de-Polonizing policies of Bismarck's *Kulturkampf;* just as in the United States organizations like the Daughters of Erin, the Daughters of Zion, and the Polish Women's Alliance arose in conjunction with male organizations. Despite her disappointment with the Zionists' restrictions on women's vote, Rosa Sonneschein herself concluded: "we well know that Israel is still pursued and persecuted by living Hamans, so also do we believe in the existence of many Esthers, who in time of trial and danger would sacrifice life and happiness for God and family, for Israel and its adherents. The loyalty of the Jewess is marvelous."[28] Sonneschein, like many of her loyal counterparts in Polonia and Irish-America, fought on one front to redefine the masculinist nation, even as she fought to liberate that nation on another.

Given this circumstance of diversity within the ranks, nationalism is best understood not as a political monolith but as an idiom, a language capable of expressing a wide range of ideals—radical or conservative, masculinist or feminist. Although some concern for state power necessarily lies at the heart of nationalism, the outermost boundaries of this shared concern are broad indeed. They comprise the bourgeois program of Theodore Herzl and the radicalism of Chaim Zhitlovsky; the parliamentary approach of the Home Rule movement and the violent tactics of Irish dynamiters; the feminist nationalism of Teofila Samolinska and the zeal to recoup the nation's injured masculinity embodied in militarist men's organizations. All of these people envisioned some kind of national rebirth or liberation. But they did not agree on why they wanted it, how it was to be achieved, or what the newly established nation should look like upon completion. Nationalism did not supplant other political or religious convictions; rather, it dovetailed with these convictions and framed their articulation.[29] The nationalist movements within each of these groups had a political left, right, and center; each encompassed diverse vintages of Old World political thought, as successive arrivals over time brought versions of nationalism distinctly stamped by the politics and circumstances at the moment of migration; each included religious and secular factions; and each was characterized by diversity—even discord.

The Larger Ireland

The affinity between departure and revolt was particularly strong in nineteenth-century Ireland. Emigration and nationalist resistance represented two responses to a single vexing constellation of issues: the inequities of land distribution under the Protestant Ascendancy, landlord-tenant relations, the dislocations of commercialization, and the power of the British imperial state to define the terms of Irish economic life and to shore up existing arrangements in times of widespread distress. Hence the leaders of Irish resistance looked upon the emigrants as natural and well-placed allies: as the emigrant community grew in size and stature in the waning decades of the nineteenth century, Irish leaders saw in Irish-America an incalculable bankroll for political projects ranging from land reform to violent overthrow. Their pleas, conversely, found a responsive audience. Because nationalists after the Famine drew so heavily upon the bitter experiences of the Catholic masses in their protests, those dispossessed and laboring Catholics now exiled in America found the nationalist polemic especially resonant.[30]

Ireland's troubles were rooted in a long history of conquest, "racial" and sectarian differences, and conflicting approaches to property rights.[31] From the earliest Norman disruption of Gaelic customs of land ownership and tribal obligation, to Henry VIII's imposition of British authority, to the accelerating cycles of resistance and reprisal in the Cromwellian and Williamite periods, a now familiar pattern had gradually emerged: a system of land tenure which was remarkably harsh to the peasantry, and a political situation which, despite its nuances, lent itself to strict sectarian interpretation. Under the last

Tudors, those who resisted British authority saw their lands confiscated and settled by Protestants from England and Scotland; and where these settlements failed, the dispossessed drifted back to their former lands with no precise legal status, and no claims which the British were bound to respect. Under the regime of the Penal Laws in the eighteenth century, the holdings of the Catholic majority were further whittled down to a mere seven percent of the island's cultivable lands.[32]

By fits and starts the elements of modern Irish nationalism emerged from these patterns of land distribution, the effects of which were reinforced by the gradual dislocations of commercialization in the late eighteenth century. On the one hand, the period witnessed a series of sporadic, localized outbursts on the part of a host of secret societies against the most accessible emblems of their discontent. Whiteboyism or Defenderism (so called after two of the more notorious groups) represented a widespread impulse to bring rough justice and intimidation to bear upon the rack-renters, evictors, tithe collectors, land enclosers, and commercial middlemen who were perceived to be behind local economic troubles. At the same time, a new political confidence and spirit of independence took hold among the Protestants. Assured of their primacy in local affairs and pinched by Britain's economic policies, many Protestants began to revise their views of the proper relationship between Ireland and England. Behind Wolfe Tone and Samuel Neilson, the United Irishmen publicized a radical program of total independence and full citizenship for the Irish of all religions.[33]

These two threads came together, however imperfectly, in the rebellion of the United Irishmen of 1798. The rising was put down quickly and brutally; and the ensuing Act of Parliamentary Union (1801) legislated an independent Irish Parliament out of existence. The Union set the terms for Irish political life for the century to come: the island was drawn more firmly into the orbit of the British imperial economy, the established churches of England and Ireland were united, and the Dublin Parliament was dissolved. Moreover, the Union set British power squarely behind existing economic relations in a manner which, over time, led many landlords to see their own security as dependent upon Ireland's continued subordination.[34]

Despite the defeat of 1798, this period had established both an arrangement of government power and an appealing mythology which were crucial in forging an oppositional political culture of Irish nationality. The Union itself ensured that a wide variety of social, economic, and political issues would of necessity be defined as "national" questions. The nineteenth century was to hear a diverse series of proposals for the benefit of Ireland—pleas for total independence, agitation for land reform, "national" literary movements, revolutionary conspiracies, and cultural initiatives for de-Anglicization. But English power was now at the center of every discussion. And the many inequities and the spontaneous moments of revolt since the days of the Gaelic chiefs yielded material for a galvanizing mythology of Irish resistance to foreign conquest and rule. Drawing selectively upon folk memory, the heroism of the Defenders, and the martyrdom of Wolfe Tone, publicists wove a tapestry of Irish unity-in-suffering and singleness of purpose. History itself was recast to forge a common cause where historically there had been none; and, as one scholar has observed, this "bad history" often made for good politics.[35]

As emigrants fled the island's deepening pauperization in the middle decades of the nineteenth century, Irish nationalism took root and flourished in a variety of forms, both in the tightly packed ghettos of the major urban centers of Boston and New York, and in smaller, more remote communities like Butte, Denver, and Sacramento. As compared with the later development of Polish and Yiddish nationalism in America, Irish nationalism was perhaps the quickest to take hold and the most prolific in its organizational expression. This mosaic included situational organizations, such as the Fenian Brotherhood and the Ladies Land League, which came and went with specific phases in the ongoing struggle in Ireland; enduring benevolent organizations such as the Ancient Order of Hibernians, whose nationalism was linked to the defense of the immigrant; and the more politically ambitious Clan na Gael camps, whose genteel appellations of "literary societies" often cloaked a fully revolutionary intent.[36]

The roots of this nationalist enthusiasm were several. As Kerby Miller explains, the rural Catholic worldview itself inclined the nineteenth-century Irish to explain the drastic act of emigration in the passive terms of "forced exile." Within an ideological frame which emphasized collectivity over individualism, patience over action, and fatalism over will, migration was seen as something under*gone*, not under*taken*. This outlook may have kept the rates of migration down during the lean years before the 1840s; and it certainly contributed to the phenomenon of the "American wake," the ritualized farewell for the departing emigrant. Those who did leave throughout the century articulated the break with tradition and immediate communal ties which migration represented in terms of breach of faith on the part of their oppressors. This perception of emigration as banishment was no doubt corroborated by the various ways the emigrants were pushed to leave by landlords and the British government. Migration became exile, and the massive exile of the mid nineteenth century in turn became the greatest symbol of Ireland's sum of suffering at the hands of England.[37]

Another source of emigrant nationalism was the mid-century political awakening across the Irish countryside. The period of greatest exodus was preceded by a movement in Ireland whose success in politicizing and mobilizing the Catholic peasantry was unprecedented in its sweep. Under the leadership of Daniel O'Connell, the quest for Repeal of the Union in the 1840s had planted the seeds for nationalist interpretations of the peasant experience. Having won a Catholic Emancipation Bill in 1829, O'Connell sought to use the newly democratized Irish electorate as a wedge for splitting the Union itself.[38] As the Repeal agitation reached its peak in 1843, "monster meetings" sponsored by the Repeal Association were said to have attracted as many as three quarters of a million at a time to hear the great Liberator.[39] Hence when the potato blight hastened the trans-Atlantic exodus in the years that followed, many who fled bore with them a newly acquired political vocabulary for interpreting and discussing the woes of the old country.[40]

Conditions in America, too, helped to kindle the sparks of incipient nationalism. Cycles of anti-Catholicism and nativism throughout the latter half of the century, for instance, not only broke down the "littleness of countyism," but also lent a certain currency to the publicists' rhetoric of Saxon oppression. "I cannot feel that America is my country," wrote Jeremiah O'Donovan Rossa: "I am made to see that the English power, and the English influence and the English hate, and the English boycott against the Irishman is to-day as active in America as it is in Ireland." The pairing of Irish suffering and Irish-American persecution was one of the engines which powered nationalist benevolent organizations such as the Ancient Order of Hibernians.[41]

In this politically hostile climate, Irish nationalism and Irish "Americanism" became mutually reinforcing. On the one hand, Irish sovereignty in the Old World was trumpeted as a means for winning respect in the New. As Michael Davitt implored a Cooper Union audience in 1880, "aid us in Ireland to remove the stain of degradation from your birth and the Irish race here in America will get the respect you deserve."[42] The dignity of race in the social arena, by this argument, rested upon the integrity of nation in the diplomatic arena. Such arguments echoed throughout the latter half of the century, particularly among the upwardly mobile whose craving for respectability was insatiable. Conversely, Anglophobia, the mainstay of Irish nationalist thinking in the post-Famine era, was a convenient idiom in which the Irish could lay claim to American citizenship. Far from being "bad" Americans, as the nativists charged, the Irish could claim the strongest attachment of all to America's historic ideals: politically, the United States was neither more nor less than a "successful Ireland." Even Tammany man A. Oakey Hall indulged in this rhetoric of dual patriotism. "The stamp act and taxations without representations are now shifted from New York and Boston to Cork and Dublin," he explained. "No schoolmaster could ever teach an American child who reads about the greed and oppression of the various English governments for the last ten centuries to live otherwise than detesting them."[43]

On this foundation—the mass politicization of the O'Connell and Land League eras, the diaspora view of migration as exile, and the utility of nationalism in an often hostile American political climate—was built an immigrant movement whose major undertakings mirrored and supplemented those of the movement in Ireland itself. As in Ireland, the nationalist constituency in the United States was fractured ideologically along two separate axes: on the question of means (violent rebellion versus parliamentary procedure), and on the question of ends (total independence versus parliamentary Home Rule). The direction and the tactics of the movement shifted throughout the latter half of the century, but its progression retained a dynamic continuity as competing factions with competing orientations rose and fell in influence. The strengths and failures of one phase in the struggle served as guideposts for the next.[44]

For the forging of the political configuration within Irish America in the 1890s, the pivotal link in the chain from Young Ireland to Sinn Fein was the era of the New Departure (1878 and after). In Ireland, the collapse of the revolutionary Fenians in 1867 had sent the nationalist movement scrambling in two directions. On the one hand, the failure of physical force revitalized the parliamentary wing, which had been more or less in eclipse since the Famine. Behind Isaac Butt and the banner of Irish federalism, and later behind Charles Stewart Parnell, the Home Rule movement became an ever more powerful presence in British electoral politics throughout the 1870s and 1880s. And on the other hand, the Fenian debacle seemed to some to demonstrate the futility of agitation for national independence. Adopting a wide variety of strategies—including rent strikes, electoral and parliamentary activity, and the agrarian violence of old—land agitators behind ex-Fenian Michael Davitt operated on the premise that the lot of the tenant and the laborer could indeed be improved regardless of the question of national independence. Home Rule and land reform came to dominate Irish politics for decades in the wake of the abortive Fenian rising of 1867.[45]

In the United States, the fall of the Fenians had a complex result. In 1867 ex-Fenians in New York had established yet another secretive, revolutionary, and ultimately more durable organization, the Clan na Gael. Like the IRB (Irish Revolutionary Brotherhood), the Clan na Gael boasted local branches across the United States and intended to work closely with conspirators in Ireland toward an armed Irish revolt. These revolutionaries, however, could not ignore the agitation of the rural Irish. Nor could they deny the political promise of the nationalist bloc which Parnell was assembling in Parliament. Under a policy devised by John Devoy and known as the New Departure, the Clan na Gael temporarily adopted a gradualist approach based upon cooperation with the moderate forces of Charles Stewart Parnell.[46]

Devoy's New Departure policy had first been articulated in 1878 and was largely abandoned by 1882, when the fragile collaborative effort splintered on the question of priorities. But the strategy made a powerful impression on the character of Irish-American nationalism over the next several years. While the agenda was dominated by constitutionalism and the land question during the 1880s, Irish-American ideology came to be heavily influenced by the revolutionary Clan na Gael. Devoy's New Departure brought the Clan to or near the center of both the Home Rule Movement and the Irish National Land League in America. The influence of the extremist Clan na Gael created a certain fractiousness in Irish-American affairs, but from an ideological standpoint it also lent a bracing stridence to the American movement as a whole.[47]

The New Departure also went a long way in popularizing nationalist politics across the class lines of an increasingly stratified immigrant community. Strategically, the alliance was finally undone by the question of which should rightly take precedence, economic justice or political freedom. Devoy, Parnell, and other orthodox nationalists gradually became disaffected with Michael Davitt's growing interest in land nationalization and other "socialistic" solutions—interests which bespoke a waxing internationalism at the expense of national liberation.[48] But for the Irish immigrants disproportionately represented among America's laborers, the radical proposals put forward by

Michael Davitt, Patrick Ford of the *Irish World*, and Ford's special correspondent, Henry George, not only addressed the trials left behind in the Old World but spoke to the daily miseries of the New. Labor politics and nationalism among the Irish in America now achieved a new and dynamic affinity. The immigrants' harsh existence in the mines and factories of America fueled an interest in the new economic bent of Irish nationalism as represented by mounting land agitation; and conversely, Irish nationalism became the language in which many labor leaders appealed to the Irish laborers on behalf of unionism or socialism.[49]

In one sense, the fears of nationalists like Devoy were well founded: indeed, the bedrock premise of Henry George's thinking was that "it is a mistake to consider the Irish Land Question as a mere local question, arising out of conditions peculiar to Ireland, and which can be settled by remedies that can have but local application."[50] George's proposals were hence distinctly antinationalist in their implications. But for Irish migrants in America, such ideas and the organizational tactics which flowed from them represented a brand of labor nationalism not altogether unlike the Yiddish socialism of the Bund. For these workers, the appeal of the universalist program rested largely in its resonance with the specifics of their national experience. The call to American working-class action rested on the basis of Irish colonial memory.

This ideological nexus was expressed both in the class politics of distinctly Irish organizations, and in the pronounced nationalism of many elements within the American labor movement. On the one hand, for Patrick Ford and his followers "land monopolism" became the key in explaining Ireland's woes. The *Irish World's* emphasis on humanitarian reform and economic agitation netted as much as $1,500 a week in reader contributions for the Irish cause in the early 1880s. Significantly, contributions were particularly heavy in the anthracite regions of Pennsylvania and the mining regions of the far west. In 1880 and 1881, for example, the small mining community of Leadville, Colorado, contributed only a few dollars less than the major immigrant centers of Chicago and Philadelphia.[51]

On the other hand, in areas with a significant Irish presence, the Knights of Labor and the Irish nationalist organizations drew together into a very close relationship. Terence Powderly, later the Grand Master Workman of the Knights, served as the president of a Scranton branch of the Irish National Land League until 1883. (Powderly was also an officer in the Clan na Gael.) "The Knights of Labor were then working secretly," he recalled, "and, as many members were Irish or sympathizers with the struggle of the Irish people for land reform, they invited me to visit cities and towns throughout the country for the purpose of speaking at Land League meetings . . . When the public, or Land League, meeting would be over a secret meeting of Knights of Labor would follow. In this way I was of use to both organizations." Indeed, as Grand Master Workman, Powderly issued a letter "to the Order wherever found" stating that Michael Davitt himself was to be recognized as a member of the Knights.[52] This link between class-based and nation-based politics would persist well into the twentieth century, as epitomized by figures like James Connolly.[53]

While Ford, Powderly, and the Knights were busy fusing national and class issues in varying proportions, an uncomfortable alliance of economic conservatives and nationalist revolutionaries cast their lot with Parnell and Home Rule. To ardent nationalists like John Devoy, the land agitation had become a diversion from the national question at best, and a full-fledged betrayal at worst. If Home Rule seemed unnecessarily tame to these revolutionaries, it at least represented a step toward national independence. And to the Irish-American middle class, for which American respectability remained an essential aim of nationalist agitation, Home Rule appeared irresistible not only because of the excesses of the increasingly radicalized land movement, but also in view of the exceptional potential of Parnell's maneuvers in Westminster. When the Irish Parliamentary Party successfully positioned itself as a decisive swing vote in the mid 1880s, Home Rule seemed to middle-class Irish-Americans as promising as *Irish World* radicalism and Clan na Gael revolutionism seemed repugnant.[54]

Out of the wreckage of the New Departure in 1882, then, emerged a peculiar coalition of conservatives, moderates, and revolutionists under the new umbrella of the Irish National League. As laid out in its charter at a Philadelphia convention, the League's chief aims included providing "moral and material aid" to the Irish movement headed by Parnell, encouraging an American boycott of English manufactures and increased import of Irish manufactures, and promoting Irish culture through education to "keep alive the holy flame of nationality."[55] Although dominated from the outset by the Clan na Gael, the National League did remain faithful to these moderate objectives. Of more lasting significance was that the League's fate and the fate of programmatic nationalism in America likewise remained tied to Charles Stewart Parnell.

This long history of factionalism and class division within the American movement made the 1890s an unproductive decade for the cause of Irish nationalism. The political configuration established in the 1880s left the American wing extremely vulnerable to the setbacks suffered by the Home Rule movement in Ireland in the years that followed: in 1886, optimistic predictions to the contrary, the first Home Rule Bill was defeated in Parliament; in 1890 Parnell himself became engulfed in scandal when he was publicly named an adulterer in the divorce proceedings of Captain and Katherine O'Shea; and in 1891 he died.[56]

Each of these events struck at the organizational strength and the strategic possibilities of an American movement which had aligned itself so thoroughly with "the uncrowned king" and the cause of Home Rule. Having abdicated, as it were, for over ten years by allying with Parnell, revolutionary nationalists were now in no position to fill the void left by Parnell's death. The Home Rule wing, for its part, was splintered not only by the ensuing struggle for power among Parnell's successors, but also by the impact of the Parnell-O'Shea adultery scandal on a staunchly Catholic constituency. Following Parnell's death, Home Rule did remain the central concern of the mainstream nationalist movement (a second bill was introduced and defeated in 1893), but the issue lost much of its urgency in a swirl of internecine warfare and a general wave of pessimism on both sides of the Atlantic. Although new organizations like the Irish National Federation of America did arise and support various Home Rule candidates in Ireland, broad-based and coordinated political activity faded markedly in the United States after 1891. As one observer lamented in 1897, no one short of "the Parnell mould" would be able to rescue programmatic nationalism in Irish-America from the self-ravaging factionalism which followed the leader's death.[57]

The 1890s have widely been considered the "dead years" of Irish nationalism in the United States as in Ireland.[58] But the decade is best seen as a period of retrenchment, not of utter quietude: Irish nationalism had not simply vanished from the American scene. Since the Wolfe Tone rebellion nearly a century before, the struggle for Irish independence had been sustained more than once by mere "sunburstry," as it was known—a vague but energetic talk of freedom, conveniently unencumbered by the damning details of practicality.[59] If Irish America's proper strategic course was unclear throughout the 1890s, impressive amounts of energy continued to be channeled into the National League's earlier aim of simply keeping alive "the holy flame of nationality." The activities pages of immigrant journals like the *Irish*

World and the *Catholic Citizen* routinely attest to the vigor of local nationalist societies across the country—the Daughters of Erin, the John Boyle O'Reilly Club, the Robert Emmet Literary Society, and the Wolfe Tone Club. Most frequently acting under the aegis of either the Clan na Gael or the Ancient Order of Hibernians, such groups organized local St. Patrick's Day festivities as well as commemorations of nearly every observable event in Irish history.[60] The Ladies' Auxiliary of the AOH, founded in 1895, established an office of National Chairman of Irish History, whose duty it was "to promote the interest in Irish History, Literature, and Music."[61]

Throughout the 1890s this network of organizations also supported and popularized the cultural initiatives of Ireland's flourishing Gaelic movement, whose object of "the de-Anglicization of the Irish people" was meant to bolster liberationist commitment among the Irish until a clear political course presented itself.[62] These organizations also coordinated the American speaking tours of Irish emissaries such as MP John Redmond, the ex-dynamiter John Daly, and "the Irish Joan of Arc," Maud Gonne. Before vast audiences, these orators recounted past Irish glories, catalogued the current sufferings of Ireland and its political prisoners, and reminded the exiles of their enduring duty to those they had left behind.[63]

The "flame of nationality" was further fanned by the resurgence of American nativism in the 1890s. The American Protective Association and the Immigration Restriction League, both emerging with particular force after the depression of 1893, once again cast Irish-American ethnic identity in especially bold relief. The threat posed to Irish-America by this "American Orangeism," as the press tended to define it, was augmented by the concurrent rise of pro-British sentiment within the American government, and the increasing official discussion of an Anglo-American alliance. This tide of nativism and Anglomania—and particularly the reliance of these groups on the doctrine of Anglo-Saxon supremacy—helped to fuel Irish cultural and pride initiatives such as the Gaelic League, and to reinvigorate the nationalists' faded arguments of Saxon treachery. By the decade's end, even the centrist Boston *Pilot* would assert that "when the putty-heads clamor for an Anglo-Saxon domination of the world, then we others protest, and should stand ready to back our protest with the last argument of kings and of republics, the resort to physical violence."[64] Although the movement was scarcely at high tide during the 1890s, nationalist discussion still continued to hold a critical position in Irish-American community life, taking the form of now a revised political agenda stressing culture over politics, now a posture of defensive Americanism in the face of an Anglo-Saxonist regime. The articulation of Irish group identity in the 1890s retained a vocabulary and logic based not upon mere chauvinism but upon versions of the long history of conquest and martyrdom, and a vision of continued struggle. As Joseph O'Halloran urged in "Close up the Ranks," his anthem of sunburstry in an era of factionalism,

> Think of the myriads who gave
>   the crimson current of their veins,
> Our darling motherland to save
>   from the Oppressor's cruel chains!
> While still one rusty fetter clanks,
> Close up the ranks! Close up the ranks![65]

Liberationist possibilities and the battle for state power remained salient in expressions of Irish-American group identity well beyond the turn of the century, despite the tactical setbacks and the internal divisions of the movement. If Jeremiah O'Donovan Rossa regretted that "No society of Irishmen exists now that [England] is afraid of," still delegates from over sixty Irish-American societies passed a resolution in 1899 that "every effort to overthrow the British dominion will be approved and supported."[66] As Robert Ellis Thompson affirmed in his "Spirit of the Irish Nation" (1898), "the larger Ireland [that is, the diaspora], which English misgovernment and deportation has created, sends its confirmation back to the old Ireland of its love and its hate. From every quarter of the inhabited world the Irish race watch and wait for the hour of deliverance."[67]

Poland's Fourth Partition

Despite certain similarities in its liberationist programs, its internal divisions, and its unifying mythologies, Polish nationalism in Europe and America presents some sharp contrasts to the Irish struggle. Polish history offers no analogue to Daniel O'Connell's "monster" mobilization of the peasantry, nor were the daily hardships of common Poles so widely attributed to "the dominion of the stranger." On the contrary, with few and fleeting exceptions the idea of *nation* in Poland denoted the nobility alone. That class of displaced peasants and laborers which dominated Polish emigration in the closing decades of the nineteenth century had had only tenuous and uneven connections to the national liberation movement before its migration. Hence while Irish activists in the 1890s attempted to keep the flame alive among a fairly well politicized community, Polish leaders were still merely kindling a sense of nationality and group destiny. Indeed, late in the century the Polish press still scolded its readers for giving Russia, Prussia, and Austria as their nations of origin when asked by various New World officials. "Let's Be Poles!" goaded *Dziennik Chicagoski*.[68]

But the awareness of Polish nationality was in ascendance, and the idea of the emigrant community as Poland's "fourth partition" did gain currency as American Polonia took shape in the 1870s and after.[69] Though the common people had played a mixed role in Poland's struggle for independence, that struggle itself gradually assumed centrality in the political life of those Poles who found themselves in America. In both its ideological content and the tenor of its leadership, Polonia's political fabric was woven of the threads of national rebellion: it drew its leaders largely from the political exiles and refugees of the failed January Rising of 1863, and many of these leaders, in turn, popularized their cause using Poland's long-standing mythologies involving the historic mission of the Pole abroad. By 1896 John Finerty would hold the Polish movement up to his Irish compatriots as a model worthy of emulation. Despite *three* enemies, he noted, Poles in America admirably held to the opening words of the song that would become the national anthem: "Poland has not yet perished, as long as we are living."[70]

Modern Polish nationalism emerged from what one historian has called the "political vivisection" of Poland in the partitions of 1772, 1793, and 1795. Plagued by internal disorganization and precariously situated at the hems of three of Europe's most powerful and ambitious empires, Poland had drifted into an ineluctable cycle of unsuccessful internal reforms followed by highly successful foreign interventions. The first partition, in which Poland ceded over twenty-five percent of its territory to the three powers, was the consequence of a failed rising of nobles against the Russian "protection" under which Poland then suffered. Thereafter each attempt at political reform in what remained of Poland provoked an intervention on the part of Russia; each intervention included the assistance of Prussia and Austria; and each act of assistance called for tokens of gratitude from Russia in the form of more Polish territories. Following the third partition of 1795 in the wake of the failed Kościuszko rising, all accounts were paid in full: the Polish Republic as a political entity simply ceased to exist. The precise terms of Poland's political existence were altered by treaty throughout the nineteenth century. For the Poles, however, these vicissitudes merely constituted variations on the single theme of political subjugation to the three partitioning powers.[71]

Polish leaders in the United States drew upon several currents of political thought in linking emigrants to the ongoing struggle for Poland. Late-century publicists were neither consistent nor systematic in tapping these currents or in citing their precedents. Two of the key political and military premises in this linkage date back to the period of partition itself. Publicized in the pamphlet *Can the Poles Rise to Independence?*, Tadeusz Kościuszko's conviction that the peasantry was indispensable to the Polish revolution had a tremendous influence on nationalist discussion throughout the nineteenth century. A liberal, democratized constitution, in Kościuszko's vision, went hand in hand with the military objective of a peasantry mobilized under the banner of national liberation. His armies of irrepressible peasant "scythemen," if elusive in historic fact, became a staple of Polish insurrectionary thinking.[72] Likewise, Jan Dąbrowski's writings on the power of foreign alliances gave rise to an enduring vision of Polish soldiers winning decisive support for the fatherland by fighting other nations' battles. "France is victorious," he had written in 1796, "*she is fighting for the freedom of nations:* let us attempt to weaken *her* enemies." "The triumphs of the French Republic are our one and only hope, and with her help, and that of her allies, we may yet see our homes, to which we bade farewell with such feeling."[73] The Kościuszko and Dąbrowski doctrines of peasant mobilization and foreign alliance were tailored to new circumstances across the Atlantic decades later, defining an indispensable political role for the peasantry-in-exile that constituted American Polonia.

A second ideological strand linking emigrants to the national cause was a highly politicized view of Polish culture itself. This was borne of the nineteenth-century cycles of rebellion and reprisal in Poland, whose chief features included anti-Polish assaults in the arenas of education, religion, and language on the part of the partitioning powers. Following the rebellion of November 1831, Czar Nicholas I had embarked on a harsh retaliatory policy: in addition to hundreds of executions and tens of thousands of deportations, over 2,000 manors were sequestered, many Polish schools, universities, and churches were supressed, millions of rubles in reparative taxes were levied, and an army of occupation was established at Poland's expense. In the estimation of French observer Jules Michelet, the Russian policy "was undertaken not only to kill Poland, her laws, her religion, her lan-

guage, literature and national civilization, but *to kill the Poles*, to an-
nihilate them as a race, to paralyze the very nerve of the population
... The Polish people, as a living, potential energy, would vanish
completely."[74] The failed rising of January 1863, too, led to a stepped
up campaign of "Russification" in the Russian territories, as well as to
similar cultural initiatives on the part of the Bismarck government,
ever alive to the dangers which the Polish nationalist spirit could pose
to Prussia.[75]

Against this backdrop a widespread tendency developed among
Poles jealously to guard cultural *Polskość,* or Polishness, as a political
treasure. For the emigrants of the 1870s and after, the questions of
New World assimilation or acculturation which inevitably arose in
emigrant communities were shaded with deeper questions regarding
political obligation to the homeland. Unlike French or German immigrants, whose countries would continue to exist with or without
them, explained *Zgoda,* "the Pole is not free to Americanize" because
faith, language, and nationality in Poland itself had been "powerfully
torn away by the enemies." "The Pole is not free to Americanize
because—wherever he is—he has a mission to fulfill." In sharp contrast to the military mission, which constituted the duty of the Polish
man, this cultural mission was framed as the central duty of the Polish
woman: "The Polish mother's milk is the poison that worries the
enemy," as one popular poem had it. The clarion call of the Society of
Polish Women (Chicago, 1898) proclaimed that "our obligation is to
guard the rearing of our young, and to train them as good Polish sons
and daughters." This gendered division of political labor did not go
uncontested, but the politicized understanding of Americanization was
nonetheless one of the central strands of Polonian nationalism.[76]

And finally, a dominant faction of Polonia's leadership drew upon
and popularized the romantic notions of armed insurrection which
dated to the November 1831 Rising, including the chivalric imagery of
the "pilgrim's" triumphant return. The failure of the November Rising
had produced an outpouring of romantic writing on the subject of
Poland's sufferings, its martyrdom, and its historic mission.[77] The poetry of Adam Mickiewicz, with its emphasis on the pilgrim's obligation, resonated most feelingly among the émigrés of later generations.
By Mickiewicz's reckoning, a national commitment akin to religious
devotion was the key to the pilgrim's existence. Poems like Mickiewicz's "Prayer" and "Litany" for the pilgrim not only articulated a
holy bond between the Pole abroad and the nation left behind, but
fully sanctified insurrection:

Lord God Almighty! The children of a warlike nation lift up to thee their unarmed hands from the various ends of the earth . . . God of the Jagiellos! God of the Sobieskis! God of the Kościusz-kos! Have mercy on our Fatherland, and on us. Grant us again to pray to thee according to the custom of our fathers, on the field of battle with our weapons in our hands, before an altar made of drums and cannon, under a baldachin made of our eagles and standards; and grant our kinsfolk to pray to thee in the churches of our cities and of our villages, and our children on our graves. Nevertheless not our will, but thine, be done. Amen.[78]

These works had originally appeared within the relatively small circle of Polish elite emigration; Mickiewicz's pilgrims were a cadre of dispersed insurrectionists, most of whom lived in Paris. But Mick-iewicz's powerful mixture of national devotion with religious feeling, of anthem with prayer, fit with the familiar patterns of devotion among the Catholic masses. Late in the century such writings were reposi-tioned and reinterpreted within the massive emigrant community in America. Political leaders discovered in Adam Mickiewicz a popular hero whose romantic vision of the emigrant-as-pilgrim could be in-fused with new meaning and deployed in the struggle to make America into Poland's revolutionary "fourth partition." Mickiewicz, argued the editor of *Zgoda*, "felt and suffered for millions."[79]

While one wing of the nationalist movement in America thus drew its inspiration from the insurrection of 1831, a powerful counterposi-tion was built upon the chastening effects of the failed January Rising of 1863. Convinced by this brutal defeat that the overthrow of foreign rule was but an unrealizable dream (or worse, a form of mass suicide), many, including a number of disillusioned veterans of the rising, re-jected earlier militarist romances and adopted a wholly new approach to the problem of the Polish nation. "There is nothing much in dreams and swordplay," wrote one poet in the wake of the defeat; "The sabre snaps and the song fades away."[80] "Positivism," as the rising brand of realism came to be known, located the nation's troubles not in Rus-sian, Prussian, or Austrian tyranny, but within the Polish people them-selves. Positivists proposed that the nation's martyrdom had little to do with historic divinity and much with the flaws of the Poles; and the solution was to be found in concrete social, economic, and moral reforms rather than swordplay. National liberation, according to this doctrine, was to be achieved through economic, industrial, and edu-cational rejuvenation—the "organic work" of nation-building.[81]

Political activists and the recognized leaders in American Polonia came largely from the ranks of the exodus of 1864 and the ensuing period of heightened Russification and *Kulturkampf*; hence political discussion and organizational life in the United States tended to replicate the overarching debate in post–1863 Poland between "romantics" and "realists."[82] While the positivists held the upper hand in Poland itself in the period of disenchantment following the January Rising, these competing programs were more evenly matched among the emigrants in the United States. The confrontation of principles in American Polonia was embodied in the orientations of the two largest immigrant organizations of the nineteenth century: in the unabashed liberationism of the Polish National Alliance (PNA) and in the moral and educational "organic work" of the Polish Roman Catholic Union (PRCU).

These organizations had their precedents in political circles like the Kościuszko Society and the Polish Commune, American auxiliaries to émigré circles in Europe during earlier Polish national movements. Several efforts at colonizing North America in unassimilated Polish settlements likewise foreshadowed the concern of these groups for cultural integrity.[83] But the decisive period in Polish associational life began in 1874, when a group of community leaders including Teodor Gieryk of Detroit and Wincenty Barzyński of Chicago proposed a nationwide federation of Polonia's existing local societies. At the initial meeting some participants conceived this federation as a decidedly nationalist one, although clearly in the positivist mold: "Discord and disunity defeated Poland," ran one declaration at the founding *sejm*; "not the enemies, but disunity and discord set the Fatherland in its grave." Under the banner "Fatherland before all, God above all," the proposed federation was to work organically toward national regeneration through Polish education, through charities and fraternal aid programs, through the establishment of a network of Polish institutions including orphanages, hospitals, and a seminarium, and through the preservation of the linguistic and cultural integrity of the emigrants in America. Poland's enemies—discord and disunity—were to be conquered through concerted social action.[84]

Early on, however, the PRCU's highest circles ran into a serious point of contention: the extent to which the young organization was to function as a Polish body or a *Catholic* body. The question of membership qualifications was the wedge which split the Polish Roman Catholic Union. Liberals like Gieryk, who agitated for a broad construction of Polishness with no bars to non-Catholic membership, ultimately lost to the conservative faction headed by Resurrectionist father Wincenty Barzyński. Under Barzyński's leadership, the PRCU's social agenda would be carried out within a strict framework of Catholicism, and membership in the organization—as in the Polish nation itself as it was conceived here—was restricted to Catholics. Perhaps best summing up the organization's shifting orientation on the national question, the slogan "Fatherland before all" gave way to "God and Fatherland," politics now firmly relegated to second rank.[85]

The supremacy of the Barzyński faction after 1875 generated a powerful and cohesive opposition. Barzyński's hard line on the questions of liberationist struggle and religious toleration left a large segment of politicized Polonia as yet unrepresented. Hence when Agaton Giller's blueprint for organizing the Poles in America appeared in *Gazeta Polska* in 1879, it attracted a number of alienated members of the PRCU in addition to nationalists in favor of forcible liberation and religious liberals who had held aloof from the PRCU from the outset. Whereas Barzyński, many felt, had betrayed the movement by convening the PRCU "for the Polish priests in America, not for the Polish people," Giller's commitment to the national cause was beyond doubt: "There is no cause which is more important to the Pole than this one," he wrote. "All other causes draw their significance and importance from the extent to which they are helpful and useful to this one."[86]

Like his Irish counterparts, Giller identified emigration itself as "a living protest against the order of things which the partitions have produced in Polish lands." Noting the large numbers and growing proportion of peasants in the migration of the 1870s, he wrote:

> It is this class of the population which is most tied to the native soil and which possesses an unconquered aversion to distant travels ... If this simple people, accustomed to want and poverty, carrying without a murmur every burden with which it is saddled, finally grows impatient and moves in order to seek bread, justice, and liberty across the ocean—how great must be the oppression which turns them away from their farmhouses!—how cutting and unbearable the poverty, which pushes them on an uncertain and dangerous journey across the ocean![87]

As the Polish population grew in the United States, Giller argued, a central aim of political activists should be to instill the overseas peasantry with a sense of obligation to the country they had been compelled to leave. As Polish peasants awoke to their cultural Polishness in a foreign environment, moreover, they were especially ripe for such political tutelage. Ultimately, the newly politicized emigrants would function as a corps of ambassadors, fostering sympathy and encouraging diplomatic action on the part of "the mighty republic" which was their adopted home.[88]

For Giller, organization was the key to consolidating this "fourth partition," and meeting the concrete, everyday needs of the emigrant was the key to organization. His blueprint involved a federation of mutual benefit societies organized at the parish level, governed by a national parliament of representatives. This scheme became the basis for the Polish National Alliance, which crystallized in 1880 to rival the PRCU. The PNA's early activists ranged from veterans of the Polish insurrections to a bloc of liberal priests led by Dominik Majer, a central figure in the earlier dissention within the PRCU. On a platform of national struggle, religious and ideological tolerance, and commitment to the material well-being of Polish immigrants, the PNA grew to nearly three times the size of the PRCU by the turn of the century.[89]

The antagonism between the PNA and the PRCU involved concrete economic issues, as the two organizations competed in a variety of local settings for Polonia's limited resources of loyalty and dollars. Although frank charges of thievery were not unheard of in this game of organizational enhancement, the animosity was most often framed in ideological terms of "proper" devotion to both God and country. Outspoken leaders of the PRCU denounced liberal nationalists as "masons" and "atheists," parodying the PNA position in the slogan, "Revenge, revenge to the enemy,/ With God or in spite of Him." Drawing parallels between Polish activists and the excommunicated Fenians, one priest commented in 1880, "we don't know which of the two evils would be worse for Polish Catholics, to surrender to the Czar, or to throw themselves into the embrace of such people [nationalists]." Partisans of the PNA, on the other hand, saw mere "impostors" behind the mask of PRCU pieties: "Our nation has paid too dearly for deference to foreign people [Rome] who are unfamiliar with our soul and who, at bottom, are indifferent to the political existence of Poland."[90]

But this antagonism did not bespeak a fundamental difference on the national question. The distinction here is not between nationalism and its antithesis, but between "religionist" and "secularist" approaches to the national question.[91] At the heart of the discord between these two organizations was their stance on the relationship between religious devotion and national salvation: the PRCU's central contention was that "not the people, . . . but a miracle will deliver Poland!" The PNA's terse response: "Faith without action is dead." Yet national deliverance was the common objective, and both organizations grew out of the same impulse to "preserve Polish emigrants for the fatherland." The original PRCU blueprint sought "to uphold the national spirit of Polish Americans" and to "develop in Polish youth love and honor for the country of their ancestors," just as the PNA vowed "to urge the discharge of duties dictated by national honor."[92]

PNA activists raised thousands of dollars for the National Fund (a nationalist coffer administered by a group of exiles in Rapperswil, Switzerland), although there were vigorous disputes over the proper aims of the Fund. And in the final years of the century, factions within the PNA developed ties to both of the parties then dominant in Polish politics.[93] PNA activists were likewise instrumental in founding the Polish Falcons, a physical fitness organization envisioned as a Polish American Army in the mold of the earlier Polish Legions. "If nothing else can bring freedom to our fatherland," commented *Zgoda*, "one thing is certain—a sword and a carbine in the arms of strong young men can help for sure." On his visit to the United States in 1899, insurrectionist Zygmunt Miłkowski urged that PNA dispense with "beautiful but costly uniforms" and save its money for weapons.[94]

Given the level of national consciousness among the mass of Polish emigrants in the final decades of the century, however, nationalist efforts in this period were largely educational and ceremonial—activities designed to foster a national consciousness among the emigrants which might later be turned to the political advantage of the nation. Like Roman Dmowski's National Democratic Party in Poland, the PNA saw the defense of Polish culture and the propagation of the national idea as necessary first steps toward liberating Poland in the era of *Kulturkampf* at home and "denationalization" abroad. Toward this end, PNA chapters across the country sponsored lectures by nationalist speakers such as Tomasz Siemiradzki ("The Professor"), worked to erect American monuments to Polish heroes, sponsored essay contests on nationalist themes, and organized massive public observances to mark the January and November risings, Kościuszko's birthday, the Third of May, and the Battle of Grunwald.[95]

This strategy of cultural nation-building in the hopes of some future, concrete contribution to the national cause in effect blended elements of both the positivist and the insurrectionary approaches. As one

"Alliance priest" argued in a November rising address in 1897, "although an ocean separates us, we can struggle and help the fatherland. But the struggle must be a struggle for our own welfare, for education, for civilization, for uplifting ourselves to a more prominent position—and then we can effectively help Poland." This address was followed by a rendition of the insurrectionary "Warszawianka": "Poland arise, cast off your irons/ Today your triumph or your death!"[96]

Inasmuch as the two organizations shared the central goal of heightening and maintaining Polish national consciousness, they did enjoy moments of cooperation. Branches of the PNA and PRCU jointly protested restrictionist immigration legislation, for instance; and they collaborated on many national observances and on the drive to erect a monument to Kościuszko.[97] But as historian Victor Greene has shown, in many cases it was the discord, not the harmony, of Polish associational life which served to heighten the sense of group feeling. Competition between these societies brought questions of group definition and direction to the very center of immigrant communal life, and perhaps more than any other single factor, these internal debates popularized the importance of Polish national identity. As partisans of each organized and challenged one another at the local level, the Polish National Alliance and the Polish Roman Catholic Union came to embrace over 40,000 emigrants in twenty-two states by the turn of the century. By the final decade of the nineteenth century, the PRCU and the PNA stood at the center of Polish-American organizational life, and nearly every other Polish body—the Polish Socialist Alliance, the Polish National Catholic Church, the Daughters of the Polish Crown, the Polish Singers' Alliance—had either overlapping membership or official ties with one or the other of these umbrella organizations.[98]

Among the most complete and telling assessments of nationalism in Polish-America for the period is the report drawn up by Zygmunt Miłkowski, a member of the National League in Europe and a writer popularly known by the pen name T. T. Jeż. Miłkowski came to publicize the National Fund and to gauge the level of political feeling among the emigrants in America. From colony to colony across the country, he sought to overcome the emigrants' skepticism toward the National Fund and to persuade them that sacrifices for the fatherland constituted an *obligation*, not a charitable act. His tour took him to Polonia's largest colonies such as Chicago, Milwaukee, and Cleveland, as well as more modest settlements like Wilmington, Scranton, and rural Wisconsin.

Miłkowski's final assessment of Poland's "fourth partition" was mixed. On the one hand, he noted, "I was heard by my compatriots with ardent patriotic favor." The emissary took heart in the size and festivity of many of his receptions, and in the fact that the Polish National Alliance had the support of a whole constellation of women's organizations, youth organizations, cultural and artistic circles, military bodies, and in some cases the clergy and the parishioners themselves. Among the emigrants in America, he noted, "There *are* those who have not forgotten Poland"; "Complete denationalization, such as the Germans achieve in Poland, cannot be foreseen." But despite this evidence of a robust nationalist sentiment, Miłkowski was worried by Polonia's seemingly limited propensity for action. He fretted over the relatively small numbers of truly committed activists (PNA membership at the turn of the century accounted for only one to two percent of the Polish population.) He was frustrated by the pervasive suspicion among Poles in America that the National Fund was so much "rubbish," not to be trusted. Most of all he was alarmed by the "selfishness" of the church and its campaign against practical nationalism—he was alarmed, that is, by the Resurrectionist view that "since Poland's fall was the will of God, all that was left to patriots was to pray."[99]

The PRCU's *Naród Polski* met Miłkowski's criticism, and in so doing neatly summed up the competing ideologies of positivist and insurrectionary politics: "Our party does not spend a penny on this [National] Fund. It builds schools, churches, homes for orphans and the elderly ... It gathers the young and teaches them and acquaints them with Polish history. In this alone is our national strength, our national life, and so the Rapperswil [National] Fund is nothing." "We are convinced," added the journal, perhaps with unusual charity, "that the road which we follow—that is, to Warsaw through Rome—is the straightest, although we do not condemn anyone of the other opinion or judgment, that to get to Warsaw one must necessarily pass through Rapperswil."[100]

While Rapperswil and Rome symbolized as well as anything the competing secular and religionist approaches to the national question, in the 1890s nationalist leaders recognized that the most pressing task before them was first to interest the emigrants in pursuing *any* path to Warsaw. During this decade Polish leaders located the struggle largely in the arena of culture—not, as was the case for their Irish counterparts, as a means of political retrenchment, but rather as a first gesture toward nation-building in exile.

Jewish Immigrants and the National Question

Nationalism and emigration among East European Jews in the late nineteenth century represented two responses to the anti-Semitic brutality of East European regimes. And like Polish and Irish nationalists, many Jewish thinkers drew heavily upon nineteenth-century currents of romantic nationalism. Emma Lazarus, for instance, struck both chords in her *Epistle to the Hebrews*, asserting that the refugees from Russia "bear living witness to the fact that the spirit of martyrs and heroes is not extinct among our people."[101] But in contrast to either of the former cases, the fact of historic Jewish statelessness seriously complicated this nationalist discussion. Jews could strive for neither the liberation of an existing nation nor the reunification of a divided one. Here polemics like Philip Krantz's *Are the Jews a Nation?* held a place similar to the Poles' unifying *Book of Polish Pilgrims*.

By the late 1890s, three competing ideologies dominated this discussion in both Europe and the United States. Zionists held that only through the creation of a separate Jewish state could the Jews of Western Europe be truly emancipated and the Jews of Eastern Europe be made safe. The Bund, a Jewish nationalist wing of the international socialist movement, held that since many Jews were oppressed as workers, true emancipation could not be achieved through the creation of a bourgeois Jewish state; but, conversely, since many workers were undeniably persecuted *as Jews*, neither could true emancipation be attained through class struggle alone. Although they remained bitter enemies of Zionism, Bundists increasingly combined elements of Jewish nationalism with a program of class struggle for state power. The third movement, cosmopolitanism, had adherents on both the right and the left who argued for the complete incorporation of the Jews into the body politic of the countries of the Diaspora. Cosmopolitanists like Peter Wiernik, Jacob Gordin, and Philip Krantz thought Jewish nationalism a mistaken surrender to the contagion of "murder-patriotism" then sweeping Europe, geared not to liberation but to the "wild instincts" of tribalism and hate.[102] Although it was the reverse of a nationalistic doctrine, by its counterlogic cosmopolitanism exerted considerable force in shaping both Zionist and Bundist arguments, and so was an essential element in the overall texture of late nineteenth-century Jewish nationalism.

These three stances represented the full flowering of the Jewish secular enlightenment, or *haskala*, of the nineteenth century: each drew from broader currents of European secular thought, and each offered a secular alternative to religious orthodoxy on the question of the Jew's proper stance in a social and political world dominated by Gentiles.[103] But so did each address the unique threats posed to Jews in the era of government-sanctioned pogroms in the East, and the spectre of anti-Semitism in the West, which was embodied most clearly in the Dreyfus affair.

The Zionist movement of the late 1890s had its roots in the czarist brutalities of the early 1880s. In the wake of the "temporary laws" of May 1882, which severely curtailed the economic life of Russian Jewry, and amid a rising tide of anti-Jewish violence in Russia and Rumania, a variety of Jewish thinkers came forward with programs for organized Jewish relocation. These proposals reflected the immediate need for a mass escape from Eastern Europe, and, often, a binding group mythology of national regeneration, redemption, and biblical promise. In the years immediately following the May laws, groups such as BILU (a Hebrew acronym for "O house of Jacob, come ye and let us walk") and Hovevei Zion (Lovers of Zion) spontaneously formed across Eastern Europe, advocating the establishment of Jewish agricultural settlements in Palestine. With some help from Jewish philanthropists like Baron Edmond de Rothschild, by 1900 such groups of "infiltrators" had established twenty-two settlements.[104]

Others, working toward a more systematic and comprehensive program than these modest colonies, envisioned a full-scale Jewish exodus from Eastern Europe. Moishe Lieb Lilienblum, for instance, promoted a return to Eretz-Israel, where Jews "would no longer be strangers but citizens and masters of the land themselves." And Yehuda Leib Pinsker, in his *Autoemancipation!* (1882), argued that *any* land—not Palestine exclusively—would serve the political needs of the stateless nation. "A people without a territory is like a man without a shadow," but this quest for Jewish lands need not become entwined with the religious quest of a "Return to the Promised Land."[105]

Jewish nationalism gained considerable force and cohesion upon the appearance of Theodore Herzl's *Jewish State* in 1896. Herzl's work shared several elements in common with these earlier tracts and movements. Indeed, though he was surprisingly unfamiliar with many of these forerunners when he wrote his own pamphlet, he later remarked on the affinity of his own ideas with those advanced by Pinsker and others a decade and a half earlier.[106] Following a brief review of the Jewish Question and a theoretical discussion of the spread of anti-Semitism, *The Jewish State* offered a logistical blueprint for the gradual but total resettlement of Jews to either Argentina or Palestine, and a preliminary sketch of the society they ought to build there. The pamphlet touched upon every aspect of the life of Zion, from its constitution and its military to its commerce, its economic structure, and its architecture. "The Maccabeans will rise again," Herzl concluded. "We shall live at last as free men on our own soil, and die peacefully in our own homes."[107]

Herzl's signal contribution to the nationalist discussion lay in his rejection of the various projects which, like that of the Lovers of Zion, bypassed questions of political sovereignty in favor of the practical work of relocating to foreign lands. Viewing the settlement of Jewish "infiltrators" in Palestine not as a political solution at all but merely the postponement of one, Herzl approached Jewish nationalism from the standpoint of international diplomacy. He expected to solve the Jewish Question "by making it a political world-question to be discussed and settled by the civilized nations of the world in council."[108] To this end—and unlike his predecessors—Herzl spent a great deal of time and energy establishing diplomatic relations with the Turkish officials who held the deed to the land that was the object of Jewish devotion and cultivating possible allies among world powers. In his diplomatic forays and in the formation of institutions such as the Zionist Congress and the Colonial Bank, Herzl sought, in effect, to create a recognized and respected Jewish state *before* securing a Jewish territory. "Great things," he remarked, "need no firm foundation."[109]

If Herzl's diplomacy proved less than perspicacious, Zionism nonetheless did gain a political impetus under his leadership which it had lacked in all previous incarnations. The first Zionist Congress in Basel (1897) tapped existing networks of the Hovevei Zion and Hibbat Zion movements, and Zionism now found an organizational strength and breadth which, factionalism aside, outstripped all earlier efforts. Moreover, Herzl not only won support among the Yiddish masses of Vilna, Sofia, and New York, who had a continuing stake in the Jews' plight in the East; but he also stirred an unprecedented interest in Zionism in the assimilationist Jewish communities of Western Europe and among the middle-class, "uptown" Jews in America.[110]

Herzl's program no doubt benefited from the sense of crisis in the West surrounding the 1895 espionage trial of Alfred Dreyfus in France, and the anti-Semitic outpouring which accompanied it. Among Jewish intellectuals, postrevolutionary France had long epitomized political emancipation and the promise of liberalism. And yet now, at the end of the nineteenth century, that promise was being revoked. According to some, assimilation itself was on trial in the Dreyfus affair, and this shaken faith in assimilationism as a solution to the Jewish Question became one of the frequent themes in Zionist polemics in the late 1890s. As Max Nordau asserted in his address to the Second Zionist Congress, the Dreyfus case "raises itself as an admonition and a lesson in the face of those Jews who still persist in believing themselves to be definitely and without reserve received into the national comradeship . . . of the most advanced Western countries." Or again, speaking of the Jews' dangerous sense of security in the United States, even Reform Rabbi Gustave Gottheil warned, "They do not know, or they do not want to know, that their new 'fatherland' does not believe them, does not desire them, laughs at and mocks their declarations of love; they do not know, or do not want to know, that their new 'fatherland' treats them not as children, not as patriots, but as vagabonds, . . . as outcasts. And [Jews] are allowed to stay only so long as they are willing to be woodchoppers and water bearers."[111]

Paired with the enormous and continuing influx of Yiddish-speaking migrants from Eastern Europe, this rising interest in Jewish nationalism among the assimilationists in America's German Jewish community lent a peculiar cast to Zionist activity in the United States. The shape which the Federation of American Zionists (FAZ) assumed upon its founding in 1898 hardly rendered it a model of political efficacy: the FAZ consisted of an English-speaking, "uptown" cadre of leaders, and a Yiddish-speaking, "downtown" rank and file. Such cultural differences greatly weakened the movement in terms of its organization, unity, and coordination: key leaders were neither familiar with the Yiddish language, nor terribly interested in tailoring their program to the intellectual style of the religious (orthodox) masses, nor, in fact, eager to bridge these differences. FAZ president Richard Gottheil, for example, was less inclined to mend this growing cultural rift than to exploit it in framing his Zionist appeals: the established Jewish community, he argued in his Aims of Zionism (1898), could take heart that the creation of a Jewish state would stem the tide of immigration from Eastern Europe, and hence the influx of these allegedly less assimilable "Oriental" Jews would cease to threaten the assimilationist aspirations of a fully Americanized Jewry.[112]

Disaffection with the style and priorities of the leadership was reflected in rival Zionist organizations more sensitive to the religious and cultural sensibilities of the newly arrived, Yiddish-speaking Jews, and more responsive to the material needs of an impoverished immigrant population. The largest of these until the turn of the century was the Knights of Zion. Founded in Chicago by Leon Zolotkoff (who had

been among the American delegates to the Basel Congress), this organization resembled the Polish National Alliance in that it combined
the ideological goals of nationalism with the practical programs of
mutual assistance, insurance, and Old World sociability. The basic
units of the Knights of Zion were the Yiddish community's pre-existing
landsmanshaften—voluntary associations formed on the basis of Old
World regional or village ties. In tapping this network, leaders of the
Knights hoped to root Zionism firmly in the fabric of immigrant communal life, and thus to reach more Yiddish immigrants, and to reach
them more meaningfully, than did their "silk hat" rivals in the FAZ.[113]

Zionism in the United States in the waning years of the 1890s was
fraught with organizational and ideological contradictions stemming
from the increasing diversity of America's Jewry. As an organized
political force, Zionism would remain relatively modest in the United
States until World War I. Nonetheless, organized Zionism was markedly on the rise from the first Basel Congress onward. By 1900, for
instance, the FAZ claimed 135 affiliated societies, spanning twenty-
five states and embracing 8,000 members. The Knights of Zion network, regional arrangements such as the Zion Federation of New
England States, and unaffiliated circles such as the the Modern Builders of Zion (Kansas City) augmented these figures modestly.[114]

Moreover, the Zionist presence shaped the terms of the debate over
a variety of questions in the immigrant community. In this respect
American Zionism enjoyed an influence far beyond its limited organizational expression.[115] So long as Jews worldwide suffered "special
Jewish *tsores* [troubles]," Leon Zolotkoff argued, Herzl's program represented one of the few attractive, realizable, and concrete schemes for
redress. Zionism, he wrote, says to every Jew, "Enough of flirting with
people who despise you! Enough talking of tolerance when you need
to talk of your rights! . . . Have self-respect!"[116] To the extent that
recent refugees from the Russian Pale were particularly concerned with
issues of group identity, social tolerance, and self-respect, the portent
of a Zionist state shaped the ways in which a range of issues were
discussed—assimilation, anti-Semitism, patriotism to the host nation,
and the immigrant's continuing responsibility to oppressed Jews elsewhere in the world.

Within the burgeoning Jewish socialist movement there was a good
deal of resistance to Herzl's Zionist program. Zionism was anathema in
these quarters, first, in that Herzl's blueprint had little to say about the
threat of Jewish labor falling prey to Jewish capital. "Private property,
which is the economic basis of independence, shall be developed freely

and respected by us," wrote Herzl, thus suggesting to some that the Zionist state would simply replicate, not redress, the economic basis of exploitation. Indeed, a Jewish Bank was to be the engine of the entire project.[117] And second, Herzl's emphasis upon creating a Zionist state through diplomatic negotiation with world powers meant accepting, rather than challenging, the legitimacy of repressive regimes. The Jewish liberation movement as he saw it ought to remain neutral on questions of domestic policy within the nations of the Diaspora. Hence to its milder socialist critics Zionism represented a misguided effort to address economic issues with ethnic responses; to more severe critics like Karl Kautsky, Zionism proved itself not merely misguided but fully reactionary, by actively blocking revolution in Russia and elsewhere.[118]

But an alternate version of Jewish nationalism, rooted in the bitter events of 1881 and 1882, did gain some currency among Jewish radicals in the final decades of the century. Until the massive anti-Jewish violence in Russia in 1881, most Jewish intellectuals and students involved in revolutionary or populist politics had been involved as Russians, not as Jews. "Going to the people," as the contemporary phrase in revolutionary circles had it, meant without ambiguity going to the *Russian* people. Since the liberation of the Jews would be an inevitable result of the liberation of Russia at large, Jewish nationalism was seen as a superfluity. But after the outbreak of anti-Jewish violence on the part of the Russian and Ukrainian peasantry in the early 1880s, "assimilation" and "Russification" took on new and troubling meaning for Jewish radicals. The unity of the imagined "Russian people" was suddenly and irrevocably called into question when many Christians within the movement applauded the anti-Jewish violence in Kiev, Elizavetgrad, and elsewhere. Jews, the Czar, and the landowning nobility represented the triumvirate of Russian oppression, the argument ran, and the pogroms beginning in the Passover season of 1881 represented the first tremors of the long-awaited revolution. The slumbering peasantry, which had taken on a mythic significance among many Russian thinkers in the 1860s and 1870s, was at last showing signs of a political awakening.[119]

As radicalism and Judaism thus came into collision, many Jewish radicals still maintained their ties with the Russian intelligentsia. Jacob Gordin, for example, who would later surface in New York as one of the premier spokespersons for the cosmopolitan position, issued a pamphlet only months after the pogroms in which he identified the Jewish bourgeoisie as the real villains of 1881. Moishe Lieb Lilienblum subsequently charged that Gordin was on suspiciously good terms with the "pogromchiks."[120] Other Jews, too, joined their Russian compatriots among the populist groups in greeting the violence as "the signs of the Russian revolution, expressing itself first on the Jews," or as the "instinctive outbreak of a revolutionary group rage [folks-tsorn] among the Russian masses against their oppressors."[121]

But others began to rethink—even renounce—their assimilationism and to discover a tie to the Jewish masses. Some now rejected the Russian language and began speaking Yiddish exclusively; some discarded their Russianized names and went back to their Jewish given names. One group of Kiev students announced to their orthodox coreligionists, "We repent of having considered ourselves Russians and not Jews . . . The pogrom in Elizavetgrad, in Balta, here in Kiev, and in other towns has shown us what a mournful mistake we made. Yes, we are Jews."[122]

While many of these activists retained their faith in political radicalism and held aloof from the proto-Zionist Am Olam and BILU societies which were then gaining currency, they nonetheless rejected the assertions of the Russian populist Narodnaya Volya that anti-Semitism represented a legitimate and necessary stage in the liberation of Russia. Out of this disaffection with the main currents of Russian radicalism emerged a new brand of leftist Jewish nationalism, which fused radical economic principles with the Zionist certainty that the Jewish Question could not simply be wished away. Although quite distinct from Zionism, this sentiment within the Jewish labor movement in Europe, and later in America, rested on the very premise which animated Theodore Herzl's treatise itself: "We are one people— our enemies have made us one without our consent."[123]

This inchoate national feeling began to crystallize as a political force only in 1897, when the General Jewish Workers' League (the Bund) was founded in Vilna; a network of Bundist leagues in the United States appeared later still. But throughout the 1880s and 1890s an informal Jewish nationalism spread among workers in both Europe and America as the Yiddish proletariat grew, and as Jews under blatant czarist policy continued to suffer (and hence to flee) as Jews. The leftist but Jewish orientation gained popularity as labor organizations increasingly came into competition with Zionist organizations for the hearts and minds of the Yiddish proletariat: the growing presence of the Zionist movement in 1898 and after would drive Bundists to ever fancier flights of nationalist rhetoric.[124]

The debate over national identity was not at every moment the central, defining conflict within Yiddish labor in the United States: it criss-crossed additional faultlines separating trade unionists and socialists and the competing cults of personality surrounding figures like Louis Miller, Benjamin Feygenbaum, and Daniel DeLeon. But the national question did surface repeatedly in a variety of labor forums in those years. As early as 1887, Jewish socialists in New York split on the question of national identity and hence founded two rival branches of the Socialist Labor Party (SLP): "Jewish" Branch 8, and "Russian" Branch 17. Practical considerations forced a similar concession to Jewish separatism upon the founding of United Hebrew Trades in 1888.[125] Most dramatically, Abraham Cahan underscored the lingering unease of Jewish socialists when he raised the Jewish Question at the International Socialist Congress in Brussels in 1891. As Point Four of the agenda, the delegate from New York entered the straightforward but finally controversial question, "How should the organized workers of all countries stand on the Jewish Question?"[126]

Point Four raised a number of objections among the delegates, ranging from the standard assertion that "such questions do not exist for socialists" to the more idiosyncratic argument that a pro-Jewish statement would leave the socialist movement dangerously vulnerable to the wrath of European anti-Semitism. Cahan then appealed to the Congress:

> The Jews are persecuted. Pogroms are made upon them. They are insulted, they are oppressed. Exceptional laws are made for them. They have been made into a separate class of people with no rights. These people with no rights want to struggle right alongside all other proletarians and they request a place in the ranks of the social democracy. The anti-Semitic Russian press attacks the Jews, and tries to create the impression that everyone hates us, including the workers. I therefore demand that you declare before the world that this is a lie—that you are the enemy of all exploiters, Christian as well as Jewish ones; that you love Jewish workers as well as Christian ones.
>
> Push back anti-Semitism! Declare before the world that you condemn every form of anti-Jewish persecution![127]

After heated debate over the unfair privileges implied by such a "philo-Semitic" declaration, the Congress's rather remarkable compromise was to pass a resolution condemning both anti- *and* philo-Semitism.[128]

Cahan's plea at the Brussels Congress antedated the formation of the Bund in Russia by six years and the advent of the Farband (Jewish National Workers' Alliance) in the United States by nearly two decades.[129] But his address encapsulated the central concerns of these later organizations, and expressed an increasingly common line of argument among Jewish socialists in the 1890s. Throughout this decade and beyond, allegiances to the host nation, to the Jewish "nation," and to the socialist International were not always easily squared with one another. To one contributor to the *Abend blatt* in 1900 it was clear that assimilationism meant to "close one's eyes, turn one's head, and to believe that there is no peril":

> [The assimilated Jew] appears to evade every especially Jewish question, to make himself deaf and blind to all that takes place in the Jewish world, and—when he is honest—to suffer deep in his heart . . .
>
> As a socialist I drop the present entirely and live in the future and for the future. For the time I shut my eyes to the entire Jewish people and see before me only a Jewish proletariat. I want to organize them, awaken them to struggle, broaden the social revolution.
>
> But when, day in day out, I must leaf through the black, gloomy record of the Jews . . .
>
> No—better to bid me to hew wood.[130]

The tactical corollaries to the socialist/nationalist fusion included the demand that world socialist leaders not harden the lines of ethnic identification by condoning anti-Semitic words or deeds while blandly insisting that Jews simply assimilate into the international community of workers. Like Zionists, the Yiddish socialists held that world history and world hostility had forged the Jews into a nation—whether or not they willed it, and whether or not they had a home. The second corollary was that the socialist movement at large had plenty to gain by approaching Jews as Jews rather than as members of some backward clan who ought to abandon their parochial allegiances. In his "Proletarishker Maggid" in the *Arbeiter Zeitung*, for instance, Cahan himself sought to broaden the base of New York's labor movement in the early 1890s by casting socialist polemics in the folk form of the East European Yiddish homily.[131]

But the bedrock of this ideology as it came to be articulated by the immigrant intellectuals Morris Winchevsky and Abraham Liessen, and by Chaim Zhitlovsky and Lev Martov in Europe, had to do not with tactics merely, but with entitlements. Not for the sake of expedience, but by *right* were Jews to be incorporated into the international socialist movement as Jews, just as other workers took their places in the ranks on the basis of national blocs. By *right* Jews were to be granted recognition and autonomy by the socialist state. "The Russian may be a Russian patriot, the German a German, the Hottentot a Hottentot," wrote Moishe Baranov, but a Jewish socialist must "presume to be a German patriot when he lives in Germany, a Russian when they break his bones in Russia, or an Austrian when they spit in his face in Austria." "How is it," he wanted to know, "that Russian or Polish or French patriotism is less *treyf* [impure] than Jewish?" The nation, in this view, was the proper building block of international socialism, and there was no question but that the Jews constituted a nation.[132]

This view did not go unchallenged, of course, nor was it the dominant view within immigrant labor circles in the 1890s. Maybe in a "broad sense" a Jewish socialist can be a Jewish patriot, quipped *Naye tsayt* editor Philip Krantz; but then, "in a 'broad sense' an attic can be a noodle-pot."[133] But while cosmopolitanists like Krantz and Benjamin Feygenbaum had the upper hand on the nationality question, they may have protested too much. Although cosmopolitan arguments were more palatable in New York and Chicago in the 1890s than in Minsk and Kiev in the 1880s, nationalism was gradually on the ascendancy. The Yiddish press, branches of the Workman's Circle, *landsmanshaften,* and labor unions became the arenas for an ongoing, if inconclusive, debate over national identity. By the late 1890s, while labor nationalism still awaited expression in a coherent party, shades of nationalist polemic nonetheless enjoyed currency in a variety of public forums including coffeehouse discussions, *Forverts* feuilletons, and the Yiddish short stories of Abraham Cahan and Leon Kobrin.[134]

Such was the political lay of the land within the active Jewish community in the late 1890s. Whereas the Irish movement was retrenching following the defeat of the Home Rule bills of 1886 and 1893, and whereas the Polish movement was rising in pitch alongside the National Democratic movement in Poland, the Jewish nationalist movement was engaged largely in an internal war of words and definitions. The FAZ and the Knights of Zion did stand on concrete platforms, aligned with the aims of Herzlian Zionism worldwide. But until well after the turn of the century, perhaps more energy was spent in the battles engaging cosmopolitans and nationalists, bourgeois Zionists and socialists, orthodox believers and secular freethinkers, than was spent in the Jews' struggle against the non-Jewish world powers for some political settlement of the Jewish Question.

Jewish nationalism was scarcely a focused movement in the waning years of the nineteenth century. Rather, the national question evoked a dynamic, complex, multivocal, almost infinitely faceted response. But no less than the more neatly delineated factional debates among Irish and Polish activists, this ongoing debate on the question of Jewish nationality did draw upon and further popularize a shared vocabulary of "peoplehood," group rights, and political sovereignty among the wanderers in North America.

The organizational history of immigrant nationalism is less important for the real power wielded by the Clan na Gael, the PNA, or the FAZ, than for the ideologies, hopes, and tactics which these organizations expressed. Successful or not, such organizations remained the primary instruments for emigrant action on behalf of their beleaguered nations, and so they mark off the range of political possibilities which emigrants of the period thought both practical and desirable.

But the significance of nationalism in Irish, Polish, and Yiddish emigrant communities must not be gauged by its limited political might. As the Gaelic League, the Polish Singers' Alliance, and Otto von Bismarck himself recognized, politics is not limited to the straightforward mechanics of government. Culture itself may be the site of domination and resistance; and cultural forms like the religious myth and the historical melodrama may embody and convey the ideals of national liberation more forcefully than even the most broad-based and best-oiled political organizations.

2

Plaintive Song, Heroic Story: Nationalism and Immigrant Popular Culture

> The awareness of being Irish came to us as small children, through plaintive song and heroic story ... As children, we drew in a burning hatred of British rule with our mother's milk. Until my father died, at over eighty, he never said "England" without adding, "God damn her!" Before I was ten I knew of the great heroes—Robert Emmet, Wolfe Tone, Michael Davitt, Parnell, and O'Donovan Rossa, who was chained hand and foot, like a dog, and had to eat from a tin plate on the floor of a British prison.
>
> —Elizabeth Gurley Flynn, *The Rebel Girl*

Chiding the Irish-American nationalists of his day for reducing the cause to a mere calendar of social events, Finley Peter Dunne quipped that "Be hivins, if Ireland cud be freed be a picnic, it'd not on'y be free to-day, but an impire, begorra."[1] To be sure, devoting a few hours to a Clan na Gael picnic or Women's Alliance entertainment did not necessarily represent a willingness to devote one's life to the cause. But emigrants' limited commitment to active political struggle should not obscure the extent to which nationalism did hold sway in other areas of day-to-day life. There is a second, critical dimension to Dunne's observation on the penchant of nationalists for sponsoring picnics: if it is true that political activism often lapsed into mere sociability, it is also true that everyday sociability was often infused with political meaning. If we consider immigrant outlooks as opposed to political outcomes, these nationalist movements and debates were not marginal but central.

Whatever his or her particular level of political commitment, the ordinary immigrant encountered the language and icons of nationalism in a wide variety of cultural forms. Proto-Zionist plots in Yiddish theatre, the martial strains of Polish Catholicism, the ceremonial solidarity of St. Patrick's Day parades—a range of cultural texts indicate the salience of national questions in the everyday dealings of these immigrant communities. As Elizabeth Gurley Flynn's autobiography suggests, nationalism was woven into the very fabric of everyday living—in riveting bedtime stories, in a parent's Anglophobic curses, in family chronicles and legends, in popular songs. Even the Irish writer of an essay on boxing might pause to reflect, "The prize fight with bare hands could only have been developed in England. It is fit only for brutalized men." Indeed, the politics of sport in general was nicely captured in the same writer's article on "Ancient Irish Athletic Games, Exercises, and Weapons."[2]

Material culture and artifice, too, prominently featured nationalist icons: commemorative trinkets and engravings of Queen Jadwiga or Tadeusz Kościuszko; prints of "Limerick Avenged" by the Irish Brigade; posters depicting "The Spirit of '98," with twenty-seven images from "the great insurrectionary movement"; and didactic calendars noting every conceivable date of national significance. One Milwaukee Avenue shop in Chicago dealt exclusively in paraphernalia to enhance the military pomp of Polish clubs and societies—flags, sashes, badges, batons, and rods.[3]

Four areas of immigrant popular culture in particular diffused nationalist ideologies beyond the limited circles of dedicated political activists: the immigrant press, popular religion, vernacular theater, and the annual calendar of national celebrations, observances, parades, and ethnic fairs. Far more than the tactical initiatives of the Knights of Zion, the Clan na Gael, or the Polish National Alliance, these elements of immigrant culture kept the nationalist idea of peoplehood and identity alive in the diverse setting of the New World.

George Lipsitz has described the late nineteenth century as a period of crisis for "traditional forms of memory." The disruptions of urbanization, the atomizing effects of industrial wage labor and new information technologies, and the break from earlier restraints which attended the rise of commercialized leisure, he argues, all added up to "the destruction of tradition" and a collective "sense of disconnection from the past."[4] Nowhere was the potential for such "disconnection" as pronounced as in the case of migrants, removed physically from their respective communities and from the locus of ethnic tradition, and in some cases removed temporally, as it were, from the pre- or early-industrial patterns which prevailed in the rural pockets of the old country.

Under these circumstances popular culture offered a salve for the dislocations of modernity. Immigrant journals redressed isolation and bridged trans-Atlantic distances by defining and addressing their readers as members of a cohesive diaspora community. The popular religio-political mythologies surrounding the Maccabees, St. Patrick, and Our Lady of Częstochowa countered American patterns of nativism and interethnic prejudice by evoking long, grand traditions and flattering notions of chosenness. And street demonstrations in memory of the Wolfe Tone Rebellion or popular plays like Moishe Hurvitz's *Eretz Israel: the Rabbi and the Czar* symbolically rerooted the emigrant within a community and a tradition which the act of migration had disrupted. In all of this, nationalist strains were particularly resonant: within a context of demeaning Anglo-Saxonism, the nationalist idiom expressed a sense of pride; against a backdrop of past hardship and present uncertainty, the nationalist idiom promised a better future; and amid the concern for the friends and relatives one had left behind, the nationalist idiom offered the assurance that their lot, too, could be improved, and that the emigrants had not simply abandoned their compatriots.

Popular nationalist mythologies and iconographies tended to obscure the social divisions within these communities, but they did not erase them. Just as nationalist narratives themselves contested the meaning of diverse "peoplehood" in the hierarchically ordered New World, so were the emblems of national destiny contested from *within*. The rogue-heroes of the Irish vernacular theater were assaulted as unrespectable by the Irish-American middle class, for instance, even though such characters often served as vehicles for a subversive (and pervasive) Anglophobia. And the liberationist legends derived from theology or military history, steeped as they were in the rites and rights of "manhood," rested upon gendered formulations of participation in the nation even as they invoked a unified group destiny. Like the stage Irishman, such exclusions and imbalances were subject to challenge— as, for instance, when Teofila Samolinska, Stefania Chmielinska, Stefania Laudyn-Chrzanowska, and others sought to refashion the constraining nationalist icon of the Polish Mother.

But if their meanings were diverse and sometimes openly contested, popular legends and emblems did give the question of national sovereignty a currency which was otherwise precluded by the demands and the limitations in the narrower arena of politics proper. The ideas of nationalism, in other words, far outreached the politics of nationalism. Predicated on the promise of national liberation, punctuated with historic and inspirational references, popular culture at once reflected and reinforced the dimensions of immigrant exile, pilgrimage, and wandering in the New World.

The Press

Circulation figures for immigrant journals are notoriously unreliable, making it very difficult to gauge the press's influence with any quantitative precision. Publishers routinely exaggerated their circulation not only to inflate their advertising rates, but also to enhance their own importance in the eyes of local politicians and business elites. On the other hand, however, contemporary memoirs and sketches of ghetto life indicate that a single copy of the *Forverts* or the *Irish World* may have reached three, five, ten, or a sweatshop-full of readers, suggesting that available figures may actually understate the extent of a given journal's reach. As Victor Greene puts it, a journal's audience "included 'listeners' as well as readers."[5]

The most widely cited figures for the 1890s provide at least a rough sense of scale. The Irish, enjoying the greatest resources by the end of the century, boasted the two highest circulating immigrant papers, the *Irish World* (125,000) and the Boston *Pilot* (75,000), and a number of more modest publications ranging from 20,000 to 50,000. By contrast, the largest of the Yiddish dailies, the *Yiddishes tageblatt*, claimed only 30,000 in 1898, although along with the rivaling *Forverts* and *Abend blatt*, it was growing rapidly as the Yiddish-speaking readership grew. And finally, in 1894 Henryk Nagiel estimated that the entire Polish-American press combined enjoyed a circulation of 100,000 and an actual readership "three or four times greater." The largest share was commanded by a few giants like *Zgoda*, *Dziennik Chicagoski*, *Wiara i Ojczyzna*, and *Kuryer Polski*.[6]

Other aspects of the journalist's reach are more certain. First, although women's participation in journalism was limited until well after the turn of the century to a few exceptions like Katherine Conway of the *Pilot* staff, or to the exceptional project of *Głos Polek* (The Polish Women's Voice, 1900), women did make up a significant part of the immigrant readership.[7] Letters to the editor, notices on women's organizational activity, and columns like the *Forverts*' "Bintel Brief" all suggest that these papers were read regularly by women as well as men. Indeed, the "Women's Page" as an institution was everywhere on the rise. Second, the largest immigrant journals are known to have reached a nationwide, even an international, audience. The *Pilot* and the *Irish World*, for example, were mainstays in the trans-Atlantic dialogue among the "sea-divided Gaels"; and one *Tageblatt* opinion survey in 1899 prompted letters from across North America, including Boston, Jersey City, Baltimore, St. Louis, Cleveland, Kansas City, Pine Bluff (Arkansas), New Orleans, and Montreal.[8]

The press of all three immigrant communities played a critical role in the diffusion of nationalism. In the three cases the most widely read, highly circulated, and influential newspapers in the 1890s were directly engaged in the ongoing debates over national questions, and most were affiliated, in spirit if not institutionally, with one or another of the nationalist factions then active. As James Jeffrey Roche wrote of John Boyle O'Reilly, his predecessor at the *Pilot*, "His *Pilot* work was more than that of mere editor; for he was also the leader and teacher of his people; not only did he gravely weigh and discuss the interests of the struggling patriots at home, but he devoted himself with minute zeal to the defense and advancement of his fellow-exiles."[9] Editors and publishers like O'Reilly, Khasriel Sarasohn, Patrick Ford, and Zbigniew Brodowski may have first been drawn to the press because of their political activism; but their stature in their respective movements resulted largely from their control of the press.

Of course, in describing ethnic journalism, the broad appellation "nationalist" takes in a whole range of journalistic opinion and style. Even in his "respectable" period at the century's end, Patrick Ford of the *Irish World* inclined at least rhetorically to the incendiary, while journals like the *Catholic Citizen* warned that "intelligent Irish nationalism" eschewed dynamite and "barrack politics."[10] Certain that "the Zionistic solution of the Jewish problem is the only practical one," the *Yiddishes tageblatt* explained to its orthodox readers that nationalism was not *treyf* from a religious standpoint; the radical *Naye tzayt* and *Forverts*, meanwhile, pondered and debated whether Jewish nationalism was *treyf* from a socialist standpoint.[11] And organs like New York's *Gazeta Polska* were designed solely to support and sustain the nationalist movement, while in the mercurial *Kuryer Polski* nationalism was secondary to—perhaps even a by-product of—the editor's concentration upon the status of Poles in America.[12] But the *Catholic Citizen* no less than the *Irish World* dutifully promoted nationalist events; the cosmopolitanist *Abend blatt*, no less than the Zionist *Tageblatt*, positioned the Dreyfus case and the crisis it represented as its lead story for weeks and months at a time; and *Kuryer Polski*, no less than the more actively nationalistic *Zgoda*, argued that the now "mighty group" of Poles in America could influence the U.S. government to intervene in European affairs on Poland's behalf.[13]

The specific contributions of these presses to programmatic nationalism may be delineated along three lines: the journals sought to fulfill a didactic function, a propagandistic function, and a strategic/tactical function. First, many editors attempted to school their respective publics in the history of their nation, often painting Old World oppression in vivid colors as a first step toward highlighting the links between Old World suffering and New World obligation. Such didactic background sketches ranged from the *Irish World's* "Diary of '98," which weekly chronicled the events of the uprising of a hundred years before, to *Dziennik Chicagoski's* lengthy history of the Polish Question from the fourteenth century to *Kulturkampf.*[14] Even the moderate *Catholic Citizen* would offer up John Finerty's recollections of "Land League Days," recount the battle of Vinegar Hill, or run a biographical series on "The Men of '48" (including a piece on Fenian James Stephens) by way of connecting readers to an unbroken past of national struggle.[15] *Kuryer Polski* patiently explained why national liberation was in the interests not only of the nobility but of the masses; and in *Zgoda* a reader's query from Ypsilanti became the occasion for a lengthy address on the November rising. *Zgoda* neatly summed up this didactic impulse in a page-one feature, "What Does the Fatherland Want from Us?" In a kind of journalistic catechism, the editors later sponsored an essay contest on the question, "What are the obligations of our youth here in regard to the Fatherland, Society, and the United States?"[16]

Perhaps the purest form of political didacticism was the English language page of the *Yiddishes tageblatt*. In its battle to protect tradition from "thick witted" Reform rabbis and from the Americanizing influences of the public schools and urban culture, the *Tageblatt* reached out with a daily page "Devoted Especially to the Younger Generation: Religion, Literature, Patriotism."[17] The English language page was designed to school the American-born in Jewish tradition, and so to keep them within the social and cultural orbit of Judaism. The spirit of the endeavor was captured in the chauvinistic assertion that "we [Jews] have greater heroes than George Washington," paired with the lament that Americanized children of immigrants were becoming ever distanced from—even ignorant of—Jewish greatness and the national aspirations which constituted its legacy.[18]

Here the editor sought to edify young readers with reports on the plight of the Jews worldwide, articles on "The Marvels of Israel's History" or "The Martyr of Martyrs—The Jew," explanatory essays by prominent figures on "Why I Am a Zionist," and instructive pieces on "Zionism and the National Idea in Judaism." Such lessons in proper identification and obligation were enlivened by bittersweet historical notes on the double-edged meaning of Jewishness: "Ever since the Babylonian captivity prejudice against Jews as a race or religion . . . has blackened the historical pages of every so-called civilized country . . . [But] the Jewish race, wonderfully virile, has conquered every obstacle."[19]

As this last passage suggests, didacticism often blurred toward the press's second nationalist function, propagandism. Both in their political editorials and in their news coverage of world affairs, immigrant journals often struck a heroic or inflammatory chord which was calculated to spur readers to political action. Articles in the Irish press decrying the "Disgusting Exhibition of Anglo-Mania" in the United States, and page-one coverage of conditions in the Old World ("Never since black '47 has there been anything like it") supplemented a political agenda based on notions of Anglo-Saxon misconduct and Celtic liberationism.[20] Fillers such as "An Incident of the Penal Laws" outlined the discriminatory inheritance laws which had decimated Catholic landholdings, keeping fresh the wounds of a period when the Irish were "treated as if they were outlaws."[21]

Less oblique calls to action included *Dziennik Chicagoski's* "Be vigilant and be prepared!" or the *Irish World's* insistence that its readers "keep alive the flames of patriotism which will yet light to her final deliverance our motherland."[22] Such calls often accompanied appeals for donations to the Famine relief drives of the 1890s, the National Fund, or the Zionist Colonial Bank as well as appeals to participate in upcoming nationalist demonstrations or festivals. Likewise, published letters from Old World political luminaries like Israel Zangwill, Max Nordau, Maud Gonne, or Michael Davitt at once kept readers abreast of political developments affecting their nation, outlined the potential emigrant contribution, and often painted a flattering portrait of the emigrants' centrality to the cause.[23]

As the *Yiddishes tageblatt's* earlier assertion of the "wonderful virility" of the Jewish race suggests, even as these journals promoted nationalist action, they also prescribed the roles which their readers were to assume. It was in this spirit that women were directed toward—and applauded for—the cultural guardianship of nation-building or the caretaking aspects of organizational activity, leaving the "virile" work of political struggle to men and boys. "The Polish woman remains what she has been for ages," remarked *Zgoda*: "a mother, a tutor of Polish children whom no government decrees and no schools can manage to denationalize." Indeed, in the period surrounding the establishment of the Polish Women's Alliance, the Polish press debated with some vigor the propriety of women's forming their own political organizations.[24] Similarly, while Maud Gonne's nationalism was predicated on a challenge to the sexual hierarchy in Irish politics, male journalists were more apt to respond to her beauty than to her words: "A brow crowned with a halo of golden hair," rhapsodized the *Catholic Citizen*, "large eyes which are now fired with indignation, now bathed in tears of pity; a graceful, slender, and supple figure; the gesture large and noble; the whole appearance stamped with a character of supreme elegance—such is Miss Maud Gonne!" While this and other Irish-American journals did report on the content of Gonne's "Appeal to the Women of America," her place in the sexualized iconography of nationalist journalism undercut her own critique of the merely "charitable" roles to which nationalist women had largely been relegated.[25]

This prescriptive dimension of nationalist propaganda assumed other shapes as well. The *Catholic Citizen*, recall, warned against "barrack politics," while *Dziennik Chicagoski* took great care in warning against secular excesses. The journal's running slogan was "Let's Be Faithful to Church and Fatherland!" and, in its competition with the secularist *Zgoda*, the religionist daily reminded readers that "the clergy was, is, and always will be the truest watchfire of healthy and authentic patriotism."[26] In this way immigrant editors often sought to rein readers in, even as they attempted to spur them on—to control and guide their respective movements, even in their efforts to heighten nationalist consciousness and unleash its potential.

And finally, these didactic outlines of group history and obligation and these emotive appeals to (proscribed) action were supplemented by concrete tactical or strategic information on when, where, and how the reader might render aid to the nation. Such public service functions began with simple announcements regarding the time and place of nationalist events, such as Miłkowski's visit on behalf of the National League or a local lecture on the Gaelic revival.[27] But these announcements often ballooned into lengthier explanatory pieces on the aims and workings of one organization or another, such as Patrick Ford's conception of the Gaelic League and its potential to "win back for our island and our race that proud position, intellectually, among the nations which she held in the early ages."[28]

The *Yiddishes tageblatt* took this institutional function to its logical extreme, positioning itself as a central clearing house of tactical and logistical information for Zionism nationwide. Early in 1898 the editors applauded "the great force which the Zionist propaganda is demonstrating in this country," and urged the Zionist federations and locals which were then emerging across the country to treat the *Tageblatt* editorial office as a center for disseminating and exchanging information.[29] Ultimately the *Tageblatt* carried full accounts of key Zionist meetings, including texts of major speeches and accounts of important debates, supplemented by a series of open letters from Chicago, Boston, and Philadelphia marking the organizational progress of the movement.[30]

These didactic, propagandistic, and tactical functions were of course crucial to the task of building a nationalist constituency in the remote setting of the New World; in fulfilling these functions the press became one of the central institutions to each of these political movements. But perhaps the most fundamental, if subtle, way that the immigrant newspaper promoted nationalist outlooks was not by the political details of its content, but by its general presentation. In its front-page devotion to Old World news, in its focus upon the ethnic enclave as the locus of U.S. news, in its regular features on the group's history and literature, in its editorials on developments affecting the beleaguered nation, and in its ethnocentric frame on American affairs, the immigrant journal located the reader in an ideological universe whose very center was Poland, Ireland, or Zion. While much has rightly been made of the Americanizing influences of the immigrant press, equally striking is the tenacity with which many of these journals positioned their readers within the envisaged "nation" and its worldwide diaspora.[31] In this respect there was a marked similarity not only among the most vociferous nationalist journals like the *Irish World*, *Zgoda*, and the *Yiddishes tageblatt*, but also among these and moderate journals like the Boston *Pilot* and even the decidedly cosmopolitan *Abend blatt*.

In his discussion of the genesis of modern nationalism, Benedict Anderson identifies the newspaper as one of the key "technological means for re-presenting the *kind* of imagined community that is the nation." In compiling and refracting world events as items of "news," and in apportioning significance to them through selection and layout, print journalism creates "an imagined community among a specific assemblage of fellow-readers" to whom *these* particular items are presumed to be meaningful.[32] The numerous and varied narratives of the immigrant journal were undergirded by an implicit political and cultural geography which at once reproduced the nation and defined the reader as one of its incommutable members.

The Socialist Labor Party's Yiddish daily, the *Abend blatt*, is especially instructive on this point, in that its stated cosmopolitanist aims were so at odds with its implicit address to a coherent and enduring Jewish community. "Our country," ran the editor's credo, "is the entire civilized world, our people, the entire struggling proletariat, and our patriotism—the solidarity of all in struggle."[33] The journal took every opportunity to emphasize that class, not *Yiddishkayt*, was the essential element of the immigrant's identity; that anti-Semitism itself had an economic basis; and that Jewish nationalism was a mistaken response to conflicts which were traceable to the ravages of capitalism. Illustrative of this outlook, for instance, was the journal's approach to the most explosive case of Jewish persecution in the period, the Dreyfus affair. Throughout the late 1890s Krantz contested the popular belief in Dreyfus's innocence, because it was based purely on outrage at French anti-Semitism. The Jewish captain, he cautioned, was neither more nor less capable than his Gentile counterparts of selling out his "fatherland for a sack of gold." This was a matter for cool logic, not "patriotic" sentiment.[34]

But while the editorial staff argued unswervingly, from its internationalist position, against the hegemonic or divisive ideologies of chauvinism, ethnocentrism, murder-patriotism, labor nationalism, and Zionism, the *Abend blatt*'s news presentation conveyed something quite different. Despite Krantz's and Feygenbaum's protestations that the Jewish Question was a chimera, the very format of the paper—the selection, placement, and language of stories—daily appealed to readers as children of Israel for whom the Jewish Question was pressing and very real indeed.

The world conveyed in the pages of the *Abend blatt* was a world whose contours and inhabitants were defined by front-page stories like "Socialism Against Jewish-Hatred [*yidn-has*]," "A Pogrom in Algiers," "More Pogroms in France," "The Dreyfus Story," "Is Dreyfus Innocent?" "The Commotion About Captain Dreyfus," "High Hopes for Dreyfus," "Dreyfus-Commotion Not Yet Calmed," "No Hope for Dreyfus," "Dreyfus Has No Tie to Germany," "Anti-Semitism in France," and "Esterhazy the Guilty One."[35] The editorial page, too, would frankly offer up "A Sermon for Jews in Honor of Passover" and routinely treat subjects like "Anti-Semitism and Anti-Frankism," "Mark Twain on the Jews," "The Jews in France," "What to Make of the Dreyfus Story," or "The Socialists in France and the Dreyfus Affair."[36] Indeed, the *Abend blatt* put out a special "Dreyfus Edition" on the day of the verdict, and among the largest headlines in the journal's history is the September 9, 1899, banner, "DREYFUS CONDEMNED." Even an ad for Triumph Pastille, which ran throughout 1899, featured a man behind bars, with the legend: "This is not Dreyfus, but he suffers a lot more than Dreyfus because he is guilty." (He is guilty, it turns out, of neglecting his health.) The paper's devotion to such ethnically inscribed material implied, at the very least, that Jewish socialism was more fundamentally Jewish than Krantz and his colleagues cared to admit; at times it seemed fully to imply an "imagined community" of members of a nation in struggle.[37]

The tendency was even more pronounced, of course, among editors who were active in promoting nationalist outlooks: the contents and address of the *Irish World*, *Zgoda*, and the *Yiddishes tageblatt* typically implied an assembly of readers—an "us"—defined not as Americans, certainly, nor even as New World hyphenates, but as members of an international diaspora community. The *Irish World*, in other words, was exactly that; and *Zgoda* typically gave more prominence to features such as "Germanization" or "The Moscovite Barbarians" than to specifically Polish-*American* issues.

While ethnic journalism undoubtedly helped to ease the emigrant's transition into American life, the politics of nationalism remained central to many journals' overt, announced agendas. And at the level of tacit assumption, the struggling nation which the emigrants had left behind remained at the ideological center of the unfolding narrative of world news.

Popular Religion

The political geography implicit in ethnic journalism was complemented by the cosmology of the immigrant church. While the penny or nickel paper, a creature of modernity, located the immigrant-as-reader in the imagined community of a nation and its diaspora, so did the immigrant church, a creature of traditionalism, locate the immigrant-as-communicant in a universe whose tenets of redemption were thoroughly bound up with mythic national histories. In Irish and Polish Catholicism, as in Judaism, the rites of religious devotion regularly invoked group identities and destinies based on conceptions of a very special relationship between God and nation.

To set "popular religion"[38] under the rubric of "popular culture" is not to imply a strict equation between a communicant's relationship to the Bible on the one hand, and to penny journalism and vernacular melodrama on the other. But the three religions are rich in the kind of stories and images which, like certain secular cultural

forms, sustained and broadened nationalist ideologies. "A warlike society will have warrior gods," notes one scholar of popular religion,
"[and] a feudal society will depict its gods as feudal lords."[39] So, one
might add, will oppressed peoples worship liberationist gods. These
three religious traditions not only furnished galvanizing stories of
historic persecution, but their very cosmologies involved formulations of the "nation"—its uniqueness, its chosenness, its particular
God-given mission among the other nations of the world—which
lent support to secular claims of national rights. Inasmuch as it was
the source for a number of nationalist themes and great deal of liberationist imagery, popular religion itself was among the cultural tap-
roots of nationalist thinking.

The precise relation between established religion and nationalism
in each of these communities was complex. On the one hand, religious
orthodoxies uniformly decried the secular excesses of nationalist politics: as Cardinal Gibbons warned in his *Ambassador of Christ* (1897),
"[Nationalism] is a sentiment as senseless as it is criminal . . . Christianity is not indigenous to any soil." Fenians had actually been
excommunicated for their political transgressions, and their excom-
munication long served as a caution for their Irish and Polish coreligionists alike.[40] Similarly, orthodox Judaism identified Zionist
politics as "hastening The Return" to the Promised Land—a sacrilege
in its implicit impatience with God to work His will.[41]

On the other hand, however, religious leaders did not in every
instance object to the aims of the secular movements. Given the
religious and sectarian dimensions of Irish colonization, *Kulturkampf*,
and the pogroms, a certain affinity did exist between religious devotion
and political aspiration. Following one appeal for the "restoration of
[Ireland's] plundered rights" on the part of the bishop and priests of the
Diocese of Cloyne, John Boyle O'Reilly had cried, "Let the words be
carried outward till the farthest lands they reach/ After Christ, the
country's freedom do the Irish prelates preach!"[42] A similar impulse to
"preach freedom" was reflected in the sermons of many rabbis and the
overt Zionism of the orthodox *Yiddishes tageblatt*, as well as in the
dictum of the Resurrectionist order, "Serve God, Poles, and God will
save Poland."[43]

As Morris Rosenfeld's ruminations on "The Little Hanukkah Candles" demonstrate, religious mythologies could dovetail nicely with
nationalist designs, even lending a certain God-given righteousness to
these secular movements. "O, you little candles! You recount histories,
stories without end," he rhapsodized.

You tell of blood,
Achievement and courage,
   Wonders of yore.

When I see you flickering,
A dream, sparkling, comes to me,
   An ancient dream speaks to me:
"Jew, you have warred once,
Jew, you have conquered once."
   God, it is scarcely to be believed!

"There was order at one time,
You once were a nation,
   You once ruled:
You once had a country,
You once had a mighty hand!"
   Oh, how deeply moving that is.[44]

However aloof organized religion may have held from organized nationalism, the political legends attached to religious figures like St. Patrick, the Maccabees, and the Holy Virgin of Częstochowa tacitly sanctioned nationalist outlooks and rhetoric. If political action on behalf of the modern nation demanded a break from traditionalism, in all three cases religious tradition itself nonetheless provided a language and a symbolism by which such action could be explained and justified.

In the case of Irish Catholicism, an extensive hagiography emphasized the Irish national mission of Catholicizing the Continent and the tyrannies of Anglo and Norman conquerors. The feast days of St. Brigid, Marianus Scotus, St. Colomba, St. Kieran and others of the Twelve Apostles of Ireland all recalled a period when the island held tremendous cultural influence in Europe. And the lives of some sainted figures—Gelasius of Armagh, Thaddeus MacCarthy, Lawrence O'Toole—fully embodied the Irish struggle against English attempts to either block or control religious worship. The lore surrounding St. Gelasius of Armagh, for instance, involves the betrayal of Ireland into the hands of Henry II by an English Pope, and the subsequent reduction of the Irish Church to beggary.[45]

The central emblem of the affinity between religious mythology and political aspiration, of course, was and remains the figure of St. Patrick. So intertwined are the mythic threads of Patrick's service to the Catholic faith and to the Irish nation, that it remains an open question whether March 17 is a national or a religious holiday. According to the typical formulation among writers, poets, and prelates in the late nineteenth century, it was both. As New York's *Irish-American* had it, "St. Patrick's Day Shows Erin's Sons Still True to Faith and Fatherland."[46]

The power of this nexus and the urgency of its recognition were forcefully conveyed in Justus J. Spreng's impressively titled homily (1898), "St. Patrick's Day: For an Irishman to Forget Patrick Is to Become Recreant to Every Duty, God and Country, Kith and Kin, Honor and Manhood." By Spreng's account, both Ireland's "purest faith and loftiest patriotism came from the teaching of Patrick." Juxtaposed against Tudor, Cromwellian, and Williamite ruthlessness, the gentle mission of Patrick symbolized both the superiority of Catholicism and, for its defense, the necessity of Irish liberation from the English heretics. By the same token, the three leaves of the shamrock symbolized the Holy Trinity, while its prolific growth suggested Irish national resilience. "Famine, pestilence and the sword mowed down the people," said Spreng, "but the 'dear little shamrock' budding forth on Patrick's Day spoke of the faith and nationality that never die."[47]

This linkage was as conventional as its power was axiomatic among Irish orators and writers. In his 1896 *Chaplain's Sermons*, a series of templated Catholic sermons for the benefit of inexperienced priests, John Talbot Smith thoroughly fused the issues of Ireland's political martyrdom and spiritual grace. "All admit," he wrote, "that the wealth and rank of Ireland among the nations might have been very high at this moment had the Irish joined the English in the deliberate treason against Christ, perpetrated by the delectable Henry VIII and his virtuous court." For rejecting the "treason" of the Reformation, Ireland itself had been crucified. But, Smith assured, "God has not deserted the faithful race, nor forgotten the apostle who carried the faith to Erin." In points seven and eight of his recommended outline, Smith went on to promise "the triumphs of the race and its religion through the very exile which was intended to destroy it," and to detail "the severe punishment of their enemies, and the vindication of St. Patrick." The twin crimes of Anglican heresy and British misgovernment will be repaid in full, as the exiles worldwide now "make known the enormities of [British] rule in Ireland and elsewhere." Ireland's history, Smith concluded, "is but beginning."[48]

Smith was careful to make clear that the "vindication of St. Patrick," though indeed political, would be primarily a spiritual, not a revolutionary phenomenon. Ireland's inevitable glory, in his formulation, "will not be born of bloody conquest or treaty-cheating, but of the peace and good will of Christ."[49] Others, however, were slower to draw such a line between the nation's spiritual and revolutionary traditions, between devotion and dynamite. According to Robert Ellis Thompson, "the Heavenly translation of St. Patrick, and . . . the birthday of [insurrectionist] Robert Emmet, coming both in March, seem to unite all that is best and most heroic in [Ireland's] earlier and later history." By Thompson's formulation, Patrick's missionary activity in Ireland "helped to awaken the nation to a sense of its collective existence and its place among the nations." In bestowing a religious mission upon the Irish people, in other words, Patrick had helped to forge the political idea of an Irish nation. And conversely, in defying British authority and insisting upon Irish independence, insurrectionist Robert Emmet had helped that nation to carry out its religious mission: "It is the purpose of Ireland to be herself, . . . to resist absorption into any and every other nationality, that it may serve them all by its independent contribution to the great cause of Christian and civilized progress."[50]

One historian has recently suggested that, given the centrality of the Catholic church in "sustaining the ongoing Irish identity" against the encroachments of Anglicization, "it was inevitable that Irish and Catholic over time would become virtually interchangeable terms."[51] As these St. Patrick's Day addresses indicate, the affinity was not limited to Irish institutional life but was imbedded in the very texture of belief. That Robert Emmet had been a Protestant was neither ironic nor terribly important, as far as Thompson was concerned: it was the spirit of his deeds, not the details of his pedigree, that counted. Most important to Thompson, as to John Talbot Smith and Justus J. Spreng, was the unity of faith and fatherland, and the way in which a devotion to each evoked an obligation to the other.

This unity was as pronounced, if not more so, in the case of the Poles. Against a similar historical backdrop of sectarian division and conquest, Polish Catholicism, too, had long taken on shades of political meaning. In their classic study of the Polish peasantry, Thomas and Znaniecki noted that Poles conceived nationality "as a part of the divine order of the world in which each nation has a particular mission to fulfill, and whoever hinders national self-determination—be it even an official church—sins against God."[52] The fusion of religious and national identities was so complete, in fact, that in the vernacular of the Polish peasant Catholicism was frequently referred to as "the Polish faith," just as speaking the Polish language was speaking "in Catholic" (*po katolicku*).[53]

It was their similar (but competing) ideological frames on Roman Catholic faith and fatherland, no doubt, which fueled the tensions between the Irish and the Poles in the United States. The most dramatic manifestation of this fusion of the sacred with the political was a series of Polish schismatic movements within the church, most notably the formation of the Polish National Catholic Church (PNCC) in Scranton, Pennsylvania, in 1897. Like smaller movements in Chicago and Buffalo which preceded it, the PNCC grew out of Polish demands for cultural autonomy in the face of an overbearing Irish hierarchy. As outlined by the movement's emergent leader, Rev. Francis Hodur, the pivotal demands were for Polish ownership and control of parish properties, and the right of parishes and their priests to choose and appoint bishops. (The PNCC later stressed the importance of the vernacular Polish liturgy.) The issue at the center of this constellation was control: under the prevailing rules of the American hierarchy, the Polish wealth represented by parish properties was severed from the Polish nation, just as Polish communicants themselves were made to adopt the "foreign" Catholicism of the Irish. "The aim of the Irish Roman Church," Hodur felt, "is to keep people in submissiveness, not to educate, redeem or make them noble."[54]

The nationalism of the PNCC must not be overstated: this was a religious enterprise, not a political one. But this schism was informed by the ethos of *Kulturkampf,* despite the irony of having hegemonic villainy represented by, of all people, the exiles from Ireland. The structure of the Roman Catholic Church in America, in which Poles remained virtually unrepresented in the hierarchy, struck an especially raw nerve among a people whose distinctive religion was ever the target of Russian and Prussian schemes of "denationalization." "What is good, singular, excellent for the Irish is not necessarily so for the Poles, whose character and past is different," Hodur wrote in the preamble to the PNCC's constitution. Polish schools, organizations, and the press in America were "dependent upon a church directed according to a system which was devised by Irish prelates and is inimical to us . . ."[55] This concern for national integrity later crystallized in Hodur's "eleven great principles" of the Polish National Catholic Church, which included the injunction that "nations are members of one great family of God on earth, therefore, it is not right for one nation to rob another nation of land, their political, religious and social freedom, their right to create a native culture; . . . The right to live and develop is the highest of all rights."[56]

At the century's end the new church consisted of some 10,000 members in ten parishes, primarily in Pennsylvania, Massachusetts, and New Jersey.[57] But the PNCC is less significant for the scope of its influence, which was but a fraction of either the PNA's or the PRCU's, than for its testimony to the Poles' powerful identification of Catholicism with *Polskość*. The PNCC's break with Rome was but the most dramatic manifestation of the more general tendency among the Poles to view Catholicism as a national, not a universal creed. This schism merely carried forward Polonia's decades-old agitation for a Polish bishop, whose appointment, according to *Dziennik Chicagoski*, was essential to the project of establishing a "Poland in America." Nearly a generation later Cardinal Mundelein, an apostle of Americanization, would continue to complain that "the Polish Catholics are determined to preserve their Polish nationality" and that there was among their clergy "a pronounced movement of Polonization."[58]

At the ideological level of Polish religious symbolism, the nexus between Catholicism and nationalism was expressed in a number of ways, including in the dual meanings attached to the idea of "resurrection." Adam Mickiewicz, in a mid-century essay on "Holy Week" (reprinted by *Dziennik Chicagoski* in 1899), averred that "Nowhere in Christendom is Holy Week observed as in Poland. Our nation seems to have a presentiment that this festival of suffering, anguish, and resurrection will someday be a symbolic ceremony of the rebirth of Poland."[59]

More politically charged still was the icon of *Matka Boska Częstochowska*, the Holy Virgin who stood at the very center of Polish religious life. Under the prevailing patterns of devotion, it was the Virgin, not God, to whom one prayed. It was the Virgin to whom one looked for protection and guidance in daily life. And it was the Virgin to whom popular legend attributed various political and military miracles in Poland's history: she had interceded on behalf of King Jagiełło against Germans at the Battle of Grunwald in 1410, for example, and had repulsed the Swedes in 1655. The power of the Holy Virgin and the political fate of the Polish nation had become so intertwined in popular understanding that the Feast of the Assumption was made into a special feast and holiday for the Polish soldier.[60]

It is therefore not surprising to find societies named for *Matka Boska Częstochowska* on the Polish National Alliance's roll of local branches, beside the frankly militaristic Society of Tadeusz Kościuszko or the chivalric Knights of the Polish Crown.[61] Likewise, nineteenth- and early twentieth-century observers often noted a distinctive connection between militarism and religious ceremony within Polish

America. Writing in 1905, Wacław Kruszka surmised that the prepon-
derance of military societies connected with the Church may have
lent the Church a stamp of the homeland in the absence of Poles in
the American hierarchy. Most important, however, "The Polish Army
in the church was a sign . . . of how deeply the idea of the struggle for
independence was rooted in the hearts of the emigrants, who had
connected this idea with deep religiosity [*religijność*]."[62]

In the case of Jewish immigrants, no single icon dominated the
religious consciousness. But the religious calendar itself, steeped in
biblical lore of oppression, exodus, wandering, and chosenness, readily
provided a sacred cloak for secular nationalism. "Their fasts," wrote
one historian, "recalled the disasters that had befallen their State.
Their Scriptures . . . filled their minds with scenes of the land in which
their kings had ruled, their prophets had taught, and their Psalmists
had sung."[63] Passover marks the deliverance of the Jews from Egyptian
bondage; the Ninth of Av marks the national calamity of the destruction of the Temple by the Chaldeans and the Romans; Sukkos has
acquired an historic association with the ancient Jews' period of wandering in the desert; Hanukkah celebrates the revolt and victory of the
Hasmoneans and the restoration of the Temple; and Purim commem-
orates Esther's rescue of the Persian Jews from Haman and Ahasuerus.
And of course the Torah itself is an often celebratory chronicle of
Jewish nationalism. Although the orthodox may have frowned on
Herzl's secular drive to recover the Promised Land, Jewish ritual and
benediction had institutionalized the belief that someday Zion would
again belong to the nation of Israel.[64]

One measure of the affinity between faith and fatherland in this
instance is the ease with which religious and political rhetoric could
blend into one another in secular polemics as in sacred rituals. Patriarchal legend and the historicized covenant of Israel easily fed into
masculinized constructions of the nation-state and militarized notions
of obligation. According to *The Jewish-American Orator*, a prescriptive
collection of Jewish toasts and orations, no great distance separated
the traditional consecration of the covenant of Abraham in the circumcision ceremony from a Zionist celebration of national resilience:
circumcision renders the boy "eternally a child of our nation, a soldier
in the ranks of Judaism." Says the father of the infant son, "I see in
him a soldier under the flag with a blue mogen-David [star of David]."[65]

The rite of passage into adulthood, too, could blur the distinction
between the devout child of Israel and the citizen-soldier under the
banner of Zion. The same prescriptive collection of orations offered a

71

series of bar-mitzvah speeches on coming of age, with a wide range of stridence and candor on the question of political obligations to the nation of Israel. In the unpoliticized versions, the son explains, "Although my people is surrounded with edicts and persecutions, I still hope that the black night of exile will vanish and give room for the dawn shining on Israel's tent. As proof of this, the Tephillin remind me how God's powerful arm liberated us from greater bondage." Here the issue of bondage and liberation is central, although cast in a logic that is clearly theological. Other addresses in the same vein include supplications to "Send thy salvation and help my people to return to their heritage," or to "gather them, while I live, and bring them back to our holy land."[66]

But in other versions of the bar-mitzvah ceremony, "God's powerful arm" is less apparent than the political resolve of the speaker. The son vows, for example, "just as any patriotic soldier upon the battlefield who follows the trumpet even unto the grave, even so I will be prepared to risk my life and follow the voice and echo of Shema Israel unto my last breath . . . More than once my childish eyes were filled with tears studying the history of my ancestors who have died as martyrs." And at the far nationalist end of the spectrum is the frankly political avowal that,

> For my God and for my faith, I shall struggle . . . to the last drop of my blood. I am in the land of liberty, in America where Jews enjoy equal rights with all other nations; but I shall always keep in mind my brethren from other parts of the world where Justice is being trampled upon. Being a good citizen of America I shall also be a good Zionist, and strive to revive our holy land . . . Bless all these assembled in this synagogue, so that we may live to see in the near future the salvation and liberation of all Israel. Amen.[67]

Such prescriptive literature does not indicate how many actual rites of male passage slipped into the rhetoric of the Zionist citizen-soldier. It does indicate, however, how closely akin this rhetoric was to certain ideas of traditional Judaism: the ideological leap from the religious to the secular ideal of Zion was not a terribly acrobatic feat.

Nor, for that matter, did Zionist publicists have far to reach in order to clothe their polemics in Biblical authority. A second measure of the kinship between faith and nation is the extent to which secular political rhetoric was grounded in the hallowed ideas of the Torah. In his

1899 "Defense of Zionism," FAZ president Richard Gottheil argued that, far from forbidding Zionism, Jewish religious practice fully sanctioned it: no less than the modern secular movement, Jewish festivals and observances themselves were "tied to Palestine." Another writer went further still: "Without Zionism, there is no Jewry."[68]

Hence each holiday represented an occasion to tap the reservoirs of Jewish belief and direct the pious toward Zionist action. Purim, according to one writer, was not merely a "carnivalic time," but served as a reminder "that slavery, whether mental, moral, or corporeal, should be resisted to the bitter end." At the heart of the festive mayhem of the holiday, he suggested, was a solemn wish to "convey our enthusiasm for our ancient brethren, who braved every danger in order that Israel might retain its freedom of conscience and action."[69]

Jacob de Haas, a close British associate of Herzl, perhaps summed up the relationship most succinctly in his 1899 Passover address in the *Yiddishes tageblatt*, "Mah Nishtanah?".[70] "Here at the Seder table assemble the visible elements of Jewish nationalism," he wrote. "The gate of Egypt meets the modern homestead."

[Passover's] national doctrine is too obvious; it haunts us with the shout: We are the men of destiny and this is the path of our future. It is of this that the Rabbis remind us when they declare that "it is incumbent upon us to discourse on the departure from Egypt." No symbol that could remind us of the past is forgotten, no token that might teach us of our claims and right of freedom. The voices of the immediate dead at Seder table . . ., the legends that stir our youth, the hope that roused the old and aged, join in one great solemn strain telling of national Jewish freedom. . . . We rise from our dormant state and join in the voice of national tradition, "next year we hope to be free men in the land of Israel."[71]

Just as the symbolism of Purim, Hanukkah, or Passover seemed to many to bespeak the righteousness of the Zionist cause, so was the traditional religious mythology of these holidays salient in the discussion of current affairs. Debate over the contemporary Jewish Question drew upon an array of powerful symbols and references from the religious calendar. Commenting on the Dreyfus affair, for instance, one editorialist remarked that "the whole history of Purim" had been replayed in France. Another emphasized the links between current anti-Semitism and the legend of Haman, "the foremost anti-Dreyfusite of his time":

> Haman made a serious mistake when he first discussed the Jewish Question with the king. He said of the Jews unto His Majesty, "There is a certain people scattered abroad and dispersed among the people in all the provinces of thy kingdom and their laws are diverse from all people, neither keep they the king's laws, therefore it is not for the king's profit to suffer them." All that was one huge lie. It was the same lie that today in France, Austria, Russia and Germany supplies the bigots and oppressors with a shield from the wrath of the people goaded to desperation by injustice and robbery. As it was in the days of Mordecai, so it is in the days of Dreyfus.[72]

Even the cosmopolitanist, socialist *Abend blatt* acknowledged and responded to the nationalist logic of traditional Judaism. In one Purim editorial, for instance, Philip Krantz explained to his readers that capitalism had produced a significant realignment since the days of Mordecai and Esther: these two Jewish nobles had since joined forces with Haman and Ahasuerus, and the four were now oppressing the poor among the Persians *and* the Jews.[73] Likewise, Morris Winchevsky, a labor nationalist and one time editor of the *Forverts*, naturally borrowed the language and cadence of a Sukkos prayer for a wandering nation when, years later, he attempted to codify his own rather complex thoughts on Yiddish nationalism. "I believe, in complete faith," he intoned in the traditional Hebrew phraseology, "that if, in a socialized humanity united in brotherhood, there is room after all for the free development of separate nations, . . . then the Jew without trouble will get back his own domain, his corner of the earth, where he can lead his own national life."[74]

Hence for Jews, as for Irish and Polish Catholics, traditional religion provided a language and a logic for discussion of the national question, even if religious leaders themselves were wary of the challenge to their authority and the threat of secularization implicit in the movements for national liberation. Questions of peoplehood, sovereignty, and national purpose were fixed in both the logic of belief and in the styles of devotion. The paeans to liberation and resurrection on Passover and Easter; the recollection of past national glories on the feast days of saints Patrick and Brigid, and of the patron saints of the old Polish Commonwealth—Stanisław, Kazimierz, and Jozafat—the martial overtones of Hanukkah and the Polish Feast of the Assumption—all of these holidays and festivals lent an immediacy and a righteousness to nationalist thinking which reached well beyond each nation's political activists. National hope and liberationist promise were institutionalized in daily supplication and in the annual rhythms of the religious calendar.

Fairs and Festivities

These nationalist cycles were further reinforced in immigrant communities by ethnic fairs and festivals such as Robert Emmet Day and Adam Mickiewicz's birthday, and secular, civic observances of some religious feasts (St. Patrick's Day, for instance). Theorists of nationalism from Ernest Renan to Patrick Ford to V. I. Lenin have long recognized that any struggle for national sovereignty can only be based upon a broadly based commonality and sense of peoplehood; and such perceptions rest, in large part, upon an understanding (or misunderstanding) of a shared history. Indeed, among the most important tools at the disposal of nationalist propagandists was history itself.[75] As Tomasz Siemiradzki implored in his *Post-Partition History of Poland* (c.1900),

> Let us read books of the martyrdom of the Polish nation! Let us read them with sorrow, because in them, at every step, we will encounter the bones of our grandfathers, fathers, and brothers. Let us read them with pride, because these are the patents on the immortality of our nation. Let us read them with hope, because on this sea of blood and tears, in fiery letters, blazes the inscription: "Poland has not yet perished!"[76]

More compelling than Siemiradzki's invitation to read, however, were the periodic invitations to partake of more lively and accessible expressions of national memory. In May, 1897, for example, New York's Irish gathered at an ethnic fair to christen the city's new Irish Palace. Although the program was rather genteel (the keynote speaker was reformer Chauncy Depew, who piously asserted that the Celtic race had furnished "some of the finest blood for the great American republic"), the fair's exhibit was neither staid in its symbolism nor assimilationist in its tone. Its displays, according to the *Catholic Citizen*, included a portion of the tree and earth from Parnell's grave; a yew tree and earth from O'Connell's grave; a box of plants from the graves of the Manchester martyrs; a fragment of the Treaty stone of Limerick; sprigs of shamrocks from the spot "where Sarsfield blew up the British"; and "one thousand shillelaghs."[77] The fair thus not only served up the Old World past for consideration in the emigrants' present; but it promoted a politicized, liberationist interpretation of the meaning of ethnic Irishness.

More common than this kind of ethnic fair, though similar in their frame of vision, were the annual observances of national holidays. Several holidays and historic anniversaries took on a festive significance in immigrant communities, bringing throngs out into the streets in displays of solidarity, or drawing them into crowded halls for poetry readings, speeches, dramatic presentations, chants, and song. This is where history was made most accessible, and it was this folk-historiography which, in highlighting the lines of obligation, continued to bind the emigrant to the suffering nation. "From California to New York, from Minnesota to Arkansas, everywhere where only a handful of our compatriots have settled down, [the November rising] was observed," beamed *Zgoda* in a page-one feature. The observances recalled "the heroic deeds of our ancestors; everywhere the outrages perpetrated by the enemies of our nation were protested; everywhere the white-amaranthine Polish flag appeared; everywhere the cry sounded, 'Poland has not yet perished!' "[78]

The range of dates and anniversaries which evoked such commemorative outpourings of spirit and emotion was quite broad in the Irish and Polish communities. It included annual observances of the greatest national holidays—St. Patrick's Day, the risings of November and January, and the Polish Constitution of the Third of May.[79] It included the birthdays of famous patriots and martyrs such as Wolfe Tone, Robert Emmet, and Tadeusz Kościuszko. It included the birthdays and deaths of national poets and artists such as Thomas Moore, Frederyk Chopin, and Juliusz Słowacki, and less known figures like Stefan Buszczyński and Seweryna Duchinska. It included centenaries, such as the widespread and massive observances of the rising of 1798, or smaller ceremonies marking Red Hugh O'Donnell's victory at the Battle of the Curlew Mountains (1599) or Jan Dąbrowski's establishment of the Polish Legion.[80] And it included a few sporadic, perhaps idiosyncratic observances of untraditional anniversaries: Queen Victoria's jubilee week in 1897 sparked a series of Irish counterdemonstrations in New York and elsewhere, some featuring mock funerals instead of the traditional fête; and Poles in Milwaukee seized upon the anniversary of King Jagiełło's restoration of the Kazimierz Academy

(Kraków) as an opportunity to protest "the arrogant pretension of German chauvinism" and its "civilizing mission" among the Slavs.[81]

The tendency toward secular commemoration and public display was far less pronounced in Yiddish culture. Perhaps because of the cultural insularity and the political caution born of ghetto life under the czars, the celebration of Jewish struggle remained tied to religious observances which took place in synagogue and at home, not in the streets. Purim did offer a tradition of anti-Christian pageantry, which exerted a powerful influence on the Yiddish theater, and an occasional fair would publicly trumpet the achievements of Zionism, as in Baltimore, where a Zion booth at a local fair presented "samples and illustrations" of the agricultural colonies in Palestine.[82] But for the most part the Yiddish political spectacle was strongest in service of causes other than national liberation. Labor demonstrations may have borrowed from the lexicon of Maccabean resistance, for instance, but they certainly did not announce nationalist aims in quite the manner of the St. Patrick's Day parade. And the bold display of the radicals' Yom Kippur ball, which openly flaunted religious orthodoxy on the holiest night of the Jewish year, was clearly meant not to demonstrate national solidarity, but to challenge the traditional lines of authority *within* the "nation."[83]

National observances in the Irish and Polish communities, however, were conspicuous and strikingly similar. In the larger immigrant communities, festivities would begin with a public procession through the city streets, featuring the uniformed and martial flourish of groups like the Napper Tandy Guards, the Sarsfield Guards, the Hibernian Rifles, or the Polish Falcons—military adjuncts to the nationalist fraternal organizations. The largest parades likewise boasted lines of carriages, and even, as in New York's St. Patrick's Day parade, "a number of floats picturing Irish history."[84] This open-air portion of the event often included rousing speeches by local ethnic leaders, by sympathetic American politicians, or by visiting dignitaries from the Old World. Reports on these events from the largest cities routinely, if perhaps hyperbolically, announced that "the parade was so enormous as to halt all movement in the streets," or that as many as "40,000" had participated.[85]

This public procession and round of speeches would be followed by a less public program in whatever large hall the group had easiest access to—a parish hall, a fraternal lodge, a local theatre. The ensuing ceremony unfolded according to a nearly identical pattern not only across ethnic lines from Ireland's Robert Emmet Day to Poland's observance of the November Rising, but also across geographical lines from the largest enclaves of Chicago, New York, and Milwaukee, to the smaller immigrant communities in North Little Rock, Arkansas, Hammond, Indiana, and Wheeling, West Virginia.

Whatever the precise occasion, the program typically included lectures on the historic significance of the event—"The Story of '98: A Thrilling Recital of Irish Heroism," or "The Cause of the 1863 Rising and the Rebirth of Poland"—as well as political advice to the emigrants and inspirational affirmations: "Love of the Fatherland is Every Person's Holiest Obligation."[86] Whenever possible, the program featured an additional address by a political celebrity such as a visiting MP, a veteran of '63, or Robert Emmet's grand-nephew.[87] Often the program featured a dramatic presentation, say a re-enactment of Robert Emmet's trial or a play, like Szczęsny Zahajkiewicz's *Marta*, set against the historic backdrop of the January rising.[88] Supplementing such visions of the past with a vision of the future, the ceremony typically included gymnastic or choral presentations by youth groups (the Falcons or the Gaelic League), as well as readings and poetry recitations by children: "To the Honor of the Defenders of Our Slandered Country," by "little Anna Malkiewicz."[89] And uniformly the festivities broke at one point or another for collections for the National Fund or Famine Relief, or for contributions toward the construction of a monument to Kościuszko or an ethnic center like New York's Irish Palace.

Equally prominent in most ceremonies were musical programs, often presented by the organized vocal groups and bands associated with various voluntary associations or the parish. Their repertoires included such insurrectionary favorites as "Do you Hear the Swords Rattle?," "The Tale of a Soldier of 1863," "On the Day of Resurrection," "Kościuszko, Look on Us from Heaven!," "March, Falcons!," "To the Defense of the People!," "They Exiled Me from the Fatherland," "The Felons of Our Land," "God Save Ireland," "Erin, Repeal, and Liberty," "My Emmet's No More," "The Manchester Martyrs," and "The Wearin' of the Green."[90] The audience often took part, as in Philadelphia, where a May Third assembly joined in encores of "Grant us, God / The return of a free country," or, more typically, when the ceremony ended with rousing anthems—"Poland Has Not yet Perished" or "The Memory of the Dead."[91] This last song, honoring the United Irishmen and undying Irish "manhood," was among the most familiar songs in Irish-America and provided the watchword in the centennial year of the United Irish Rebellion, "Who Fears to Speak of '98?" The anthem nicely captures the martial spirit and the political promise which characterized these celebrations from beginning to end:

They rose in dark and evil days
　　To right their native land.
They kindled here a living blaze
　　That nothing can withstand.
Alas, that might can vanquish right,
　　They fell and passed away.
But true men, like you men,
　　Are plenty here today.

In its third verse the anthem likewise articulates the bond between homeland and exile which the national celebrations were meant to foster:

Some on the shores of distant lands
　　Their weary hearts have laid . . .
But though their clay be far away
　　Beyond the Atlantic foam—
In true men, like you men,
　　Their spirit's still at home.[92]

It was on a note of this sort that national celebrations typically ended, sometimes as many as seven hours later.

As one scholar wrote recently, parades, demonstrations, and other forms of civic spectacle were crucial forms of communication in the nineteenth century; they communicated, above all, ideas about social power. In this respect Old World national observances were not without their New World significance, especially in cities like Chicago and New York, where the festivities involved truly impressive numbers of people. In laying claim to civic space in nationalist processions and rituals, immigrants were countering similar public displays by nativist organizations and ethnic rivals such as the Orange Order, and they were demonstrating their solidarity and their numbers to employers, to unions, and, not least of all, to local politicians.[93]

Hence in Brooklyn, St. Paul, Chicago, and Philadelphia observances of the Wolfe Tone Rebellion in 1898 became massive public outcries against the Republicans' drift toward a policy of Anglo-American cooperation. Surrounded by impressive throngs of Irish-American voters in Chicago, John Finerty denounced the administration for attempting to raise the Union Jack, "those ghastly blended crosses that look like scars waled on the back of martyred Ireland by the thong and whipcord of the British executioner." Similar Polish "manifestations" in observance of the January rising supplemented efforts to get the Polish Question on the American delegation's agenda for the international peace conference of 1899.[94] Toward these New World ends, national celebrations often adopted a bi-national symbolism: stars and stripes would fly prominently beside the Irish harp; renditions of "Poland Rising" and "On the Twenty-Second of January" would be followed by "An American March."[95]

Just as public displays communicated solidarity and group will to politicians and other ethnic outsiders, so the structure of these events legitimized and regularized the lines of social authority *within* the immigrant group, and thus sustained internal power relations. Parades, ceremonial speeches, songs, and recitations typically celebrated a militarism which defined men and boys as national actors, for instance. Women's roles were more static. Lectures "To Polish Mothers—On Raising Sons as Heroes" or "On the Need for Enlightenment and Rearing Our Youth as Good Polish Patriots" defined their part in nation-building as maternal. Or they could serve as living icons, as in the 1896 St. Patrick's Day parade in Butte, Montana, when the AOH invited "32 handsome ladies from the Daughters of Erin" to portray Ireland's thirty-two counties. By providing for women's participation, this common formula of the woman-as-icon ritualized the national commitment of the community as an indivisible whole. Yet by removing them to a separate plane of representation, it also enforced the view that the *politics* of nationalism was really none of their business. Women, that is, represented feminized counties or abstract principles like Liberty and Virtue; men, meanwhile, represented themselves, that is, citizens.[96]

These gender prescriptions, along with didactic lectures on the relationship between the clergy and the nation, political homilies "To the Polish Child," and the precedence given to "men and women of standing"—usually petty entrepreneurs or the clergy—embodied and regularized existing patterns of social authority along the lines of gender, age, and class.[97]

The capacity of these celebrations to communicate power relationships generated friction from both within and without. Within each group, the political message to be conveyed by a local celebration often became a point of contention between rivaling organizations, or between opposing factions on a planning committee. Would the program or the parade formation favor the PNA over the PRCU, insurrection over Home Rule, the clergy over secular political leaders? The Irish in Milwaukee bickered over the stridence of past St. Patrick's Day celebrations, some arguing that a more assimilationist program ought to be put together by a panel of "professional and businessmen." Poles in Hudson, Pennsylvania, split so violently that one year they had to hold two separate observances of the November rising; and the PNA secretary in Duluth, Minnesota, reported with shame in 1897 that three of the city's five Polish organizations had withdrawn from the local May Third festivities. The very institution of the national celebration was in danger, lamented *Zgoda* in 1898, because of the "disharmony and discord" born of conflicting interpretations of proper observance.[98]

Moreover, wary of immigrant power and its display, local governments too often sought to control these celebrations. In the latter half of the nineteenth century civic leaders in many cities covertly subverted St. Patrick's Day by co-opting the event and refashioning it into the now familiar ceremony of civic pride, or manipulating parade routes to the benefit of local commerce. Lamenting the passage of the *real* St. Patrick's Day in Chicago, Finley Peter Dunne wrote in 1896 that "now it might as well be th' anni-varsary iv th' openin' iv th' first clothin' store in Chicago." More directly, in 1897 Illinois passed a "disarming act" to demilitarize civic demonstrations. According to the *Catholic Citizen*, the act was "clearly aimed against the Irish quasi-military organizations" like the Hibernian Rifles and the Clan na Gael Guards. (In response, the Clan na Gael planned an armed parade to test the legality of the act, and John Devoy himself denounced the legislation at an Irish picnic held, appropriately enough, at Chicago's Sharpshooter Park.)[99]

But despite political contests over meaning, the central message conveyed by these ceremonies pertained to the political obligations of the emigrant and to his or her place in the broadest tapestry of the nation's history. "Let us celebrate this anniversary as it is fitting Poles in exile," intoned one May Third orator in Hammond, Indiana.[100] And indeed, such ceremonies not only became the very embodiments of emigrant obligation and "fitting" political bearing, but also brought to life the nation's history of heroisms and martyrdoms more effectively than could any other medium: the fête was not constrained in its reach by the limits of emigrant literacy or the boundaries of organizational membership.

A PNA essayist in 1898 was probably overstating the case when he claimed that, "Today, thanks to our celebrations the names Kościuszko, Pułaski, Sobieski and others have been so popularized that there is not a Pole who does not know them or could not tell of several deeds of these Polish fighters."[101] But even so, there is no question that these popular demonstrations went a good deal farther than history books and didactic editorials in popularizing and bringing to life the mythologies of national struggle. As Rhode Island laborer Batt O'Conner recalled, it was during the civic St. Patrick's Day procession in Providence that "I awoke to the full consciousness of my love for my country."[102] Certainly, of all the tens of thousands who attended such observances over the decades, O'Conner was not alone in his Old World political awakening.

The Vernacular Theater

A common feature of national commemorations among the Poles and the Irish, as mentioned above, was the dramatic re-enactment of key historic moments in the national struggle. A centenary celebration in Milwaukee might include a production of *The Rebel of '98*, for instance; and a Chicago observance of the January rising might feature the "Cadets of the Holy Trinity" in *The Revolution of Poland against the Moscovites in Warsaw*.[103] Such staged rebellions were not peculiar to national holidays, but were rooted in the broader traditions of Irish and Polish vernacular theater. In *Maggie*, his outsider's view of Irish ghetto life, Stephen Crane describes the Fenian undertones of a music hall variety show on the Bowery:

> As a final effort, the singer rendered some verses which described a vision of Britain being annihilated by America, and Ireland bursting her bonds. A carefully prepared crisis was reached in the last line of the verse, where the singer threw out her arms and cried, "The star spangled-banner." Instantly a great cheer swelled from the throats of the assemblage of the masses . . . Eyes gleamed with sudden fire, and calloused hands waved frantically in the air.[104]

Although this vein of popular entertainment has left only a faint impression on the historical record, Crane's depiction is corroborated by the fleeting accounts and descriptions in the contemporary immigrant press. Before moving on to discuss the Yiddish theater, the most active and the most institutionally developed of the three, the Polish and Irish vernacular stages do warrant some attention. Parish halls, saloons, fraternal lodges, and the modest professional stages in these communities frequently became the site of emotionally charged political melodramas and national romances. The immigrant theater, as one Polish observer noted in 1890, "is a pillar of national sentiment," fulfilling a political function which Polonia "understands perfectly well."[105]

Polish theater in the United States was a modest affair until well after the turn of the century. Not until the advent of professionalized theatres in Chicago, Detroit, and Buffalo (1909–1914) did Polonia have anything approximating the established troupes and the formalized circuits which the Irish-American and Yiddish stages had boasted for decades. But the amateur theater was robust indeed. Wacław Kruszka went so far as to venture that by the 1880s "in almost every parish there was some kind of theatrical hall" where amateurs put on "beautiful dramatic works." And by the 1890s Polish drama circles had formed in Brooklyn, Buffalo, Chicago, Cleveland, Detroit, Grand Rapids, Milwaukee, New York, Philadelphia, Pittsburgh, St. Paul, Scranton, Wilmington, and Winona, including groups directly linked to the PNA, the PRCU, and the PNCC.[106]

Polish-American theater remained relatively isolated from the current nationalist trends in Polish drama, embodied most forcefully in the Old World works of Stanisław Wyspiański. In the words of one critic, in his nationalist trilogy of *November Night, Varsovienne,* and *Lelewel,*[107] as well as his turn-of-the-century staging of *Forefather's Eve,* Wyspiański "fulfilled the last will of Mickiewicz." Taken up by other writers such as Stefan Żeromski and symbolist Tadeusz Maciński, this late-century rethinking of mid-century Polish romanticism gathered force as a nationalist literary and dramatic movement known as "Young Poland."[108]

Although, as historian Emil Orzechowski has discovered, such plays did occasionally find their way into production in the United States, Young Poland was not the typical fare of the turn-of-the-century Polonian immigrant stage.[109] Yet Polish-American theater remained faithful to Mickiewicz's dictum that the destiny of dramatic art is to "force lazy spirits into action."[110] Among the titles which survive from the early period of Polonian theatre are *Jadwiga, Queen of Poland, Kościuszko, Kościuszko in Petersburg, Kościuszko at Racławice, Sybiracy* [The Deportees], *I Die for My Country* (based on Henryk Sienkiewicz's novel, *With Fire and Sword*), *The Uprising of 1863, Sobieski at Vienna, The Relief of Vienna,* and *The Defense of Częstochowa* (adapted by Szczęsny Zahajkiewicz of the PRCU from Sienkiewicz's novel of Poland's war with Sweden, *The Deluge*).[111]

Given the affiliations of many Polish-American theater groups, it is not surprising that the immigrant stage not only articulated nationalist themes but also reflected the dual currents of religionist and secularist nationalism which ran through so much of Polish culture. In Act V of one parish production of *Shepherds of Bethlehem* (La Salle, Illinois, 1879), "a herald announced freedom to all nations."[112] At the far insurrectionist extreme, Zbigniew Brodowski's *A Member of the Alliance* (1897) included scenes of the "revolution in Poland, and Polish armies in America marching out under the command of the Censor [of the PNA]." The play ended with a tableau of "the Alliance unshackling the irons and lifting Poland from captivity."[113] But despite these competing visions, Karol Estreicher was nonetheless moved to report that, "As in Prussian Poland so here, the amateur theaters uphold the national spirit; they are schools of patriotism and the mortar cementing the Polish community."[114]

In the Irish diaspora two forces were at work to politicize the stage in the late nineteenth century. The first was the drive of middle-class Irish-Americans to gain control of the popular image of the Irish by expelling popular stage rascals like Harrigan and Hart's Mulligan Guards and Dion Boucicault's Shaun the Post from the American theater.[115] And second was the emergence in Dublin of the Irish National Theatre, linked in its cultural nationalism to the Gaelic Athletic Association and Douglas Hyde's Gaelic League. In the estimation of William Butler Yeats, as trumpeted in the Milwaukee *Catholic Citizen*, the theater would "give not merely enthusiasm, but definite intellectual ideas and new forms of literary expression to what is a most interesting awakening of national life."[116]

The assault on unflattering depictions of the Irish would have its greatest influence in the professional theater, and even there only after the turn of the century. The movement reached its crescendo in Irish-American demonstrations in 1911 against the Abbey Theatre production of John Millington Synge's "immoral" and "anti-Irish" *Playboy of the Western World*.[117] And the National Theatre, too, would contribute to nationalist discussion in works such as *The Countess Cathleen*, Yeats's thinly veiled tribute to Maud Gonne; but, again, the Dublin project would have limited influence on the amateur stage in the United States.

Most influential and still pervasive in amateur entertainments and parish productions in the 1890s was the long-standing tradition of national romance and historic melodrama, dating back to the 1820s and to plays like *Brian the Brave* and *Ireland Redeemed*. From a Sedalia, Missouri, production of *Ireland as It Is*, J. H. Amherst's indictment of the oppressive system of Irish land tenure, to a New York parochial school presentation of *Robert Emmet* or *The Shamrock and the Rose*, Ireland's distress and resistance were among the staples of vernacular entertainment. Even Ned Harrigan's *The O'Reagans*, more noted for its racism and its raucous depiction of boss politics than for its Irish themes, pivoted on the plot point of the Wives' Mutual Protective Association and its involvement in Home Rule politics. One variety production at People's Theatre in New York included "a smashing prison escape scene," most likely excerpted from one of the many plays of Irish political life.[118]

The playwright with the greatest longevity on the Irish-American popular stage was Dion Boucicault. Although his writing career had peaked in the 1860s and 1870s, his plays were still commonly in production in the late 1890s and beyond. In the single month of April 1898, for instance, the *Irish World* noted that Boucicault's *Robert Emmet* and *The Shaughraun* were in production in New York, and *The Colleen Bawn* was playing in Detroit. Years later, in his handbook on *The Parish Theatre* (1917), John Talbot Smith fully credited *The Colleen Bawn* with energizing the Irish amateur stage, which had been but a modest and sporadic affair until that play's appearance; and he identified *Robert Emmet* as "a favorite with amateurs for forty years."[119]

Boucicault's plays were among those attacked by the Irish-American middle class late in the century. Significantly, however, one of his plays had been banned by Queen Victoria for its dangerous nationalist content and its potential to cause "ructions." As one critic has noted, in the context of English-language drama, Boucicault's work stood out in that "it had been the fashion to laugh over Ireland, never to weep over her."[120] Boucicault's subversion ranges from relatively tame comic exchanges between the English and the Irish on issues of culture and ethnocentrism, to more pointed political commentary on British rule and Irish resistance. Much of the comedy of *Arrah-na-Pogue* and *The Shaughraun*, for instance, hinges on a relatively playful treatment of cultural difference:

MAJOR: *[Filling out form] Shaun, that's the Irish for John, I suppose.*
SHAUN: *No, sir; John is the English for Shaun.*
. . . . .
MOLINEUX: *Is this place called Swillabeg?*
CLAIRE: *No; it is called Shoolabeg.*
MOLINEUX: *Beg pardon; your Irish names are so unpronounceable. You see, I'm an Englishman.*
CLAIRE: *I remarked your misfortune. Poor creature, you couldn't help it.*
MOLINEUX: *I do not regard it as a misfortune.*
CLAIRE: *Got accustomed to it, I suppose.*[121]

This pervasive playfulness, like Boucicault's care to offer unsympathetic Irish characters as well as sympathetic English ones (as Molineux turns out to be), may bleach the deepest shades of rebellion from his work. But historic backdrops such as the Rising of '98 and the Fenian Rising do bring a serious undertone even to the comedies, and these plays are not without their moments of political stridence and tribute to Irish defiance. *The Colleen Bawn* pivots on tenant-landlord relations and the threat of eviction; *The Shaughraun* features the political intrigues surrounding a Fenian refugee; *The Rapparee* involves the treaty of Limerick; and *Arrah na Pogue* (along with its musical version, *Shaun the Post*), is set in Wicklow against the backdrop of the Rising of 1798. This last production also featured the insurrectionary "Wearin' of the Green," which was banned in English productions and revived and sung among the exiles in the United States in commemoration of Ninety-Eight.

> I met with Napper Tandy,[122] and he took me by the hand,
> And he said, "How's poor old Ireland, and how does she stand?"
> She's the most distressful country that ever yet was seen,
> They are hanging men and women for the wearing of the green.

The song concludes with this note on exile:

> O Erin, must we leave you driven by a tyrant's hand?
> Must we ask a mother's blessing from a strange and distant land?
> Where the cruel cross of England shall nevermore be seen,
> And where, please God, we'll live and die still wearing of the green.[123]

Boucicault's *Robert Emmet*, though also softened by fleeting touches of humor, depicts the Emmet rebellion (1802) with unambiguous sympathy and reflects Boucicault's political earnestness on the Irish question. The play reaches its political climax in court, where Emmet has been brought up on charges of conspiracy to betray Britain into the hands of France. "Were the French, or any other foreign nation to come here as invaders, I would meet them on the shore," he replies; "I would dispute every inch of Irish soil, every blade of grass; and my last entrenchment should be my grave. I did not seek to free Ireland from one foreign power—Great Britain—to deliver her into the hands of another." Before a closing tableau of Emmet and the feminized figure of Ireland in mutual adoration, Boucicault taps the history books for Emmet's famous speech from the dock: "Let no man write my epitaph, for as no man who knows my motives dares now to vindicate them, let not prejudice or ignorance asperse them; let my tomb be uninscribed until other men and other times can do justice to their character! When my country shall take her place amongst the nations of the earth—then—and not until then, let my epitaph be written!"[124]

The power of the Irish stage as an institution had been diluted, as it were, by the group's access to an English-speaking host culture. And the political meanings of various plots and characters themselves were highly contested—particularly at a time when Irish nationalism had come by necessity to focus largely upon the politics of culture. Even so, one can well imagine plays like Boucicault's *Robert Emmet* evoking the passionate applause and the waving of hands described by Stephen Crane on Maggie and Pete's night out.

The Yiddish theater had developed along lines quite different from the Irish and the Polish, and institutionally it was on an entirely different order. By the turn of the century the Yiddish stage drew an audience of roughly two million a year in New York alone, and many key actors, actresses, and playwrights had immigrated from Europe, making New York a veritable world center of Yiddish theatrical activity.[125]

The Yiddish stage in the 1890s did share some of the Irish and Polish characteristics of historic re-enactment and even nationalist bluster. Lulla Adler Rosenfeld described the turn-of-the-century audiences as "patriotic about America, nationalist in their devotion to the promised *Palestina*, remembering always the lost home, the lost life, the *shtetl* of their past." Popular playwrights of the day were quick to appeal to the public's appetite for Judaism's history of martyrdom and triumph, with plays ranging from the ancient subjects of *Judah Maccabee* or *The Miracle of Hanukkah*, to the up-to-the-moment *Captain Dreyfus, Dr. Herzl*, or *Son of His People*, a Yiddish adaptation of George Eliot's proto-Zionist *Daniel Deronda*. "When the lion roars," ran one operetta in a fiercer tone, by Moishe Hurvitz, "the tiger gnashes his teeth, the leopard springs and bites and fire rains down from the skies, then shall justice triumph at last, and the Jewish nation shout, 'Shema Isroel Adonai Elohenu!' "[126]

The content and style of late-nineteenth-century Yiddish drama had developed along two independent axes, both of which, however, pointed the theater toward the politics of nationalism and "people-hood" by the 1890s. First, the entire enterprise of Yiddish drama was rooted in the religious folk tradition of the Purim play (Purim *shpiel*), the festive re-enactment of Esther's rescue of the Persian Jews from destruction at the hands of Haman, dating back perhaps as far as 415 A.D. By the early 1700s the Purim play had become increasingly elaborate in some parts of Europe, including full costume, props, and stage effects. Under the influences of *haskala* in the nineteenth century the Yiddish drama evolved in scope far beyond the biblical pageantry of the Esther story. Yet Yiddish theater did retain the anti-*goyish* tint of the Purim play for some time. According to Yiddish writer and historian Bernard Gorin, until Jacob Gordin brought European realism to the Yiddish stage in the 1890s, Christian characters were typically drawn "blacker than the devil."[127]

But the lingering Purim flavor of Yiddish theater was not limited to this chauvinistic treatment of non-Jewish characters. Indeed, among the early productions in America were N. B. Bazilinsky's *Esther* and Joseph Lateiner's *Esther and Haman;* and on through the 1890s plays like *The Beautiful Esther, Esther-ke,* and *Haman the Second* would continue to run.[128] When Avram Goldfaden had set out to establish a professional theater for the Yiddish masses in Romania in the 1870s, he had quickly arrived at the crowd-pleasing formula of the historical and Biblical melodrama. Although there was a great deal of experimentation among those who followed Goldfaden in the ensuing decades (including Hurwitz and Lateiner's quick, superficial refashioning of *goyish* plays into Yiddish ones), religious and historical dramas along the lines of the Purim *shpiel* did become a staple. Alongside the popular dramas of the ghetto, Romeo-and-Juliet romances, and tragedies of family life, various moments of Jewish history were told and retold in plays such as Joseph Lateiner's *Destruction of Jerusalem,* N. M. Sheykevitch's *Last Jewish King,* Moishe Zeifert's *Heroes of Israel,* and in operas like Jacob Bilder's *Liberation of Jerusalem.*[129]

So established were these patterns, in fact, that when writers such as Jacob Gordin, Abraham Cahan, and the *Abend blatt's* anonymous "Kritiker" sought to "educate" the tastes of the masses, they met with some resistance: according to Lulla Adler, Gordin's early foray on the Yiddish stage, *Siberia,* was received rather coldly precisely because "there were no heroic scenes [and] no nationalist speeches." Upon seeing Gordin's first play, in fact, Zelig Mogulesko of the People's Theatre had flatly declared, "This Jew with the black beard is an anti-Semite!"[130]

For his part, Gordin jabbed at both the patchwork plagiarisms and the hollow sensationalism of the Yiddish stage in a one-act parody of the Hurvitz-Lateiner formula, *Yokel the Opera-Maker* (c.1892). The typical method of the Yiddish playwright, by this account, was to piece together "a scene from here, an act from there, two acts stolen from an old operetta, an epilogue snipped out of a French melodrama, a prologue with wit for the comic, from Barnum and Bailey's Circus." What the drama lacked in intelligence and care, Gordin argued, it made up for in spectacle. Says Shlumiel the director:

> Today we have to read through a new play, make from that play a historical opera, adapt to that opera a snappy name, hold a rehearsal, and already this Sabbath produce it on the stage with magnificent scenery, surprising effects, Oriental singing, African dancing, Arabian horses, Spanish sheep, genuine Yiddish historical goats, Turkish costumes, Chinese shoes, Russian nihilists, Italian melodies, Indian marches, [and] German swords.[131]

In *Siberia*, then, as in his later plays, Gordin was attempting to introduce the vernacular stage and its mass audience to the tenets of "serious" European art, and particularly to the tenets of literary realism. Dissatisfied with its two-dimensionality and parochialism, Gordin sought to broaden the vision of the Yiddish stage in true cosmopolitanist fashion—not only in his even-handed treatment of Jews and non-Jews in *Siberia* and *The Pogrom*, but in the depth of character and the "broad humanity" of his subjects in reworkings such as *The Yiddish King Lear* (from Shakespeare), *God, Man, and Devil* (from Goethe's *Faust*), and *The Kreutzer Sonata* (from Tolstoy).[132] If Gordin's new approach was not an immediate hit with immigrant audiences, who seemed to prefer "genuine Yiddish historical goats," it did create excitement among the intelligentsia. This, over time, would significantly alter the tone of the Yiddish drama. The artistic possibilities inherent in Gordin's early works drew a number of other *belletristen*, or "serious" writers, to the stage for the first time, and sparked a number of similar ventures in realism by young writers like Leon Kobrin, Bernard Gorin, Joseph Bovshover, and even the poet Morris Rosenfeld. The mid-to-late 1890s have been regarded as the critical juncture in this shift, the beginning of "the First Golden Epoch" of the Yiddish theater.[133] It was then that the intelligentsia staked its claim to the vernacular theater, countering the Hurvitz-Lateiner tradition with Yiddish reworkings of Ibsen's *Doll's House*, Schiller's *Robbers*, Shakespeare's *Oth-*

ello and *The Merchant of Venice,* and treatments of the American labor movement and ghetto life presented in the realistic mode.

The high literati would not transform the Yiddish stage overnight. In 1900 the "Kritiker" in the *Abend blatt* would still wonder whether the campaign to drive Purim-*shpieleray* from the Yiddish stage was "a war with windmills," and he continually complained about the Yiddish theater's pandering to the audience's unrefined appetite for sensationalism and melodrama. (He even lamented that Gordin's own drama of the Spanish Inquisition, *The Beautiful Miriam and the Tortured,* had reduced serious actors to Purim-players.)[134] But if the entrance of the intelligentsia into the dramatic field did not immediately overturn the tradition of the Purim *shpiel,* it did introduce a second sort of nationalist discourse to the popular stage: the young writers now turning to the stage were actively engaged in the debates over Jewish nationalism which were then raging within the Jewish labor movement and in the pages of the Yiddish press. Thus in the mid 1890s and after, these very debates gradually began to be replicated in the Yiddish theaters of New York, Chicago, Boston, Baltimore, and Philadelphia.

Gordin's achievements in bringing the cosmopolitanist argument to the Yiddish stage were not unalloyed. One unintentional consequence of portraying ghetto life in the realistic mode was that such portraits tended to evoke the sense of ethnic persecution and indomitable *Yiddishkayt* which had been born of that life and which cosmopolitanism was meant to overcome. Gordin's *Mirele Efros,* for instance, explored the issues of tradition and assimilation in a manner which, according to one critic, attracted "nationalists and apostates, Zionists, the rich, and the proletariat," and forged them into "one Jewish people." Indeed, in his 1901 prologue to the play, Morris Winchevsky was prompted to write, "You will again see that country/ Where the knout reigned over humanity;/ Where Hannah Deborah's collected curses/ Are the sound of a Jewish lamentation."[135] Moreover, Gordin was strangely prone to moments of Jewish chauvinism, notwithstanding his vehemence on the national question. The staunchest of nationalists could have scripted the scene in *Kapitan Dreyfus* (c.1899) when Gordin's Dreyfus declares: "[the French] have forgotten that I stem from a people who, as 'the Eternal Jew,' have the ability to suffer eternally and to remain alive eternally."[136]

More characteristically, however, Gordin did fashion his plays according to solidly cosmopolitanist designs. In his *Jewish King Lear,* the two malicious daughters (corresponding to Shakespeare's Goneril and

Regan) were married to orthodox Jews and remained well within the Jewish tradition, while the faithful Cordelia character had married an atheist and embraced the cosmopolitan world of St. Petersburg. And despite his fleeting chauvinisms, Gordin defined even the historic events surrounding Dreyfus as a *human* crisis, not a specifically Jewish one:

DREYFUS: . . . *I must live to purify the shameful blot on my innocent, suffering brothers, the Jews. Not only the Jews! A shameful blot lies on all of civilization, on all of humanity, and I must live until that blot is washed away. Not I alone, not Alfred Dreyfus alone languishes in captivity here on Devil's Island. All that goes by the name "humanity" languishes here along with me.*[137]

The nationalist counterargument to Gordin's work in the Yiddish drama took shape under the pens of a rising generation of writers at the turn of the century and after. The nationalist impulse in "serious" drama reached its sharpest expression in the early years of the twentieth century, in plays such as Leon Kobrin's *Return to His People* and *The Eternal Fire*, and David Pinski's treatment of Jewish martyrdom, *The Mute Messiah*. The continuing nationalism of the potboiler tradition was embodied in plays like Itzak Zolatorevsky's *The Jewish Flag: or, My Nation*. Even Israel Zangwill's *Melting-Pot* (1909), though most often remembered as a comment on America's immigration question, flowed from the playwright's involvement in the Jewish Territorial Organization and drew on the decades-long tradition of exploring the Jewish Question through the drama.[138]

Hence the Lower East Side's Thalia Theatre was a most fitting locale for the famous debate (1905) between cosmopolitanist Jacob Gordin and Yiddishist Chaim Zhitlowski on the issue of Jewish nationalism. The Thalia, like the other major Yiddish theaters in New York, Baltimore, and Philadelphia had been the site of implicit debates on the national question for some time. Yiddish theater, Gordin pronounced on this occasion, was mere caricature when it was nationalistic, and it outgrew this limitation only when it took on "the dramatic forms of the literature of gentile nations." "This sympathetic lyricism of nationalism," he said, "smells of patriotic *kvass* in Russia, of less-than-fresh limberger cheese in Germany, of Catholic incense in France, and of noodle kugel left over from a week ago Saturday in our case."[139]

For the most part the Yiddish stage, like its Polish and Irish counterparts, had not "outgrown" this nationalist lyricism in the 1890s. Gordin's periodic protestations, like the observations of a seemingly bemused Stephen Crane and a fully heartened Karol Estreicher, testify to the extent that the immigrant stage joined the penny press, the pulpit, and the holiday fête in helping to circulate the ideological currency of immigrant nationalism.

This distillation of a single aspect of immigrant cultures—their nationalism—undoubtedly makes for a distorted or monochromatic image. It bears emphasizing here that a great many popular plays had nothing to do with national questions, and that many facets of popular religion evoked a universalism which cut against the current of the national exceptionalisms sketched out above. By none of the foregoing do I mean to argue that the political fate of their "nation" constituted the single overriding concern of ordinary immigrants, that immigrant communities were hotbeds of insurrectionary activity, or that the politics of liberation were the object of unceasing and obsessive meditation on the part of the transplanted masses.

Moreover, to point out the nationalist currents running through various areas of immigrant culture is to say nothing of their reception by individual immigrants. The popularity of some plays might have been incidental to their nationalist themes, not dependent on them; and for many, St. Patrick's Day was likely more meaningful for its carnival atmosphere than for its farthest-reaching political promise. The perpetual hazard of scholarly inquiry into popular culture, like much of its interest, derives from the the multiplicity of interpretations and the fluidity of meanings which become attached to cultural material in the process of transmission.[140]

But this political sketch of immigrant popular culture, if one dimensional, does call into question the presumed "abstraction" of world affairs for the mass of laboring immigrants.[141] The pervasiveness of nationalist icons and themes in popular culture does not necessarily indicate that nationalists maintained an unruptured hegemony over their respective communities, or that nationalist thinking went unchallenged. Their pervasiveness does suggest, however, that the distinction between "bread-and-butter" issues and "ideological" issues is at best misleading: nationalism surfaced and resurfaced in a myriad of cultural forms, infusing a wide variety of social activities which are rarely considered as remote to the daily routines of immigrant life as the distant and nebulous affairs of international politics proper.

While Finley Peter Dunne and Zygmunt Miłkowski may have worried over the difficulty of translating inchoate national sentiment into meaningful political action, the sentiment itself remained a salient feature of many immigrant windows on the world. As one Polish immigrant told a WPA interviewer years later, "I was born in East Galicia, under the reign of mean Austrians."[142] The political consciousness evinced by such a statement, if less sophisticated than what the fondest insurrectionary schemes called for, does suggest both a keen, immediate awareness of Old World power relations and a perception of their injustice. It was an awareness nourished in large measure by the common idioms of popular culture.

This awareness was also nourished by immigrant literary life—that cultural realm halfway between the political blueprints of the intelligentsia and the most popular and accessible nationalist legends. Widely distributed in cheap pamphlets and reprinted in the penny press, ethnic poems, short stories, and novels took up national questions from a variety of angles and in a multitude of voices, constituting one of the chief sites of resistance to arrogant power. As Teofila Samolinska put it in her celebration of Polish writer Józef Ignacy Kraszewski, "The enemies of the nation will recognize/ That the sword of the people is—the pen."[143]

3

Pillars of Fire:
The Comparative Literatures
of Immigrant Nationalism

> Yes, he was a mighty poet,
> Star and beacon for his age,
> Light and lamp among his people,
> And a wonderful and mighty
>
> Pillar of poetic fire
> In the vanguard of all Israel's
> Caravan of woe and sorrow
> In the desert waste of exile.
>
> —Heinrich Heine, "Jehuda ben Halevy"

"Happy is the nation which boasts a poet," writes Czesław Miłosz, "and in its toils does not march in silence."[1] The link between national ideals and galvanizing poetics is a common one. To the extent that most movements have adopted some version of Ernest Renan's definition of nationality as "a spiritual principle," nationalists have traditionally accorded the writer and the poet exalted positions as agents of "the people's spirit." Literary figures become the guardians of the language itself (often considered the most important basis of national unity); their artistic merit reflects no less than the "national genius"; and their creations tap and represent the "national memory." Hence a literary history of national bards ranging from José Rizal and Rudyard Kipling to Czesław Miłosz himself parallels the history of diverse nationalist movements since the nineteenth century—movements both of aggrandizement and of resistance.[2]

Nineteenth-century Ireland, Poland, and Zion fit this pattern, as the veneration of writers like Chaim Nakhman Bialik, Maria Konopnicka, and William Butler Yeats attests. World Jewry in the late nineteenth century experienced a national literary awakening on two separate fronts: writers like Bialik, David Frischman, and Menakhem Dolitsky self-consciously fashioned a Hebrew literature whose combined romantic, Talmudic, and political strains aimed to move a nation to action. The flowering of serious writing in Yiddish, meanwhile, lent a new confidence and legitimacy in many quarters to the notion of a valued and viable national culture. In Poland the mid-century works of Adam Mickiewicz, identifying political devotion to Poland as a sacred pursuit, continued to dominate the field of literary nationalism; but writers like Henryk Sienkiewicz and Maria Konopnicka had also taken up the cause toward the century's end, composing historical epics and national lyrics as the last bulwark against denationalization. And Ireland's tradition of literary resistance stretched from Jonathan Swift's *Modest Proposal* in the eighteenth century to the strident Anglo-Irish poetics of Thomas Davis and Young Ireland in the nineteenth to the Gaelic Revival at the dawn of the twentieth.[3]

The development of *immigrant* nationalist literatures, however, was complicated by several features of enclave culture. Here literary nationalism reflected more than Old World conventions, individual temperaments, and political circumstances; nor did it simply reflect thematic variations emerging in response to social conditions in the diaspora. Literary nationalism was further subject to the structural forces of cultural production. Specifically, immigrant literatures were determined in part by the number of active writers in the New World and their degree of mutual engagement; by the instability of enclave publishing enterprises; by the class background, tastes, and aims of the group's booksellers and publishers; and by the degree of the group's isolation from, or absorption into, the English-speaking host culture. The extent to which each group established a distinct diaspora literature thus depended upon the volume of literary productivity in the New World. The *manner* in which these diaspora literatures departed from their Old World relatives, however, depended upon the demographic, linguistic, and economic circumstances of cultural production in the New World ghetto.

The comparative literatures of Yiddish-American, Polish-American, and Irish-American nationalism mark three disparate courses of literary nation-building in a diaspora setting. The Yiddish community, characterized by a large and active intelligentsia, quickly developed its own, distinctly American themes and styles. Like the Yiddish theater, literary production in this community was dominated by political activists; the works of popular writers like Abraham Cahan, Morris Rosenfeld, and Leon Kobrin reflected the ongoing conflict between nationalists and cosmopolitanists. Tales of ghetto life and American-ization were encompassed by deeper disputes over *dos pintele yid*, the contested notion of the "quintessence of the Jew" and its implications for Jewish political life worldwide.

Polonia's active intelligentsia, by comparison, was positively tiny. While a handful of writers like Teofila Samolinska and Stanisław Dangiel did forge a modest Polish-American tradition, journalists and booksellers relied far more heavily upon reprints of Old World liter-ature to fill their columns and stock their inventories. The romantic nationalism of the Polish classics—*Pan Tadeusz, Kordjan*—dominated Polonia's literary life; the nobility's poets of past generations ironically became the most popular writers for this community of peasants-in-exile. In this instance the creation of books through acts of manufac-ture and distribution was as consuming as the creation of texts through acts of imagination.[4]

And Irish-American writing, ever influenced by the accessibility of the English-speaking host culture, assumed yet a third configuration by the 1890s: a broad spectrum of literary-nationalist stances, varying in their continued Irish orientation or their absorption in American concerns. Writers like Louise Imogen Guiney wrote primarily for a genteel and cosmopolitan audience, touching on the Irish Question only occasionally and in strains more sentimental than insurrection-ary. Jeremiah O'Donovan Rossa, at the far nationalist extreme, spun a sensational memoir of Irish martyrdom, calculated in its intensity to compel the continued allegiance of the exiles' American-born chil-dren. Works like *Rossa's Recollections* and James Jeffrey Roche's *John Boyle O'Reilly* were companion volumes to the *Book of Irish Martyrs* and *Speeches from the Dock*.

Nationalism assumed diverse shapes and shades as Old World con-ventions met New World conditions. The present chapter concerns not only the most strident nationalist expressions—Morris Rosenfeld's salutes to Maccabean militance, James Jeffrey Roche's romance of Fenian insurrection. It also concerns what Mary Poovey has called the "ideological work" of literature in both meanings she attaches to that phrase: "the work of ideology" in shaping narratives which presumed a distinct and unified "peoplehood"; and "the work of making ideol-ogy," as diverse writers constructed and contested images of the "na-tion."[5]

Literature was more than a useful venue for the contest of political *ideas*; it was also a forum for protesting present conditions, for glori-fying the past and formulating visions of the future, and for challenging the oppressors' legitimating narratives of persecution and conquest. Even more fundamentally, it was in part through literature that the notions of group coherence and distinctiveness upon which nationality rested were maintained. Mobilizing various languages of lineage— "race," "nature," "history"—literary work underwrote the opposition between the nation's insiders and outsiders. Further, by extolling certain virtues, condemning certain vices, celebrating certain kinds of deeds, and advancing certain versions of the heroic, literary work fabricated and enshrined the "national character." Indeed, the nineteenth-century conventions by which authorship was discussed reified such constructions, in that "genius" was supposed to reside precisely in the author's capacity to "comprehend" and represent that "national character."[6]

In this respect literary work exerted a normative influence upon the social relations within the group and upon the relation of each member to the group itself; this constitutive power was especially important in the diaspora, where national identity and political allegiance were ever in question. Stock literary conceits such as the unassimilable greenhorn, the romantic revolutionary, and the Spartan mother were intricately linked with, and indispensable to, the grander public fictions of national collectivity. Literature, in short, represented one of the critical practices by which these now global scatterings of people proclaimed their unity as discrete populations, defined their distinctive virtues, policed their boundaries, sustained their enmities, and projected themselves as candidates for political self-determination.

Literary *Yiddishkayt*

During a heated critical exchange over the nationalist poetics of Morris Rosenfeld—was he a labor poet or a folk poet?—Jacob Milkh concluded, with some ambivalence, that Rosenfeld was "a labor poet in whose work, in a Jewish mirror and with Jewish coloring, the suffering, the struggle, the striving, and the hope of the working-class is reflected."[7] Critics on the left could assert the primacy of class identity in Yiddish literature, just as figures on the right, denying the legitimacy of Yiddish altogether, could assert the Jewish capacity for genteel (gentile) respectability. But the persistent and undeniable "Jewish coloring" which characterized the work of Jewish writers haunted such commentators all along the spectrum. Within the context of the pogroms, the Dreyfus affair, the Jewish exodus from Russia, the lures of assimilation, and the debates over Bundist and Zionist conceptions of nationhood, this "Jewish coloring," pointing ever toward a distinct Jewish peoplehood, was as politically charged as the most frankly Zionist poems.

As it blossomed toward the century's end, Yiddish literature generally did not replicate the nationalist defiance of Hebrew writers like Bialik. "Nothing but your fierce hounding/ has turned us into beasts of prey," Bialik wrote of the Czarist regime. He went on to promise revenge "with cruel fury."[8] Rather, this was a literature of quiet, perhaps inexplicable survival, devoid of vengeance and blood-letting. But from the folk idioms of Sholom Aleichem's *shtetl* sketches to the realist urban sketches of Abraham Cahan to the bardic poetry of Abraham Liessen, Yiddish writing of the 1890s did explore and so consolidate notions of Jewish peoplehood, which quietly bolstered Zionist-Bundist visions of Jewish political separatism.

The task of forging a "high" cultural tradition from the vernacular language of the ghetto was an oppositional act in itself: it challenged the Russifying cultural decrees and regulations of the Czar, and, later, it resisted the definitions of "the people" advanced by assimilationists on one side and Hebraist purists in the Zionist movement on the other. As Irving Howe and Eliezer Greenberg have argued, Yiddish writers approached their subject "with an instinctive conviction that their purpose was something other than merely to entertain and amuse"; theirs was "the task of reweaving the fabric of national consciousness."[9] Mendele Makher Sforim captured the political-spiritual dimension of the enterprise when he explained, "It seems heaven had decreed even before I was born that I was to be a writer for my people, for my poor, unfortunate people, and God wanted me to learn their customs and observe their ways. Therefore He said: Wander, little bird, over the world, unfortunate among the unfortunates, a Jew among Jews."[10]

Early Yiddish writing in Europe was thus inseparable from the social and political climate of the ghetto which created it. Folk narrative forms and conventions of address irretrievably merged individual characters into their broader social groupings. This was a literary cosmos whose inhabitants were sharply divided, as one character put it, into "Jews, and—to be exact—others." A character in one sketch is described as plunging "into the crowd of Jews and gentiles, no comparison intended." So deep, indeed, was this social chasm that Sholom Aleichem could describe an assimilated Jew as "a Jew who has been transformed into a German, and who could later be transformed into a wolf, a cow, a horse, or even a duck."[11]

These writers did, on occasion, take up political questions directly. Sholom Aleichem's "Red Headed Little Jews," for instance, satired and indicted the dismissal of Zionism among the orthodox East European Jews. The choice, as he posed it, was either to accept the wisdom of Herzl's blueprint, or merely to "talk, talk, and again to talk" while Jews were beaten in the streets of Eastern Europe. In tales like "The Golem" and "The Shabbes-Goy,"[12] I. L. Peretz, too, explored questions of passivity and resistence in the face of anti-Semitic violence.[13]

More typically, however, the Jewish Question was borne in the very texture of the tale, not in pointed challenges from the narrator. Peretz's "Three Gifts," for instance, explored the theme of Jewish martyrdom and devotion with an irony that cut directly to the core problem of Jewish social identity in the age of rising secularism. In this story a soul is sentenced to "wander" the world when, upon judgment, his good deeds are found to weigh exactly as much on the scales of eternity as his bad deeds. If, he is told, he can present three gifts betokening three deeds "unusually beautiful and good," then the gates of paradise will swing open and he will be allowed to enter.

Cast in the homely idioms of oral tradition, the piece then recounts the history of the three gifts, each deriving from religious and folk conventions of Jewish heroism. The first tells of a Jewish man murdered by thieves as he fearlessly defends a "most precious treasure," "a bit of earth . . . from the Holy Land intended for his grave." The second tells of a Jewish woman who, denounced as "the Devil in a beautiful shape" and condemned to be dragged to her death behind the horse of an anti-Semitic *hetman*, pins her skirts to the flesh of her feet so she will not be exposed to the eyes of the soldiers. And the third tells of a Jewish man who prolongs his brutal run through a gauntlet of Russian soldiers in order to retrieve his *yarmulke* fallen midway through. The wandering soul presents the three gifts at the gates of heaven—the bit of earth, the pins, and the *yarmulke*,—and he is indeed allowed to enter.

The tale ends on a note of jarring irony: looking upon the three gifts which so powerfully symbolize love of Zion, unconquerable devotion, the bitter mission of the Diaspora, and Jewish chosenness and its responsibilities, God is heard to remark, "Truly beautiful gifts, unusually beautiful. They have no practical value, no use at all, but as far as beauty is concerned—unusual."[14] In collapsing these cherished symbols to mere curiosities in the eyes of a bemused God, Peretz devalues Jewish martyrdom and devotion, and even challenges the orthodox conceptions of Jewish peoplehood which rest on the covenant of

Abraham. But at the same time he relies on the reader's sharing in the traditional cosmology which produced the three gifts in the first place. The power of the story lies precisely in this tension between the depth of Jewish conviction *and* the simultaneous recognition that such conviction might be entirely mistaken.

The tale springs from and epitomizes the same moment which produced the Jewish secular movements of Zionism and Bundism, a moment when the historic weight of Jewishness was at once heavier and lighter than ever before: the secularizing forces of modernism had altered the traditional, religious basis of Jewish social identity, and yet Russia's May Laws of 1881 and the ensuing pogroms enforced with violence the "unalterable" condition of being a Jew. The three gifts are heart-wrenchingly meaningful; the three gifts may be entirely meaningless.

This narrative tension was the mainspring of much Yiddish literature of the period. Tightly strung between the poles of folk ingenuousness and *haskala* skepticism, between traditional piety and modern irony, Yiddish literature vibrated with the question, "what is it to be Jewish?" This concern was posed with a fundamental disregard for finer points of character, psychology, and manners—a narrative strategy which implicitly enforced the primacy of social groups. As Howe and Greenberg have observed, "What matters most to the Yiddish writers is the context, the contour, the choreography of social behavior: in short, collective destiny."[15] Although each wins our sympathy, for instance, the wandering soul and the three heroes of "The Three Gifts" remain entirely faceless; they command attention solely by their relationship to weightier circumstances. By convention Yiddish literature dealt not with finely drawn personages after the fashion of an Isabel Archer or a Daniel Deronda, but with social *types*—the *yente*, the *schlimazl*, the Chelmer.[16] Every interplay of types evoked the larger tapestry of East European Jewry and the underlying, defining chasm between Jewish and non-Jewish worlds.

In the final decade of the century, a growing body of Yiddish-American writing left the *shtetl* behind and took up the concerns of the American ghetto. Yiddish-American writers and poets like Abraham Cahan, Jacob Gordin, Leon Kobrin, and Morris Rosenfeld did not, however, leave behind the question of "collective destiny." In keeping with the Russian literary tradition of Chernyshevsky, Turgenev, and Dostoyevsky, from which they drew so heavily, these men viewed literature as an arena for exploring political and philosophical premises. Not least among them was the question: were the Jews, in fact, a nation? What tied the Jewish freethinker to the Jews as a *folk?* Was assimilation desirable or even possible? They pondered these matters, moreover, in a style still influenced by Mendele, Sholom Aleichem, and Peretz, which tacitly emphasized ineradicable difference between the Jew and the Gentile.[17]

The incompatibility of standard, enduring Yiddish narrative forms with cosmopolitanist arguments surfaced most vividly in the polemic short stories of Jacob Gordin. "He who will make of a man a nationalist will drag that man back," Gordin insisted; and yet he had a difficult time convincingly casting such ideas in the form of the Yiddish short story.[18] In "What Sings the Jew" a festive, motley gathering of emigrants entertained themselves on shipboard en route from Hamburg to New York by performing their national anthems for one another. When the cry went up that it was the Jews' turn, "Only a mournful, ironic smile played on their lips." There was, of course, no anthem to sing. But to everyone's surprise (and the Gentiles' derision), "Israelik the pauper" agreed to sing. He chose to sing the Kol Nidre, and Gordin's jeering onlookers were transformed by the Jewish song: "Unwillingly each of the *goyim* began to feel and to understand that he was hearing an old, holy, historical song which told of many human troubles and sufferings, which bitterly lamented the lost past and asked with pain what would be found in the future . . . [A] melancholy feeling stole into the heart of everyone."[19]

Here the promise offered up in the story's polemic content—that humanity may be united above the narrow divisions of "Germany Over All" and "Poland Has Not Yet Perished"—is broken by its Yiddishist narrative frame. Like "The Three Gifts," Gordin's story is founded on types and prototypes. Israelik can only be understood to represent "a Jew," and hence the transcendent power of his song can only suggest the superior culture and ethics of Judaism. With its emphasis on group identity even as it describes a universalizing sentiment, the tale is chauvinistic in spite of itself: in sharp contrast to the *goyim,* whose behavior is mean-spirited and whose songs are divisive, "the Jew" emerges as the moral superior in the social relations aboard ship, just as only the *Jewish* tradition has the power to unite humanity.

Again, "In Prayer Garments: A Fact" was Gordin's answer to those for whom Jewish socialism was solidly rooted in Judaism. Here a persistent ethnic attachment led only to despair: "[Jacob] knew that he was a Jew, and, as a Jew, he was born only to have worries, he got married only to have worries, he lived only to have worries, had children only to have worries. In Russia he lived only to have worries, and with his troubles he *shlepped* himself over from Russia to America—to have worries." One morning, as he stood by the window with his prayer garments on, watching the "worried and depressed" passersby and listening to his children begging for food in the next room, and as he asked himself whether there was no other joy in life but "the love of one's God," he opened the window and leapt out. Fully comprehending this man's life and his death, those who gathered around his body in the street "dared not tell a lie"—they dared not utter the prayer for the dead, "Blessed be the true judge."[20] Through the refusal of these passers-by to "tell a lie," to recite the prayer, Gordin rejects the Jewish tradition as politically paralyzing. Nonetheless, his tale conveys a totalizing experience of uniquely Jewish "worries," which undermines the argument that Judaism can be shed like an unwanted garment. "This little song about the Jewish quintessence and about the Jewish soul is very beautiful and sweet," Gordin would argue in his debate with Chaim Zhitlowsky, "but it is no more than a lyrical feeling." Yet his own stories portrayed a Judaism which ran much deeper than sweet little songs.[21]

Gordin's political adversaries, particularly Abraham Cahan and Leon Kobrin, embraced the tenet of an unshakable Jewish quintessence—*dos pintele yid*—with considerably less ambivalence. Here the message emerged directly by polemic content. The inner coherence and outer boundaries of *Yiddishkayt* were rendered immutable by their grounding in the terrain of "nature": works in the realist-naturalist vein took up the Jewish Question in the lexicon of sexuality and blood relations—homely themes of "natural" family bonds overarched by schemes of "race" and "physiognomy." In "Yankel Boyle," Leon Kobrin's Romeo and Juliet novella of the *shtetl*, the romance of a Jewish youth and a Russian peasant woman strikes the village with the secular force of a "race question"; in the story's climactic storm scene, in fully Shakespearean undertones, Yankel attributes the horrors of the night to his own transgression against the natural order.[22] Cosmopolitanism is bankrupt, these authors argued, because Jewish identity is etched in the very stone of the natural order.

The inescapable grip of "nature," the futility of transcending one's *Yiddishkayt*, was the very crux of Cahan's first major literary success, *Yekl.* The plot centers on a blustery and misguided immigrant bent on shedding his Russian-Yiddish self and becoming a true Yankee. So intent is he on this transformation that when his wife and son join him in America after a prolonged separation, he recoils, ashamed of their "foreign" demeanor. Under the spell of his Yankee aspiration, Yekl then falls in love with Mamie Fein, a partly Americanized, royally pretentious woman whom he has met in an East Side dancing school. Yekl ends as a "defeated victor," achieving his freedom from the greenhorn Gitl through divorce, yet sensing vaguely that he has been duped by his own elusive measures of success and happiness.

It was Cahan, recall, who had brought the Jewish Question before the Socialist Congress in Brussels a few years earlier. In this character sketch of a familiar ghetto type he challenged the tenets of cosmopolitanism on two counts. First, *Yekl* countered the cosmopolitanist reasoning that nationalism was necessarily divisive and that assimilation was necessarily a unifying principle, the key to workers' solidarity across ethnic or national lines. On the contrary, in the American context assimilation itself was among the supreme expressions of bourgeois aspiration. Yekl's quest to become "an American feller" led to Mamie Fein, her money, and the petit bourgeois dream of opening a dancing school of his own. Far from engendering the humanitarian spirit described in cosmopolitanist tracts, assimilationism led to self-absorption and Yekl's sense of superiority to his coworkers. Finally, it led to his truly inhuman attitude toward his wife and compatriot, Gitl: "I am an *American feller*, a Yankee—that's what I am. What punishment is due me, then, if I can not stand a *shnooza* like her?" " 'Ah, may she be killed, the horrid greenhorn!' he would gasp to himself in a paroxysm of despair."[23]

Cahan underscored the theme of assimilationism as a regressive impulse by the recurrent equation of Americanization with nobility, an unambiguous intimation for his largely socialist readership.[24] In the world of *Yekl* assimilation offered no "broad" alternative to "narrow" nationalism. On the contrary, kindness and decency themselves depended upon a humble acceptance of *Yiddishkayt*: one of Yekl's rare moments of clarity, a momentary resolution to reform and fulfil his obligations to Gitl, was attended by Old World memories of "the Hebrew words of the Sanctification of the Sabbath" and a homely vision of "a plate of reeking *tzimes* [a sweet dish made of carrots]."[25]

Cahan's argument that assimilation was undesirable, moreover, was underpinned by an iron contention that it was in fact impossible. This second layer, Cahan's version of *dos pintele yid*, comprised a constellation of images of which this "plate of reeking *tzimes*" was but one element. The complex as a whole linked naturalized notions of lineage and kinship ("race" in the broadest instance, "parentage" in the narrower instance) to naturalized conceptions of patriarchal order. Cahan locates *dos pintele yid* within the rhythms of nature, firmly lashed to notions of race and sex also presumed to be natural.

Yekl's bid to become a Yankee feller is futile. On the grounds of "race," the thin veneer of Americanization is ever betrayed by "his Semitic smile" and his "strongly Semitic" eyes. As one of his sweat-shop rivals chides, "He thinks that *shaving* one's mustache makes a Yankee!"[26] Indeed, it is his attempt to transcend his "natural" self which renders Yekl the buffoon that he is. On the question of whether Judaism is a system of religious belief or a more fundamental element of one's being, *Yekl* is unequivocal: a Jew, even if fallen away, will always be a Jew. Hence when William Dean Howells identified Cahan as "a Hebrew" and described his ghetto sketches as "so foreign to our race and civilization," he was not merely expressing an Anglo-Saxon parochialism.[27] This racialist view was embraced on both sides of the presumed barrier (see Chapter 5).

Further, as critic Susan Kress has observed, the institution of mar-riage is perhaps the foremost arena for the thematic treatment of assimilation throughout Cahan's fiction. Kress is most interested in the social options for immigrant women and the ways in which Cahan portrayed them. But the issue might fruitfully be put another way: for Cahan, as for many of his male colleagues, notions of *Yiddishkayt* invariably intersected notions of masculinity, femininity, maternal duty, and patriarchal authority.[28] In the case of *Yekl*, sexuality, like race, naturalized the Jewish quintessence: the buffoon-hero's hope of transcending his Old World self is limited by overlapping and envel-oping complexes of parentage-as-race, and parentage-as-patriarchy.

Yekl's doomed quest to escape his own *Yiddishkayt* is played out almost entirely on the terrain of gender and sexuality. The question of identity which so plagues him is cast as a choice between two women: the cultural conservatism of Gitl, or the rather thin assimilationism of Mamie Fein. Yekl's momentary surrender to "the grip of his past," his fleeting acceptance of *Yiddishkayt* and his memory of "reeking *tzimes*," is attended by a very particular image of Judaism and the Jewish home: "seated by the side of the head of the little family and within easy reach of the huge brick oven, is his old mother, flushed with fatigue, and with an effort keeping her drowsy eyes open to attend, with a devout mien, her husband's prayer."[29] And in the closing scene, Yekl dimly acknowledges his mistakes and imagines undoing them in these terms: "What if he should now dash into Gitl's apartments and, de-claring his authority as husband, father, and lord of the house, fiercely eject the strangers, take Yosele in his arms, and sternly command Gitl to mind her household duties?"[30]

The gender relations evoked throughout the novel replicate precisely and literally the sexual division of labor which constitutes an essential prop of traditional Judaism. Women were to supply men's physical needs, freeing men for more important matters of the spirit—including the spiritual needs of women themselves.[31] It was because of their biological function as mothers that women were discounted as legal members of the quorum in prayer; and it was this maternal capacity and its "natural" limitations which Jewish men were to acknowledge in their daily benediction, thanking God "for not having made me a woman."[32] Cahan thus taps a powerful current of social authority—at once Talmudic and biologic—answering cosmopolitanist designs not only with racial certainties but with an eternal Judaism rooted in patriarchy and the eternal feminine. Yekl's futile assimilation-as-denial is ultimately contrasted to Gitl's more organic transformation: with her neighbor Mrs. Kavarsky's help ("Be a mother to me"), Gitl loses her "rustic, 'greenhorn-like' expression" without betraying Judaism.[33]

To be sure, in the late-nineteenth-century Jewish community the idea of a reified sexual order was the site for a number of conflicts other than purely national-cosmopolitanist ones. Contested representations of gender in this period reflected the complex social reality of a multicultural milieu—competing moralities, the lure of the "modern," the erosion of traditional mores surrounding love and marriage, and the consequent generational conflicts in the immigrant community. But the overlap between national questions and urban social questions was substantial. As Irving Howe has written of the Yiddish drama's most famous matriarch, "In some deep way *Mirele Efros* spoke to the common Jewish perception, grounded in a sufficiency of historical experience, that the survival of a persecuted minority required an iron adherence to traditional patterns of family life. Mirele represents the conserving strength of the past, which alone has enabled the Jews to hold together in time."[34]

The extent to which this was in fact a "common Jewish perception" was later belied by women authors like Anzia Yezierska and Anna Margolin. But it is true that in this most patriarchal of literary traditions (Mendele wrote of the Yiddish language, "[I] wedded her forever," "she became an attractive helpmeet and bore me many sons.")[35] Jewish identity and tenacity were often located in the figure of the Jewish maid/matron/matriarch. For the secularized male writers of the 1890s, the image of the Jewish woman was a cultural anchor.

Hence these were the scenes which most captured the unconquerable spirit of *Yiddishkayt*: a once-pious woman, having fallen under America's ungodly spell, reawakens on Yom Kippur and again feels at one with "the children of Israel . . . massed together in every corner of the globe." An Americanized, "fallen" woman of the ghetto reclaims her Old World self when the chant of the Kol Nidre, drifting up from a *shul* across the street, awakens in her a nearly pious "sadness in the soul." "I am not Jenny," she cries; "I am Zlate!" A daughter of the ghetto, a freethinker overcome by melancholy on Passover, can only ask herself, "Why is this night different from every other night?"—and yet be certain that it is. A mother of the Old World, upon hearing that her emigrant daughter has married a Christian, rends her garments and recites the prayer for the dead. And as the grip of her parental authority loosens in the New World, another matriarch angrily denounces her daughter as a *shikse*—a non-Jewish woman.[36]

There is some overlap, clearly, between the complementary themes of the culture-bearing power of the feminine, and the recuperative power of Jewish ritual (the power of the Kol Nidre in "What Sings the Jew?"; the power of the Hebrew words during Yekl's fleeting reawakening). But in his controversial sketch, "What Is He?" Leon Kobrin developed the gendered aspect of the argument even as he captured the contentious nationalist spirit of much Yiddish-American literature. He had originally written the story in the first person of a man, but he soon recast it and added the subtitle, "From the Diary of a Socialist Mother."[37]

"What Is He?" is a monologue in the voice of a Jewish freethinking socialist, who begins to suspect that in casting off Judaism she has robbed her little boy of his childhood's rightful magic. "What does my little five-year-old Nikolai Chernyshevsky,[38] my darling boy, know of *Yiddishkayt*? What kind of Jew is he?" she asks. As she reflects on the beauty, the mirth, and the depth of feeling in the Jewish religious tradition, her question becomes, "Where is the poetry of my Nikolai's childhood?" What is there in socialism and the freethinker's concern for broad humanity that could take the place of Hanukkah, Pesach, and Purim in the lives of the activists' children? The *sotzialistke* finally works herself up from this simple reflection to a plaintive accusation leveled at the cultural tenets of Jewish socialism: "How come the socialists among other peoples do not take their national holidays away from their children?"

In response to the wave of letters which flooded Philip Krantz's editorial office in response to the sketch, Kobrin wrote a second, even stronger statement entitled "Yes, What Is He?" "Yes, what is my Nikolai?" asked the *sotzialistke* again. "What will he grow into in this indefinite gray reality?—in this mish mash of ours, without life, without light, and without the sunny warmth of a festive childhood?"

Reviewing the Jewish calendar of holidays and recounting its joys at length, Kobrin's *sotzialistke* exclaims, "What poetic nectar for the spirit of a child!"[39] *Yiddishkayt*, these sketches argued, was being unnecessarily sacrificed on the altar of cosmopolitanism. Like young Nikolai, the Jewish socialist in the age of Dreyfus was "cut off from his own people, but had no bonds with the stranger." And again, it was the Jewish mother, never to be estranged from tradition, who stepped forward to make the case.[40]

Abraham Liessen [Abraham Wald] and Morris Rosenfeld, America's bards of Yiddish nationalism, carried this literary polemic to its extreme, complementing in many ways the sketches of the ghetto realists. Whereas the Yiddishism of the sketch writers stopped at anti-assimilationism, Liessen and Rosenfeld suggested a positive nationalist program. Rather than emphasize the power of the feminine as a force of national preservation, Liessen and Rosenfeld celebrated a militarist masculinism aimed at national fulfillment. As Kobrin wrote of Liessen, the "Maccabee-spirit" itself "spoke out through the spirit of this young scholar from Minsk"; and it was Rosenfeld, recall, who reveled in the symbolism of Hanukkah, "Jew, you have warred once! Jew, you have conquered once!"[41]

Liessen was described by one countryman as "the father of nationalist thought in the Bund." He had early defected from the radical project of "going to the [Russian] people," embracing instead an idealized version of the Jewish masses.[42] At least as important as his Maccabean politics was a cosmology in which poet and folk were depicted as inseparable and unconquerable. Like the narrative "I" of Sholom Aleichem and I. L. Peretz, Liessen's poetic voice reflected a conception of self which bespoke collectivity: "Another little page, *mayn folk*,[43] another terrifying picture / From your life's book have I known." Not only did Liessen conceive the individual lifetime as but one page in a greater tome, but indeed the meaning and value of that page were measured precisely by its contribution to the overarching "life's book":

> In the fervor of a powerless wrath,
> I've managed only to groan, nothing more;
> I've thirsted for vengeance so longingly
> And have had to sate myself with a tear.
>
> Another tear in the abyss of tears
> That marks your way upon the earth;
> Another groan in a wide world of groans—
> What to you, then, is it worth?[44]

This vision of the Jew's living out one "terrifying picture" in Jewish history was a constant in Liessen's work. In contrast to the naturalists, however (and in spite of his going on to become the most highly regarded nature poet in Yiddish), he cast this link between the lone individual and *mayn folk* not in racial but in historical terms. In "A Martyr's Blood" and "In Battle" he invoked a defining tradition of heroism whose "example will long give light,/ through generation after generation."[45] In "From the Dark Past," on the other hand, he portrayed a dynamic of history and psychology in which pain was identified as the galvanizing force of Judaism. As if entranced, the poet regards the momentous sufferings of his people as treasures to be cherished.

> I think, *mayn folk*, of the terrors of the past,
> I am captured and overwhelmed by your grief—
> The magnificence of your garland of thorns among the
>   nations,
> The fateful sentence of three thousand years.
>
> And I think, *mayn folk*, of a better future,
> I become so heavy with regret:
> Will you vanish in good fortune? To what end, then,
> The sufferings of thousands of years?[46]

Finding a threat in good fortune, demanding some cohesive meaning from the sufferings of thousands of years, the Jewish people wills itself into the future by clinging to the beloved terrors of the past. The Jewish spirit is kept alive in part by a macabre romanticism: "Oh, dark, great, heroic past," Liessen concludes, "How dear to me, how beloved you are!"

But the essence of Judaism is no less real for being founded merely on memory. "The Eternal Jew," Liessen's popular manifesto on the persistence of the Jewish character, locates the Jewish essence above what is human, above what is natural, and finally above what simply *is*.

> . . . The greatest states have been lost,
> The mightiest peoples have been decimated,
> And world-cities have been ploughed under in salt,
> And gigantic mountains have fallen in shadow,
> And eternal woods have rotted, been trampled.[47]

"I live and endure everything!" he concludes; "Blunt is the tooth of time." Hence an ineluctable circularity was at work in Liessen's conception of the Jew. History (as opposed to nature, race, or the sparks of Jewish mysticism) was the mainspring of *Yiddishkayt*. Jews were made, not born—they had been made by historical "terrors," and they remade themselves by acts of memory as they sought meaning in the heroism and the pain of the past. Yet ultimately they were exempt from history's ravages. The paradoxical corollary to historical determination was the absolute transcendence of history itself.

The poet Morris Rosenfeld, too, located the eternal Jew in the workings of history, although he was primarily interested in the secular political power of traditional religious mythology.[48] While he was most widely praised for his ability to translate and sing the common sweatshop experience in pieces like "Be Proud, Laborer" and "The Sweatshop," Rosenfeld was also an ardent Zionist.[49] Zionism, as he described it upon his return from the Congress of 1900, hoped to recover "the Crown of the Torah, the Crown of the Kingdom, and the Crown of God's name—all of which Exile has covered with the dust of generations and with the blood of innocent Jewish victims." Herzl himself was "the architect of the new Jewish history."[50]

More than most socialist writers, Rosenfeld invoked specific moments in the Jewish past and drew strength from the themes and imagery of religious tradition—traits which prompted one critic to dismiss his poems as "good-looking sermons in rhyme."[51] In this vein "Sephirah"[52] defined the Jew's contemporary suffering as part of a narrative which has been unfolding "ever since his enemies have shattered and broken the sweetest instruments of music in his Temple." Poems like "The Little Hanukkah Candles" borrowed heroes and precedents for militarized resistance from religious lore:

> We have lost our courage
> in exile among the wicked,
> And yet in our blood is preserved
> the fire of the Maccabees.

Or again, in "Judus Maccabeus":

> Love for the Creator in his heart,
> Sword in hand, he takes the field
> To save his people and his Torah:
> Jerusalem's last hero.[53]

Although secular logic infused the mythologies of Moses and the Egyptians, the Babylonian exile, and the Maccabees, still all roads led to Jerusalem: Rosenfeld's conceits of *Yiddishkayt* became increasingly territorial and combative. He lamented that "We are slaves in foreign lands,/ recognized by no one"; he goaded his compatriots, "The earth has been robbed from under your steps,/ The light has been taken from over your head"; and he refused to give up on the Promised Land: "Oh, no, I cannot go begging with shame for a home in foreign lands."[54] "A Diaspora March," founded on an almost parodic dissonance between plaintive words and martial cadence, decried the vulnerability of the stateless Jews at the hands of ruthless foreign states:

> With a walking staff in hand,
> Without a home, without a country;
> Without a savior, without a friend,
> Without a tomorrow, without a today,—
> Not endured, but chased,
> In one place by night, another by day,
> Always woe, woe, woe,
> Always go, go, go,
> Always step, step, step,
> As long as strength holds up.[55]

This singular "Jewish coloring" greatly perplexed doctrinaire socialist critics. Unlike the works of Liessen, Kobrin, and Cahan, Rosenfeld's national poems did not stop at the Bundist insistence upon Jewish recognition in the international. Rosenfeld, perhaps the most acclaimed of labor poets, fully embraced the Zionist dream. In his compelling march toward the Promised Land, he differed but little from Hebrew poets like Menachem Dolitzky, whom Hutchins Hapgood regarded as "a champion of race," or Chaim Nakhman Bialik, the poet laureate of Zionism, who urged, "Rise, desert wanderers, leave the wilderness,/ Far is the way, many are the battles." If Jews seemed to have lost the "ancient audacity of giants," Rosenfeld wrote, nonetheless "an ideal lives on in us—and that, nations, you cannot conquer!"[56]

Overall the relationship of Yiddish literature to Jewish nationalism was deeply mixed. Herzl himself discounted the significance of this literary awakening, and indeed denied the legitimacy of the Yiddish language. "We shall give up using those miserable stunted jargons," he wrote, "those Ghetto languages which we still employ, for these were the stealthy tongues of prisoners."[57] Yet this body of writing addressed and upheld the very notions of peoplehood which were critical to Jewish nationalism, and it did so in the "stealthy tongue" of the masses upon which both Zionism and Bundism depended.

The nationalist work accomplished by Yiddish literature was acknowledged by combatants on both sides of the question in America: the cosmopolitanist press denounced writers like Leon Kobrin as best suited to the nationalist *Tageblatt;* and Kobrin, for his part, would later recall that it had been primarily novelists and poets who had breathed "a national-Yiddish atmosphere" into the Yiddish radical press in the United States.[58] Chaim Zhitlowsky later codified the politics of Yiddish cultural production in his political-sociological theories of "Yiddishism." "The Yiddish language," he posited, "is the breath of life whose very inhalation renews the existence of the Jewish people. As long as Yiddish lives, there can be no doubt that the Jewish people will live."[59]

The Bards of Polish Literature

In the Polish literary cosmos nationalism required no defense; the Polish national spirit, unlike *dos pintele yid,* required no explanation. On the contrary, instances of its absence had to be accounted for. As Maria Rodziewiczówna wondered in her romance of the 1863 Rising, *Fire and Ruins,*

> Where do a nation's traitors come from?
> One land nourishes them, one sun shines on them, one spirit of tradition and principle teaches them, and yet at a certain moment they fall away from society or corrode it like gangrene.
> They have everything in common with heroes; they lack only heart, warmth, and fire.[60]

The heart, warmth, and fire of Poland's natural and abundant heroes, set off against a backdrop of partition and rebellion, was the very stuff of nineteenth-century Polish literature: the importance of national struggle to this tradition can scarcely be overstated. Within a social context where the direct avenues of political expression were blocked for long periods of time and where harsh censorship codes underscored at every turn the power of the word, the Polish intelligentsia had long viewed literary pursuits as acts of resistance, literature itself as a political resource. As one Polonian poet wrote in a paean to the Polish language, "Our virtuosos in Polish volumes / Show the world that ever we live on, / That anti-Polish thunderbolts are naught."[61]

It was in this spirit that *Kuryer Polski* could ask in all sincerity, "who has rendered more to the fatherland than Adam Mickiewicz?" It was in this spirit that one critic hailed Henryk Sienkiewicz's historical fiction as a patriotic "deed rather than a word," and that another admirer, learning of the writer's worldwide renown, cried, "That's it. As long as Sienkiewicz lives, Poland has not perished!" It was in this spirit that Sienkiewicz's "The Lighthouse Keeper," by a self-reflexive turn, depicted the power of literature to stir national passions.[62] And it was in recognition of this spirit, indeed, that the unveiling of a monument to Mickiewicz in Warsaw could take place only under the vigilant gaze of Russian troops, "without oratory, [amid] an army of bristling bayonettes, spades, and knouts."[63]

Emigrant writers like Teofila Samolinska and Stanisław Dangiel generated over the years a modest body of nationalist tales and lyrics for the nation's fourth partition, and so carried forward this Old World tradition. They will be taken up below. More pressing, however, and in sharp contrast to Yiddish literary life in America, is the extent to which the writings of Old World authors were seized upon, repositioned, and infused with new relevance by Polonian publishers—the extent, that is, to which Polish classics like Mickiewicz's *Pan Tadeusz* and *Konrad Wallenrod* became the staples of the New World literary diet. The routine appearance of Mickiewicz, Juliusz Słowacki, and Maria Konopnicka in Polish-America's penny papers not only confounds any proposed distinction between "high" and "popular" culture; it also muddles the boundaries presumed by the notion of "immigrant" or "ethnic" literatures. From the standpoint of the Polish-American reader in the 1890s, émigré poet Adam Mickiewicz lost nothing in immediacy beside the emigrant writers in Chicago and Milwaukee. True to the contours of Polonia's literary scene, Stanisław Osada's 1910 overview of "Polish and Polish-American Literature for the Poles in America" covers little that is "Polish-American" in the strictest sense.[64]

Tapping the well of Old World literature solved several problems at once for Polonian editors and publishers. In contrast to the Yiddish migration, which included a sizable and wildly prolific intelligentsia, the overwhelmingly working- and peasant-class profile of the Polish migration set limits on the amount of literary activity to be found in the communities of the fourth partition. The use of Old World classics redressed the shortages created by Polonian demographics themselves. Given the political nature of so much Polish writing, moreover, editors could draw upon the elegant phrases of Poland's best-loved poets and novelists to advance their own political agendas. And not least of all, coopting Mickiewicz and Słowacki eliminated the need to pay author's fees, and so eased the financial burdens that came with enclave publishing.

Under these conditions, the volume of nationalist literature written in Poland and made available in America either in cheap editions or in the penny papers was considerable. In an ad for the *Gazeta Katolicka* bookstore (1898) featuring ninety titles and brief descriptions, for example, thirty-nine dealt with Poland's history of oppression, resistance, and military valor, or with themes of bondage or persecution.[65]

Setting aside divisions separating romanticism from positivism, anticlericalism from religionism, or right from left, three broad categories of nationalist literature are discernible. The first includes direct literary treatments of Polish history. In 1885 *Zgoda* became the first newspaper on either side of the Atlantic to serialize Józef Kraszewski's novel of the January Rising, *A Child of the Old City*; over the following decades the immigrant presses ceaselessly reprinted such accounts of nationalist rebellion. This class includes sweeping novels like Henryk Sienkiewicz's *With Fire and Sword* (on the Polish-Cossack wars) and *The Teutonic Knights* (on the fifteenth-century clash between Poland and Prussia); short historical sketches, such as Anna Lewicka's "A Brave Lad" or "As a Blacksmith Is Able, So He Serves the Fatherland" (both on the January Rising); and topical poetry, such as Maria Konopnicka's "Hymn of New Poland" (celebrating the Polish National Alliance) or Józef Szujski's "Under Your Protection" (on the defense of Częstochowa against the Swedes). An untitled piece in *Zgoda* (1897) bewailed the latest piece of anti-Polish legislation: "for the increase of our sorrow,/ The Moscovite has invented new fetters."[66]

The second category, reflecting both the Polish impulse to create a usable past and the force of censorship under Russian and Prussian rule, included works which tacitly commented on Poland's history by drawing analogies with other nations, often in distant periods. Most familiar in this vein among non-Polish readers is Henryk Sienkiewicz's treatment of Nero's Rome, *Quo Vadis?*, at once a condemnation of imperial arrogance and a celebration of moral fortitude in the face of persecution. (Not surprisingly, the novel was translated and popularized in the English-speaking world by Jeremiah Curtin, an Irish nationalist.)[67] Bolesław Prus's *Pharoah* was an analysis of political power and its workings in ancient Egypt, which, as *Kuryer Polski* commented, clearly reflected its authorship "under the knout of the Czar." Słowacki's "Agamemnon's Grave," Kornel Ujejski's "Maraton," and Lambro's "Greek Rebel" all drew on Greek history; others drew upon the persecution of Catholics in England or upon *The Bondage of the Moors* to explore the broad themes of domination and resistance.[68]

And finally, the third category consisted of romantic elegies and mythic, sometimes mystical legends whose constructions of heroism were founded upon these same ideals of resistance and liberation. Juliusz Słowacki's "My Testament" encompasses in a pithy quatrain the Polish idealization of political self-sacrifice:

> I adjure—let the living not lose hope
> And before the nation carry the torch of learning;
> And when it is needed, go to their death in their turn
> Like stones thrown by God against the rampart.[69]

Mickiewicz's "Grażyna" tells of a woman who discovers that her husband, a Lithuanian Prince, has made a traitorous pact with the Teutonic Knights; she disguises herself in the prince's armor and leads his army into battle against the Teutonic Order. The hero of his *Konrad Wallenrod* is a Lithuanian boy who has been captured during a military raid and raised by the Teutonic Knights. Over the years he has risen to the top of their hierarchy, yet Konrad undergoes an ethnic reawakening when he hears the song of an old Lithuanian minstrel. True to his newly recovered identity, he leads the German Knights into battle in such a way as to ensure their demise. And Słowacki's *Kordjan* is a fanciful exploration of romantic *angst* which finally centers on a plot to assassinate Czar Nicholas I. The editors of *Zgoda* ran this particular work in its entirety, they explained, because it "is so soaked through with love of the Fatherland, so filled with extreme images and the terrible power of suffering."[70]

The penchant for "extreme images" and "terrible power" among Polish writers had gathered particular force in the wake of the failed November Rising of 1830. Czesław Miłosz has described this period in Poland as a time "of criss-crossing currents, of madly daring ideas, of self-pity and national arrogance, and of unsurpassed brilliancy of poetic technique."[71] It was then, in the 1830s, that the theme of Poland's suffering became immortalized in a national aesthetic; it was then that a national concern became a literary obsession. At the center of this romantic nationalist awakening was Adam Mickiewicz (1798–1855), who explored Polish martyrdom and redemption in a torrent of plays, verses, epic poems, and literary essays.

His political contribution to Poland was twofold: as one critic has aptly put it, "Mickiewicz's works nationalized poetry and catholicized patriotism."[72] His nationalization of poetry was reflected in works like "Grażyna" and Konrad Wallenrod, in which political rebellion became the purest expression of romantic heroism. His catholicization of patriotism, on the other hand, emerged in a messianic ideology which linked the political redemption of Poland with the moral redemption of humanity. Written in a biblical, parabolic style, the Book of the Polish Nation established a symbolic parallel between the political purity of Poland and the moral purity of Christ. "Whoever shall come to me shall be free and equal, for I am FREEDOM," cries the Poland of this parable. Both the nation's martyrdom at the hands of the partitioning powers—the "satanic trinity"—and its redemptive powers for all of humanity echo the themes of martyrdom and redemption in Christian symbology:

> And they martyred the Polish nation and laid it in the grave, and the Kings cried out, "We have slain and we have buried freedom."
>
> [But] the Polish nation did not die: its body lieth in the grave, but its soul hath descended from the earth, that is from public life, to the abyss, that is to the private life of people who suffer slavery in their country and outside of their country, that it may see their sufferings.
>
> But . . . the soul shall return to the body . . .
>
> And as after the resurrection of Christ blood sacrifices ceased in all the world, so after the resurrection of the Polish Nation wars shall cease in all Christendom.[73]

Here and in the companion piece, the Book of the Polish Pilgrims, Mickiewicz established a national commitment akin to religious devotion as the very key to the Pole's—and especially the exiled Pole's—existence. "The pilgrims' guiding star is a faith in heaven; and their compass is a love of the Fatherland." Emigrants, in this politico-religious fusion, were the nation's apostles.[74] "The Pilgrim's Litany" captures in their complexity the intertwining themes of exile, bondage, prayer, insurrection, and redemption:

> God the Father, who didst lead thy people out of the
> Egyptian bondage and didst restore them to the Holy Land,
> Restore us to our Fatherland.
> Son of God and Savior, who wast tortured and crucified,
> who rose from the dead and dost reign in glory,
> Raise from the dead our Fatherland.
> Mother of God, to whom our fathers gave the name Queen
> of Poland and Lithuania,
> Save Poland and Lithuania.[75]

After some twenty more verses of call and response, the Litany ends with the pilgrims' prayers "For a happy death on the field of battle," "For the burial of our bones in our own land," and "For the independence, unity, and freedom of our Fatherland." The "national arrogance" and the "madly daring" political vision of Mickiewicz's mid-century works defined the terms of Polish artistic aspiration for generations to come.

As in politics, so in literature the period after the failed rising of 1863 witnessed a backlash against what were now perceived as the suicidal tenets of Polish romanticism. Polish literature after the January Rising of 1863 tended to dim the color and dull the edges of romantic messianism and insurrectionism. But the extent to which the period could sustain a nationalist literary vision was demonstrated by Maria Konopnicka (1842–1910), according to *Zgoda* "the most sublime poet not only in our literature, but perhaps in the literature of [all of] Europe today."[76]

Konopnicka paid tribute to Mickiewicz both in poems and in critical works. Pieces like "The Third of May" and "There, in My Country" embraced not only the nationalism, but even the romantic mysticism which the earlier generation had established.[77] But Konopnicka's singular contribution was a populist revision of the most common nationalist themes. Whereas Mickiewicz had presented Polish history in its grandest sweep, Konopnicka now brought the national question to the earthier level of the wholly imaginable sorrows and deeds of wholly ordinary people. If Mickiewicz "catholicized" nationalism, then Konopnicka democratized it.

"The Heart of a Peasant," a wrenching portrait of a mother whose son has been conscripted, typifies this angle on the national question. The opening of the poem, which focuses on the woman as she stands outside the recruitment hall, at once represents a poetic keening on behalf of the nation, and lays claim to the nation on behalf of the common folk:

In a crowd, in the frost, she stood beneath the wall,
Wrapped in an old russet coat of her husband's.

A dreary thing is this grizzled red coat,
Later soaked through with tears,
Torn in the back—the back bent from the adversity and
    toil
Of a wretch, who from the darkness never reaches
Out toward the light
With one single animating hope.

And a grievous thing it is, this coat,
Melancholy and by itself so mournful,
As though not a rag at all, but a fresh wound
On the body of the nation, bleeding.

Sometime, when the storms and gales blow through
And a century of sunlight wraps itself in azure,
The world will talk of this russet coat
And it will be named in epic folk histories.

And maybe then even we, we ourselves,
Will save this miserable, woolen, torn remnant
Among the national treasures and monuments
—Maybe we ourselves will bathe it in tears.[78]

The poem goes on to describe the last moments spent together by mother and son, and finally to describe the mother's death—"They say her peasant heart was broken." Here Konopnicka overturns long-standing conventions of the nationalist canon: she relocates the moment of national "sacrifice" from a hero's death on the battlefield to a mother's loss at the recruitment hall, and so reconnects glory to its inevitable shadow, grief. Likewise, she storms the shrine of national memory, questioning the contours of "epic folk history" and urging a redefinition of "national treasures."

Konopnicka's particular brand of populism everywhere bore traces of her perspective as a woman; but overall it was the populist-nationalist statement, not the feminist, which broke through most powerfully in her work. "Let's Build a House for Our Fair Fatherland" exhorted Poles to look to one goal only, "the goal of a great resurrection"; "O Wrześniu" protested the treatment of Polish schoolchildren by Prussian teachers in that city; and "The Fate of Stanisław" highlighted the contrasting experiences and fates of peasant and noble men in battle. In "The Germans Have Walked Here" she decried the colonization of western Poland in a manner which, like her portrait of the russet-coated peasant woman, emphasized the grassroots, face-to-face dimensions of national struggle. Here in the first person of a peasant man, Konopnicka envisioned a "cemetery grown over with wild brambles, like the orchards where our ancestors lay in their graves." If the Germans took the land, "my children ... would not know where to look for their father's grave."[79]

Given the circumstances of late-nineteenth-century Poland, this sympathy for the masses could only lead across the seas to the growing assemblies of Poles abroad. Like Henryk Sienkiewicz, who sought to stem the tide of emigration by his horrific portrait of life in America, *After Bread*, Konopnicka increasingly addressed the fate and welfare of the overseas migrants. "A Chorus of Polish Children Abroad" affirmed in optimistic tones the emigrants' undying spirit of *Polskość* ("Don't cry, Father, Mother,/ Looking across the sea—/ Here in the name of God your children have created a New Poland.") And "A Hymn to New Poland," written in honor of the PNA, likewise promised that "... although distant,/ your people gather together under your flag/ Faithful of heart now and forever."[80] These were but dim foreshadowings of her emigration epic *Mr. Balcer in Brazil*, published in 1910 after twenty years in the works.

Hence Konopnicka's populism, like Mickiewicz's catholicized nationalism, bridged the social distance between the intelligentsia in Poland and the emigrant readership in America. The relevance of *The Book of Polish Pilgrims* or "A Chorus of Polish Children Abroad" to the displaced peasantry was not hard to find. Nonetheless, the reliance of New World editors upon Old World literature did call for some explanation. The interpretive comment was perhaps the fastest growing genre in Polish-American writing, as PNA and PRCU intellectuals sought to position these works in the lives of the emigrants. Lest they misread "Maraton," a portrait of Greek rebellion, for instance, *Zgoda* supplied the orthodox PNA reading: "Kornel Ujejski chose this glorious moment in the history of the Greeks, wanting to lift the spirit in our nation ... In the struggle for freedom the greatest military might, brutal and disciplined, matters less than the strength of the spirit and the thirst for freedom."[81]

This tendentious mode of literary comment led to a war among Polonia's political factions for stewardship of Poland's literary canon. *Dziennik Chicagoski* described the centenary of Mickiewicz's birthday and the silver jubilee of the PRCU as two momentous and intimately related events. In "The Relationship of Mickiewicz to the Resurrectionists," the journal not only acknowledged a debt to the poet, but fully claimed him as "in a certain respect, the founder of [the] congregation."[82] Later, drawing upon *Pan Tadeusz, Forefather's Eve*, and *Konrad Wallenrod*, Stanisław Szwajkart demonstrated Mickiewicz's reverence for the Holy Virgin and traced the development of national-religious themes over the course of the poet's career. Mickiewicz's work was not merely nationalistic, he argued, but properly Catholic, defending Poland against the "unhealthy" influences of modern European literature.[83] Such assertions countered similar exercises in *Zgoda* which positioned the poet squarely within the PNA-Falcon camp. Citing Mickiewicz's own declaration that he saw in literature "the means of redemption for my Fatherland," the liberal *Zgoda* declared that the poet's significance was not religious but purely insurrectionary.[84]

Despite the prominence of Old World writing, Polonia did boast a number of its own writers who kept alive the literary traditions of the homeland and added a variety of New World tones to the political aesthetics inherited from Mickiewicz. As early as 1876 a literary journal in Lwów greeted "the rise of Polish literature in America" as "a very important sign": "The thousands of Poles who have been driven to the United States either by persecution or by poverty would quickly lose their Polish national character among the foreign peoples if, without organization and literature, they lived in isolation, occupied only with their daily bread." One of the guarantees "that they will preserve their nationality and will be saved for Poland," according to this writer, "is the creation of Polish literature among them."[85]

Although more candid in its nationalism than most Yiddish fiction of the time, Polonian literature did contain a constitutive element of nation-building akin to the naturalizing treatments of *Yiddishkayt* in the works of Kobrin and Cahan. "The Christmas Gift," for example, probably by *Zgoda* editor Stefan Barszczewski, paints a Christmas Eve scene in which a mother explains the empty place-setting at the table to her son. The husband/father, it seems, has died in the struggle for Polish independence—a fact which the boy not only comprehends, but enthusiastically embraces as he listens to his mother's words. He then recites the roll of the nation's martyred heroes, and basks in the warming notion that his own father is numbered among them. "In how many Polish homes on this day, so great for the Christian world, is there an empty third setting on the Christmas Eve table?" asks the narrator. Christmas has come, and "we, a nation of twenty million, suffer in the prisons of bondage! We, who through five centuries . . . defended the ideas of Christendom!"[86]

Like the Yiddish ghetto sketches which traded on gender and sexuality in establishing certain particular images of *Yiddishkayt*, this sketch quietly conveys as much about the internal workings of the "nation" as it does about the nation's clash with external enemies. The story regularizes certain relationships among the nation's members by locating the male child in a long history of militarist heroics; by enforcing the image of the Spartan mother; and by identifying the disruption of the domestic idyl as the chief crime of the oppressors. Likewise, in linking the politics of nationalism to the figure of Christ and to the defense of Christendom, the tale at once signals the God-given character of the movement and limits its membership to Polish Christians.

But these constitutive elements are most often overshadowed by the unabashed liberationism of Polonian writing. Poems and stories were often not only transparent pleas for Polish independence, but also rather transparently joined the partisan conflicts which then divided the emigrant community. Although occasionally conveying hints of the "terrible power" of Poland's most revered writing, much of the literature of the fourth partition read as though the position papers generated by the PNA, the PRCU, and the PNCC had merely been projected through a thin gauze of aestheticism. Works like "Exiles, to the Nation" gave poetic voice to both the PNA pledge of emigrant loyalty and the romantic ideal of political sacrifice: "Death for us holds no terror . . . / To die for Poland, that is our most beautiful dream." Such pieces found their inevitable rebuttal in the literary religionism of *Dziennik Chicagoski*—in poems like "A Prayer for the Fatherland" or "Under Your Protection We Betake Ourselves."[87] Elsewhere, religionist constructions lapsed from themes of divine protection into a chauvinistic national cultism:

> Onward brothers, hand in hand,
> To uplift our poor land,
> Let the whole world bow
> In admiration of God's people.
> And marvel at the apparent miracle:
> The resurrected Polish people![88]

Among the earliest and most highly regarded poets in Polish-America was Teofila Samolinska, known, significantly, as "the mother of the Polish National Alliance." It was Samolinska who, in her tribute to Kraszewski, identified the pen as "the sword of the people." Her poetry helped to bridge the gap in sensibility between the political exiles of 1863 and the waves of peasants arriving in the 1870s and after. Her first attributed submission to *Orzeł Polski* (1870), for instance, set the tone for much of the literary production in Polonia in the following decades: "Here one is free to fight for the Fatherland; / Here the cruelty of tyrants will not reach us, / Here the scars inflicted on us will fade."[89] With the "magnificent thought" of victory inscribed on its standard, *Orzeł Polski* would "lead the emigrants to armed action."

Samolinska's successors echoed this call in the ensuing decades, stressing the Poles' vigilance against the corrosive cultural influences of life abroad and reminding them of the martial promise of mass mobilization for an assault on the oppressors. Pieces like "To a Polish Mother" exhorted emigrant women to "stand guard over our children,/ Stand strong, invincible," while songs to the nation's youth promised that "The Pole will not be extracted from the Fatherland,/ An orphan cast among foreign breeds."[90]

Nor was the aim of all this vigilance ever in doubt: seeds sown in America by Polonia's dutiful Spartan mothers would come to fruition in Poland itself. In "The Falcons' Banner" Stefan Barszczewski trumpeted the martial spirit of Polish-American youth, promising in some eighty lines, "Poland, the night has passed, the Falcons are in flight!"[91] "How Many, How Much?" set out the meaning of exile its starkest political terms: "O enemy of Poland! Can you count / These bones of ours, which God will plough up / In every part of the world at the hour of judgment?" The piece went on to define, just as starkly, the duties incumbent upon Polonia's young men:

> O son of Poland! Do you know how many
> Herculean tasks await you here?
> Do you know how many lucky days of youth
> You have to offer in sacrifice?
> How many hours to meditate in despair?
> To listen to the groans of your fellow wanderers?
> And how many broken nests you have to restore?
> And how many flowers of bright fortune to scatter,
> And how much life to sacrifice to Poland,
> To struggle and perish in hope and belief?[92]

In answer to these programmatic PNA and PRCU poetics, Francis Hodur and Stanisław Dangiel produced a body of work in the nationalist mold of the Polish National Catholic Church. In his novel *Pharisees and Sadducees*, Hodur referred to the divine inspiration of the schismatic movement. Dangiel, meanwhile, spun a minor subgenre of resistance poetry decrying the oppressive Irish Catholic hierarchy. "The Last Shirt" laments that the Poles' lot (bad enough already, by any estimation—"No tomorrow, no merriment, without any future/ Without fortune, family, or any joy") has been made even worse by "priests and bishops" intent on "tearing the last shirt from their backs." In "Behold the 'Patriots'!" Dangiel condemned the Irish hierarchy's accomplices among the Polish clergy, and their willingness to dissipate Polish wealth under the rules of the Irish dominated church: "In order to tear dollars from the people" the clergy had hoisted the banner of "the harp, the snake and the three leaf clover!"[93]

The poetics of the PNCC journal *Straż*, however, were not strictly limited to the concerns of the National Church. In an 1898 hymn to his followers, Hodur struck the broader theme of Polish, as opposed to Polish-American, travails. "Let no one lose hope/ That we will liberate ourselves and our brothers," he wrote; then, in a line reminiscent of Słowacki, "we will hoist the standard of freedom, . . . A people once pushed, like a stone moved, will no longer turn back."[94] "When Will We Arise?" (1900) bespoke a darker view of the nation's prospects, although here, too, Hodur called for Poland's *zmartwychpowstanie*—a form of the word "resurrection" which, in this context, clearly has connotations of *in*surrection as well:

> . . . small peoples, in some corner of the world
> Thunder today their hundred cannons of
>   (insur)resurrection
> And we Poles are silent, dumb,
> As if condemned to eternal agony.[95]

If this seriousness of purpose was characteristic of nationalist literature, and if the prospects looked grim to many, not all Polonian writing was so dour. In a moment of lightheartedness, Zbigniew Brodowski offered up a humorous sketch of "The Discovery of America" which, in the tradition of *Quo Vadis?* and *The Pharoah*, explored power relations and resistance through historic parallel. In this version of the Columbus expedition, the King calls for Columbus, and asks simply, "are you ready to discover America?" After the two haggle over how many ships he will be allowed, Columbus indeed sets sail, and he indeed finds the New World, where American Indians not only wait in anticipation of his arrival, but actually greet him by name.

Although merely fey on the face of it, the politics of the piece are revealed by the subtitle: "Translated from the German." By this gentle manoeuver, Brodowski emphasized the telling of the tale over the tale itself, historical consciousness—and German historical consciousness, at that—over historical fact. "Do I have the honor," asks one Indian as the Spanish ship docks, "of speaking with Mister Columbus, who has to discover us? . . . 'Oh Jesus,' he sighed, 'no one, not even a poor Indian, can escape his fate! Come ashore then, Mister Columbus, we surrender completely because we've been discovered by you!'" The whimsy of the piece's anachronism and illogic becomes a biting satire on the German political outlook: this is the *German* understanding of the relationship between strong nations and weak. The sense of the absurd which is evoked by the sketch is precisely the absurdity of German political arrogance.[96]

The range, then, of nationalist expression in Polish and Polonian literature was quite broad. From the recycled romanticism of Mickiewicz and Słowacki, to the postinsurrection soul-searching of Prus and Kraszewski, to the optimistic lyrics of Konopnicka and the blustery military epics of Sienkiewicz, and to the partisan poems which laid out in rhyme the reasoning of Polonia's leading political organizations, literary expression and political aspiration remained inseparable—as they had been in Poland for generations. In his 1910 overview of Polish and Polonian writing, Stanisław Osada suggested that the greatest honor was due those writers "who from their own souls produce that power of genuine (insur)resurrection."[97] From mid-century Warsaw to late-century Chicago, Milwaukee, and Scranton, the consensus on this point was impressive.

Irish Literary Culture

Irish literature shared in some measure the insurrectionary motifs of the Polish tradition. The ballads of Thomas Davis and Young Ireland looked to a United Irish future when "The Orange and Green will carry the day"; politicized novels like *The Vultures of Erin* rehearsed the litany of Irish wrongs and projected idealized visions of Irish rural life and character. *Knocknagow* (1879) captures both the political spirit of much Irish fiction of the period, and the place of emigration in the Irish literary imagination:

An' the English Viceroy tells us that Providence intended Ireland to be the fruitful mother of flocks and herds. That is why our people are hunted like noxious animals, to perish in the ditchside, or in the poorhouse. That is why the floating coffins are crossing the stormy Atlantic, dropping Irish corpses to the sharks along the way, and flinging tens of thousands of living skeletons on the shores of this free country.[98]

Physical-force nationalist Jeremiah O'Donovan Rossa expressed the relationship between Irish politics and Irish art most succinctly, claiming that his early exposure to recitations from Davis's *Nation* "had a hand in making a 'bad boy' of me."[99]

One historian has recently described the nationalism which flourished among the exiles in America as "the culture of *Speeches from the Dock*, and the ideal of rural Ireland propagandized in novels like Charles J. Kickham's *Knocknagow*."[100] The characterization conveys some important partial truths. The literary reference is not simply casual: like their Polonian counterparts, Irish-American publishers throughout the century peddled politicized romances such as *The Boyne Water, Forty-Eight and Ninety-Eight, The Book of Irish Martyrs*, and *The Black Prophet: A Tale of the Irish Famine*. For the centenary, even the moderate *Irish-American* ran short stories like "The Gap of the Corpse—A Tale of '98."[101]

Moreover, the demographics of the post-Famine migration freed Irish-American writers from the ideological strains and the logical contortions of those Anglo-Irish writers in the old country, like Samuel Ferguson, for whom preserving Protestant privilege had been an integral part of building an Irish "nationality." Whereas Ferguson had walked a treacherous tightrope between vilifying England and yet pitying the "seduced victims" of Catholicism, writers in exile had no such delicate tasks before them.[102] If O'Donovan Rossa, John Boyle O'Reilly, and others did promote the ideal of an Ireland united across religious lines, in the overwhelmingly Catholic community of Irish-America they did not have to worry about who the "real" Irish were. O'Reilly could comfortably identify Catholicism as the prime mover of modern Irish nationalism: the words of the Catholic priest, he wrote, "Flash from Donegal to Kerry, and from Waterford to Clare, / And the nationhood awaking thrills the sorrow-laden air."[103]

The strongest literary appeal of *Speeches from the Dock* was limited, however, in its power and in its longevity, by the lure of an English-speaking host culture. Irish nationalism had faced from the outset what one critic has called the "almost ludicrous necessity" of forging an oppositional literary culture in the language of the oppressor.[104] Their commonality of language with the English undermined Irish claims of distinct cultural identity, and so, to many, negated nationalist arguments for political sovereignty. The Gaelic Revival, which listed language itself among the national treasures which England had plundered, was one response to precisely this circumstance. As Seamus Deane suggests, James Joyce's "vengeful virtuosity" in English was another. Irish nationalist writers in English had long struggled with the contradictions inherent in addressing an audience which comprised both the proposed nation and its oppressor.[105]

The task was doubly demanding—or ludicrous—in the diaspora community of the United States. Here the nationalist project was not only hampered by the cultural blurring between oppressor and oppressed, but it was also sapped by an American literary culture which was omnipresent, accessible, and attractive to both the exiled writer and the exiled reader. By the 1890s most Irish-American writers had been drawn away from purely Irish subjects and themes. The heyday of nationalist writing lay largely in the past, represented by works such as *The Irish Widow's Son* (1869), on the pikemen of 1798; *Moondyne Joe* (1879), based in part on John Boyle O'Reilly's experiences as a British political prisoner; or *The King's Men* (1884), a fantasy about the overthrow of "George the Fifth" and the triumph of Irish republicanism under "President O'Donovan Rourke."[106]

But if literature was a less certain avenue for political comment for Irish immigrants than for their Yiddish- and Polish-speaking counterparts, Irish-American literature still bore thick traces of the nationalist tradition. Irish-American writing of the 1890s fell along a spectrum from one side of the hyphen, as it were, to the other; and while the canon was heavily weighted toward more American themes and concerns by 1890, literary nationalism of the Irish sort had not vanished altogether. In *Pere Monnier's Ward* (1898), William McDermott satirized the tendency among the mobile Irish not only to forget their origins, but fully to renounce them in the name of "respectability." Although he aimed plenty of barbs at Irish nationalists, McDermott used commitment to, or betrayal of, the Irish cause as a moral barometer of his characters.[107] Even Mr. Dooley, Finley Peter Dunne's wag-philosopher most often recalled for his wry comment on American life, worried from time to time over the fate of Ireland and the disposition of the exiles. "There's Mac's an' O's in ivry capital iv Europe atin' off silver plates," he observed, "whin their relations is staggerin' under the' creels iv turf in th' Connaught bogs." Much of his satire—his complaint of the nationalists' penchant for picnics, for instance—carried sincere political commentary, whether or not leaders like John Finerty were willing to listen.[108]

British misrule remained the defining cataclysm in Irish-American history even for the second and third generations, and even characters devoted to matters American were drawn as creatures of a bitter colonial past. Katherine Conway's *Lalor's Maples*, a tale of mobility and social manners on the pattern of Howells' *Rise of Silas Lapham*, recalls Ireland's history through essentialist notions of ethnic "Irishness." John Lalor had "the irresistible impulse of his Irish blood towards political agitation"; Margaret's "Irish blood showed itself in a sincere, if aggressive, clan and tribal passion."[109] And just as the fighting, clannish spirit of the Irish national character is eternal, so the post-Famine diaspora is divinely ordained. On the subject of marriage, Winnie Blackitt explains to the American-born Mildred Lalor,

> ". . . all men are divils. But when all's said and done, the Irish divils are not so bad. But beware of the foreign divils."
> "But Winnie, the Irish are foreigners, too."
> "Not they, Miss Mildred. They belong everywhere, but especially in America."[110]

Defined by a past of "political agitation" and tragedy, and now having found wonderful asylum in America, the Irish were *especially* American for being ineradicably Irish.

This logic was a staple among a generation of Irish-American writers for whom the hyphen produced a number of ambiguities. Louise Imogen Guiney, another in the Catholic literary circle associated with the *Pilot*, later codified this wonderful comportment of the Irish past with the American present in her "little historical descant" titled *Robert Emmet: A Survey of His Rebellion and of His Romance*. "To be unbiassed and Irish is to love Robert Emmet; to be generously English is to love him; to be American is to love him anyhow."[111]

One critic described Guiney's sensibility as "compounded of English, French, Irish, Scotish, and American feelings, influences, and aspirations, all fused in the crucible of her Catholicism." Hers was scarcely the political stridence of the fiercest nationalist writers: indeed, she spent a great deal of time in London, and a "devotion to England burned in her a steady flame."[112] But despite her Anglophilism, and despite her self-identification with the English poetic tradition, Guiney did turn her attention periodically to the plight of Ireland, the land of her father and grandparents.[113]

"The Vigil in Tyrone" locates the Irish struggle within the lives of the exiles in a way which conveys both its proximity and its distance. The poem describes the magical slumber of Hugh O'Neil's[114] army— "Earl Hugh's men that never have died"—as they await the call once again to rise up and battle the British. Having long ago marched against "the demon Elizabeth," nine hundred and ninety-nine soldiers in armor now sleep in a cave near Tyrone, needing only the leadership of O'Neil himself.

The legend is framed, in its opening and closing quatrains, as a bedtime story told by a grandfather to his granddaughter. The old man claims to have seen the cave with his own eyes when he was a boy; and he breaks the tale off abruptly, pained that the time has not yet come for Hugh's army to arise. In the poem's last line, the granddaughter peers into his face, and sees "the far-off, idle, eternal tears" of Ireland's suffering. The immortality of Hugh O'Neil's army is thus paralleled by the permanency of feeling for the nation's tragedy; and the national "vigilance" of the title refers in part to the transmission and emotive force of the tale itself as it passes from elders to the young. But if Ireland's tears are "eternal," so are they "far off" and "idle": from the perspective of the granddaughter nationalism is a compelling but finally ambiguous presence.[115]

The Irish cause is more fossilized still in an essay simply titled "Irish," a mournful elegy to the Celtic spirit of old Ireland, whose genius, Guiney fears, is unsuited to encroaching modernity. She lauds the island's "charming futile bravado," and discovers in the Irish spirit the tacit boast that "My ancestors were plotting treason, while yours were keeping sheep!" And though she sees the world as deeply indebted to Ireland, she concludes that "Venerable Ireland has failed, as the world reckons failure . . . Abominably misruled, without a Senate, without commerce, she has fallen back into the sullen interior life, into the deep night of reverie." Finally Guiney can only say, along with an anonymous sage of the Wicklow highlands, "We have not been conquered: we are unconquerable. But we are without hope."[116]

For Guiney, a cosmopolitan at heart, Ireland's subjugation was more a matter of dark romance than of explosive polemics, even if England's "abominable misrule" was openly addressed. Writing in and for the metropole, Guiney treated the Irish Question as but a literary motif. The battle is ever present; but the battle is not hers.

In *Erin Mor: The Story of Irish Republicanism* John Brennan squarely faced the problem of Americanism, hyphenism, and Irish nationalism. In his scheme the Irish cause was not as remote as it was to Guiney. The novel is a storied treatment of Irish-American history and politics in which the life of the central character, Andy Dillon, weaves in and around the lives of historical figures like Horace Greeley, Patrick Ford, and Thaddeus Stevens. The "Erin Mor" of the title refers to the hero's single greatest animating idea: "Andy Dillon's sweetest consolation in exile was the contemplation of a 'Greater Ireland.' His liberty-loving soul yearned to gaze upon his exiled race in its trans-Atlantic home, where free institutions, unlimited opportunities, and equality before the law afforded ample scope for the exercise of the 'cloudy and lightning genius of the Gael.' "[117] The bulk of the novel is given over to the development among the emigrants—referred to throughout as "exiles"—of a "free Ireland" on American shores.

Erin Mor is steeped in the nationalist ethos of the Old World: emigration itself, for instance, is described as the "grist" which inevitably resulted as "the upper and nether millstones of English rule kept grinding human hearts."[118] But this is as much a book about American electoral politics as about Irish liberation. In a brief dedication to Benjamin Harrison, whose election he sees as the crowning achievement of Irish-American political endeavor, Brennan explains that his purpose is not to "excite any form of foreignism," but rather to help create "a deep, intense, and fervid American National spirit." And in a brief introduction, he insists that "while foreign rule has been the crowning and all-encompassing curse of Ireland," the actual root of Irish suffering has been Britain's free trade policy—a policy dangerously replicated by then-current economic thinking within America's Democratic Party.[119]

A political tract in fiction, then, *Erin Mor* tells the twin story of the republican ideals brought over from the Old World, and their compatibility with the Republicanism of Blaine, Harrison, and McKinley. Free trade offers the key to "The True Causes of the Famine," just as the McKinley Tariff will later "[cement] the alliance between Greater Ireland and American nationality." The Democratic Party, meanwhile—a "factory" whose gears were greased by corruption and liquor—represented no less than "the graveyard of the Irish race" in America.[120]

Ultimately it is Thaddeus Stevens who points out the inconsistency in the liberty-loving Irish emigrants' attachment not only to a party of slaveholders, but to a party whose economic policies can only (in Brennan's view) bolster British power. The novel then traces the rise of the Republican insurgency among the Irish, by fits and starts, from the era of Reconstruction to the triumph of Benjamin Harrison, bemoaning along the way that "Ireland's hope for liberty" had been usurped by the cheap diversions of Democratic politicians. But now "Greater Ireland . . . swelled beyond the measure of her chains." The election of Harrison represented "the consummation of Andy Dillon's hopes. The Irish exiles scraped away the parasites and barnacles that fed and fattened on the race in American politics while they befouled it in the eyes of the American people." Drawing heavily upon the language of respectability and the rhetoric of gender so characteristic of Irish-American nationalism, Brennan concluded that in electing Harrison, the Irish "extended their hands in sympathy and fellowship with the soul, the brain, the manhood, and the conscience of American national life."[121]

Still further along the nationalist spectrum was James Jeffrey Roche, editor of the Boston *Pilot* from 1890 to 1904. Like Louise Imogen Guiney, Roche won significant recognition beyond the pale of the strictly Irish literary scene. But like William McDermott, he scoffed at those who betrayed their Irish kin in the name of American respectability—the Scotch-Irish, in his view, represented a "hypothetic race" which traced its origins to the impossible locale of "Tipperary-on-the-Clyde."[122] And like John Brennan, he saw no conflict between Irish and American political sensibilities. Indeed, as an officer of the American Irish Historical Society, he sought to revise American history to reflect the tremendous debt of the United States to Erin.

At once a trenchant wit and an ardent nationalist, Roche displayed an extensive emotional range in his writings on Irish matters. His nationalism was at times merely playful, as in *Her Majesty the King*, a fable of the "Orient" whose political barbs only occasionally pierced the surface of an otherwise innocuous literary jest. Among the fabricated epigrams at each chapter head, for instance, this bit of wisdom: "Every nation has just the government for which its people are fitted; at least, that is what is said by the rulers who are piously engaged in misgoverning it."[123] Or again, in a transparent reference to the Anglo-American alliance which was then the point of so much rancor, Roche toyed with the political pomp and illogic of his fictional Middle Eastern states. A political orator waxes eloquent on the necessity of friendship between the people of Ubikwi and those of Nhulpar, citing their commonality of race, language, and religion. "A quarrel between two such peoples would be a crime against humanity," he says. "If the speaker overlooked the fact that such crimes had been committed once or twice already, with the enthusiastic consent of both parties, that was neither here nor there. The sentence was well turned, and that is enough to expect of a state oration."[124]

But light satire frequently gave way to a sharper, angrier, more accusatory polemic. Poems like "Babylon" register Roche's protest and level his charges against the Empire in an idiom far removed from the mere quipping of Her Majesty the King. Like much of Roche's poetry, "Babylon" is more important for its political venom than for its artistry.

> Her robes are purple and scarlet,
> And the kings have bent their knees
> To the gemmed and jewelled harlot
> Who sitteth on many seas.
>
> They have drunk the abominations
> Of her golden cup of shame;
> She has drugged and debauched the nations
> With the mystery of her name.
>
> Her merchants have gathered riches
> By the power of her wantonness,
> And her usurers are as leeches
> On the world's supreme distress.
>
> She has scoured the seas as a spoiler;
> Her mart is a robber's den,
> With the wrested toll of the toiler,
> And the mortgaged souls of men.
>
> Her crimson flag is flying,
> Where the East and West are one;
> Her drums while the day is dying
> Salute the rising sun
>
> She has scourged the weak and the lowly
> And the just with an iron rod;
> She is drunk with the blood of the holy,—
> She shall drink the wrath of God![125]

Whatever Roche's intentions here, friend and foe alike interpreted "Babylon" as an assault on the British Empire: the London Spectator complained of its coded Anglophobia, while a friendlier reviewer in the Catholic Citizen cheered that the piece "lashes the capital of British pharisaism with a scorn and hatred that are positively magnificent." Although such an interpretation was reasonable within the context of Roche's politically charged satires and frankly nationalist *Pilot* editorials, the poet himself apparently enjoyed the political implications of the poem's ambiguity. With an if-the-shoe-fits smirk, Roche simply wrote that the *Spectator's* reading of modern-day Britain into ancient Babylon "has made a grave subject suddenly humorous."[126]

Roche's boldest nationalist stroke was his hagiographic treatment of *John Boyle O'Reilly: His Life, Poems and Speeches.* Along with Jeremiah O'Donovan Rossa's *Recollections,* Roche's life of O'Reilly represents the far nationalist extreme in Irish-American writing at the century's end. Both address Ireland's political struggle directly; both treat the "heroic" which was supposed to be at the very heart of the Irish cause; and both are products of a nationalist cosmology in which the enmity between England and Ireland is a development not of human but of natural history—as if Irish Anglophobia could be found on the periodic table alongside cadmium or zinc.

Whereas Katherine Conway merely mentioned "tribal passion" and the Celtic penchant for "political agitation" by way of illuminating emigrant life in America, Roche and Rossa became engulfed in an all-embracing and highly politicized Irishness. "Unfortunately for the wretched people of Ireland," wrote Roche, "they were not slaves. When they died by the thousands in the dark year of famine, when they fled the country by millions in following years, their masters were unmoved by the one calamity; they rejoiced at the other."[127] For Roche and Rossa, the history of Irish struggle *contained,* as it were, the history of emigration.

Roche's portrait accomplishes its political work on two levels. On the one hand, inasmuch as *John Boyle O'Reilly* is the biography of a poet-rebel, it derives a great deal of political vigor from the words and deeds of its central character. Just as Polonia's editors imported midcentury Polish romanticism into the literary life of the later pilgrims, so in this volume Roche repackaged O'Reilly's nationalist works ("My Native Land," "Ireland—1882") for readers of the 1890s.

More than this, however, the biography also carries Roche's own indictment of British rule. In Roche's narrative O'Reilly is but a vessel for the heroism, the greatness, the courage, and the yearning for justice which—inevitably, one suspects—animate the whole of the Emerald Isle. "Drogheda is a town with a history," runs the opening line, "and, as it is an Irish town, the history is mainly a tragedy." Within the first few pages Roche ennumerates some of the details of that tragedy—

from the Norman and Danish conquests, to Cromwell's assault on the "Papists"—and launches into the familiar strains of national martyrdom: "the victors fell upon the defenseless people, massacring in cold blood twenty-eight hundred men, women, and children."[128]

Conspicuous among the defenders of Drogheda for his "generous and chivalrous acts" was one O'Reilly of Cavan. At this point national martyrdom meets political genealogy, and the figure of John Boyle O'Reilly emerges as an inevitable product of Ireland and the Irish struggle. He not only descends from a clan "ever distinguished as soldiers, prelates, and scholars," but is also born into one of the most history-soaked and glorious districts on the island. Surrounded by relics and ruins recalling St. Patrick, King James, and ancient Gaelic royalty, O'Reilly spends his youth "unconsciously absorbing the poetry and romance whose atmosphere was all around."[129] If Roche acknowledges O'Reilly as a rare sort, still he never dissociates the hero from this spirit of place; O'Reilly's political stature is predestined.

But what sort of hero is he, precisely? The key is in the masculinist ethos of Irish nationalism: as David Cairns and Shuan Richards have noted, writing against an intellectual tradition which characterized the Irish as "an essentially feminine race," many (male) nationalists responded with a poetics of the masculine.[130] When Roche personified Empire as an evil woman ("the gemmed and jewelled harlot who sitteth on many seas") in "Babylon," this may have conjured images of Britannia, or even of Queen Victoria; but it also set the feminine, wanton Empire in opposition to the "manliness" which was to be its political antidote. *Her Majesty the King*, a farce of gender confusion, ends with the hero-prince proving "his manhood" on the battlefield.[131] *John Boyle O'Reilly* is Roche's most complete development of this theme: to be truly Irish is to be by nature a rebel; and to be an Irish rebel is to be a very particular kind of *man*. Just as it defined and naturalized *Yiddishkayt* in works like *Yekl* and *Yankel Boyle*, a complex of racial and sexual ideology defined and naturalized Irish nationalism in Roche's work, although here more stress was laid upon the masculine hero than upon the feminine culture-keeper.

O'Reilly himself had written on the matter of gender and politics, "Woman suffrage is an unjust, unreasonable, unspiritual abnormality . . . It is a quack bolus to reduce masculinity even by the obliteration of femininity." Politics, at bottom, was founded on might: the voting population, O'Reilly felt, "ought to represent the fighting population," and by their very natures women were not fighters at all but "the guardians and the well-spring of the world's faith, morality, and tenderness." Lest anyone doubt the extent to which these polarities were rooted in nature, O'Reilly, in a flourish of suggestive imagery, had added: "Fie upon it! What do they want with a ballot they can't defend? with a bludgeon they can't wield? with a flaming sword that would make them scream if they once saw its naked edge and understood its symbolic meaning?"[132]

It was in the spirit of masculinist heroics, then, that O'Reilly's life took on all the drama of "the pages of a romance," and that he appeared as a "young hero of a romantic revolutionary movement,— [a] poet whose whole life was a poem."[133] The highlights of this lived poem include a Fenian cabal within the British Tenth Hussars; O'Reilly's consequent servitude in a series of British prisons and later in an Australian penal colony; his daring escape and passage out aboard a New Bedford whaler; and his coverage of the Fenian invasion of Canada as a war correspondent for the *Pilot*. A Clan na Gael plot to free several more Australian prisoners was "as gallant and chivalrous a deed as ever loyal knights had dared."[134]

Indeed, where O'Reilly's memoirs do not conform to the pattern of masculinist romance, Roche borrows from elsewhere. O'Reilly's own rather bland, even homely, reminiscences of prison life are martialed toward the construction of the iron hero ("only a man of the strongest constitution" could hope to survive such an ordeal), while more chilling details, pulled from the memoirs of Michael Davitt, sustain the conventions of the Irish prison narrative. "Many a still living wreck of manhood," wrote Davitt, "can refer to the silent system of Millbank and its pernicious surroundings as the cause of his debilitated mind." And on the British care of Irish prisoners, " 'It was quite a common occurrence at Dartmoor,' says Michael Davitt, 'for men to be reported and punished for eating candles, boot-oil, and other repulsive articles.' "[135] Despite O'Reilly's own remark that he regarded his prison cell "with affection," under Roche's pen *John Boyle O'Reilly* still generates the "extreme images" and "terrible power" so prized among literary nationalists.[136]

Jeremiah O'Donovan Rossa, a physical-force advocate and another veteran of the British prisons, shared many of Roche's views on Irish nature, manhood, and romantic rebellion. It was he, recall, who complained of Ireland's late-century reliance on the politics of culture— "until England is made afraid, she will do nothing for Ireland." Literature, for Rossa, was a means to ignite a movement which might once again "make England afraid." In the preface to *Rossa's Recollections* he spelled out his aim of making "the Irish-blooded children of this country [the United States] and this generation grow up to be men proud and helpful of the land of their fathers."[137] Like the O'Reilly biography, Rossa's "storied memories" often flowed in the harshest rhetoric of oppression: "Gladstone starved me til my flesh was rotting, for want of nourishment; Gladstone chained me with my hands behind my back, for thirty-five days at a time; Gladstone leaped upon my chest, while I lay on the flat of my back in a black hole cell of his prison."[138]

Under Rossa's pen the memoir becomes a remarkably fluid genre. Rossa the propagandist pontificates on political strategy; Rossa the folklorist recalls ballads from his youth about Daniel O'Connell ("The Kerry Eagle") or about an eighteenth-century battle between the Orangemen and the women of Ross; Rossa the Young Irelander and Fenian recounts the triumphs and failures of those movements; Rossa the exile paints sentimental portraits of a sorely missed landscape. And as one narrative mode gives way to the next, even Rossa the narrator, dizzied, loses his way in the loops and twists: "Why do I make these remarks? I don't know."[139]

What unifies this otherwise shapeless narrative is an unyielding nationalism, an incendiary political vision of Irish national affairs which is apt to burn its way to the surface in virtually any context. Like Roche, Rossa regards Irish nationalism as a product of natural history. On the proposition that his "mad" hatred for the British stemmed from his experiences in British prisons, he simply remarks, "That kind of talk is all trash of talk. What I am now, I *was*, before I ever saw the inside of an English prison. I am so from nature."[140] Elsewhere he defines his own political temperament as an instinct which he shares with an entire people:

> 'Tis my mother and father, God be good to them, that had the true Irish natural feeling about those Englishmen governing Ireland.
>
> I can see now how relieved they felt whenever they'd hear of a landlord being shot in Tipperary or anywhere else in Ireland.
>
> It was like an instinct with them that an enemy of theirs had been done away with. That kind of instinct is in the whole Irish race to-day.[141]

Nationalism is not merely a political topic; the thirst for rebellion is not merely an isolated trait. Rather, these are the most fundamental elements of the Irish character, shading and informing every other topic and trait. The Irish Question is extraordinarily salient for Rossa;

nationalist politics is not merely near the surface of his consciousness throughout the narrative, but it *is* his consciousness—or it is the consciousness of that persona which he projects as the narrator.

Hence the *Recollections* will lapse into nationalist polemic at any time and without notice. His father's use of dead crows to keep other birds away from the family crops brings Rossa to reflect on British villainy: "could he have learned that from the English, who spiked the head of Shawn O'Neill on Dublin's Castle tower, and the heads of other Irishmen on other towers, to frighten their countrymen away from trespassing upon England's power in Ireland?" A boyhood memory of chasing and catching birds—and particularly the mother bird's tactics for outwitting the boy—remind Rossa of how Gladstone ("the prime hypocrite Governor of Ireland") outwitted the Irish and lured them away from revolution. Memory of a certain Irish lane reminds him of his boyhood encounter with Daniel O'Connell. The architecture of the Irish countryside—and particularly the walls surrounding the grandest manors—becomes a comment on "the imprint of the invader's footsteps": "The old saying has it that a guilty conscience needs no accuser. Those walls were not built around the castles of Ireland 'til the English came."[142]

In their political directness and in the salience of the national question throughout their narratives, Rossa and Roche were the exceptions, not the rule, among Irish-American writers of the 1890s. More typical were expressions of nationalist sympathy—like Guiney's "Vigil of Tyrone" or Mr. Dooley's complaint that "there's no soil in Ireland fr th' greatness iv th' race"—which, however sincere, reflected a considerable social and temporal distance from the seat of Irish struggle. But as Charles Fanning has noted, throughout his Dooley sketches Finley Peter Dunne routinely mentioned details of Irish nationalist history without feeling compelled to offer his readers any background—whether on the Battle of the Boyne in 1690 or the dynamite campaigns of the 1870s. The level of familiarity which Dunne assumed among his readers, like the reflexive assumption that Roche's "Babylon" was actually England, signaled that, even in a late-century Irish America oriented largely toward New World concerns, there was still a heavy trace of what Yeats would call the collective, "multiform reverie" which distinguished a nation "from a crowd of chance comers."[143]

Although never so sure an arena for political evangelism as the more accessible parish dramas, street fairs, or St. Patrick's Day sermons, poetry and fiction did supplement the nationalism carried in these other immigrant cultural forms. The masculinist ideals celebrated in "Little Hanukkah Candles" and *John Boyle O'Reilly* buttressed the quasi-militarism of the Knights of Zion and the Clan na Gael. The Spartan motherhood endorsed by "The Christmas Gift" echoed and so underwrote the ideal of the Buffalo, New York, address "To Polish Mothers—On Raising Sons As Heroes." Naturalistic portraits of *dos pintele yid*, like the reifications of a bellicose "national character" in *Rossa's Recollections* or Konopnicka's "Chorus of Polish Children Abroad," defined the emigrants as "saved for the Fatherland" in precisely the manner called for in PNA, FAZ, or Clan na Gael blueprints.

To be sure, the idea of Americanization did exert a gravitational pull. Yekl's pathos was rooted in his familiarity as a ghetto type: for many (not least of all Cahan himself) becoming a "true Yankee" did seem to be a road to all sorts of social benefits. But the politics embedded in the major voluntary organizations, in the vernacular theatre and the press, in popular religion, and in popular Old and New World literature countervailed the ideology of Americanization. While emigrants did learn English, change the cut of their clothes, marry out, and form alliances with other emigrants and with Americans in the workplace, in labor organizations, or in temperance circles, the political *idea* of Ireland, Poland, or Zion retained centrality in each group's culture. In a multitude of ways each immigrant culture articulated group identity as national identity, and enforced the idea that this national identity entailed a lasting commitment to certain cherished loves and hatreds.

Immigrant discussion of America's rise to world power at the century's end bore the tint of this political sensibility. José Martí's efforts to unify and stir the Cuban diaspora in the 1890s were observed against the backdrop of very similar undertakings on the part of Theodore Herzl, Zygmunt Miłkowski, and John Devoy. News of the overmatched but dauntless Cuban guerrillas, some fighting the Spaniards only with machetes, was received within a cultural context where symbols of militarist defiance (the Maccabees, "Grażyna," the pikemen of 1798) were familiar and highly valued. The cry of *Cuba Libre!* and the clamor for U.S. intervention evoked the Fenian aim of enlisting U.S. aid in the Irish cause, or General Dąbrowski's appeal to the Polish Legions to fight for Polish liberty through the liberation of others. Because of their liberationist political cultures, these communities were especially receptive to McKinley's pious, if misleading, declaration that "in the cause of humanity" the United States would step in "to put an end to the barbarities, bloodshed, starvation, and horrible miseries" then existing in subjugated Cuba.[144]

Yet it was also within the framework of liberationism that many immigrants would assess the storm of self-congratulation and the expressions of unbounded U.S. entitlement unleashed by success in the war with Spain. How did exiles, pilgrims, and wanderers respond when America's prophets of Empire, like Senator Albert Beveridge, began to celebrate the country's "resistless march toward the commercial supremacy of the world"? How would refugees from the policies of Anglicization, *Kulturkampf,* and Russification greet the proposal that the United States was obliged to bring "soap and water, common-school civilization" to Cuba? How would migrants whose organizations, popular ballads, dramas, and poems so exalted the ideal of sovereignty react to increasingly popular American assertions that only select peoples were "capable of self-government"? How would members of these subcultures—wary of imperial power and its grandiose encroachments, yet also entertaining strong chauvinisms of their own—respond to the slogan of the expansionists, "Fellow Americans, we are God's chosen people"?[145]

II

Nationalist Sensibility and American Expansionism

4

Cuba Libre! Immigrant Versions of Spanish Tyranny, Cuban Rights, and American Power

Let the present war be for us a school for the future! Let Poland's part be taken someday just as Cuba's is taken at present!

—Stefan Barszczewski, *Zgoda*

The golden glory of Spain began to pale four hundred years ago, when it unchained religious fanaticism and persecuted the Jews.

—Rosa Sonneschein, *American Jewess*

Old Knute (Tom) Galvin, formerly a policeman, is in my room trying to convince the boys that we ought to stop in Ireland on the way home and free the Irish.

—Letter home from D. F. McCarthy, C Company, 13th Minnesota Volunteer Infantry

Amid deafening American expressions of sympathy with Cuba and a growing clamor for war with Spain, the *Yiddishes tageblatt* prankishly announced in its April Fools edition of 1898, "Extra! A Jewish Kingdom in Cuba. Rothschild Bought the Island." The piece went on in great detail and with apparent mirth to describe territorialist designs for colonizing Cuba as a Jewish state, including blueprints for a Jewish government based on the British parliamentary model. Spain, meanwhile, in penance for past sins, had signed a contract turning the island over to the Jews *"in eybik"*—forever.[1]

This piece may have been idiosyncratic in its whimsy, but the turn of mind which linked Cuban liberation with other national questions was not at all unusual. Immigrant fraternal organizations passed resolutions supporting Cuba in the familiar idioms of Irish, Polish, and Jewish nationalism. The Irish-American press denounced the Spanish garrison element in Cuba as "Iberian Orangemen," while the Yiddish press routinely vilified Spain as the "inquisition country." Editorials and popular plays depicted the Cuban war as a rehearsal for the liberation of the various immigrant homelands. National festivals like the Polish May Third now included speeches and lectures on Cuba. And ethnic regiments departed for war amid much Old World flag-waving and singing of "Poland Has Not yet Perished" or "The Wearin' of the Green."

Cuba's second war for independence began in early 1895, led by rebel-exiles of the failed Ten Years' Revolution of 1868–1878. Having established during their years of exile a revolutionary political party, an insurgent Cuban press, and an international network of sympathizers and financial backers, José Martí, Antonio Maceo, and Máximo Gómez returned to Cuba early in 1895 to lead an assault on the island's Spanish rulers. The *insurrectos* minimized Spain's advantages in numbers and arms by mounting a guerrilla offensive which allowed them largely to dictate the pace of the war and the time, place, and circumstances of its battles. Despite being overmatched in military resources, they won many victories; most important from a political standpoint, they demonstrated again and again Spain's incapacity to bring the island under control. Under Gómez's leadership, the insurgents also adopted a "scorched earth" policy designed to halt sugar production and make the island unprofitable to the Spaniards. "The chains of Cuba have been forged by her own richness," Gómez argued. Together, these military and economic strategies were designed to break Spain's imperial will. The *insurrectos* held their own throughout 1896 and 1897.[2]

The motive behind the U.S. intervention in Cuba has been a point of some contention since the moment it occurred. The immediate factors contributing to America's "war fever" in the spring of 1898 have been widely rehearsed: they include a notoriously active yellow press, whose daily revelations about Spanish General "Butcher" Weyler inflamed public opinion even as they boosted circulation; the publication of an indiscreet letter from Spanish Minister Depuy De Lome, insulting President McKinley as a "low politician" who "caters to the rabble"; the hope in some quarters that a wartime economy would usher in the coinage of silver which had been defeated along with William Jennings Bryan in the election of 1896; a rousing speech on the floor of the Senate by Redfield Proctor, an eyewitness who asserted that the situation in Cuba was every bit as dreadful as the yellow press had portrayed it; and the explosion aboard the U.S. *Maine* in Havana harbor, which killed two hundred and sixty-four Americans. This litany has become standard in American historiography.[3]

But the economic spoils of the war have raised vexing questions. Was this an imperialist intervention from the outset?—or did U.S. dominion over Cuba, Puerto Rico, and the Philippines come as an unexpected fruit of victory, as so many contemporaries claimed? Clearly, argues Philip Foner, many in the United States could not have been surprised by the results of McKinley's "splendid little war": talk of "new markets" for U.S. production had become commonplace in the depression-plagued Gilded Age, and this concern for foreign markets had been attended by discussion of transithsmian shipping routes, naval power, coaling stations, and the global extension of "the blessings of civilization." José Martí himself had been frankly wary of enlisting the aid of his giant neighbor to the north, asking, "Once the United States is in Cuba who will get her out?" Similarly, antiexpansionists in Congress were suspicious enough to introduce a "self-denying ordinance" clarifying that, in aiding the Cuban rebels, the U.S. had no designs "to exercise sovereignty, jurisdiction, or control" over Cuba.[4]

Controversies regarding U.S. aims in the Caribbean have complicated the assessment of American public opinion in the months leading up to war. Given the conflict between the administration's humanitarian rhetoric and the war's aggrandizing results, what, precisely, does it mean that Americans so enthusiastically marched off to war, in Thomas Bell's fine phrase, "as to a picnic"?[5] The common image of war hysteria, immortalized in Richard Hofstadter's thesis of "psychic crisis," connotes an irrational public whose concerns could not have been strictly humanitarian.[6] On the other hand, the waves of protest and the realignment of opinion once the expansionist terms of victory became known suggest a public whose war cries had not been hysterical but considered, and whose expansionist appetite was hardly out of control.

Historians seeking to reconcile the liberationist and imperialist impulses at work in the years 1898–99 have often painted an ambiguous picture. Hofstadter himself concludes, for instance, that "the humanitarian impulse behind the war was strangely coupled with a taste for battle." Ernest May asserts that a "stubborn," "willful" cadre of imperialists orchestrated public opinion using "the rhetoric of piety"; but he then quietly slides into a contrary argument that "mass hysteria" forced the administration reluctantly to adopt expansionism against its better judgment. And Foner, wary of any suggestion that the public had simply been duped, concludes that "at the root of the nationwide support for Cuba was admiration for a people struggling for freedom against overwhelming odds." Elsewhere, however, he castigates Abraham Cahan, Morris Winchevsky, and other "so-called Socialist leaders" for having supported U.S. intervention, presumably on the grounds that they should have known better.[7]

The present chapter seeks not to judge various positions on the war from the safe haven of hindsight, but rather to assess the texture of political argument and to analyze the intellectual and ideological currents which were tapped by discussants along the political spectrum. Among Irish, Polish, and Yiddish immigrants—as among the American public at large in these years—there were many who wildly applauded the aims of war and yet later recoiled at the terms of peace. None was as fervently in favor of U.S. intervention in the spring, yet as alienated and outraged in the fall, as James Jeffrey Roche of the Boston *Pilot*. Others, like Kazimierz Neuman and Philip Krantz, demonstrated a marked skepticism toward McKinley's "humanitarian" aims from the outset. But in each case the discussion of Cuba flowed from broader, ongoing immigrant discussions of nationalism and national rights, of the role of the exiles in winning the United States as an ally for the homeland, or of the martial ("manly") virtues of political rebellion. Though the purported subject of debate was the triangular relationship among Cuba, Spain, and the United States, polemic throughout the spring of 1898 borrowed rhetorical and logical power from the political circumstances of Ireland, Poland, and Zion.

The Old World political sensibilities evident in the responses to the Cuban crisis were reflected in the editorials, the short stories and poems, the novels, and the plays of each group's most articulate and active intellectuals, and in the nationalist symbolism of the massive rallies, parades, and ceremonies in honor of immigrant men who enlisted in the cause of Cuban liberation. Editors and writers may not have been representative in the positions they articulated, and they certainly were not representative in their means to articulate these positions. But the enthusiasm for enlistment and the popular ethnic rallies in cities like Boston, New York, Chicago, and Milwaukee do suggest that men like Roche and Neuman were not alone in viewing the Cuban situation through a nationalist lens. The flag-waving, the anthems, the speeches, the insurrectionary names of the ethnic regiments all suggest that the Spanish-Cuban-American War represented something more complex to many immigrants than simply an opportunity to serve Uncle Sam. Decades earlier immigrant militarism had carried a strong trace of the Old World during the American Civil War. "Two countries we love, and two mottos we'll share," ran the "Song of the Irish Legion" (1861):

> And we'll join them in one, on one banner we'll bear:
> Erin, mavourneen! Columbia, agra!
> E pluribus unum! Erin, go bragh![8]

This sentiment held not only for the exiles from Ireland, and not only for the war between the states. Immigrant participation in the war for Cuban liberation at the century's end reflected a similar meeting of Old World sensibility and New World political activity.

Nationalism and the Cuban Cause

To note the prevalence of nationalist idioms in immigrant discussions of Cuba is not to suggest a unanimity of opinion on the question of U.S. intervention. The American Civil War offers the starkest demonstration of how nationalist logic could lead different thinkers to quite divergent conclusions: having emigrated to the United States in the wake of Young Ireland's failures at mid century, Thomas Francis Meagher and John Mitchel, two of Young Ireland's most radical and fiery leaders, found themselves on opposite sides of the Civil War in their adopted country. Significantly, Mitchel, a Confederate, argued that the rebel states merely sought Home Rule—a humble and wholly reasonable aspiration. Meagher, on the other hand, felt that if Ireland had ever tasted the freedoms currently enjoyed by the southern states, then the island would never have developed such a tradition of political rebellion.[9] Though their conclusions were diametrically opposed, the two men shared the fundamental touchstone of the Ireland analogy in addressing the question.

As in the Civil War, so in the Spanish-Cuban-American War nationalist sensibilities did not fully determine immigrant opinion; there was plenty of room for disagreement. Indeed, in a short story titled "War Silhouettes" (c.1900) Jacob Gordin seized on the war with Spain to illustrate immigrant sensibilities in collision. The tale focuses on a Spanish immigrant father and his "true Yankee" son whose sympathies come in conflict when war breaks out in Cuba. They volunteer for opposing armies, and finally they face one another in a fatal confrontation in Cuba.[10]

"War Silhouettes" was of course another of Gordin's literary condemnations of divisive nationalism: nations at war, for Gordin, were the extreme manifestation of that absurd spirit which enabled governments to turn natural allies (classes, families) against one another. But the story also served as an allegory for the internal struggles which the Cuban question had provoked within the Yiddish left. Yiddish debate over Cuba fed upon the longstanding antagonisms between Daniel De Leon and the anti-De Leonists of the SLP; these factions' opposing stances on the war provided new and broader horizons for internecine invective.[11] Playing upon the historic Jewish hatred of Spain, the prowar Forverts no less than the orthodox Tageblatt took the occasion to denounce the SLP leader as "Cardinal DeLeon" or "The Spanish Inquisitor," and his followers as "Spaniards."[12] Tensions were heightened on May 1, 1898, when the De Leon faction had its May Day parade permit revoked by city authorities for fear of incendiary antiwar protest. With the authorities' blessing, meanwhile, the anti-De Leonists paraded in sympathy with Cuba and in support of American intervention.[13]

This strife on the Jewish left merely dramatized a more general atmosphere of disagreement within immigrant communities regarding the Spanish-Cuban-American War. As the question of U.S. intervention loomed throughout the spring of 1898, other points of dispute included qualms about giving the Cubans priority over other struggling nations and classes; discomfort with the inconsistencies in the U.S attitude toward Spanish empire and, say, British empire; distrust of McKinley's true intentions in the Caribbean; and, among the Irish and the Poles, a vigilant anxiety about the anti-Catholicism which surfaced in much American rhetoric regarding Catholic Spain.

The cluster of key questions at the center of polemic exchanges regarded the worthiness of the Cuban cause, the legitimacy of U.S. aims and the trustworthiness of McKinley's articulated intentions in the region, and the extent (if any) to which U.S. intervention would affect the cause of each homeland. The polemic terrain and the range of opinion reflected in the immigrant presses were strikingly similar across ethnic lines. At one end, journals like the Pilot, the Tageblatt, and Zgoda struck an enthusiastic prowar stance founded on the rhetoric of a nationalist empathy with the oppressed. At the far opposite extreme were journals like Dziennik Chicagoski and the Abend blatt, whose positions on the national question led them, albeit along very different routes, to look askance at U.S. aims and priorities. And in between, expressing various degrees of ambivalence, were journals like the *Forverts*, whose editors seemed to wince as they supported the war, and the *Catholic Citizen*, whose editors seemed to wince as they opposed it.

But if nationalist idioms and concerns did not fully determine or unify the substance of opinion on the Cuban question, nationalism did powerfully pattern and give shape to political expression. In the commentary surrounding the wars of 1898 and 1899 four issues in particular served as points of reference, mooring the discussion and marking off the boundaries within which political debate took place. These four recurrent themes included, first, Cuba's colonial plight and the perceived parallels between oppressed Cuba on the one hand and Ireland, Poland, or Zion on the other; second, the symbolic significance of Catholic Spain as the named enemy in the conflict; third, the dual hopes of winning the United States as an ally of the particular "nation" in the international political arena, and winning respect for the community of exiles in the domestic political arena through sacrifices made on the battlefield; and fourth, the opportunity which war presented for the expression of the masculinist gender ideologies which underpinned the nationalist vision in many quarters. While various writers and editors diverged greatly in their specific stances on the questions raised during the spring of 1898, commentary on the Cuban crisis in the immigrant papers was nonetheless bound together by these four pervasive and intertwining ideological threads.

Discussion of the colonial situation in the Caribbean was thus enveloped in the larger, ongoing discussion of nationalism and national rights. A certain empathy was embedded in the very vocabulary employed to describe the struggle in Cuba: *Zgoda*, for instance, described the activities of "the Cuban Kozmians and Tarnowskis"[14] in the struggle for "their Poland"; the *Catholic Citizen* coined the phrase "Iberian Orangemen" to describe the Spaniards in Havana; and the *Tageblatt* worried over the possibility of a "pogrom" in Havana, and routinely referred to the need to "drive Spain out of Cuba"—employing the same highly charged verb, *oystrayben*, which was used in describing the expulsion of the Jews from Spain centuries earlier.[15]

In addition to these isolated words or phrases, entire arguments, too, were founded on a telling nationalist logic. "If Ireland is a constant source of trouble and weakness to England," averred the *Pilot*, "it is because the former has been for centuries robbed and bullied by the latter. Cuba is a constant source of trouble and weakness to Spain for precisely the same reason."[16] Responding to McKinley's assertion that the plight of Cuba represented a singular case on the world scene, the *Tageblatt* snapped: "[the president] knows very little about the world. The Jews in Russia are 'reconcentrados,' just like the Cubans. The May Laws proclaimed this sort of tyranny, and Ignatiev discovered it even before General Weyler."[17] And in January 1897 the PNA donated $250 to the Cuban rebels because, as Stefan Barszczewski explained, "if the Polish nation wants to be free, it must work for the freedom of others."[18] The text of the PNA resolution ran,

> Ourselves exiles, who have felt the hand and the hostile knout of oppressors, whose hearts ever fill with bitterness at the sight of the oppression of our brothers remaining under the scepter of barbarians, and who are able to value the blessings of liberty; from the depth of our souls we send out a voice of sympathy and compassion to all oppressed nations of the world, and above all to the brave sons of Cuba, who, like the Polish heroes of yore, sacrifice their blood, property, and life for Cuban liberty—we wish them the speediest rising of the star of liberty.[19]

Nationalists in the emigrant communities of America were not alone in expressing enthusiasm for the Cuban cause within the framework of these strict Old World parallels. In Ireland Michael Davitt and John Dillon also registered their enthusiasm for U.S. intervention, and the hope that a similar hand might someday "be extended to liberate Ireland from another European oppressive power." An item picked up from *Kuryer Lwówski* and reprinted in *Zgoda* detailed the participation in the Cuban revolution of several Polish soldiers who had fled Poland after the debacle of 1863, including the minister of war, one general, one commander, and three colonels. And, as Abraham Cahan reported, prayers were said for McKinley and the U.S. Army in synagogues throughout Russia during the war.[20]

By the same token, however, many discovered an uncomfortable double-edge in the Cuban cause and in American sympathy. An Irish letter-writer in Syracuse, New York, encapsulated a common ambivalence when he explained to Patrick Ford, "Our people here see no difference in the cause of the starving peasantry of Mayo and the reconcentrados of Cuba."[21] The assertion of "no difference" cut two ways: the exiles identified with Cuba and found vicarious satisfaction in the island's imminent liberation; and yet they wondered why the Cuban tragedy had stirred so much interest when Ireland, Poland, or the "reconcentrados" of the Russian Pale had not. Humphrey Desmond of the *Catholic Citizen* could assert unequivocally in 1896 that "Spain should get out of Cuba . . . [and] if she won't go willingly, we should assist her exit"; and yet, the day after the first U.S. shots were fired in the Caribbean, he remarked that "as a matter of personal preference we would sooner see the United States punish perfidious Albion, which has been so cruel to poor Erin."[22]

The radical nationalist press, too, viewed the venture with a mixture of approval and skepticism. The *Forverts* presented the Cuban struggle in positive, liberationist terms (asking, for instance, "Will the U.S. Cut the Chains in Which Cuba Is Shackled?"), yet reminded its readers that the world's workers were no less in need of liberation. The *Forverts* finally solved this problem of priorities in much the way of *Zgoda* and other nationalist journals, which identified Cuba as "a school for the future," a vast liberationist rehearsal. Workers who were willing to put their lives at stake for a neighbor's freedom, argued Cahan, would sooner or later be able to put their lives at stake "for true freedom of their own."[23]

Chicago leader Leon Zolotkoff, a socialist and a Zionist, wavered too. On the one hand, Zolotkoff the Zionist identified Spain's grip on Cuba as a vicious nostalgia for "the good times of old, when her colonies sent plenty of good things from across the sea, and she lived by bullfights, sung serenades, and burned heretics." Yet Zolotkoff the socialist questioned McKinley's humanitarianism. He located the conflict with Spain within the context of American imperial designs as reflected by the Monroe Doctrine. American monopolies, he argued, wanted "to consume the earth and a scrap of the moon besides"; in this opportunity to take Spain's Caribbean pearl, "the capitalists in America . . . know a good thing when they see it."[24]

Such qualms often gave way to outright protest against American interventionism, even among writers whose hearts went out to the Cuban insurgents. An "Ireland first" approach to the conflict, for example, gradually crystallized in the editorials of the *Irish World*. Although Ford noted at times the promise implied by American willingness to take up arms against an imperial aggressor, forcefully and frequently he wondered at the world's alarm over Cuba when Ireland had so long been in distress. Professed sympathy for Cuba was rendered most suspect, in Ford's eyes, in that it was piously voiced even by the British. In response to one British M.P.'s expression of anti-Spanish indignation, Ford rather coolly pointed out that *of course* there were plenty of horrors across the Cuban landscape to describe and lament—

Cuba was at war. British protestations were but "a spice of that canting hypocrisy in which John Bull is such an expert." Ireland, after all, was officially at peace, and yet "men, women, and children at this moment are enduring sufferings as great and as horrible as any recorded in our consular reports from Cuba."[25] (Robert Ellis Thompson fashioned *Irish World* sentiment on Britain's enthusiasm for American intervention into this convenient axiom, "If England wants you to do anything very much, that is a good thing not to do.")[26]

Similarly, a Yiddish writer in *Der nayer geyst* (signing simply "Politicus") broke the Cuban question into its component parts of humanitarianism and materialism, "haggadah"[27] versus "dumplings." Many good and sincere people had been won to the prowar position by the appeal of high principles, he wrote, but these people should not fool themselves into believing that such principles actually drove administration policy. He bolstered this point by listing some peoples whose equally dire causes did not particularly interest Uncle Sam, including Filipinos, Hindus in the British empire, Poles in Russia, Indians in North America, and blacks in the southern states.[28]

Kazimierz Neuman of *Dziennik Chicagoski* challenged America's professed commitment to the abstract principle of political self-determination. Citing a jingoistic Chicago *Chronicle* editorial, he pointed out that if Cuban freedom were truly the issue, "we should conscript ourselves at once for the liberation of Ireland from English rule, and then for the liberation of India and Egypt from their oppression." After reeling off a list of colonial situations much like the one compiled by "Politicus" in *Der nayer geyst*, Neuman added, perhaps coyly, "And the *Chronicle* still forgets Poland."[29] The editor of *Swoboda* gave these same misgivings a decidedly chauvinistic edge. That U.S. aid to Cuba was disinterested and altruistic, he argued, was "nonsense": only Poland and France have such high ideals, "and today this spirit is dead even in France."[30]

Notwithstanding the attraction of liberationist logic, significant opposition to U.S. intervention emerged within all three groups over the spring months of 1898. Earliest among the nay-sayers was the Yiddish organ of the Socialist Labor Party, the *Abend blatt*. Cool to the assertion that Spain was every Jew's hereditary enemy (and outright hostile to the equation of Cuba with Zion), Philip Krantz and Benjamin Feygenbaum hammered out antiwar themes throughout the first half of 1898. They deplored the proposed war's cost in lives to the working class; they warned that when the dust of war settled Cuba would not be liberated at all, but would suffer under the "criminal" and "cruel" stewardship of America's ruling classes; and, in tones typical of their hostility to "murder-patriotism," they explained that "the love of Fatherland is the aim" of the American capitalists, "the hatred of Spain is the means." Worker, asked Feygenbaum, what will you have gained "when Cuba belongs to our ruling classes?"[31]

Far slower to voice their anti-interventionism, but ultimately no less strident once they did, were Irish and Polish Catholic journals like the *Irish World* and *Dziennik Chicagoski*. The Polish journal began by simply taking a cautious line on the *Maine* disaster; Neuman scolded the yellow press for its jingoist enthusiasms and for playing on readers' naiveté. By early March, however, he went as far as to suspect that the point of U.S. aid was that "this island must belong to the United States."[32] The *Irish World*, perhaps more strident in its criticisms of U.S. policy, arrived at a similar editorial position by way of Anglophobia: in the context of Anglo-American rapprochement, McKinley's intentions could scarcely be pure. Robert Ellis Thompson wrote, "We have made partnership with a power which has waged more petty and unjust wars this century than all the other powers taken together; and yet we expect to get credit for magnanimity in trying to liberate the Cubans from Spanish rule!" After a litany of England's political crimes around the globe, he concluded, "it is in this company that we step into the arena as the vindicator of the oppressed Cubans, boasting at the same time of our kinship by blood with the greatest oppressor on earth."[33]

That the oppressor in question was, of all possible countries, Catholic Spain, further patterned discussions of the Cuban plight and American proposals for intervention in all three groups. Viewed through an Old World lens, the tyrant's identity carried a great deal of significance: it is possible that interventionist passions would have run cooler among Yiddish immigrants—and especially within the Yiddish left—had the imperial power in question not been associated with the expulsion of Jews and the tortures of the Inquisition. Conversely, many Irish and Polish observers might have been less ambivalent had the war in the Caribbean not been attended by a popular demonization of Catholicism in the United States.

Khasriel Sarasohn's *Tageblatt* led the Yiddish press in its steady stream of anti-Spanish invective: "What is the duty of our brethren?" asked the editor. "Can they forget the martyrs of the Inquisition? Can they forget the rack, the wheel, the auto-da-fe, the stake and the flame? Can they forget the holy men and women, the flower of the race, who died with 'Shema Israel' on their lips? Can they forget those who died for God and Judaism? Can they forget the expulsion, when 80,000 perished in one day? No, no!"[34] The *Tageblatt* staff never tired of describing and decrying "WHAT THE INQUISITION IS CAPABLE OF!" Background sketches of Spanish history attributed Spain's decline from former greatness to "ignorance," "wildness," and "fanaticism"—traits for which the country could thank "her inquisition and her fanatical priests." The country was a "hotbed of religious intolerance and blood-thirsty persecution," and the war in Cuba would be "a holy thing." When the Pope made a last-ditch attempt to work out a settlement between Spain and the United States and so avert war, it was "only because he knows that Spain will have a bitter end, and the inquisition-country is very dear to him."[35]

Nor did the *Tageblatt* staff tire of painting current events in the distinctive hues of Jewish history. An article on the experiences and tortures of a refugee from Butcher Weyler's Cuba explained that he had undergone "the most horrible inquisition's pains, truly like the martyrs of yore." As U.S. intervention seemed imminent, the journal found satisfaction in the prospect that Spain would now "[pay] back with interest the money she borrowed from Jews to discover America before she drove them out [*oysgetrayben*]." Likewise, the editors took some pleasure in the notion that "the country that at one time burnt Jews for their religion" now depended upon the house of Rothschild to finance a war; and that the commission investigating the *Maine* disaster in Havana Harbor was headed by a Jew named Merix—perhaps a descendent of a victim of the inquisition. Spain, the *Tageblatt* concluded, was "lower in civilization than China"—perhaps the harshest estimation possible in Euro-American discourse at the time (see Chapter 5).[36]

But if the *Tageblatt* showed unusual zeal for this kind of talk, it was scarcely alone. Sarasohn was joined in this festival of revanchism by spokespersons at every point of the Jewish political spectrum. Rosa Sonneschein reviewed the treatment of Jews in "Evil Spotted Spain" for the *American Jewess*; a rabbi in New Orleans offered a sermon on "the intensely patriotic subject 'Remembering the *Maine*,'it being directly in line with the suffering of the Jews as undergone at the hands of the Spanish Inquisition"; and in a historical series for the *Forverts*, even Abraham Liessen recalled the "passionate, bloodthirsty" Spanish inquisitor who "annihilated every trace of heresy and foreign religion in his country."[37]

According to a ghetto sketch for the *Commercial Advertiser* by correspondent Abraham Cahan, such sentiments were common even in everyday discussion in the streets and cafes of the Lower East Side. "Apart from considering themselves Americans and loving their adopted country as the only one in the world where the unhappy children of Israel find a home, [the emigrants] have an old account to settle with the Spaniards." "They tortured the Jews and banished them from their land," said one East Side tailor, "and now the God of Israel is getting even with them."[38] An observer in Chicago wrote that "There is a wonderful war excitement among the 25,000 Russian Jews in Chicago": "All the [Zion] societies have decided to abandon Palestine and go to Cuba instead, and to go with rifles in their hands to fight Spain . . . Our people do not forget that it was Spain which banished 1,000,000 Jews, and treated them with inhuman barbarity. It will be to avenge this that we go."[39]

The Spanish tyrant became a popular and omnipresent figure in the Jewish arts. In his sprawling, thousand-page treatment of Cuban history, Moishe Zeifert described how "since the island was discovered by Christopher Columbus in 1492, it had not ceased to bleed. By fire and sword the Spaniards had occupied it; and by fire and sword they have governed there to the present day." Nor were the Cuban Indians anywhere to be found: the Spaniards had " 'civilized' them for so long that they were raked under the earth . . . The pious, Christian Spaniards!"[40] Throughout the spring and summer of 1898 the *Tageblatt* ran Meyer Lehman's *The Grand Inquisitor: Burned for Belief*; and in the fall, *Spain's Blood Bath: How the Cruelest Country in the World Tormented People with Sword and Fire in One Hand and the Cross in the Second*. The *Tageblatt* also popularized these lines on the Cuban crisis by the English-language poet, Joaquin Miller:

> And the kind who forged these fetters?
> Ask five hundred years for news.
> Stake and thumbscrew for their betters?
> Inquisitions! Banished Jews![41]

By 1900 even cosmopolitanist Jacob Gordin had produced a play on the Inquisition, *Beautiful Miriam and the Tortured*.[42]

The Jewish community, of course, held no monopoly on anti-Catholicism in its discussion of the Cuban crisis. Talk of "Pope-ridden Spain" was equally common among prominent native politicians and Protestant clergymen. The mainstream metropolitan presses frankly entertained suspicions regarding the sympathies of American Catholics; sermons like Reverend J. H. Lieper's "Popery, the Foe of the

Republic" presented the war as a clash between Protestantism and Catholicism; while tracts like Justin D. Fulton's *Washington in the Lap of Rome* ominously proposed that McKinley's indecisive posturings throughout February and March were owing to Catholic intimidation.[43]

That Spain had become a national enemy, was as momentous for Irish and Polish Catholics as it was to the descendents of Spain's banished Jews. Circumstances called for a certain finesse among Irish and Polish commentators, whose sympathy for Cuba was generally matched by a healthy apprehension at the mounting anti-Catholicism of American war fever. A speaker at the 'Ninety-Eight celebration in Denver simultaneously conveyed stridence and defensiveness: "as Irishmen and Irish-Americans . . . our cordial sympathy goes out to all people struggling for freedom." Then meeting head-on the popular charge that Catholics were secretly rooting for Spain, he assured, "We stand for America against every other country on earth."[44]

The Catholic press was active in combating anti-Catholicism on several fronts. James Jeffrey Roche, in his usual wry fashion, pointed out to the "A.P.A. idiots who clamor for a war with Spain because it is a Catholic country" that Cuba, too, was a Catholic country. Articles like "The Duty of Catholics in the Case of War" and "A New Slander on Catholics" reflected the tension for the coreligionists of Spain as that country drew more and more rhetorical fire in American public debate. Editors like Roche and Neuman not only protested and challenged current stereotypes of the priest-ridden Catholic blindly pledging allegiance to Spain, but, just in case, they also outlined immigrant obligations to the United States for the benefit of their readers.[45]

Humphrey Desmond of the *Catholic Citizen* was perhaps most cautious about the prospect of war and most active in the editorial campaign to redeem Spain and Catholicism. When news of the inflammatory De Lome letter hit the front pages of the American press, Desmond smoothed over the fracas with an alternative, unusually generous translation of the letter. The Spanish minister had not called McKinley "a low politician," but merely a "politician," he explained; nor had he called the President "one who caters to the rabble," but merely "one who seeks popularity."[46] And upon the sinking of the *Maine*, Desmond employed the England-Ireland analogy to blunt the more menacing edges of American enthusiasm for war. The U.S. response to Spanish "treachery," he charged, was rooted in anti-Catholic stereotypes: "[But w]here in all history since Nero's time was there a bloodier and more treacherous king than Richard III? And who excelled

Elizabeth in craft, Walpole in duplicity, or Pitt in intrigue? So far as bloodthirstiness goes, England's treatment of Ireland is worse than the record of a dozen Spanish Inquisitions."[47] Desmond later pled, "Let us be magnanimous toward Spain," and intervene not in hatred.[48]

The advice of the immigrant press on the proper response to the Caribbean crisis was also based largely upon nationalist logic. To be sure, much of their counsel did bespeak an Americanist orientation— concerns for the fate and status of the emigrants in America, for how the war might improve conditions in exile, and for proving their American loyalty. Many immigrants had cancelled plans for a visit to Ireland in celebration of '98, announced the *Pilot,* because "Irishmen of America are so anxious to stay here and fight for their adopted land." Buffalo's *Polak w Ameryce* remarked that, after the "surprising" patriotic outpouring in Polonia, "no one will be able to charge that we are worse citizens than people born here, but [they] will have to concede our superiority to others in the matter of patriotism and sacrifice to the country."[49] The *Catholic Citizen,* embracing the war as a great social equalizer in the hierarchical New World, at once cheered the loyal immigrants and lashed out in parody against the spirit of American nativists: "The audacity of those Catholics, crowding into positions of danger in our navy, is something intolerable. It threatens the integrity of our institutions. We believe that these places at the front should be reserved for those only upon whose loyalty to the flag we can depend. How can a man like Murphy, who owes allegiance to the Pope, be trusted to scuttle the *Merrimac?*"[50]

The question of allegiance was no less salient among Jewish immigrants, notwithstanding their relative ease in vilifying Spain. Anti-Semitic stereotyping in the period had come to include blanket charges of Jewish "cowardice" and of a nearly treasonous Jewish indifference to the political fortunes of their host countries. In *Harper's,* for instance, Mark Twain wrote of the Jew's "disinclination patriotically to stand by the Flag as a Soldier." "By his make and his ways he is substantially a Foreigner, and even the Angels dislike a Foreigner."[51] Hence the *Tageblatt* urged its male readers not only to volunteer for service, but, more important, to help make that service widely known. The journal pledged to print every scrap of information sent in regarding Jewish military participation, so that "there shall be no question as to the patriotism of our brethren." Likewise, publicizing the patriotic resolutions passed by Yiddish fraternals in New York, Baltimore, St. Louis, Chicago, and Pittsburgh, the *Tageblatt* cheered that such activity had "bettered the reputation of Jews in this country."[52]

But the discussion of immigrant duty to the adopted country was more intricately textured than these straightforward assertions of American loyalty. Commentary on immigrant mobilization reflected a complex negotiation between Old and New World outlooks. Soon after the *Maine* disaster the *Tageblatt* captured the double-edged quality of Jewish participation in the war: if Spain were indeed guilty, the United States would be obligated to "blot Spain from the map; and we, the Jews of this country, will have an opportunity to repay America for her hospitality and to pay Spain an old debt." Throughout the spring the *Tageblatt* increasingly linked the issues of immigration and U.S. foreign policy, arguing that America's role as an "asylum" for the oppressed was of a piece with its emergent role as an intervening liberator. In this construction Jewish enthusiasm for the war was overdetermined: "We Jews who have found our shelter and our home in these United States, we Jews who have always been on the side of those who struggle for justice, of those who defend the weak, we have more reasons to blow all patriotic sparks into one fire and serve this country in the present crisis."[53] In retrospect a year later the journal consolidated this connection between Jewish nationalism and Americanism in the contention that "in our late war the majority of our volunteers enlisting in the army were fiery Zionists."[54] Likewise the *Pilot* feature on the notable verve of Irish men in "PROVING THEIR PATRIOTISM" included the remark, "Ireland's day of liberty, it is asserted, will come as Cuba's has come."[55]

The Old World ramifications of New World military participation were even more pronounced in Polish-American polemics. The relative triumph in Polonia of romantic militarism, coupled with the hallowed ideal of Polish soldiers fighting for just causes worldwide and so winning the benevolent recognition of other powers, translated into direct commentary on the fruits which Poland stood to harvest from the Cuban war. The enthusiasm on this score was not unanimous, certainly: the Polish press in Europe registered its dismay at Polonia's eagerness to expend its youth on the battlefields of the Caribbean. "Let's not enlarge the cemetery" of Poles dying abroad, complained one journal. At least one Falcon official, too, Casimir Zychlinski, wondered at the chivalric monster he and his colleagues had created: Poland, not America or Cuba, was the Fatherland, he argued; Polish youth should not risk their lives in any conflict other than Poland's.[56]

But Zychlinski's dissent notwithstanding, the overall debate highlighted the cultural distance which had developed between Polonia, where romantic insurrectionism was still a powerful current, and the homeland, where Positivism had largely triumphed over this "suicidal" ideal. In answer to those who complained that "enough blood has been shed for the freedom of others," or "your blood belongs to the Fatherland!" Stefan Barszczewski waxed rhapsodic on the virtues of military sacrifice: "Oh, undoubtedly, a hundred times better is this noble-minded enthusiasm to serve a good cause, than cold calculation and indifference. A hundred times more agreeable is it to Poland to pour out the blood of her sons on foreign soil, than excessively sparing this blood out of selfish considerations." Of the soldiers fighting under the American flag, he commented:

> It could be that their deeds, their names, written down beside Kościuszko and Pułaski in American history, will come to this: that sometime America will look into the matter of Russia, Austria, and Prussia, and will assert the right of liberty for our Fatherland. We did not condemn the French who fought for our Fatherland at the time of the Confederation of Bar, and so we do not condemn our compatriots fighting for the liberation of Cuba. Indeed, we are honored that in the present war Poles take part as defenders of freedom and progress![57]

Barszczewski further propagated these views in his popular melodrama, *Cuba Libre*. A tribute to both the American government which dared to liberate Cuba and the Polish Falcons who answered the call, the play carries an unmistakable political message: after Cuba, the standard of freedom will be borne to other countries—including Poland—and for the soldiers of the fourth partition the war in Cuba will be but a rehearsal for the battle which they have been anticipating since the most recent defeat of 1863.[58]

Given the range of arguments offered in favor of intervention—parallels between the homeland and Cuba, the potential of the Caribbean island as both a proving ground for immigrant patriotism and a training ground in military maneuvers, the importance of Cuban liberation as a stroke for the broad principle of self-determination—immigrant interest in the conflict ran extremely high when the United States finally did intervene. Once McKinley had delivered his war message to Congress in April, all three groups took a rather proprietary interest in the proceedings.

The symbolic significance of the conflict and the perceived stakes of immigrant involvement were reflected in a stream of wartime "firsts" heralded by the immigrant presses: fifteen Jews had been aboard the

Maine, according to the *Tageblatt*, and two Jewish soldiers were among the first casualties of the war. "Their blood has fulfilled the wish of our people in the entire world, namely to show that Jews are patriots in the country where they live and that they shed their blood under the flag that gives them rights and protection." *Zgoda* attributed the first shot of the war to a Polish sailor aboard the *Nashville*, the son of a PNA official in Duluth, Minnesota. The Irish press, meanwhile, reveled in the news that the first shot had been fired by Patrick Mullen—as James Jeffrey Roche quipped, "an Anglo-Saxon, of course." The *Catholic Citizen* reported that Captain O'Connell, John Daniels, Daniel McKeon—Irishmen all—were among the first to land in Cuba, the first to die, and the first to be wounded, respectively. And the first "over the summit of San Juan Hill" was, of course, one Private Hoolihan.[59]

This American war for Cuban liberation was to be a war for Jewish rights, for Polish glory, and for Irish honor as well. Not least of all, it would prove to be a war for the conceptions of "manhood" which were so crucial to the popular visions of these nations and their liberation.

War and Manliness

Activities which are said in the vernacular to "separate the men from the boys" often accomplish the more portentous cultural work of separating the boys from the girls. War is unequalled in this respect. If, as George Mosse suggests, nationalist culture defines war as "an invitation to manliness," many of the men in these communities were particularly eager to accept. Reviewing a regiment of Irish volunteers in May, the San Francisco *Chronicle* reported, "the men are wild with the promise of warlike experiences amid new scenes."[60] The war of 1898 tapped a powerful nationalist-masculinist current in each of these three immigrant communities—a current long manifest in political-religious symbolism and lore, in festival and commemoration, in militarist drama and poetics.

As Margaret Higonnet and others have argued, war is a "gendering activity," a grand civic ritual which consolidates and even augments preexisting definitions of gender and systems of gender relations.[61] War accomplishes this work of gendering, first, by ritually separating the nation into defenders and defended—as one scholar puts it, into "warriors" and "beautiful souls"—and so heightening cultural ideals of "male" valor and "female" vulnerability. The culture of war defines violence as masculine, and exalts the masculine capacity for violence as a political virtue.[62] "War tests the fibre of the man," asserted a popular poem of 1898; a World War I editorial in *Ladies' Home Journal* later announced even more suggestively, "the biggest thing about a principle or a battle or an army is a man! And the biggest thing that a war can do is bring out that man." The Allied objective of the Great War, according to this writer, was "to demonstrate the right kind of manhood."[63]

The right kind of manhood, of course, demands its counterpart in the "right kind of womanhood"—or the right *kinds* of womanhood. One wartime advertisement for a social advice manual (1898) accentuated the power of war to define sexual difference, evoking the feminine mother/nurturer as a necessary counterpart to the male warrior:

Every male fighter, however brawny and heroic, was born of a woman; was once a feeble infant drawing—along with his very breath of life from his mother's own physical resources—the hardihood, mental stamina and high courage that becomes a nation's final and impregnable defense in the last dread arbitrament of war.

Shall we say that women contribute [only] the bandages and the provisions? No: they contribute the fighters![64]

Stefan Barszczewski put a similar sort of speech into the mouth of the heroine of his popular play, *Cuba Libre!*:

A Polish woman loves her Fatherland, loves freedom, loves the greatness of her nation. When an enemy of the nation would press you to the ground, would want to wrest from your soul the last trace of Polishness, then a Polish woman will each time deliver to the world a new generation of heroes and martyrs; she brings before the face of the enemy each time new regiments of swordsmen for freedom; by the fireside, by cradle and primer, she conspires against the enemies of the nation, she suckles avengers at her breast, and when war comes she does not despair, but blesses the sons, husbands, and brothers who go to bedew with their own blood the battlefield—the field of glory and immortality for the Polish nation! Such is a Polish woman, and so would I myself like to be.[65]

(Marja's soliloquy is followed immediately by the song, "O Polish Woman, Angel of the Nation.")

An alternate image of wartime womanhood emphasizes not nurturance or the capacity to produce males of "high courage," but feminine vulnerability and sexuality. According to this representation women first rely upon the protection of their warriors, then sexually reward them for their service to the nation. Henryk Sienkiewicz portrayed this most succinctly in *With Fire and Sword*, whose plot not only pivots upon the continual endangering and rescue of the fair Helen, but whose epic cast includes one Lithuanian knight who, it is said, can break his vow of chastity if he manages to sever three enemy heads with a single saber-stroke.

By their peculiar erasures and revisions, moreover, popular conceptions of "front" and "homefront" exaggerate these representations of sexual difference and enforce the notion that only male combatants (as distinct from the women who inhabit cities under siege, for example) really do or can experience the horrors of war. As Cynthia Enloe has argued, just as the "front" is masculinized in popular perception, so is the "homefront" feminized in a manner which corresponds more with preconceived assumptions about the sexes than with the facts of a given case. Legislative and popular debates over what constitutes "combat" at the front and "support" at the rear, she argues, have mostly to do with "how to make use of women's labor without violating popular notions of femininity, masculinity and the social order itself."[66]

In 1898 feminization of the homefront was manifested in the rituals surrounding the soldiers' departure: in San Francisco, for instance, high school girls were excused from classes in order to line up along Clay Street and wave to the men of California's volunteer infantries as they departed for Manila. The band, meanwhile, played "The Girl I Left Behind Me."[67] Popular press accounts augmented the gendering impact of these rituals through a selective vision of who, exactly, was left behind to be "defended." "Mothers, Sweethearts and Wives Miss the Boys Who Have Gone," announced the *Chicago Daily News*; the *San Francisco Chronicle*, in a portrait of the farewell parade in that city, described "whole rows of women . . . out in the street with eyes streaming," while above, "windows were alive with women and children."[68] Many accounts maximized this effect in what Paul Fussell has called the "high diction" of wartime writing: in journals like the *Pittsburgh Post* and the *New York Times*, the volunteers were "bronzed and hardened" as they paraded for public review, while "demure maidens stood on tiptoe" to see them. "Woman wore her best and brightest to wish the First [California Volunteers] godspeed," wrote one reporter; women

wiped their tears with "dainty mouchoirs held in white gloved hands."
By both ritual and reportage, U.S. aid to Cuba would take on some of
the knights-and-damsels quality of popular romance—what Amy Kaplan has called "the spectacle of masculinity."[69]

In addition to the gendering aspects of war in general, moreover,
this particular war with Spain was especially characterized by a rhetoric and iconography of sexual melodrama. Debates on the Cuban
revolution and American intervention were especially rife with sexual
imagery, often with the added emotive charge of Progressive Era racialism. Many of the gems of the yellow press which so inflamed
American public opinion had to do with "womanhood" dishonored,
and so appealed to a sense of ("Anglo-Saxon") chivalric duty. They
included the harrowing Spanish captivity of Evangelina Cosío y Cisneros, "the Cuban girl martyr"; the alleged strip search of three women
aboard the American *Olivette* by Spanish customs officials; and the
"dance of Guaimaro," a newly popularized incident of the Ten Years'
War in which "the ferocious hordes of negroes" under Weyler's command were ordered to strip the "defenseless women" of Puerto Prín-
cipe, and then perform an African dance before them.[70]

The overlapping languages of international conduct, sexuality, and
race influenced American debate on several levels. As one historian
has noted, the furor over Evangelina Cisneros had the effect of pro-
jecting an image of Cuba as "a pale-skinned, upper-class virgin waiting
breathlessly for a broad-shouldered American to rescue her and make
her his."[71] One popular poem of the period adopted the sexualized
imagery of the Cuban crisis (the United States-Cuba partnership is
proposed as a "marriage"), yet the poet's seeming eagerness to identify
this "dark-eyed" maiden as sufficiently *akin* to Uncle Sam ("little
sister") gives the piece a strangely incestuous overtone:

> Our little sister Cuba
> Rebelled against old Spain
> That treacherous old tyrant
> Blew up the warship Maine.
> The little dark-eyed fairy
> Has laid a secret plan,
> She may elope and marry
> Long-legged Uncle Sam.
>
> Our little sister Cuba
> Appeals to us for aid,
> And Uncle Sam should be a man

And draw his trusty blade—
In name of God and freedom
Strike down the tyrant Spain—
Avenge our gallant seamen
Who went down with the *Maine* . . .[72]

In popular cartoons, too, a gallant Uncle Sam was typically pictured stepping in, with the bold flourish of contemporary melodrama, to rescue the maiden Cuba. Significantly, whereas Cuba in violent revolt was often portrayed as a black man, Cuba the candidate for American statehood was portrayed as a white woman. *Kansas City Star* editor William White captured the complex interplay of these sexual and racial themes most succinctly: after expressing horror at the prospect of spilling "good Anglo-Saxon blood" for the sake of Cuba, he explained that "Cuba is like the woman who lets her husband beat her the second time—she should have no sympathy."[73]

This sexualization of empire and rebellion tapped the masculinist ideas of national liberation which were already current in Irish, Polish, and Yiddish politics and culture. As one Polish folksong asked,

War, Sweet War,
What sort of mistress are you
That you can be pursued
By all those beautiful boys?[74]

It was the gendering ideological work of war, at bottom, which had encouraged revolutionists like Boyle O'Reilly to define "manhood" and "womanhood" in relation to violence, and to conclude that "the voting population ought to represent the fighting population . . . A vote, like a law, is no good unless there is an arm behind it."[75] Critic Susan Jeffords has put the matter this way: "it is the crystallized formations of masculinity in warfare that enable gender relations in society to survive."[76]

It was thus with a certain masculinist bravado that volunteers under the banner "The Poles Are Ready" crowded into a Chicago recruiting station, emboldened by the song, "Fight, brothers, though a hundred will fall I will feel no defeat,/ Glory will be your legacy, and so march! to Cuba!"[77] Likewise, it was with a certain reverence for Maccabean heroics that a poet in the *Tageblatt* cheered, "In battle the mighty, eternal Jew will be manifest."[78] And almost as if in answer to the *Kansas City Star*, a gallant interventionist writer in the *Irish World* declared that "if I am satisfied that either in malice or in madness [my neighbor] is killing his wife or his children, then I have no further respect for the limitations which keep his home outside my sphere of responsibility. I kick in his door and take him by the neck."[79]

In the festival of masculinism which accompanied war fever, "manliness" became a litmus for political legitimacy. Striking the defensive posture of the dove in wartime which has become so familiar in more recent years, the *Abend blatt* felt compelled to declare that "The socialist martyrs of all countries have sufficiently demonstrated that the socialists are courageous and valiant men."[80] *Kuryer Polski*, for its part, scoffed with similar bravado at the widely held American view that the sailors aboard the *Maine* had been "heroes." Merging the chauvinisms of gender and nation, Michael Kruszka explained that a genuine hero "can only be a fellow who, knowing the immensity of a given danger, [yet] animated by some noble idea or motive, throws himself forward in spite of it to render someone some service." The best example of genuine heroism was "a soldier standing amid a hail of bullets and fighting in defense of the fatherland." The American casualties of the *Maine* were simply "unlucky victims and nothing more."[81]

Wartime's rampant masculinism was not entirely unchallenged by immigrant women, although women's thoughts on these issues are more difficult to recover than men's. In part, women's commitment to militarist liberationism could in itself call into question certain gender conventions. In an address before the Pennsylvania state convention of the Daughters of Erin, for instance, Catherine Flood donned the mantle of heroism on behalf of Irish women, even as she deferred to Ireland's male political leadership:

Let England learn from Spain the lesson which America is teaching the world. To the true and good men of our race we confide Ireland's future. As in the past, so in the future will Irish women be found ready and willing to follow them like the Betsy Grays, the Miss Sheares, the Miss Byanes, and . . . Eliza Bryson, who, taking a green flag, rushed out to meet the redcoats in '98, exclaiming as she held it aloft, "Follow this!"[82]

A second line of argument accepted the gendering terms of war, but challenged the male exclusivity of political life on the grounds that women, as "beautiful souls," might exert a "civilizing" influence over the polity. An antiwar essay in the *Forverts*, signed simply "Sofie

Hoyzfroy" [Housewife], remarked that every perishing soldier "will leave behind the broken hearts of a mother, of a wife, of a bride to be, of a sister." Inverting the masculinist logic that the voting public should represent the fighting public, Sofie suggested that, on the contrary, the world would be a more peaceful place—and the nation more secure—if the voting public represented the *grieving* public.[83] Irish women in California worked to organize an ethnic nursing auxiliary to the 1st California Volunteers—at once challenging gender segregation of the theater of war, yet conforming to more traditional conceptions of the feminine caretaker. (Said the Chief Surgeon during the war, "Nursing is a woman's special sphere . . . Her sweet smile and gentle touch are often of more benefit to the patient than the medicine she administers.")[84]

As immigrant men and their sons responded to the war with Spain, however, their enthusiasm reflected the resonance of both the nationalist and masculinist dimensions of the Cuban cause. "What glories does a regiment composed of soldiers of Irish blood call from the past!" rhapsodized Major Edward McCrystal of the Irish 69th of New York. "In every clime, under every flag, in every war has this green flag of a people—not of a nation—been crowned with honor, fame, and victory—alas, and baptized in most precious blood; what splendid fighters the Irish have always been, in every cause except their own: unsurpassed by the sons of any age, nation, or race."[85] *Zgoda* applauded that "Polish youth, fighting under the star spangled banner, gives an example of the valor for which Poles have been famed for all time"; while the *Tageblatt* chimed, "our fathers were always distinguishing themselves as gallant and skillful soldiers."[86]

The convergence of nationalist and masculinist ideals in the Cuban cause translated into feverish activity in the recruitment centers of the immigrant communities. "I've been knocking around the camps for two weeks," wrote a Kentucky colonel in the spring of 1898, "and, by the blue smoke, I believe a third of the soldiers are Irish."[87] To hazard from the immigrant presses, the other two-thirds must have been Polish and Yiddish. Reports from immigrant enclaves across the country were uniform: in New York "thousands rushed to the recruiting stations" of the Lower East Side; in Boston, "Faneuil Hall was jammed to the doors" with AOH members anxious to join the Boyle O'Reilly Battalion; in Buffalo, when *Polak w Ameryce* put out a call for volunteers, the answering crowd "was unexpectedly large, like the Krakowiaks of yore in answer to Kościuszko"; several hundred had to wait outside the overflowing hall. In the enlistment proceedings for the

Illinois 7th, whose ranks were limited to 1,200, "[Kavanaugh] could have enlisted twice 1,200 if he had been given the power to take all the men who wanted to go with an Irish regiment." Even the native-owned metropolitan papers took note of immigrant enthusiasm for the cause: the Chicago *Tribune* described the "scores of young Irish lads" eager to go to war; the Milwaukee *Sentinel* exclaimed, "The martial spirit is rampant among the Polish-American citizens of Milwaukee."[88]

Men in several immigrant enclaves aspired to muster in a solid ethnic regiment under the dual standards of the Old World and the New. Organizations like the Guards of Zion and the Hibernian Rifles hurriedly petitioned state governors across the country, pledging to fill regimental scrolls and requesting a place among the state units of the National Guard. Irish and Irish-American soldiers did dominate the ranks of the 7th Illinois Volunteer Infantry, the 9th Massachusetts, and especially the 69th New York, which boasted over four hundred Irish-born members. The 1st California, too, was Irish by tradition if not by birth (most companies had only one or two foreign-born Irishmen in their ranks).[89] Eighty-four Poles from Milwaukee and environs formed Company K of the 1st Wisconsin Volunteer Infantry—nicknamed the Kościuszko Guard—of which forty-five were foreign-born.[90] Jews were concentrated in the largest numbers in the 1st California Regiment; the 1st and 2nd Illinois Volunteer Infantries from Chicago; and the New York State Volunteer Infantries from the New York, Brooklyn, and Buffalo areas.[91]

These were only the most noted immigrant units among the U.S. forces, however; enthusiasm to enlist ran high elsewhere as well. In Colorado the call went up for an Irish regiment under the banner "Faugh a Ballaugh [Clear the Way] and Remember the *Maine*"; the Rocky Mountain Irish insisted that "the regiment must be Irish-American from the Colonel to the drummer boy."[92] In one Boston synagogue "two thousand men, young and old" rallied to offer their services to the governor; one hundred members of the Zion Association of Chicago formed the Guards of Zion, two companies of a non-Jewish regiment of Illinois Volunteers.[93] And after the rolls of the Kościuszko Guard had been filled, Milwaukee Poles, too, quickly laid plans for an additional regiment to be ready for McKinley's second call for volunteers. At a mustering-in ceremony in Pittsburgh, a *Post* reporter noted a group of Polish men "gaudily dressed in red and carrying great curving sabers[;] they were imposing," he opined, "and there were cheers for them unknown though they were."[94] Even Teddy Roosevelt's much-celebrated Rough Riders included five Irish-born and two Russian-born soldiers. Roosevelt himself singled out a young Jew nicknamed "Pork Chop" as "one of the best fighters in the regiment"; a biographer later described Captain Bucky O'Neill of troop "A" as being "Irish as a brickbat."[95]

Much of this enlistment activity was coordinated through the existing machinery of various immigrant fraternal associations. At the national level, organizations like the Irish National League and the Clan na Gael worked to assemble an "Irish Brigade" consisting of regiments from the country's largest enclaves (Chicago, Boston, and New York).[96] Far more feverish (and prolific) was the activity at the local and regional levels. A group of Russian Hussars from New York and the Knights of Maryland, a Jewish youth group in Baltimore, petitioned their respective governors to form ethnic regiments; the men of the Baron de Hirsch agricultural colony of Woodbine, New Jersey, volunteered en masse, as did a Boston *landsmanshaft* of immigrants from Janausohek; and several Yiddish benevolent associations actually pledged to pay a cash fee to any member who enlisted.[97] Local Polish leaders in Chicago used existing networks—both fraternal associations and the Democratic Party's ward and precinct machinery—to organize Polish recruits.[98]

Most impressive, however, were the local recruitment drives among the Irish. The California AOH, for instance, resolved that "whereas millions of our race who were compelled by inhuman laws to leave the land of their birth found a home and a field for their labor in this land of liberty," the California Irish would raise an entire regiment. An officer of the Rhode Island AOH, too, offered the services of that branch, explaining that "the down-trodden of all races and peoples should receive the aid and assistance of all good men, and particularly, that of Irishmen and sons of Irishmen."[99] In addition to the famed Irish regiments of New York, Massachusetts, Illinois, and California, Irish immigrants and their sons—often clustered in units like the Hibernian Rifles or the Emmet Guards—were a distinct, noteworthy ethnic presence in the Volunteer and National Guard units of Connecticut, Delaware, Maine, Minnesota, Ohio, Pennsylvania, and Rhode Island. The Irish press reported further enlistment rallies and attempts at establishing ethnic regiments in Baltimore, Denver, Lexington, Nashville, San Antonio, and Savannah.[100]

The very names of the immigrant units suggest the ideological tenor of military enthusiasm: although it is true that Tadeusz Kościuszko had fought in the American Revolution, no one who had ever attended a Third of May celebration, for instance, could have missed the Old

World significance of the name "Kościuszko Guard." Among the most popular plays in all of Polonia, recall, was *Kościuszko at Racławice*, which recounted Kościuszko's mobilization of the peasantry and his first victory in the insurrection of 1794. Likewise the Irish 69th in New York included companies named for James Fitzmaurice Fitzgerald, who led an Irish invasion against Elizabethan settlers in 1579; Patrick Sarsfield, who defended Limerick against the British in 1690; Napper Tandy, a rebel of 1798; Robert Emmet, who led a rising in 1802; Thomas Francis Meagher, who fought in the Irish rising of 1848 and in the American Civil War; and one company was named "Faugh a Ballaugh." (Two others were named for Michael Corcoran and James Shields, leaders of the Irish Brigade during the Civil War.)[101]

More telling still were the enlistment rallies across the country, and the communal celebrations—soaked in nationalist symbolism and Old World allusion—in honor of local immigrant units once they did muster in and depart for camp. "The sons of Erin thronged Faneuil Hall last night," reported the *Boston Globe* of one such enlistment rally; "The hall was packed solid and there were many hundreds who could not get in." After telling the crowd that "Irishmen are born soldiers (applause)," the chairman of the meeting asked, what more fitting way could the Irish of Boston celebrate the anniversary of '98 than to form an Irish regiment for the Cuban cause? "Through four hundred years of struggle for freedom, whose light has just dawned on fair Cuba, the sons of that other fair, green isle have learned to love to fight for this cause." Later in the proceedings, when Mayor Josiah Quincy announced that the regiment which emerged from this rally was to be called the Boyle O'Reilly Battalion, the hall erupted in "tremendous applause and cheers." Thomas Gargan added that the members of the meeting would be "disloyal" if "we do not remember that land over the sea where rest the ashes of our ancestors."[102]

The city of Worcester, meanwhile, "was turned upside down with enthusiasm" as the Emmet Guards marched out to join the 9th Massachusetts Volunteers. Ten thousand people reportedly turned out to review the troops, who themselves each wore a sprig of green; and " 'The Wearin' of the Green' brought a joyous gleam into almost every eye."[103] The Irish 9th Massachusetts was seen off by the Boyle O'Reilly Cadet Band and an Irish throng of several thousand singing "Auld Lang Syne," and they were greeted upon arrival in Camp Alger, Virginia, by a second Irish throng waving U.S. and Irish flags while "the band played 'The Wearin' of the Green' and other Irish melodies."[104] Similarly, before a crowd of several thousand who had turned out to see off the Irish 7th Illinois in Chicago, Brigadier General Charles Fitzsimons complimented "the Irish race for the bravery shown on many a historic battlefield."[105]

As the Fighting 69th of New York made its way south by rail, the soldiers were feted in "monster receptions" along the way. As many as 10,000 greeted them in Lexington, Kentucky, where, according to the *New York Times*, "about a hundred of the handsomest young women" of the community presented them with flowers. Private Józef Nowalski of the Kościuszko Guard described a similar, though far more modest, reception arranged by Stefan Barszczewski as the Guard passed through Chicago en route to their camp in Florida.[106]

But the grandest of these fetes for immigrant units were the New York send-off for the Irish 69th, and the Milwaukee send-off for the Kościuszko Guard. Contemporary accounts in both the immigrant and the metropolitan press convey the symbolic and ideological freight of this "splendid little war" for the exiles. "An immense throng of visitors" turned out for the mustering-in ceremony of the 69th, where the Friendly Sons of St. Patrick presented the regiment with a stand of colors including the Stars and Stripes, the New York State, regimental, and Irish flags. According to the *New York Times,* the "long pent-up enthusiasm of the 'Fighting Irishmen' at once began to show itself."[107]

When the regiment departed for Chickamauga Park, Georgia, throngs of people lined the streets ("20,000," according to the *Irish World*) waving American, Cuban, and Irish flags. The regiment paraded through the city, changing its route to visit St. Patrick's Cathedral to receive the benediction of Archbishop Corrigan. The band played "The Wearin' of the Green," then onward the volunteers marched "through a crowd that came from no one knows where, but that seemed to grow in numbers as the regiment progressed." Finally the 69th boarded the ferry *Joseph J. O'Donohue,* and, as they sailed through the harbor, a passing British steamer "saluted with her whistles and by lowering her flag."[108]

Milwaukee festivities for the Kościuszko Guard began with confession and mass for the soldiers, as one English-language paper put it, "following the custom of the army of Poland in the glorious days of her kingdom."[109] The Church had been decked out in flowers and Polish flags for the occasion. After communion, Father Szularecki addressed the volunteers on "the grandeur of their mission." Invoking the military tradition of Sobieski and Kościuszko, Szularecki implored soldiers to fight "righteously" and "courageously" like "our national heroes," and to bring "fame to yourselves and to the Polish nation." "As Poles and as Americans," he intoned, the men should fight for the United States and in so doing build a monument to Kościuszko. Amid "the painful tears of mothers and the heartfelt tears of girls," each of the soldiers was presented a bouquet of white and amaranthine roses (matching the Polish flag), and schoolchildren numbering "toward a thousand" paid tribute to the Guard with Polish patriotic songs.[110]

A few of the immigrant soldiers may have found a little of the glory which was promised by such auspicious and politically charged beginnings. Mayer Benjamin Dodek, for instance, an immigrant from Berdechev, Russia, and once a member of the First *Aliyah*,[111] was presented two medals for his contribution to the Spanish war—one by the U.S. government, and one by the Cuban government. For Morris Mendelsohn the war was something of an initiation into civic life. After losing his arm in Cuba at the age of seventeen (he had lied about his age to get into the army), Mendelsohn's involvement in Jewish veterans' affairs led to a long and influential career in both Zionist and American politics.[112] And the Irish of the First California were lionized in banner headlines back home, as the outfit figured prominently in the early fighting against the Filipino rebels in February of 1899. (Among their comrades in arms, however, they were derided as "laughing stocks" and "the butt of the whole island," evidently because of their quickness and bluster in warming up to the heroes' role.)[113]

For most, however, romance evaporated quickly. "All the fellows now say that if they had known beforehand that it would be like this," wrote one Polish soldier to his cousin, "then none would have gone, even if they were promised a farm, because really this is the life of a dog, not a man."[114] The logistical snags during wartime have become legendary. The food was not merely bad; some of it was in fact tainted. Troops were ill equipped (soldiers in the sweltering heat of Chickamauga Park, Georgia, for instance, were issued winter underwear), and others were not equipped at all (many had no weapons). Railroad cars full of supplies, meanwhile, sat on nearby sidetracks. And since some states had trouble meeting their payrolls for weeks at a time, volunteers were often unable to buy the necessities which the government had failed to supply. More than one observer joked that the U.S. army now replicated "Coxey's Army." By June of 1898 organizations like the Friendly Sons of St. Patrick and the Polish National Alliance had already begun receiving pleas for financial aid from their compatriots in the camps of the south.[115]

Other rather inglorious aspects of the wartime experience included rampant health problems, as war fever all too often gave way to yellow fever, hysteria to malaria, both on the islands of the Caribbean and in the camps of the south. In the one month period between July 31 and August 31, for example, twenty-five of the eighty-four soldiers in the Kościuszko Guard spent sick time in quarters or in the camp hospital—a few spent as much as two weeks. *Kuryer Polski* described another southern camp as "one giant hospital."[116] Nor did wartime assignments quite live up to the promise of martial song and heroic story. While American gunships bombarded the Spanish fleet at Santiago, Private Nowalski and his comrades of the Kościuszko Guard passed the time drearily bombarding paper boats on the tremendous puddles of Jacksonville after a Florida rainstorm. Many within the ranks felt that their assignments, like military promotions, were dictated by a politics of favoritism, and that the war had become a factory for the deliberate fabrication of Republican heroes.[117]

The experience of the Irish 69th was perhaps the most disheartening of all. In addition to the common payroll and supply problems, the regiment was in a railroad wreck which killed two on the way to Huntsville, Alabama; the rank-and-file filed a petition protesting their assignment to a Cuban garrison; and over the course of the summer and fall, a nearly mutinous resentment mounted against Colonel Duffy. The leader was ultimately charged with several formal offenses, including misappropriation of funds (including those furnished by the Friendly Sons of St. Patrick), drunkenness, falsifying records, and "coarse and inconsiderate" treatment of inferiors. By the end of 1898 the 69th, in the estimation of one bitter soldier, was "fit only for disbandment."[118]

Nonetheless, the extant evidence, sketchy though it is, suggests that the often unromantic quality of army life during the war did not altogether dissipate the ethnic-nationalist significance of the venture. "We are Poles to a man," wrote Private Nowalski in July, "and if not for the English commands, we could be marching on the Moscovite, like a Polish army."[119] In a series of letters to *Zgoda* over the course of the summer, Nowalski, a twenty-four-year-old carpenter from Sejny, Poland, continued to strike Polish national themes. When Tadeusz Wild, the captain of the Kościuszko Guard, returned to Milwaukee early in the summer to drum up more recruits, Nowalski noted the importance to the men of the Guard's remaining 100 percent Polish.[120] He likewise noted with pride the high (though unspecified) number of PNA members among the National Guard units at camp, and claimed that half of them belonged to the nationalist Polish Youth

Alliance; he described the verve of the Falcons in leading the Polish soldiers in calisthenics; and he wrote of the Guard's meeting with a local Jacksonville Pole named Działynski, "a veteran of '48"[121] who addressed the troops.[122] And on one June afternoon members of the Guard met just outside the camp's official boundary (where liquor was allowed), drank beer, and "spent several hours talking and singing patriotic songs. Poles from other units also took part in the party."[123]

In his memoir of Philippine life with the 13th Minnesota Volunteer Infantry, John Bowe, too, noted the Irish nationalist significance which the war had taken on for many of his Irish-American comrades. "The boys were celebrating the seventeenth of Ireland [St. Patrick's Day]," he wrote, when word spread that the regiment had been sent to the front. "Then pandemonium broke loose; half the band got out and went up the street, piping, 'St. Patrick's Day in the Morning.' " The impromtu parade featured "the Irish contingent, consisting of the McCarrens, the McGuinesses and the McMuds, decorated with green ribbon resurrected by Jimmy Brown." Although Bowe never fully explained it, he also noted a tendency on the part of the Irish soldiers to identify at least in part with the Filipino insurgents. Perhaps it was because of the rebelliousness which the Filipinos demonstrated, first against Spain and later against the United States, which prompted the Irish soldiers in Bowe's unit to refer to them as "smoked Irish" and "the O'Hooly's."[124]

And despite the prosaic cast of the wartime experience for many of those who had enlisted, so, too, were the receptions for the returning soldiers steeped in nationalist symbolism and charged by the same liberationist energy as the mustering-in ceremonies months before. If anything, their welcome back was even more festive and politically charged than their send-offs had been. According to the *New York Times,* New York "was a gayly fluttering wilderness of flags and bunting, and wherever the red, white and blue was flung to the breeze, the green of Erin floated by its side." Despite the bitter January weather, "unnumbered thousands of wildly enthusiastic spectators" lined the streets, wearing green ribbons and waving flags of green with the Irish harp; half a dozen bands played "alternate strains of 'Yankee Doodle,' 'The Wearin' of the Green,' 'Dixie,' 'The Green Above the Red,' and 'Gerryowen.' " An AOH delegation had met the regiment at Weehawken station and presented each member with "a sprig of green plucked from the historic battlefield of Oulart Hill";[125] and the regiment was then escorted through the streets by nearly every prominent Irish organization in the city. Although Colonel Duffy was traveling separately and would not arrive until later, one women's organization had turned out to present him with a large floral harp (notwithstanding the complaints which had been made against him).[126]

In advance of the Kościuszko Guard's return to Milwaukee, *Kuryer Polski* set about planning and publicizing their welcome. "The reception will be short, but enthusiastic and huge," wrote Kruszka, "because without a doubt all of Polonia will turn out to greet our brave fellows." Among the features of the celebration, a chorus of schoolchildren were to sing "Poland Has Not yet Perished," and a hundred twelve-to-fourteen-year-old girls were to present bouquets to the soldiers.[127] And indeed, when the Guard finally arrived, even though their train pulled into Milwaukee at six in the morning, "in dishabille" several hundred residents—"particularly women—welcomed them with joyous cries and waving kerchiefs." The greeting was followed by a brief ceremony at Kościuszko Hall, where the schoolchildren, the patriotic songs, the girls, and the bouquets all materialized.[128]

Even in San Francisco, where the reception for the 1st California Volunteers had the flavor of a general civic, not a specifically ethnic Irish event, the parade featured 2,000 members of the AOH and the Ladies' Auxiliary in carriages; the Knights of the Red Branch; the Celtic Union; the Knights of St. Patrick; the Knights of Tara; the St. Patrick's Mutual Alliance of California; the Gaelic Literary Society; and county organizations from Monaghan, Leitrim, Tyrone, Fermanagh, and Donegal.[129] Reprising the theme of the war's gendering cultural work, the *Examiner* described the "Unconditional Capitulation of the California Volunteers to the Girls They Left Behind Them."[130]

The entire experience of American intervention and the war for Cuba was quickly absorbed into the dramatic and bardic repertoirs of immigrant popular culture. Moishe Hurvitz, who had dashed off a play on *Cuba: or, General Maceo* in 1897, had *The Spanish Victims: or, Uncle Sam and Miss Cuba* written and in production by the first week of May, 1898. By the following January he had added *The Heroes of Santiago*.[131] Popular ballads, too, struck both masculinist and nationalist chords in trumpeting the immigrants' participation in the war. One Yiddish poem, "The Jewish Soldier in Battle Against Spain," averred that "He fights for revenge/ He fights for the flag"; and "He laughs when death winks at him."[132] A popular Irish ode to "The Fighting Race" wove Irish losses in the *Maine* tragedy into a longer history of martyrdom beginning at Vinegar Hill (1798). Another, "Fag a Ballagh," celebrated in over fifty lines "Those fighting, daring sons of

Erin,/ Those dashing, smashing sons of Erin" and their contribution to
the Cuban cause:

> Were all over in death and drill—
> At Bloody Lane, at San Juan hill;
> At Las Guasimas, Siboney,
> Porto Rico, and El Caney;
> The earth is pillowed with the graves
> Of old Ireland's sons, Erin's braves . . .
>
> Against old Spain their strength they hurled—
> Stars and Stripes and the Green unfurled,
> Irish blood to avenge the *Maine,*
> Till Irish brows, besprent like rain,
> Were mixed all in a bloody brew,
> Where swords and guns in flinters flew,
> Where cannister hot, grape and shot,
> Hissed o'er that awful bloody spot
> Where floated grand Old Glory . . .
>
> See their charge on hill and valley,
> In wood and dale, Old Glory's rally;
> Hear the war cry, "Fag a Ballagh!"
> O'Boyle, O'Neill, McCoy, McCalla,
> The stubborn Spaniard backward bearing,
> Those fighting, daring sons of Erin,
> Those dashing, smashing sons of Erin . . .
>
> They left their bones on Bunker Hills,
> At Stoney Point, and the Antilles;
> They fought and bled at New Orleans,
> Mexico, and the Philippines.
> 'Neath Pekin's walls they rest unseen,
> Blossoms of blood their sprigs of green.[133]

Other tributes to the valor of immigrant soldiers included a New
York appeal to build a monument to the Jewish volunteers. In a Lower
East Side sermon which was later circulated as a pamphlet, Rabbi
A. E. Hirschowitz honored "the martyrs of Israel fallen in battle" who,
he felt, had "sanctified the name of Israel among the nations by the
zealous sacrifice of their pure-hearted, youthful lives."[134] And looking
back years later in a short story titled "At Santiago" (1913), Stefan

Barszczewski immortalized a fair-haired soldier, shot in the chest, whose gaping shirt revealed an icon of the Holy Virgin of Często-chowa.[135]

In the years immediately following the defeat of Spain, Cuba, for some, continued to symbolize both the promise of national liberation and the political righteousness of the adopted country. Such was the power of nationalist culture: the war for Cuban independence may have failed to strike a blow for oppressed nations everywhere, but many productions of nationalist culture did not fail to absorb and recast the war as a significant victory for the immigrants, their warriors, and their nation. Paeans to "the dashing, smashing sons of Erin" or "the martyrs of Israel fallen in battle," like the celebratory parades in New York and Milwaukee, fixed the Cuban war as a nationalist event in a way which smoothed over the logistical nightmares, the dreary Jacksonville afternoons, and, not least of all, the hegemonic articles of the Platt amendment.[136]

For observers like J. C. O'Connell, the salient aspect of the "splendid little war" in the Caribbean was the military experience it provided Irish-American youth. "Irishmen," he cried in his revised history of the Irish in the U.S. military (1903),

> you, with the sons of Irishmen, are 20,000,000 freemen. You help to wield the destiny of the greatest Republic that the world has ever seen or heard of. The country that gave you birth is writhing under the galling Saxon yoke. Her bleeding breast heaves with the breath of returning life. Why not win for her what you won for your adopted country, the inalienable rights of life, liberty, and the pursuit of happiness? . . . The starry banner will smile encouragingly on her sister, Sunburst, in grateful remembrance of the heroic bravery of her sons in the cause of American liberty.[137]

For others, it was not the newly proven military competence of the immigrants, but the newly "liberated" island of Cuba itself which held the most promise, the Platt Amendment notwithstanding: the island seemed a suitable refuge for the exiles of the world's conquered nations. In his 1902 travelogue for *Straż*, Władysław Wagner, a member of a Polish colonization society which had sent a fact-finding delegation to the island, asserted that "the Polish people should search for their good fortune on the land, and not in the subjugation of mines or factories; and Cuba is a promising land, flowing with milk and honey."[138] This view of Cuba's potential to solve Polish woes recalls the *Tageblatt's* April Fool joke at the outset of the war—"Extra! A Jewish Kingdom in Cuba!"

But not everyone was so sanguine about what had taken place in Cuba. The socialist *Abend blatt*, which had questioned U.S. intentions all along, was among the most vociferous in decrying the results of the war. "Now comes the hangover!" the journal announced in July of 1898; "now that a bit of Cuba has finally been captured and the American flag flies there on every spire, Cuba's own flag must not be shown." Elsewhere, in a satirical piece titled "The Diary of a Patriot," the journal sighed with mock disappointment, "What a shame that the earth-kugel is so small!"[139]

But the Yiddish socialists were not alone in identifying U.S. treatment of Cuba as a betrayal of liberationist principles. For Kazimierz Neuman of *Dziennik Chicagoski*, also among the early skeptics with regard to the humanitarian aims of the United States, Cuba came to symbolize not liberation but betrayal. After Spain's defeat, the journal noted with some foreboding that the Cuban army did not take part in the victory parade in Havana.[140] The journal's view of Cuban "liberation" was summed up in a front-page cartoon in 1900: a Cuban is seated on a bench reading a newspaper; a poster behind him proclaims that the U.S. army will remain in Cuba only until law and order reign, while the screaming headlines of his newspaper announce various lynchings across the United States. Comments the Cuban, "When I read of these atrocities, I come to the conclusion that my old, bloody friend Weyler is now the chief commander of the United States."[141]

Even *Zgoda* and the *Pilot*, once so enthusiastic about American intervention on Cuba's behalf, protested the expansionist turn which U.S. policy had taken. In an essay on "The Future of Cuba" *Zgoda* lamented that "at present there is hardly a larger city in the U.S. in which joint-stock companies would not form for the exploitation of the Pearl of the Antilles. And the field for exploitation is enormous."[142] In late 1898 the *Pilot* wanted to know what had happened to the *reconcentrados* who had been the focus of so much humanitarian concern only a matter of months before. "The Cuban reconcentrados have disappeared from the earth as effectively as they have from our policy," noted one editorial; "but the earth remains, and we can take that." Wavering between satiric wit and sober protest, the journal argued that "It is one thing to rescue a man from robbers, and quite another to reward our own virtue by robbing the rescued one."[143]

"Who fears to speak of '98?" asked James Jeffrey Roche at year's end, echoing the famous song in tribute to the Irish rebels of 1798.

> We think our children and our children's children will fear to speak of 1898 with much pride in the years to come. America, the hope of humanity, the refuge of the oppressed of every nation, if it become permanently seized with the lust of Empire, is no longer the beacon light of liberty, but the wrecker's bale fire of destruction. If that be its mission, God save the Republic![144]

Denunciations of American expansionist policy became more venomous still over the course of 1899, when U.S. hegemony was enforced, not by legislative amendment merely, but by force of arms.

5

Windows on Imperialism: Nationalism, Race, and the Conquest of the Philippines

Our generals in Cuba and Puerto Rico have two tasks: to learn how to rule over the liberated peoples and to teach the liberated peoples how to rule over themselves. Their first task is easy, because, with several tens of thousands of American soldiers nearby, they can rule even without learning how, as is demonstrated, for example, by the Russian Czars.

—Ben Efrim, *Abend Blatt*

Today the Filipinos are treated in their own country by their would-be foreign masters the same way the Irish were treated by the English in 1798. Like the Irish, they see their religion insulted and their most sacred rights infringed on by insolent foreigners, who are trying to steal their country from them. They would be deserving of contempt if they did not resist to the last the "benevolent assimilation" William McKinley would force upon them.

—Patrick Ford, *Irish World*

For us Poles, this war is not necessarily pleasant. Traditionally we always stand on the side of the oppressed; since we have repeatedly taken up arms in defense of our independence, we naturally sympathize with all other peoples struggling for independence—even if they be half-savage Malays.

—Michael Kruszka, *Kuryer Polski*

Beginning with Admiral Dewey's victory at Manila in May 1898, the political ground in the United States shifted dramatically. Journals like the *Catholic Citizen* had confidently proclaimed that "America is not in the business of plunder or in the game of destroying the independence of weak peoples"; yet by early summer the nation's "hurrah element," as Humphrey Desmond called the expansionist camp, was loudly enumerating America's just territorial desserts for having defeated imperial Spain.[1] Regarding the Philippines, suddenly central to American interests, Finley Peter Dunne's Mr. Dooley quipped, "tis not more thin two months since ye larned whether they were islands or canned goods." But the unresolved fate of these and other hitherto obscure islands were "makin' puzzles fr our poor tired heads" nonetheless. "Ivry night, whin I'm countin' up the cash," Dooley moaned, "I'm askin' meself will I annex Cubia or lave it to the Cubians? Will I take Porther Ricky or put it by? An' what shud I do with the Ph'lippeens? Oh, what shud I do with thim?"[2]

The vexing question of overseas expansion was not new, to be sure; islands in the Caribbean and the Pacific had been the focus of much interest and speculation in the United States since well before the war with Spain. Decades of American business practice were distilled, for instance, in Secretary of State James Blaine's 1891 identification of Cuba, Puerto Rico, and Hawaii as "three places that are of value enough to be taken." Two years later an annexationist faction of American planters staged a Hawaiian "revolution" of sorts, which would have given the United States political control of the islands had the in-coming Cleveland administration not rejected the revolutionists' claims to legitimacy. Cleveland and his Secretary of State, Walter Gresham, forestalled for a time the momentum of overseas expansion, declaring that "it would lower our national standard to endorse a selfish and dishonorable scheme of a lot of adventurers."[3]

But the imperialism question regained its force in the months following Admiral Dewey's victory over the Spanish fleet. Over the course of the summer cries of "Cuba Libre!" gradually gave way to debate over America's newly discovered "responsibilities" and the ultimate disposition of Spain's colonies. In ousting Spain, had the United States not rightfully won control of Cuba, Puerto Rico, and the Philippines? Arguments for the annexation of Hawaii, too, now resurfaced: the islands were hailed as an indispensable waypoint for the U.S. fleet in the Pacific, notwithstanding the objection of Congressman Champ Clark that if Dewey's "great victory proves anything at all about these islands, it is that we have no earthly use for them, for he could not have done better if we owned all the islands in all the seas."[4] Congressional opposition to Hawaiian annexation creaked and collapsed in July, in part under the weight of a grandiose rhetoric of national destiny, in part under the weight of the compelling (if specious) argument of "military necessity."[5]

The debate over American imperialism further intensified in the fall of 1898, as it became clear that Spain's cession of the Philippines to the U.S. would be one stipulation of the peace treaty between the two countries. The Treaty of Paris, providing for U.S. control of the islands, provoked a heated public debate and a vigorous fight in the Senate over ratification.[6] But discussion reached its starkest polarities only in February 1899, when fighting broke out between Filipino nationalists and American soldiers in the outskirts of Manila. The imperialism question now hinged on competing and highly emotional allegations of the Filipinos' savage ingratitude on the one hand, and the McKinley administration's brutal arrogance on the other. As one popular anti-imperialist tract couched the polarity, *Criminal Aggression: By Whom Committed?*

For immigrants, as for the American public at large, the Philippine question was divisive and often bitter. When Father McKinnon, the chaplain of the First California Volunteer Regiment, lectured in favor of expansion on the grounds that Filipino leader Emilio Aguinaldo was another "Nero" and that his followers were incapable of "understanding what freedom means," he was heckled for making "the English argument." "Why shouldn't they be free?" one member of his largely Irish New York audience challenged before being escorted from the hall.[7] Likewise, letters to the editor of the *Yiddishes tageblatt* worried over the militarism necessarily involved in expansion: "we see from enslaved Russia that a great army impoverishes the people," argued one writer; another warned that the United States would become a great military power "like France"—a charged analogy in the emotional days of the Dreyfus affair. Yet another argued that it is impossible to "beat freedom into someone's head with cannons and rifles." But the editor, for his part, scolded, "It is . . . a sickness to hate the country where one has rescued oneself from Russia"; he took every occasion roundly to denounce "the Aguinaldos in the United States."[8]

Arguments on both sides of the question were framed in part in the favored language of masculinism. Once fighting had broken out between Americans and Filipinos in Manila, commentators like Humphrey Desmond and Michael Kruszka concluded that "We must not retreat from our difficulty in the face of present Filipino bravado." The United States must leave the islands only with its "honor" intact; to withdraw under Filipino attack would make the Americans look like

a "laughingstock" or "cowards."[9] Others, on the contrary, saw in the
Filipinos an admirable model of nationalist-masculinist valor. "Can we
call these people bandits," asked Stefan Barszczewski, "who would
rather die than lay down the arms which they took up in defense of
their native land? The most zealous adherents of annexation must tip
their hats to these 'rebels.' " And indeed, one of annexation's most
zealous adherents did exactly that: ever alert to manifestations of
Maccabean spirit, the *Tageblatt* commented, "One thing the Filipinos
have shown is that they are courageous in battle and they can die like
heroes."[10]

But while familiar masculinist strains informed immigrant men's
discussion of Filipino rights and American power throughout the war,
an emergent tension between nationalist and racial political identifications exerted more influence on the debate. In a proclamation on
the Philippines in late 1898, President McKinley had asserted that
"the mission of the United States is one of benevolent assimilation,
substituting the mild sway of justice for arbitrary rule."[11] McKinley's
policy and the terms of its articulation held wildly complex resonances
for immigrants. On the one hand, the bitter histories of Anglicization,
Russification, and *Kulturkampf*—histories kept current by the Gaelic
revival, poetic protests like "Jerusalem," or observances of the Third of
May—promoted an interpretation of "benevolent assimilation" as ma-
levolent indeed. Was McKinley's policy not "arbitrary rule" after all?
The dominion of "Anglo-Saxondom" abroad, moreover, mirrored a
fierce Anglo-supremacism at home: the underlying philosophy of "as-
similating" the Philippines to superior Anglo-Saxon culture was not
without its implications for America's non-Anglo residents, including
Hebrews, Celts, and Slavs.

And yet, as white Europeans in a context where white supremacy
and European centrality were the founding assumptions of so much
public discussion, many immigrants could distance themselves from
the Filipinos and adopt American "responsibilities" in the Pacific as
their own. Many were particularly eager, too, to identify as Americans
and to prove themselves loyal American citizens, as the rallies at the
outset of the Spanish-Cuban-American War had demonstrated.

Hence when Michael Kruszka balanced the clauses, "we naturally
sympathize with all other peoples struggling for independence—even
if they be half-savage Malays," he nicely encapsulated immigrants'
perceived stake in the Philippine Question. The "natural sympathy"
professed by Kruszka suggests immigrant nationalism's potential as an
oppositional voice in national politics, beyond the narrow scope of

mere ethnocentrism. While the patricians of the Anti-Imperialist League decried imperialism for the threat it posed to American institutions, and while commentators on the left worried over the threat which Philippine "coolie" labor posed to American workers, immigrant nationalists forged a damning critique of American empire-building based upon a rare empathy with the Filipinos themselves.

Equally important, however, is Kruszka's qualifying *even if*. While the logic of nationalism defined a great deal of immigrant discussion and framed immigrant outrage regarding McKinley's Philippine policy, this empathy did not preclude Eurocentric, racialist conceptions of "civilization" and "savagery" which comfortably cast the Filipinos as "other." Through the prism of race, an unthinkable sympathy with the conquering nation became thinkable for many. *Kuryer Polski* itself, for instance, ultimately went on to describe the Filipinos' character as the chief obstacle to Philippine independence, concluding that these "Malays" had "nothing to lose" by the "protection" of the United States. "In regard to civilization," the journal clarified, "the Polish nation stands higher beyond comparison than the Filipinos." Or, as one letter to the editor of the *Tageblatt* asserted, betraying at once a hierarchical view of racial diversity and an exclusive view of the United States as a nation of white Europeans, "The United States, which was able to educate the Indian and the Negro, will also be able to educate the Filipino."[12]

"My Father saw the whole picture clearly, way back in 1898," recalled Elizabeth Gurley Flynn in her autobiography. "When one understood British imperialism it was an open window to all imperialism."[13] Not all observers saw quite the same thing as they peered at the struggle in the Pacific through their nationalist windows. Swept up by the "glorious" advance of Judeo-Christian civilization, and bowing, in part, to the Herzlian imperative to remain on the best terms possible with all existing powers, the Zionist *Tageblatt* literally joined the nation's "hurrah element": "Our flag now flies over Manila! Hurrah for our flag!"[14] Irish nationalist James Jeffrey Roche, on the other hand, had only harsh (if often comical) words for the imperialists: "The 'White Man's Burden' . . . is never so heavy that he cannot carry it out of the door or window of the house which he has just burglarized." Flynn, too, looked in retrospect upon McKinley's Philippine policy as "ruinous." "As children, we came to hate unjust wars, which took the land and rights away from other peoples."[15]

The varied immigrant responses to American expansionism highlight the complexities of what sociologists like Milton Gordon have called "identificational assimilation."[16] Like the initial campaign for Cuban liberation, the Philippine crisis resonated with the liberationist strains of immigrant culture. Far more than the Cuban cause, however, the Philippine crisis tested the strengths and limits of New and Old World political identifications, bringing the two into logical collision. That immigrant commentators like Patrick Ford, James Jeffrey Roche, Stefan Barszczewski, and Ben Efrim were among the most vociferous, consistent, and empathetic protesters on behalf of Filipino rights is testimony to the salience of Old World aspirations in assessing New World political conduct. That race emerged as the dominant motif by which others resolved this tension suggests the extent to which, for Celtic, Slavic, and Hebrew immigrants, "becoming American" depended upon "becoming Caucasian."

Between Whiteness and Anglo-Saxondom

In December of 1898, before the question of imperialism had flared into guerrilla war at Manila, Humphrey Desmond published a point-by-point manifesto in the *Catholic Citizen* on "Why We Don't Want the Phillipines." Two points in particular revealed the tension between the politics of nation and the politics of race. Point two rejected annexation "Because it is playing England's game in the Orient"; and point four, "Because it means that American citizenship is to be diluted by Malay citizenship, and that America's democracy is to stand the trial of working itself out among inferior people."[17] Although Desmond did direct these arguments of nation and race toward the same anti-imperialist conclusion, the two themes were nonetheless in conflict: one expressed empathy with the potential victims of "England's game" of imperial politics, the other expressed a racialist contempt for those same victims.

Desmond was singularly glib in his racialist dismissals of Filipino rights and in his estimation of peoples of color generally. His support for Cuban intervention itself had been based, in part, on the premise that, by virtue of its racial composition, Cuba was entitled to better treatment than Spain was according it. The colonial politics of plunder "may do in the case of a barbarian or savage race," he had written; "but the Cubans are white men." Later, under the banner "Are They 'Niggers?'" Desmond refuted the claim that Cuban independence would mean "negro rule" over the island. "The heads of the Cuban army and state are white men, and the Cuban centers in this country are also civilized and able men of pure Caucasian blood."[18]

As attention now shifted to the Philippines, Desmond rejected annexation by a similar racialist logic. "Probably the majority of Americans would prefer to be excused from loading this country with another 'negro problem,' " he wrote. "We may swallow a small black morsel like Hawaii; but if we must expand largely, our acquisitions should be civilized Caucasian communities, such as can adapt to our democratic system. Barbarian dominions can never be amalgamated with the American republic; and we want no such satrapies."[19] More directly still, he would cry, "No new negro problem! No Malay annexation policy! No coolie citizens!" or blithely judge that "In the southern states the black population hamper and clog the working of the American system of government." The Philippine population, he argued, would be still worse.[20]

Desmond's judgments were not altogether unique, and perceptions of race thus commonly became a mitigating influence on immigrants' insistence upon Filipino rights. Such racialism was echoed in periodic references to the archipelago's "savage" or "half-savage" population in the *Tageblatt*, the *Abend blatt*, or even in typically sympathetic journals like *Zgoda* and the *Pilot*. " 'The Philippine vote' will become an important, possibly a decisive, factor in a national election," warned the latter. "Dost like the picture?"[21] Others, like Michael Kruszka of *Kuryer Polski*, fully endorsed the U.S. mission of "civilizing" the Filipinos. "The partition of Poland brought the Poles slavery," he asserted, "[but] the taking of the Philippines will bring the Filipinos freedom."[22]

But while some immigrant writers were quick to identify this as a conflict between "white" and "non-white" worlds, others saw the matter much less starkly. "Those miserable foreigners in Manila, Cuba, Porto Rico or wherever you please," commented one sardonic writer in the *Pilot*,

> if they are not ready to accept and adopt every "Yankee notion" offered them, are manifestly unfit for self-government, and our equally manifest duty and destiny is to pitchfork our institutions down their throats, or, failing that, to govern them ourselves in the good old time-honored "Anglo-Saxon" way.
>
> Was it for that end that the war was begun? Ostensibly it was undertaken in the interests of humanity: to put an end to the intolerable sufferings of the Cuban reconcentrados and to rid the western hemisphere of a tyranny at our doors only equalled by that which afflicts another island on the extreme western border of Europe.[23]

As this writer's bitter reference to Anglo-Saxondom suggests, the overall map of immigrant sympathies was complicated by a late-nineteenth-century racial taxonomy which, in this context, nuanced the opposition between "white" America and the "non-white" Pacific islands. It was not just that dearly held principles of national rights and popular Euro-American conceptions of racial hierarchy cross-cut one another in the instance of the Philippine conquest. Rather, the period's conventional articulation of "race" in and of itself offered Irish, Polish, and Yiddish immigrants several possible avenues of self-identification—and hence suggested several different ways of positioning themselves in relation to McKinley and the "Anglo-Saxons" on the one hand, and Aguinaldo and the "Malays" on the other. To the extent that the Philippine war was cast in popular discussion not only as a war of white against nonwhite or of civilization against savagery, but of *Anglo-Saxon* against *non-Anglo-Saxon*, these immigrants could summon alternate logics to locate their interests on either side of the conflict.

The ambiguity derived from the slippage between two distinct but coexisting terms of racial identification in turn-of-the-century America: "white" and "Anglo-Saxon." On the one hand, immigrants from all three European groups were considered (and considered themselves) white—a crucial distinction under the terms of the century-old naturalization law which limited naturalized citizenship to free "white" immigrants. By American law and by less formal conventions of social consensus, immigrants from Ireland and eastern Europe were "white," belonging to a community of whites separate from other communities of non-whites.

The salience of this racial conception was reflected not only in the rights and privileges bestowed upon European immigrants in the United States, but also in the terms of their own identifications of Self and Other in a variety of contexts. The California Irish of the 1870s, for instance, had felt sufficient footing as members of the white community to spearhead an anti-Chinese movement without fear of its lapsing into more generalized agitation against the foreign-born.[24] Similarly, in his memoir of the Indian wars, *Warpath and Bivouac* (1890), Irish nationalist John Finerty drew the line between "whites" and the "aborigines" of North America in the sharpest, most virulent terms possible. Chapter headings like "The Invincible White Man Carries His Point" or "Never Trust a Horse or an Indian" left little doubt as to which side of the racial divide he favored, while the tone of much of his narrative indicated just how wide, in his view, that divide actually was: "The Sioux must be descendants of Cain, and are veritable children of the devil. The rest are a very little behind them, except in point of personal appearance and daring, in which the Sioux excel nearly all other Indians. Most of them are greedy, greasy, gassy, lazy, and knavish."[25]

Conversely, James Jeffrey Roche invoked the same categories of "white" and "other" to decry exactly this kind of virulence. In Roche's poem "The White Wolf's Cry," white supremacist thought is cast as a *self*-indictment:

> We are the Chosen People—look at the hue of our skins!
> Others are black or yellow—that is because of their sins!
>
> We are the heirs of ages, masters of every race,
> Proving our right and title by the bullet's saving grace;
>
> Slaying the naked red man; making the black our slave;
> Flaunting our color in triumph over a world-wide grave;
>
> Wearing the lamb's pure vestment to the unsuspecting feast;
> Flinging it off to show them the conquering Mark of the
>   Beast;
>
> Unto the tropic Edens, where shame was a thing unthought,
> Bearing the fruit of knowledge with the serpent's venom
>   fraught.
>
> Indian, Maori, and Zulu; red man, and yellow, and black;
> White are their bones wherever they met with the White
>   Wolf's pack.
>
> We are the Chosen People—whatever we do is right—
> Feared as men fear the leper, whose skin like our own is
>   white![26]

But "whiteness" in this period did not carry the same meaning that it does in the late twentieth century: both in nineteenth-century science and in popular understanding the white community itself comprised many sharply distinguishable races. The categories "Celt," "Slav," "Hebrew," and "Anglo-Saxon" represented an order of difference deeper than any current notions of "ethnicity." The perceived chasm between them was indicated by Thomas Nast's simianized caricatures of Irish immigrants, by political debate over the "natural" propensities of various peoples for adaptation to American institutions, by phrenological tracts on the European races and their relative merits, and, ultimately, by the concern of biologically minded nativists—Theodore Roosevelt among them—that the high birthrate of "the inferior European races" threatened to alter the essential character of the United States. It was within this framework of racial difference that Charles Francis Adams could worry over the electoral influence of a "Celtic proletariat on the Atlantic coast," or that, in a survey of the Irish countryside, an English observer could remark, "to see white chimpanzees is dreadful."[27]

The term "race" was highly unstable and was applied with a staggering imprecision. It could connote a social difference whose basis was biological, historical, political, psychological, physiological, linguistic, or some combination of these, depending upon the speaker and upon the moment. What did remain stable, however, was the *degree* of difference which the term was understood to describe. As racial theorist Alfred Schultz put it in his early-twentieth-century tract, *Race or Mongrel?*, "The principle that all men are created equal is still considered the chief pillar of strength of the United States. It is a little declamatory phrase, and only one objection can be raised against it, that it does not contain one iota of truth." Schultz employed a variety of vivid analogies to make the point that what are now regarded as ethnic, or cultural, differences were not a matter of culture at all, but of *stock:* "The opinion is advanced that the public schools change the children of all races into Americans. Put a Scandinavian, a German, and a Magyar boy in at one end, and they will come out Americans at the other end. Which is like saying, let a pointer, a setter, and a pug enter one end of a tunnel and they will come out three greyhounds at the other end." Even Schultz's favorable comments on the various races hinge upon this notion of biological difference: "Why do the Jews succeed?" he asked. "Because they deserve to succeed. They belong to a great race, and they kept and do keep that race pure."[28]

Significantly, it was not only from the "Anglo-Saxon" side of the racial divide that Celt, Slav, and Hebrew were held up as coherent and meaningful categories. Recall, for instance, Abraham Cahan's portrait of Yekl as unassimilable, his conception of a *Yiddishkayt* rooted in biology and ever betrayed by the Jew's immutable Semitic features. Years earlier Emma Lazarus had asked whether Judaism was a race or a religion and had emphatically concluded, "*it is both.*" She went on to congratulate the Jews on having "adapted ourselves to the practical requirements of American life without ever losing the fire of our

Oriental blood."[29] And well on into the twentieth century Morris Winchevsky could write of the "historical physiognomy" and "facial distinctiveness" of nations. "I believe in complete faith," he wrote of Jewish identity, "that even if the melting down of other races were to be wished, such a national suicide would be simply impossible for us. The Jewish race is simply stronger by far than the others—and while the other side of the contest would sink into the concoction, the Jew would not."[30]

Likewise, Polish nationalist leader Agaton Giller had described the German colonization of western Poland as a contest between the Teuton and the Slav in which Germany hoped to "distort the Polish-national face of our land" with "Teutonic features."[31] The underlying assumptions of this assessment were shared by the otherwise unsympathetic Alfred Schultz. "One hundred fifty years ago the Poles of Prussia were German-Slavic mongrels," he wrote, "and their worthlessness is proved by every page of their history. The Germans are not anxious to replace the Polish-speaking mongrel with a German-speaking mongrel. They want Germans there. And they are succeeding."[32]

And despite an overall social profile which reflected their earlier arrival and a higher level of acculturation and mobility in the United States, the Irish, too, remained racially distinct in the eyes of many. In his novel of Irish republicanism, *Erin Mor*, John Brennan described assimilation as a cultural veneer overlaying a stubborn biological difference: emigrant children "wore clothing after the manner and form of the wealthiest Americans; until soon, at the theatres and other places of amusement, in the political meetings, and places of assembly generally, it was only by the physiognomy, or the color of their countenances, that one was enabled to distinguish between the children of the Irish exiles and those of the wealthiest Americans."[33] In response to the rampant Anglo-Saxonist agitation for an American alliance with England, a poet for the *Irish World* in the spring of 1898 had likewise struck the chord of immutable racial difference. "Alliance? Never!" he announced to the Anglo-Saxon:

> . . . you are not of the self same race
> Nor blood of the self same clan,
> But Celt and Teuton face to face
> Talk back to you man to man,
> That they never will trust you, hypocrites base,
> And know that no freeman can.[34]

The indignant tone of this protest also indicates that while Celtic or Slavic immigrants accepted the basic categories of differentiation among the white races, many grew increasingly uncomfortable with the rhetoric of the Anglo-Saxon side of the divide in the late nineteenth century. The ascendent definition of the United States as an Anglo-Saxon nation held ominous portents for both the social position of non-Anglos in the domestic sphere and for the nation's conduct in the international sphere. Various spokespersons on both sides of the Atlantic—politicians, reformers, and Protestant clergy—now referred to a natural harmony of interests between the two leading Anglo-Saxon nations, and of a "patriotism of race" by which all Americans should be favorably disposed toward Great Britain. One likely result of America's entrance in European power struggles, according to Chauncy Depew, for instance, would be "the union of the Anglo-Saxon race." A Protestant minister in Brooklyn hailed England as "bone of our bone, flesh of our flesh," while a Boston preacher trumpeted Anglo-Saxondom as "the one great race to whom God has given the endowment to civilize the world." The United States and England, by these lights, were "destined by the Most High to rule this earth."[35]

Political Anglo-Saxonism met with a powerful and manifold resistance on the part of immigrants. The question was especially salient for the Irish, of course, whose historic struggle for sovereignty had long been understood in the racial terms of oppressive Anglo-Saxon privilege and Celtic misery. Such protest included, first, a straightforward objection to the proposed Anglo-American alliance in the familiar nationalist idiom.[36] An Anglo-American alliance, warned the *Pilot*, would mean "that the army and navy of the United States should be used, if necessary, to put down an insurrection in Ireland against English misrule. How do you like it, you who thought you were escaping tyranny forever when you became American citizens?"[37] Throughout 1898 and 1899 popular demonstrations against the entente were staged by the Irish across the country (often as part of their '98 centenary observances). "There are those, born on this soil," cried John Finerty at a rally in Chicago, "who would raise [the Union Jack] up again and unfurl it to insult the American sky, which it had too long disfigured." A mass rally of Poles in Chicago, too, registered opposition on the grounds that "we, Polish-American citizens, can see no reason at all for an alliance between this government, for whose establishment Kościuszko fought and Pułaski died, and that of England or any other monarchical power."[38]

A second, frequently enunciated objection to Anglo-American entente was the racial logic which lay behind it. The remarkable elasticity of the category "Anglo-Saxon" as applied to the United States rendered it an easy target for ridicule. Finley Peter Dunne jested that when the worldwide alliance of Anglo-Saxons is completed (including "the Ancient Ordher iv Anglo-Saxon Hibernyans," "the Pollacky Benivolent Society," and the "Benny Brith," among others), it will be hard going for "th' eight or nine people in th' wurruld that has th' misfortune iv not bein' brought up Anglo-Saxons." In the same vein, James Jeffrey Roche quipped that the Dowager Empress of China's name, Tsi An, was "evidently a corruption of Betsy Ann. Thus does the onward march of Anglo-Saxonism wend its westward way." Those who were foremost in condemning "hyphenated Americanism," he later jabbed, were "always perfectly willing to call us all 'Anglo-Saxons' with the hyphen in full view."[39]

But at the heart of such parody was the wholly serious question: Who is an American? Among the seventy-five million "Anglo-Saxons" in the country, immigrant writers routinely pointed out, were "about 20,000,000 of Irish blood, nearly as many of German, 7,000,000 of African, and at least a dozen million of French, Italian, Polish, Scandinavian, Spanish, Portuguese, etc. . . . No wonder that the Anglo-Saxon race is so powerful."[40] New York's '98 Centenary Committee passed a resolution which denounced Anglo-Saxonism as "an insult to the intelligence of the American people, not one in twenty of whom is, or ever was 'Anglo-Saxon.' " And in an editorial piece striking in the light of late-twentieth-century curricular debates, the *Irish World* questioned the Anglo dominance of public education, which taught "each rising generation of Irish, German, French, Scandinavian, Polish, Italian, and other children that they were the descendants of a class of commercial marauders in England styling themselves the great 'Anglo-Saxon race.' "[41] Patrick Ford elsewhere decried the schemes put forward by "your narrow-minded, little-souled Puritan," and called on immigrants and their children representing every non-Anglo "element" to unite in order to "block the Anglo-Saxon game. We will not be Anglicized!"[42]

Against a backdrop of massive immigration and increasing American diversity, popular Anglo-Saxonist arguments contained two contradictory but finally inseparable impulses: a recognition of (or an insistence upon) racial difference, reflected in the polemics of Anglo superiority; and a denial of racial difference, reflected in a stubborn erasure of American diversity. The ardent Anglo-Saxonist could bemoan the increasing number of racial "inferiors" in the country while at the same time defining the United States unproblematically as Anglo-Saxon. Irish activist T. St. John Gaffney sought to lay bare the political dynamic of this Janus-faced racialism. "The 'Anglo-Saxon race,'" he argued,

> which, according to the best informed ethnical students, is but one tenth of the population of this country, is accredited with a much larger portion of the upbuilding of this Republic than it deserves . . . The moment a Teuton or a Celt achieves fame in the world of letters, art, or professional life, the moment he wins a victory on land or sea, he is hailed as a new product of "Anglo-Saxon" civilization! But if he winds up in the police court in the morning, he is regarded simply as a drunken German or Irish-man.[43]

But, again, while immigrant writers may have dismissed Anglo-Saxonism as a "solemn and persistently asseverated piece of nonsense" or "an ethnological lie,"[44] at bottom they rejected neither the fundamental racial distinction between "Anglo-Saxon" and "other" nor the level of perceived difference such racial distinctions represented. Most accepted the fundamental categories, and challenged only the Anglo-Saxonists' imprecise application of the racial scheme and the presumption of Anglo supremacy. Thus, an article under the banner "Two Race Elements That Should Unite" called for a political alliance of Irish and French Canadian immigrants, because "in the veins of both flows the Celtic blood." Another writer complained that "the great currents of Teutonic and Celtic blood flowing through the veins of the nation count for nothing" in the current climate of rampant Anglo-Saxonism.[45] And James Jeffrey Roche could counter the Anglo-Saxonist denunciation of the highly prolific "lower races" and their biological impact on the nation without altering that argument's fundamental premise. "Let the Anglo-Saxon call the roll of his relations," Roche wrote with some satisfaction, "and confess, with shame, that a grand race like that of the Puritan and pilgrim is vanishing . . . The fittest will always survive, when they care to do so."[46] These writers thus identified the contest between Saxon and Celt in the very same terms of the staunchest Anglo-Saxonists.

As the United States stepped onto the stage of international politics at the century's end, racialist assumptions of fundamental difference, of Anglo-Saxon greatness, and of the nation's racial "duty" to the "lower races" served as a mainspring for public discussion of U.S.

policy. As early as 1885, enthralled by a vision of the religio-racial destiny of *Our Country*, evangelist Josiah Strong had predicted that the world was to "enter upon a new stage of its history—*the final competition of races for which the Anglo-Saxon is being schooled. If* I do not read amiss," he had ventured, "this powerful race will move down upon Mexico, down upon Central and South America, out upon the islands of the sea, over upon Africa and beyond."[47]

Similar conceptions of the racial order of world politics now guided the debate over the Philippine Question. William Howard Taft, for instance, allowed that the Filipinos would need a hundred fifty years of U.S. tutelage to develop "Anglo-Saxon political principles and skills." Theodore Roosevelt concurred, doubting that independence alone could transform the "pirates and headhunters" of the Philippines into "a dark-hued New England town meeting." For Roosevelt, moreover, U.S. military adventure and ultimate control of the Philippines was as necessary for the Anglo-Saxon as it was for the Malay: imperialism was but one manifestation of that "masterful instinct which alone can make a race great."[48] And none was as unbridled in his enthusiasm for racial conquest as Senator Albert Beveridge of Indiana. In a gloss of American history fully Whitmanesque in its sweep and its energy (and, indeed, in its capacity for global absorption), Beveridge celebrated "the Anglo-Saxon impulse" whose "watchword [in Jefferson's time] and whose watchword throughout the world today is 'Forward!' "[49]

Anglo-Saxonist versions of the Philippine crisis and of the necessities of U.S. policy were not limited to the political podium but infused American popular culture as well. As one popular souvenir book of *Exciting Experiences in Our Wars with Spain and the Filipinos* (1899) had it, "[the Filipino is] capable of considerable physical effort, yet much indisposed to make it, and not possessing a disposition for prolonged exertion, being utterly devoid of the faculty of steady, persistent pegging away at things, so characteristic of the Anglo-Saxon."[50] Other Anglo-Saxonist representations ranged from the racialized depictions of the war in political caricature to the hierarchical taxonomy presented in the ethnological exhibits of the Pan-American Exhibition in Buffalo (1901). One turn-of-the-century soap advertisement rather suggestively promised, "Anglo-American Alliance and Pears' Soap: Changing the Complexion of the World."[51]

Hence the framing of trans-Pacific expansion as a meeting of the white and nonwhite worlds coexisted with its alternate definition as a contest between Anglo-Saxons and their pitiable inferiors. By the terms of this latter definition, the interests of Celts, Slavs, and He-brews by no means rested unequivocally with the United States. When, upon reviewing the American troops in the Philippines, Albert Beveridge lauded "these thoroughbred soldiers from the plantations of the South, [and] from the plains and valleys and farms of the west," he was distinguishing the "Saxon type" not only from the "Malay" enemy but from the non-Saxon types of the United States as well. "The fine line is everywhere," he wrote, reflecting the (typically exclusionary) aesthetic of male beauty which so often accompanies militarist na-tionalism: "The nose is straight, the mouth is sensitive and delicate. There are very few bulldog jaws. There is, instead, the steel-trap jaw of the lion. The whole face and figure is the face and figure of the thoroughbred fighter, who has always been the fine-featured, delicate-nostriled, thin-eared, and generally clean-cut featured man."[52]

One rejoinder to this racialized view of American military impera-tives and successes was to publicize the fact that war heroes like General Funston and Captain Byrnes were members of "the fighting race."[53] "The American is neither Anglo-Saxon nor Celt, nor Ger-man, nor French, nor anything else individually," commented the *Pilot*, and, certainly, whatever successes the country enjoyed were due to its diversity and not to Anglo-Saxon pluck.[54]

More common, however, were direct challenges to the righteous-ness of "Anglo-Saxon principle." "Either it is or is not a good and desirable thing for the United States to join with England and 'rule the world,' as the clap-trap phrase goes, on 'Anglo-Saxon principles,'" wrote James Jeffrey Roche; "but it is surely a better thing to obey the eleventh commandment and mind our own business, leaving the rul-ing of the world to its Ruler."[55] Elsewhere, in a fit of Celtic despair, Roche lamented the interventionist policies in Samoa and especially the participation of Irish-Americans in the ranks of the U.S. military there. "The superior 'Anglo-Saxon' . . . will let the foolish 'foreigner' do the work," he remarked, "while he . . . 'sits on the fence and does the heavy work of supervising.' That is what Anglo-Saxon civilization means the world over, and we are not sure that it is anything other than the 'inferior races' who submit to it deserve."[56]

Responses to the cross-currents of national and racial politics varied a great deal within each of these immigrant groups. On the one hand, Robert Ellis Thompson could heartily reject Anglo-American entente, but then let slip this telling piece of Eurocentrism: "it is sixty years too late for this talk of an identity of either blood or interest between the two countries. America is a great composite nation, in which all

European nationalities are represented."[57] Writers in the *Pilot*, on the other hand, true to the memory of Boyle O'Reilly's crusades for racial justice—whether on behalf of Modoc Indians, the California Chinese, or African-Americans—generally showed a greater sensitivity to questions of diversity and a greater empathy with the oppressed of all colors. (As O'Reilly himself had put it on the occasion of a skirmish between the U.S. government and the Modoc Indians, the Irish had "too much and too old a sympathy with people badly governed, to join in this shameful cry for Modoc blood.")[58] Likewise, letters to the editor of the *Tageblatt* ran roughly half-and-half on the Philippine Question. While some denounced the islands' "half-savage revolutionaries" and despaired of ever bringing order to this "savage country of mulattoes," others felt that America must not enslave those who were "beautiful and right before God." Still others agreed with the administration that the Filipinos were not ready for self-government: the Filipino rebel was "like a sick child who will not take the medicine the doctor prescribed."[59]

But despite the considerable range of opinion, a few broad patterns are discernible. Given the emotive power which the very word "Anglo" held for the Irish, commentators in this group were more likely than the others to dwell on the language of Anglo-Saxonism and on the connections among the British empire, Anglo-American rapprochement, and McKinley's "large policies" in the Pacific. Poles, less obsessed with notions of specifically Anglo-supremacism, shared with the Irish a certain bitterness on questions of racial supremacy as expressed in the discourse on "civilization." Both groups had been long-standing objects of a rhetoric of "barbarism" and "civilization" in their homelands. The phrase "unfit for self-government" had long been in operation to describe the necessity of English rule in Ireland: the Celt, as Matthew Arnold summarized, was "undisciplinable, anarchical, and turbulent of nature." And Bismarck, for his part, had urged the Poles of the Prussian territories to participate in "the benefits of civilization offered to you by the Prussian state." One instance of national sensitivity on this issue came up in 1899, a few weeks into the Philippine war, when, during one of their many political observances, the Poles of Milwaukee denounced "the arrogant pretension of German chauvinism" and its "civilizing mission" among the Slavs.[60]

Hence writers in these two groups were particularly zealous in their criticism of the reigning notions of civilization which came into play as the United States sought hegemony in the Pacific. This bit of political doggerel, cast as an exchange between Uncle Sam, still "green" when it comes to imperialist methods, and the expert John Bull, exposed the brutality behind the civilizing mission and the thievery behind open door economics:

> Said Samuel Green, a 'prentice hand:
> "I don't exactly understand.
> Suppose this heathen locks his store,
> and don't give us an open door?"
> But Burglar Bull he winked his eye:
> "Open a winder then, says I.
> And if he kicks when we surprise him,
> Let's take our clubs and civilize him!"[61]

James Jeffrey Roche was especially prolific on this subject, both in his editorials and his fiction. "The Samoan language is queer," ran a characteristic barb in the *Pilot*. "It has no word to signify inhospitality or ingratitude . . . When we shall have sufficiently civilized them, their vocabulary will be enlarged even if they have to learn English in order to comprehend the fullness of baseness."[62]

His novel of the "Orient," *The Sorrows of Sap'ed* (1904), was Roche's fullest (and last) parodic treatment of this theme. As in his earlier work in the same vein, *Her Majesty the King*, much of the humor of *Sorrows* is cast in the form of anti-imperialist irony. When a ship is sighted off the coast of Roche's fictional Asian land, for instance, a wave of terror overtakes the villagers as word spreads of its identity: "I fear me much it is the *Helping Hand*. She has been cruising in these waters of late, after her performances in the China seas, and I have little hope but that her mission is civilizing." Everyone is much relieved to discover that it is only a pirate ship, and that it is on no such (hostile) civilizing mission after all. ("You will do well another time," remarks the indignant pirate captain, "to think twice ere you make rash judgments about a ship which has done you no injury—as yet." But, he has to admit, "Maybe the mistake was natural . . .")[63]

The Polish press, too, routinely featured this kind of satire. *Straż* pointed out the much publicized abuses and frauds within the U.S. military as "a good example of civilization for the Filipinos"; and the journal printed its own satiric ballad, "Oh, Civilization Is with Us!", a catalogue of the inglorious features of American civilization—the Kentucky lynch-law, the hypocrisies involved in the persecution of Mormons in Utah, the fleecing of the poor by bankers, the gunning down of workers who "driven by poverty went on strike." The poem ends with a bitter comment on race-as-justification for U.S. domination of the Philippines:

> Oh, civilization is with us,
> And those Tagalogs are savages!
> You don't believe it? You can doubt it?!
> They look dark, like a shoe.[64]

Dziennik Chicagoski raised similar objections in an editorial on "The Americans as Culture-Bearers" [*kulturtraegerzy*]. The word *kulturtraegerzy*, a Polonized version of a German word, brought the full range of Polish liberationist connotations to bear on McKinley's proclamation that the United States would be "supreme" on the archipelago. A piece on Aguinaldo's protest against the establishment of English as the "official" language of the Philippines carried similar symbolic freight from the de-Polonizing era of Bismarck's *Kulturkampf*. In denouncing the arrogance of McKinley's imperial policies, the journal cited Admiral Dewey's own favorable estimation of the political capability of the Filipinos (from an earlier time, when he and Aguinaldo had been allies) and questioned the logic by which the United States seemed willing to kill off half the Filipino population in order to "lift" the other half out of "barbarism." In Manila, as in Poland, violence and victimization seemed to be among the chief "blessings of civilization."[65]

Jewish immigrants, by contrast, had a very different perception of the question of civilization and savagery. Anti-Semitism had generated a range of negative images and had branded the Jews in a variety of ways, but the charge of savagery was not chief among them. On the contrary, where Jews were despised they were most often despised for a kind of overcivilization: they were seen as shrewd manipulators, Europe's (and now America's) scheming middlemen and usurers. (The ancient "blood libel"—that Jews needed Christian blood for their Passover rituals—was an exception.) Their alleged crimes were more often conceived to be crimes of intellect and cunning, not of violence or brutishness. Shylock, in short, was no barbarian.[66]

Jewish commentators did occasionally question the premise of America's civilizing mission in the Philippines. The *Abend blatt* noted with some irony that "Aguinaldo, whom the Americans represent in the shape of a murderous and ridiculous savage . . . wrote two long letters to General Otis about human rights and international jurisprudence."[67] A cartoon in the *Nayer geyst* depicted McKinley's exported civilization as a Filipino card game taking place in the jungle.[68] And a *Naye tzayt* essay entitled "Are the Filipinos Savage?" dismantled the *noblesse oblige* at the heart of much expansionist polemic. At the time Spain took the Philippines under Philip II, the piece explained, "in Manila rifles, swords, bayonets, and spears were already being made (what better sign do you need of civilization?)"[69]

But Jewish observers were generally far more detached than their Irish and Polish counterparts on this question of political tutelage. Some, indeed, fully embraced the notions of civilization and savagery as legitimate descriptions of the Judeo-Christian world on the one hand, and the allegedly heathen world on the other. A colony, wrote A. Manenbaum in an explanatory piece for the *Tageblatt*, is "a country or an island, it doesn't matter which, where savage or half-savage, uncivilized people live, whom a civilized government wants to civilize."[70] Here as elsewhere the very terms of discussion, the unquestioning acceptance of hierarchical categories, precluded any analogies between the Jewish and Filipino struggles for political sovereignty.

The disinclination of Jews to identify with the Filipinos was reflected, on one end of the political spectrum, by a wholehearted endorsement of the civilizing terms of American expansion. The *Tageblatt* editorial staff drew an ingenious Biblical analogy to equate McKinley's policy of imperial conquest with Mosaic *liberation*. The Filipinos, in this configuration, played the Levites to McKinley's Moses:[71] Moses himself had to "fight with swords against those he freed from Egypt because they did not understand his plan and the path along which he led them." Likewise, Aguinaldo and his followers were "so savage and confused by their freedom that they do not recognize their liberators and their friends." The transition to true freedom, explained the journal, "works like the emergence from a dark cellar into a bright, light place where the sun warms and shines. It dazzles the eyes and raises a clamor in the head and causes one to mistake a friend for an enemy."[72] If the Filipinos of this representation were implied to be perfectible, they nonetheless had a long, long way to go in relation to their "civilized" counterparts: "the savage people there are like babies who break the bottle which nourishes them."[73]

This rhetoric of civilization and its underlying assumptions of difference allowed Jewish spokespersons not only to side with the United States, but fully to participate and glory in the imperialist achievement. Zionists such as Gustave Gottheil applauded the extension of religious rights to the "Jews" and "infidels" of Spain's former colonies. The *Tageblatt* reveled in the prospective fruits of cultural imperialism:

"The time is not far off," the journal cheered, "when the *Yiddishes tageblatt* will be sold on the stands in Manila; and naturally, where the *Tageblatt* is read, all Jewish feelings and ideas live on." And a writer in a prominent Reform organ, *The American Israelite*, remarked that the United States should not Christianize the inhabitants of the former colonies, as so many Protestant spokesmen seemed to want, but should Judaize them. In any case it was the specifics of the mission which were questioned or modified; the hierarchical relationship existing between the United States and the Philippines and the righteousness of the mission itself were beyond reproach in the eyes of these commentators.[74]

On the Yiddish left, meanwhile, two very different lines of political argument reflected a similar distancing from the plight of the Filipinos. Inasmuch as the archipelago was to serve as the United States' stepping-stone to the commerce of China, first of all, the Philippine Question reignited American labor's fear of the "yellow peril" (*geler shrek*, in Yiddish)—imported "coolie labor" from Asia. Writers in the Yiddish socialist journals characteristically regarded imperialism as a tragedy for the American worker, with relatively little concern for the matter of Philippine independence and the protection of Filipino rights. What will happen, one writer in the *Abend blatt* wanted to know, "when the American capitalists import the Filipinos to America as scabs?"[75]

Benjamin Feygenbaum warned that Asia's further integration into Euro-American economic networks would have dire consequences not only for workers but for small entrepreneurs as well. Citing the case of San Francisco cigar manufacturers in the 1850s, he asserted that "the native small businessmen will also know a little song to sing about the Chinese competition." As for white workers, "protected" for the moment by the Chinese Exclusion Act, "what will Exclusion help if the Philippine islands become 'ours' and through them 'we' 'open China'?" Like the white workers of the 1870s who had agitated against Chinese immigration, the Yiddish left in 1899 tended to look upon Filipinos not as fellow proletarians but as potential tools of capital in America's ongoing class struggle.[76]

A second argument, staked out on a more theoretical plane and not necessarily consistent with the first, took a cold, scientific view of the struggle between American capitalists and Filipino rebels. Rooted in the logic of the evolutionary stages of civilization and the developmental stages of capitalism, socialist arguments often wrote off the Filipino peasantry as necessary casualties to the "natural" progression of industrialization. As Karl Kautsky had framed the issue, the taking of the Philippines and the opening of China were both inevitable and good: "Each step forward that capitalism makes in Asia," he asserted, "means a step forward toward socialism in Europe and America." Hence Benjamin Feygenbaum concluded that, "It is not our place to join hands with either the expansionists or the anti-expansionists in the struggle either for or against colonial rule." There was little to be done on the behalf of the Filipinos until they had become a true, industrialized proletariat.[77]

Across the Yiddish political spectrum from right to left, then, there was an implicit consensus on racial hierarchy limiting expressions of empathy with the Asians who had become the objects of American imperialism. While the *Tageblatt* endorsed the scientific principle that the world's diverse races all "stem from one father,"[78] most Yiddish comment departed from the empathy (albeit ambivalent) which characterized Irish and Polish writings of solidarity with the "Malay" rebels. The *Abend blatt* described one Philippine tribe as "very dirty and savage," and declared that many among the Filipino population "remain in the same state of savagery [*wildkayt*] in which the Spaniards found them."[79] The journal lapsed into the crass Americanism of referring to Chinese people as "John Chinaman"; and even favorable comment on the peoples of the Pacific basin reflected the essentialist, Orientalist "othering" typical of the period's travel writing. Maoris, for instance, were "the most beautiful race in the world": "They love fresh flowers, the blue sky, the golden rays of the sun, the little silver clouds which run high-high overhead and become hidden behind the mountain . . . [they love] all of beautiful, fresh nature, to which they are bound with the devoted feeling of true nature-children."[80]

The Filipino rebels, however, were characterized in the *Tageblatt* early on as "half-wild men about which every barbaric action can be believed." Significantly, as it became clear that the war in the Philippines was to be more than a mere skirmish—that the savages could hold their own against the civilized United States—the editor did not question his own assumptions about them but rather *re-racialized* the Filipinos to bring their image into line with known racialist "truths." "In the appearance of his face and the skeleton of his head," the *Tageblatt* now announced with certainty, "Aguinaldo looks like a European rather than a Filipino Asiatic. He is not tall, but he can pass for a handsome man even in a civilized country."[81]

As the *Tageblatt's* nimble revision of Aguinaldo into a European suggests, consistency was not necessarily among the hobgoblins which plagued political commentary on the Philippines. The immigrant presses differed little from the mainstream, English-language press in this respect—this was, after all, a time when Theodore Roosevelt could boast that he had "not a drop" of English blood and yet fully partake of the glories of triumphant Anglo-Saxondom.

To be sure, the broad generalizations sketched out above are not without their instances of contradiction. Yiddish commentators were on occasion as sympathetic to the Filipinos as their Polish or Irish counterparts. Despite the Asians' backwardness in industrial evolution, Benjamin Feygenbaum (after Kautsky) was able to cite certain traditions of collectivity in Asian culture and suggest that the proto-socialist savage had a thing or two to teach the civilized Yankee individualist.[82] The generally sympathetic Polish papers, on the other hand, ran occasional letters to the editor rehearsing the familiar "coolie labor" argument, or described the "Polynesian race" as "distinguished by extreme ugliness of body and by savagery." Like the *Tageblatt*, *Zgoda* associated the islands' political activism and activists with "European blood."[83]

Or again, side by side on the very same page, the *Irish-American* ran columns which denounced "Saxon 'Civilization'" on the one hand and the "Filipino Banditti" on the other. The first column exposed the military brutality of the Saxons in the Sudan and denounced John Bull as "the same brutal savage, to-day, that he was when he burned the French heroine, Joan of Arc, at the stake in the marketplace of Rouen." And yet the second urged the United States to settle the "bandit demands" of Aguinaldo and the Filipino insurgents "with powder and lead, which are the only arguments which will bring such savages to their senses."[84]

Despite such inconsistencies and the overall diversity of opinion, however, it is clear that immigrant allegiances in this conflict between the imperial United States and the insurgent Philippines were largely mapped out on the terrain of race and racialism. Positions varied dramatically from one observer to the next—from Khasriel Sarasohn, who genuinely believed that only American tutelage could liberate the Filipinos, to Stanisław Szwajkart, who saw Prussian arrogance and villainy in every instance of imperial "culture-bearing." But each argument regarding the "benevolence" of McKinley's Philippine policy hinged upon how the speaker chose to locate him or herself in relation to the white community as a white European, and in relation to the Anglo-Saxon community as a Hebrew, a Slav, or a Celt.

That the cultural manufacture of Caucasians seems to have depended upon moments of divisiveness like Chinese Exclusion or the conquest of the Philippines bespeaks a certain malevolence inherent in the terms of American assimilation. But many immigrant spokespersons rejected white supremacist or Eurocentric arguments and went on to forge bitter, heartfelt, and empathetic polemics on Filipino rights. Indeed, the cartoon in *Dziennik Chicagoski* that embodied America's aspirations of aggrandizement in a nearly bestial caricature of Theodore Roosevelt may have been both a response to, and a rejection of, the racialist terms of the imperialism debate. Bedecked in self-promotional labels such as "The hat I wore at Santiago" or blaring slogans like "Long Live Me!", the Roosevelt of these depictions is toothy, wild-eyed, uncontrolled, unspeakably silly, and yet unmistakably dangerous—much like the popular racialist imagery of Aguinaldo, in other words. These fierce depictions of Roosevelt, or the same cartoonist's quip, "in cannon we trust," indicate the vehemence with which immigrants—as non-Anglos, as nationalist partisans, as citizens of an imagined community whose scope was international—could break with their adopted country, however dearly held was the prospect of "becoming American."[85]

The Question of National Independence

"Uncle, why do the Americans call their war with Spain a 'war of liberation?' " a child asks in an editorial sketch by Ben Efrim. "Because the war has liberated the American people from many illusions regarding their economic and political masters; because it has liberated Spain from her colonies; and because it has liberated Cuba from every hope of independence."[86] Ben Efrim was but one of many who saw the denial of independence as the gist of his adopted country's policy in the former Spanish colonies. Even when the objects of domination in this case were identified as racial Others, immigrant commentators in all three groups recognized and understood the dynamics of imperialist "benevolence" from a victim's perspective.

When the possibility of Hawaiian annexation was under discussion in 1897, Patrick Ford had argued that to adopt such a policy would be "to copy the worst precedents set by the British and other nation-destroying empires."[87] When some had objected to U.S. intervention in Cuba on the grounds that the Cubans were "[merely] mongrel negroes, Indians, and Spaniards, savage and disorderly," Stefan Barszczewski answered that Poles, as Poles, were bound to fight for the *principle* of liberty in every known instance—regardless of the specifics of race or clime.[88] When China became the object of imperial rivalry among the Western powers, *Kuryer Polski* announced flatly that, "What is happening in China is what happened in Poland a hundred years ago."[89] When the question arose as to how the United States would learn to rule Spain's newly freed colonies, Ben Efrim had likened American militarism to that of the Russian Czars, who, "with several tens of thousands" of soldiers at hand, "can rule without learning how."[90]

The hallmark of immigrant anti-imperialism as events unfolded in Manila was an undying insistence upon the broad principle of national rights, whose emotive, logical, and polemic energy derived from the narrower specifics of Old World cases.[91] Francis Hodur of the Polish National Catholic Church found an analogue of his own schismatic movement in the emergent Philippine National Church—a similar effort to free local liturgical practice and church properties from "foreign domination."[92] The *Pilot* remarked that the United States had "adopted with the Filipinos the English way of treating Irish Home Rule . . . viz., 'killing with kindness.' " And Roche seemed to speak for activists of all three groups when he asked frankly, "If it is sweet and glorious to die for one's country, is it not bitter and shameful to die for the enslavement of another's?"[93]

The parallels were evidently as deeply felt as they were sharply drawn. In an agonized, page-one editorial during the early weeks of fighting in Manila, Barszczewski took up the question of the PNA's official position on American imperialism. By charter, he acknowledged, *Zgoda* was to avoid mixing in America's partisan politics and was to concentrate purely on Polish nationalist politics. But American imperialism *was* ultimately an issue of Polish nationalist portent, he concluded: not as a Republican, Democrat, Populist, or Socialist, but as a Pole, he wrote, he could not remain indifferent to those "new currents" in American politics which might lead "the United States along a completely new path, completely change the relationships of all the states of the world, and influence the fate of the Polish cause." Barszczewski conceded that some might regard America's ascendence to world power as a potential benefit to Poland; but, he concluded, as Poles, "we do not agree with the trend of a politics of conquest, which has appeared on American ground."[94] "Our opinion, at any rate," he later explained,

is that the Filipinos are defending their independence, and our government should not be treating them as it is. Before the beginning of the war every American newspaper called the Cubans revolutionaries fighting for freedom, and now the same papers call the Filipinos a band of rebels. It does not jibe. It could very well be that the Filipinos are completely incapable of self-government; but that does not exclude their right of fighting for the liberty of their native land.[95]

This concern for Filipino rights united Barszczewski with his cross-town rivals in the religionist PRCU. In assessing the stakes of the 1900 presidential election, for instance, Kazimierz Neuman asserted that "First and foremost is the matter of the Filipinos, the Puerto Ricans and other 'conquered' nations. What does that have to do with us? Oh, it concerns us enormously." "Poles, as Poles," he echoed, "knowing what bondage to an alien country means, drawn to the United States by the liberty and equality of *all* peoples," must condemn a politics of national bondage. The Filipinos "demand, and have a right to demand, that their liberty is honored"; America's "beautiful-sounding phrases" regarding Spanish tyranny and Cuban independence would mean nothing if McKinley were merely to throw a new yoke over the necks of the liberated colonies.[96]

Patrick Ford similarly saw in American imperialism not only an injustice, but a very familiar kind of injustice. "There is a certain amount of fitness in having the era of imperialism inaugurated with this blood guiltiness," he intoned at the outbreak of hostilities. "It is a forecast of what is to come. If we choose to follow in England's footsteps it may be expected that we shall duplicate her crimes against God and humanity." Ford was especially prolific in his *Irish World* comparisons between the aims, logics, and methods of the United States in the Philippines and of England in Ireland, India, and the Sudan. McKinley, he later summarized, "takes England for his model."[97]

In its reluctance to paint parallels between the plight of the Filipinos and the plight of the Jews, the Yiddish press departed significantly from the Irish and Polish presses. As noted earlier, the most vocal Zionist organ, the *Tageblatt*, found ways of approving and applauding American expansionism as Mosaic liberation. Socialist journals denounced American imperialism, from their perspective, as the logical outgrowth of capitalism. "Murder-patriotism" had been masquerading as a "love of humanity" in the crusade for Cuba; but now, as events unfolded in the Pacific, "The Mask Is Off!" "The whole story," remarked the *Abend blatt*, "shows once again clear as day that all the talk about justice, humanity, freedom, holy traditions, morality, and all beautiful things has all the substance of wax in a hot spell."[98]

Yet commentators like Krantz and Feygenbaum had few words of sympathy for the Filipino independence movement. Cosmopolitanists, indeed, treated Filipino nationalism in much the way they treated Bundist nationalism among the Jews: in the face of the inevitable and mechanistic forces at work in class struggle and the progression from feudalism to capitalism to socialism, Aguinaldo's uprising was an irrelevance at best. In March 1899, Krantz predicted that the Filipinos would lose, and that over the course of generations they would "melt together with the Americans, like all the immigrants who come to our republic."[99]

The *Forverts* did bewail McKinley's intention, namely, to "kill off an innocent nation, the Filipinos, in order to give the capitalists a market for the wares which their slaves, the workers, have produced for them."[100] But expressions of solidarity with that "innocent nation" in the Pacific were rather scarce overall. Likely because the earlier predictions of its bitterest rival, the *Abend blatt*, had come true—the glorious U.S. intervention in Cuba, that is, *had* become an imperialist crusade—the editors of the *Forverts* sought to bury the entire issue of expansionism. In a prevailing climate of competition and rivalry in which, for instance, the editors of the two journals might haggle over whose May Day parade was the larger and more successful, the *Forverts* staff had good reason in the spring of 1899 to hope that their prowar stance of a year earlier might be forgotten.[101] When the journal took up the Philippine Question at all, it most often did so in a language which collapsed imperialism and monopolism, granting little special attention to the Filipinos as such.

The *Forverts* did, however, demonstrate a marked skepticism toward American claims of early and easy victory over the Filipinos, and comments on the military prospects were one barometer of any given observer's degree of empathy toward the Filipino insurgents. The enthusiastically expansionist *Tageblatt*, for instance, repeatedly predicted an early end to the fighting. The journal ran without question what one scholar has called General Otis's expressions of "sublime optimism": that each skirmish would be "the last stroke of the war," and that victory was ever at hand.[102] Though far less charitable toward Otis, the *Abend blatt*, too, saw no chance for a Filipino victory. Journals like *Zgoda*, *Dziennik Chicagoski*, and the *Forverts*, on the other hand, immediately doubted Otis's reports that "order" had been restored and consistently presented Aguinaldo's guerrilla tactics as ensuring a long, protracted war. *Dziennik Chicagoski* expected "yearlong guerrilla battles" which would be more difficult than the American "chauvinists" supposed. The Filipinos would fight for their freedom "with the same doggedness against the Americans as they fought against the Spaniards," and this unexpected war would be more trying and costly than the battles against Spain in Cuba and Puerto Rico. (Even if the United States won, commented Szwajkart, lobbing shells "at naked savages armed with bows" would not bring much glory to U.S. troops.)[103]

James Jeffrey Roche raised skepticism toward U.S. claims of "progress" to a minor satiric art form. He remarked in April: "Dispatches from the Philippines show that our forces have advanced at least one square mile after each victory. At this rate we should be able to overrun the whole country in about a thousand weeks, or, say, twenty years, if we continue to win victories." In May he reiterated, "The Philippine 'rebels' have been conquered again, for about the twentieth time since the breaking out of hostilities. They are evidently getting used to being annihilated. But how long can our troops survive such a series of victories?" And in July he mocked: "If we keep putting down the 'rebellion' in the Philippines at the present rate, our forces, or as many of them as escape, will be able to evacuate the islands before many weeks."[104]

More somber were commentators in *Zgoda*, who sighed, "Every day a handful of young people dissappear from the ranks, all because the Filipinos want to be free." Here American deaths were defined as the result of legitimate Filipino aspirations, and Filipino deaths were often the product of atrocity, not valor: the U.S. army, noted the journal, shoots "not only at fighting Filipinos, but also destroys every coastal hamlet, killing off unarmed residents, women and children." *Zgoda* charted the dubious progress of the war within a framework of nationalist legitimacy and its antithesis; American expansion meant primarily the extension of violence and oppression.[105]

The *Irish World*, too, questioned the benevolence the United States extended to the former Spanish colonies. Noting the high emigration rates from Puerto Rico, Ford wondered why " 'benevolent assimilation' is driving the natives into exile." And as the fighting in the Philippines became fiercer, so did both the *Irish World's* denunciations of U.S. conduct and its open identification with the Filipino rebels. As incidents of the brutal conduct of the troops under General Adna Chaffee and "Hell Roarin' Jake" Smith came to light, Ford commented that, while "England long since was steeled to such horrors," proper Americans could only be appalled.[106] Under the headline "That Benevolent Assimilation" in 1900, the *Irish World* reported that

U.S. soldiers had employed torture to discover the locations of Filipino arms caches. The soldiers in the Philippines looked upon the water cure as "a huge joke," confessed one American. "A little over a hundred years ago," commented Ford, "similar 'huge jokes' were perpetrated in Ireland by British soldiers ... Your 'Anglo-Saxon' has on more than one occasion shown himself an adept at such 'jokes.' "[107]

Ford likewise pronounced General Chaffee "The Cromwell of the Philippines," and averred, "Today the descendants of the Irishmen who fought Cromwell are proud of their brave resistance just as future generations of Filipinos will feel proud of their fathers, who are now fighting Chaffee."[108] And when General Jacob Smith's infamous "kill and burn" order came to light, revealing the U.S. resolve to make Samar "a howling wilderness," Ford was quick to note that Smith's defenders were largely vocal "Anglo-Maniacs." In a defense of Smith offered by Henry Cabot Lodge, for instance, Ford heard "an echo of the nasal cant of his Puritan forebears who in Cromwell's time defended the atrocities perpetrated upon the Irish."

> In Ireland, as in the Philippines, the murderers of unarmed men, of defenseless women and of innocent children were foreigners bent upon robbing a people of their country and of their liberty. History repeats itself. The Filipinos are tortured as the Irish were in Cromwell's time, and a descendant of the Puritan lifts his voice in a defense of this method of treating a people who are unwilling to surrender voluntarily all that men hold dear.[109]

It was this interpretation of events which prompted the *Pilot* to counsel Irish-American volunteers to leave the ranks as soon as possible. "The American soldier who enlisted for the freeing of Cuba did not enlist for the enslaving of the Philippines," Roche insisted.[110] At least one Irish soldier who had fought to free the Philippines from Spain now refused to support an "unjust U.S. policy now that Philippine liberation had been achieved"; and the *Irish World* reported with some satisfaction that, despite huge bonuses being offered by the army, the reenlistment rate among American volunteers in the Philippines was a slim seven percent.[111]

Such open identification with a national enemy could not stand without considerable comment and justification. As Senator John Spooner (Wisconsin) had said during the final debate on the Treaty of Paris, "while our boys over there, your brothers and mine, are fighting for life against a wanton and willful attack upon the part of the

Filipinos, it is not for us to send messages of comfort to their enemies." The logic that "our boys' " lives depend upon this or that political stance has ever had a considerable power to chill dissent. If anti-imperialists in the Senate and among the New England Mugwumps dodged frequent charges of "copperheadism" or "treason," then the newest, as yet "unproven" American citizens were more vulnerable still to the various charges of insufficient Americanism.[112] Even the vociferous Roche had backpedaled momentarily after the Senate's ratification of the Treaty of Paris: "We do not agree with the ultra imperialists who maintain that it is treason to question the purposes of the Senate or of the Administration," he sighed, "but we recognize the fact that the decision is final under the Constitution, and must be accepted by all loyal citizens."[113]

In their national *sejm* in Grand Rapids, Michigan, in 1899, the Polish National Alliance went further, passing a resolution of unalloyed devotion to its adopted country and its policies. "We . . . express our highest respect, love, and attachment to the flag of the United States," the resolution began, "under which we can enjoy liberty, and live in freedom and equality, as, unfortunately, our foe does not allow us in our Fatherland."

> The United States will ever find in us loyal and faithful citizens, who in every necessity are prepared to stand up in defense of liberty and in defense of the star-spangled banner.
>
> Just as Kościuszko and Puɫaski fought under this flag, just as the Kościuszko Guard of Milwaukee, Wisconsin, went to the field in Cuba's war of independence, just as hundreds of our countrymen fought on that island, pouring out their blood in defense of liberty, just as hundreds of our countrymen are currently fighting for the honor of the flag of the United States in the Philippines— always and everywhere the Polish people of the United States will so stand, where the honor of the country in which we live demands it.[114]

But the PNA perhaps protested too much. Such emphatic professions of loyalty and faithfulness could not conceal the fact that the PNA's own organ, *Zgoda*, questioned the "honor" of U.S. policy in the Philippines. In a piece on the possibility of U.S. hegemony in the Caribbean and Pacific in the summer of 1898, *Zgoda* had taken a subtler, more nuanced position on Polish political sensibilities and the duties of American citizenship. The obligation of Polish-American citizens "is to point up the faults which are glimpsed in our government"; but "as citizens of the world," they should aspire to "uplift humanity" by rolling back autocracy. On the one hand, Polish-Americans must guard against their adopted country's becoming a "military state" and a colonial power; yet on the other, "we cannot help but feel an inner joy at the idea that the free, star-spangled banner of the United States is fluttering somewhere over a new clime, diminishing the power of monarchism!"[115]

As U.S. activity in "new climes" came ever more obviously in collision with the ideals of true national liberation, immigrant commentators held fast to their obligation of pointing up "the faults which are glimpsed in our government." But to be at once an immigrant and a dissident was not an altogether appealing position, as, perhaps, the PNA resolution at Grand Rapids attests. The weapon best-suited to this task of dissent from the ethnic margins was a rhetorical genuflection to hallowed American icons—protest from the high ground of an impeccable Americanism. The pithiest defense of immigrant anti-imperialism was the *Pilot's* one-line credo, "We do not believe in Imperialism because we do believe in Americanism, the very best ism ever devised." Or again, in response to McKinley's assertion that "wherever the flag is assailed" it would be carried to triumph, the journal simply remarked, "Ah, Mr. McKinley, it is assailed chiefly at Washington. Save it from dishonor there, and it will suffer none elsewhere."[116]

Such formulations of anti-imperialism as quintessentially American served a dual function. First, American history itself did offer salient counterarguments to current Philippine policy, and the proposed contrast between hallowed political tradition and McKinley's arrogant departure from it was fraught with rhetorical power. Not least among America's anti-imperialist precedents was the crusade for Cuba Libre, from which the garlands of national self-congratulation had not yet faded. "We who have been the destroyers of oppression are asked now to become its agents," cried Senator Bourke Cockran, an Irish nationalist; "We who have been the builders of freedom are asked now to become the architects of tyranny." Cockran and others could denounce imperialism as a national "heresy," and wonder, "Is it part of the principles of our free, independent government to proceed to civilize a weaker people by first shooting and then robbing them?"[117]

Likewise, very particular versions of "America" as both a political ideal and a practical ally had become intricately woven into both the lore and the agenda of immigrant nationalisms. It is not just that immigrants were anxious to prove themselves good Americans; they were also anxious that America remain faithful to its anti-imperialist pedigree. The United States, after all, had at one time been an oppressed colony; its revolutionary past now rendered it a "beacon of liberty." In nationalist culture, it was emphatically *this* America to which the exiles and pilgrims had migrated. Fenian attempts to draw the United States into a war with England; J. C. O'Connell's assertion that "the starry banner will smile encouragingly on her sister, Sunburst"; the PNA's vision of the "fourth partition" mobilizing the adopted country on behalf of the Fatherland—such nationalist visions all represent a tremendous stake in the anti-imperialist currents of American history and politics. As *Dziennik Chicagoski* commented in its piece on Americans as culture-bearers, the imperialist powers of Europe "rub their hands in glee" at the prospect of the United States' taking up the spurious mission of "civilizing," because in so doing the upstart power had forfeited its right to intercede in local struggles on behalf of "the liberty of peoples."[118]

Appeals to George Washington and the national icons of revolution became a staple of immigrant dissent, invoked under the double influence of defensive "good" Americanism and the anxious desire that the nation remain true to its origins as a colony-in-revolt. Such appeals to American tradition early characterized the Irish response to Anglo-Saxonism and its corollary, "patriotism of race." George Washington would have been "no less astonished than disgusted" by talk of Anglo-Saxonism and alliance with the "mother country," the *Irish World* asserted; the *Pilot* identified "pure-minded, single-hearted, patriotic Benedict Arnold" as the "original advocate of Anglo-American union."[119]

Immigrant commentary on the Philippines drew on similar patriotic motifs. "The love of Fatherland," commented *Straż*, "is a crime in that foreign land which this country wants to grab . . . Tagalogs, in the eyes of Americans, are rebels, criminals, because they do exactly that which . . . Washington and those who fought along with him did."[120] In response to a dispatch from Manila which cited the factionalism and internal quarrels of the Filipinos as evidence of their unfitness for self-government, the *Pilot* commented, "Change the date and the place of address, and the above dispatch would apply with equal truth, and equal falsity, to any people at any time in the world's history. For Aguinaldo write Washington, and you have the secret history of the American Revolution in a nutshell."[121] After describing an occasion of state, where the lecture hall was decorated with pictures of Washington, Lincoln, and McKinley over a sign reading "Liberator," *Dzi-ennik Chicagoski* chided,

> It is to be hoped that our current president is embarrassed, seeing himself beside Washington and Lincoln, as well as seeing this inappropriate expression 'Liberator' applied to his own name, at the very moment when out there in the west he is leading a bloody war against a defenseless nation, in which he is engaged in the disgusting work of converting Filipinos by the sword and civilizing them at the mouth of a cannon.[122]

And Patrick Ford cleverly duplicated the charges leveled at George III in the Declaration of Independence in describing the situation in the Philippines: "He has erected a multitude of new offices and sent hither swarms of officers to harass our people and eat out their substance . . . He has combined with others to subject us to a jurisdiction foreign to our constitution and unacknowledged by our laws."[123]

Even the most energetic and damning of anti-imperialist critiques, however, were not easily translated into political influence or into practical steps toward reversing administration policy. Organized protest against American imperialism unfolded in two phases: direct appeals to McKinley and to Congress, spearheaded by the New England Anti-Imperialist League and lasting until the ratification of the Treaty of Paris, followed by efforts to piece together an electoral coalition with an eye toward the election of 1900 as a referendum on "the paramount issue" of American Empire. Each of these phases presented considerable organizational challenges—even for "mainstream" anti-imperialists like Senator George Frisbee Hoar, Gamaliel Bradford, and Andrew Carnegie, whose resources and access to the halls of power were obviously far greater than those of the Polish National Alliance or the United Irish Societies. But each phase presented its own special problems to the anti-imperialists of these immigrant communities.

During the first phase of the fight (from soon after Dewey's victory at Manila Bay in May of 1898 to the ratification of the Treaty of Paris in February of 1899), immigrant participation in the anti-imperialist movement was limited by the social and ideological distance between the League's patrician leadership and the immigrants themselves. The League, conceived as a coalition of the nation's most prominent men, was antidemocratic in both social bearing and strategy: as far as officers like Charles Francis Adams were concerned, the Imperialism Question was not a matter for massive political mobilization, but something that would best be settled in cool counsel by the "better elements" of society. It had been, after all, the "fighting mob hysteria" and the "savage instincts" of the common people in the spring of 1898 which had opened the Pandora's box of American imperialism in the first place.[124]

Boasting a monstrous board of forty-one vice presidents—an eclectic *Who's Who* that included industrialist Andrew Carnegie, university president David Starr Jordan, aging Mugwump reformer Gamaliel Bradford, ex-U.S. president Grover Cleveland, white-supremacist Senator "Pitchfork" Ben Tillman, and labor leader Samuel Gompers—the League remained a top-heavy gentlemen's club which ultimately relied upon the stature of its officers rather than the breadth of its following. If the coalition model is evidence that reform-minded League leaders were willing to "put aside" their "upper-class" aversions and prejudices, as one historian has perhaps too generously concluded,[125] the League's track record suggests that this was never a fully successful cross-class, inter-ethnic partnership. A petition drive in late 1898 to collect and deliver to McKinley's desk "ten million" anti-imperialist signatures, for instance, turned up only thousands, not millions, of names. The drive's dismal failure says less about grassroots anti-imperialism than about the League's capacity or inclination to tap it.

Some links were indeed achieved between the League and various immigrant enclaves, particularly among the politically established Irish of the Northeast. The *Pilot* initially greeted the League in a headline as "An Important Movement to Save the Republic," and as David Noel Doyle observes, Irish-Americans directly active in the League included "a fair cross-section of the Irish American elite at the time"— ranging from conservative Democrats like Bourke Cockran and Patrick Collins, to the erstwhile radical Patrick Ford.[126] Ethnic rallies in affiliation with the League included a New England Clan na Gael affair presided over by Patrick Collins, and a Cooper Union rally described in the *Abend blatt* under the banner "Three Cheers for Aguinaldo." *Dziennik Chicagoski* and *Kuryer Polski*, too, occasionally covered or reprinted anti-imperialist speeches by Senator Hoar or William Jennings Bryan.[127]

In general, however, given the vehemence with which men like Roche and Neuman protested the direction of American policy, the general absence of the League from the pages of immigrant journals is more striking than its occasional presence. It was more than mere neglect which distanced many immigrant anti-imperialists from the patricians of the League, or which persuaded immigrant editors to "go it alone" in their dissent, in the words of one scholar.[128] As the scroll of the League's forty-one vice presidents itself indicates, galvanizing anti-imperialist sentiment entailed the bringing together of very strange bedfellows indeed—Carnegie and Gompers, for instance, or southern racists like Ben Tillman and heirs of northern abolitionism like William Lloyd Garrison, Jr. In some cases these animosities may have been prohibitive. Any effective organization of an immigrant wing of the League would have entailed, among other things, political truces between Irish Catholics and New England Brahmins, and between Jewish workers of the metropolis and populists of the hinterland who were given to a rhetoric of anti-Semitism.

It was not just social distance or language barriers which limited the scope of immigrant participation in the movement, but ideological distance as well. The racial, religious, and class assumptions of the Anti-Imperialist League, no less than those of the most evangelical expansionists, came under scrutiny and attack in immigrant discussion. As far as one Irish letter-writer to the *Pilot* was concerned, the figureheads of the League were among the worst of the "Anglomaniacs." "We are with Senator Hoar in his steadfast opposition to imperialism," the editor affirmed. "But was it not a slip of the tongue which made him give away his reasons . . . that the people of the Philippines are 'aliens in race and religion'? The United States has no national religion. The Fathers of our country were too wise for that."[129]

Irreconcilable, too, were the differences between the centrist, reform-minded capitalists of the League, who saw imperialism as a frightening *departure* from American tradition, and radical critics on the Yiddish left, who saw imperialism as a lamentable export of American business-as-usual. The *Abend blatt* proposed that anti-imperialists were as dangerous for what they tolerated at home as imperialists were for what they perpetrated abroad. Was not Manila but the logical extension of Homestead?

> Our anti-expansionist demagogues want to convince us that the application of violence abroad will lead us to the application of violence domestically; that our government will learn to oppress its own people with rifles and cannon once it has so oppressed a foreign people. But this is fundamentally false; and the development has been just the opposite. Our government first applied violence to the worker at home; it first oppressed its people domestically; and from that it learned how to oppress other peoples as well.[130]

The inherent difficulties of coalition politics became still more pronounced when, in the wake of the ratification of the Treaty of Paris, faced with an imperialist *fait accompli* and now a war between "our boys" and the Filipino "banditti," anti-imperialist activists set their sights on the election of 1900 as a referendum on McKinley's Philippine policy. The stark either-or of election day has often proved an inadequate peg for voters' complex sensibilities; more often than not foreign policy questions, not domestic or economic ones, are first to go by the wayside as voters try comfortably to hang their convictions on the too-simple spindle of this party versus that. If it had been so hard for the diverse elements of the anti-imperialist movement to "stand shoulder to shoulder," in Erving Winslow's phrase, during the fight over the Treaty of Paris, then how could Winslow's patchwork coalition of "Republican, Democrat, Socialist, Populist, Gold-man, Silverman, and Mugwump" possibly agree on a presidential candidate?[131]

In November of 1898, the *Irish World* had confidently pointed to the mid-term elections in Minnesota (where a Democratic governor had surprisingly won) and New York (where various Republican candidates had won by surprisingly narrow margins) as proof of the electorate's will to "censure" McKinley for his imperial ambitions. Patrick Ford, like Winslow, felt sure that imperialism would prove to be the "overshadowing issue" of the campaign.[132] But Finley Peter Dunne came closer to identifying the dynamics behind the tenuous coalition of not merely strange, but mutually *unbearable* bedfellows which constituted the anti-imperialist movement. "No wan is going to vote th' way he believes," he quipped.

> Says me friend Binjamin Harrison: "Th' condict iv th' administhration has been short iv hellish. Th' idee that this gover'mint shud sind out throops to murdher an' pillage an' elope with th' shrugglin' races iv the boochoos Ph'lipeens makes me blood bile almost to th' dew point. I indorse ivrything that Willum J. Bryan says on th' subject, an' though it goes hard fr me to say it, lifelong Raypublican that I am, I exhort ivry follower iv mine to put inmities aside, frget his prejudices, an' cast his vote fr William McKinley."[133]

J. Sterling Morton, a former Cleveland Administration official, expressed the same ambivalence when he wrote to Cleveland, "It is a choice between evils, and I am going to shut my eyes, hold my nose, vote, go home, and disinfect myself!"[134]

Immigrant communities, too, were subject to the kind of ideological cross-currents which dissipated the anti-imperialist movement's electoral strength generally. As Paul Kleppner noted in his study of Midwest politics, Bryan's evangelical moral style seems to have undercut his popularity among Catholics, including some immigrants who might otherwise have been attracted by Democratic appeals to a working-class sensibility. While the Democrats of 1896 and 1900 sought a political realignment along the economic lines of class, Kleppner argues, what they in fact manufactured was a realignment along the socio-cultural axis of "pietist" and "ritualist" religious groups. America's "civilizing mission" in the Pacific notwithstanding, on the strength of his oratory and his social vision William Jennings Bryan, not McKinley, appeared to many to be the candidate of evangelical zealotry or intolerance.[135]

For Poles, another complicating factor was McKinley's perceived warmth toward the Polish cause. McKinley had held a (very brief) audience with the visiting Polish insurrectionist, Zygmunt Miłkowski, prompting some to scoff at the anti-imperialists' attempts to portray the American president as a "despot." Prominent Polish leaders like Władysław Dyniewicz of the PNA and Tadeusz Wild, the wildly popular Captain of the Kościuszko Guard, publicly and emphatically endorsed McKinley, empire or no.[136]

Because of their powerful ties to the Democratic Party, particularly in the Northeast, Irish-American anti-imperialists were perhaps slightly more wholehearted about their vote. Longtime Irish Republicans like Patrick Ford, John Devoy, and Patrick Egan jumped the fence to support Bryan, making much of the importance of international affairs as the defining issue.[137] In cities like Boston and New York, where the Irish were well established within the Democratic machinery, immigrant voters found their prevailing electoral traditions compatible with anti-imperialist imperatives. In the context of rampant Anglo-Saxonism, Anglo-American alliance, the Philippine War, British and American machinations in Samoa, and British aggression in the Transvaal, the *Irish World* could proclaim "A Vote for McKinley a Vote for England"—an alarm echoed across the Atlantic by the Dublin *Freeman*. A letter to the *Irish World* likewise celebrated the election as an opportunity for the Irish-American voter simultaneously to "save his adopted country" and "give a crushing and effective blow to the ancient enemy of his race." Here the local custom of serving the tigers of Tammany was in wonderful accord with the broader ambition of fending off the British lion.[138]

Given the conflicting endorsements before the election and the claims and counterclaims of immigrant partisans afterwards, it is difficult to say with precision how the Philippine Question affected immigrant voting. *Dziennik Chicagoski*, for instance, painted the election as a choice between McKinley's "captivity, war, oppression, domination, trusts, subjugation, [and] paupers" on the one hand, and Bryan's "freedom, peace, prosperity, equality, [and] glory" on the other, suggesting that no loyal Pole could possibly support the Republicans. And yet after the election *Kuryer Polski*'s Michael Kruszka could claim with both satisfaction and certainty that most Poles had done precisely that.[139] Indeed, given the disparate views of anti-imperialists on other pressing questions of the day—trade and monetary policy, the economy—leaders of the Anti-Imperialist League insisted in the wake of McKinley's victory that "[the League] does not and can not recognize that the question of Anti-Imperialism was settled by that election."[140] Practically speaking, in fact, the election did seem to settle the question. Within days of Bryan's defeat the *Pilot* proclaimed that "the battle for 1904 begins today. Long live the Republic!"[141] But for all its emotional power, imperialism had not been the "overshadowing" issue of 1900, and it would not be so in 1904.

If electoral politics ultimately proved an impossible arena for anti-imperialist dissent, still the depth of dissent among many immigrants and its basis in Old World nationalist culture cannot be missed. Just as the cause of the Cuban *reconcentrados* had resonated with the nationalist strains embodied in stories like "The Pikemen of '98" or in the public rituals commemorating the November and January uprisings; just as the pageantry surrounding the immigrant regiments evoked a nationalist mythology of Maccabean or Fenian heroics; so the struggle in the Philippines evoked visions of the nationalist defeats and the civil oppressions endured in the Old World. In the wake of the election the *Irish World* declared in a banner, "ENGLAND'S CANDIDATES TRIUMPHED," adding in a subhead, "PRONOUNCE IT A DEFEAT FOR THE IRISH."[142]

Tammany regular George Washington Plunkitt later regretted that the Democrats had spent so much energy on the Philippine Question. "[The Democrats'] position was alright, sure, but you can't get people excited about the Philippines. They've got too much at home to interest them; they're too busy makin' a livin' to bother about the niggers in the Pacific."[143]

This may have been a sound, practical assessment of voters' general tendency to vote pocketbook above principle, and his active "other-ing" of the Filipinos may reflect the broader power of imperialism to transform European immigrants into Americans on the basis of race. But Plunkitt's was nonetheless a hasty view of immigrants' capacity to get "excited" about struggles like the one then taking place in the Philippines. Immigrants had in fact demonstrated such excitability again and again: when Chicago's United Irish Societies passed a res-olution announcing, "we look with disgust upon the operations of our Government in the Philippines"; when the Robert Emmet Literary Society of Butte, Montana, staged a debate on the proposition "Irish-men in general . . . favor the expansion of the United States," only to find that the Irishmen of Butte favored no such thing; when the Poles of Chicago protested on Noble Street against Anglo-American alli-ance and "monarchism"; or when the Guards of Zion, the Gallant 69th, and the Kościuszko Guard mustered in under the banner of Cuba Libre.[144]

Again, immigrant communities were hardly characterized by mo-notonous agreement; there was plenty of room for individual idiosyn-cracy and for heated debate. Elizabeth Gurley Flynn recalls that her father "was greatly wrought up over the cruelties inflicted upon the people of these faraway islands of the Pacific," while some branches of the Friendly Sons of St. Patrick openly favored expansion and enthu-siastically greeted Admiral Dewey as a hero.[145] One Polish-American soldier managed to see himself in righteous opposition to the statist power of the Czar, even as he fought to put down the Filipino rebel-lion. "Five more regiments of the regular army are to arrive here," he wrote to his brother from the Philippines, "and so we do not fear the Russian Czar himself . . ." He was evidently untroubled by his position in the ranks of a counterinsurrectionary force rather than an insur-rectionary one.[146]

Diverse immigrant responses to American interventionism and to the Cuban and Philippine causes highlight the complex personal ne-gotiations entailed in international migration and resettlement. Relo-cation across national borders demanded a certain redefinition of self: a negotiation of the imagined community left behind in the Old World, the national community imagined in the New World, and one's imagined relationship to each. What did unite diverse commen-tators were their visible attempts to reconcile a sense of rights and entitlements based upon their Old World nationality with an emerg-ing sense of participation in New World civic rites—they were united, that is, in that each somehow had to translate the common political lore, expressed in local '98 celebrations or in Sienkiewicz or Kobrin short stories, into some understanding of "America" as a political idea. Nationalism, gender, and race constituted the ideologies upon which these translations were founded.

The debates and rituals surrounding these turn-of-the-century wars indicate the implicit political dimension of what is most often considered a purely cultural process: assimilation. Like George Washington Plunkitt, historians have tended to assume a vast distance between the humble, everyday concerns of ordinary immigrants, and the grand, abstract questions of world politics. But insofar as it requires the reconciliation or integration of competing national mythologies, assimilation *is* world politics. Conversely, the world political landscape itself has been affected by the nationalist ideals of international migrants and their heirs, twentieth-century America's largely assimilated but ultimately "unmeltable" ethnics. Indeed, there is a historical continuity worth noting from the migrating generations' cultures of exile to more recent manifestations of a transnational or diasporic ethnic sensibility: the "Israel lobby," Noraid, and the anti-Soviet passions of Polish-Americans.

Conclusion:
The Diasporic Imagination
in the Twentieth Century

We are proud that our Poland is again called by destiny to become the bulwark of democracy and Christianity and we pledge our lives to the Polish cause. Five million Poles in the United States are ready to sacrifice their lives for the sacred cause which Poland is ready to defend.

> —Cable sent by the Polish Falcons to
> Marshal Rydz-Śmigły in Warsaw, 1939

The American Volunteer Brigade is being mobilized to assist IRA freedom fighters should Ireland call out to us. We realize the IRA must continue to wage their war for independence as they have for over a century—themselves alone. But if British policy produces a situation in which Republican civilians are left unprotected and threatened with extinction, we won't stand idly by.

> —Advertisement, *Frisco* magazine, 1982

What does Jewish mean now anyway except fussing for holidays and arms for Israel?

> —Melanie Kaye/Kantrowitz, "The Woman in Purple"

Years after World War I, Stefan Korbonski recalled being seated at a Polish-American banquet between two veterans of Haller's Army, a regiment of emigrant Poles from both Europe and America who had fought against the Central Powers on the promise of an independent Poland.

> Learning that both had been born in America, I wondered what had decided them to enter the army.
>
> "It was through Sienkiewicz," said one. "When my father used to come back from the coal-mine, I had to read him the *Trilogy*[1] aloud. This happened every day for an hour. When I'd finished *Pan Wolodyjowski* I would start *By Fire and Sword,* and so on. This made a Polish patriot of me."
>
> "My mother told me to," said the other . . . "One Sunday Mother shut herself in a room with me and said, 'Son, go and join the army to free Poland.' So I went."[2]

Although the political lineage from one generation of "pilgrims" to the next may be unusually direct in these instances, these veterans' answers do underscore a certain ideological continuity in nationalist culture—in this case from the earliest PNA blueprints of the 1870s to the opportunity for their fruition in the European war four decades later. Like more recent interest among American ethnics in the IRA, Arab-Israeli relations, or Lech Wałęsa, Korbonski's banquet-table exchange raises questions about the political dimension of ethnic identity as immigrant communities become ethnic communities over time. For example, read within the narrowed context of a strictly American political culture, late twentieth-century ethnic gestures to an overseas homeland may seem peripheral, even baffling. But read against the broader history of "the sea-divided Gael" or Poland's "fourth partition"—histories in which each group represents not a tile in the American mosaic, but rather one wing of a transnational diaspora—such concerns take on a markedly different coloring. A persistent (if occasionally submerged) cultural thread links immigrant nationalism with twentieth-century ethnic symbolism, such as the posthumous election of hunger striker Bobby Sands as the Grand Marshall of New York's 1982 St. Patrick's Day parade.[3]

A single chapter, of course, cannot treat the full scope of twentieth-century ethnic nationalisms and the full range of nationalist or Zionist expressions on American soil, nor is this one meant to. The intent here is simply to suggest some continuities in ethnic political cultures, and to raise some seldom asked questions about assimilation and American identities. This conclusion seeks briefly, first, to indicate the tenacious diasporic orientation of these three groups and their lasting aspirations to enlist American power in the aid of their respective nations; and second, to point out the diasporic, nationalist strains in ethnic literary and cultural life which have endured despite the undeniable movement toward Americanization.

A sea change, no question, has occurred on every front since the events and debates described in the first five chapters. In the intervening decades Poland has been (twice) reborn; twenty-six of Ireland's thirty-two counties have been liberated from English rule; and a Jewish state has risen from the ashes of a Holocaust whose dimensions would have been beyond the imagination of even the most urgent turn-of-the-century Zionists. Given the perpetual state of war in Israel, the unleashing of anti-Semitism in Solidarity-era Poland, and the continued strife in Ireland, these three cases argue most eloquently that nationalism, as a liberationist program, is perhaps most effective when left unfulfilled. Recalled in light of the *Intifada*, Golda Meir's 1948 description of Jewish desperation captures the sour irony of nationalism's capacity to generate new sorrows even as it alleviates old ones: "If we have something to fight with we'll fight with that," she promised. "If we don't we'll fight with stones."[4]

So, too, have orientations shifted dramatically in these ethnic communities in the United States, despite modest infusions of Old World energy provided by continued immigration. Granddaughters and grandsons of the many exiles, pilgrims, and wanderers of the 1890s have become Americans by any meaningful measure of that national appellation. The national births and rebirths of Ireland, Poland, and Zion failed to draw torrents of exiles back home across the Atlantic; group experience has indeed become normalized under the influence of a political culture which, in Haim Chertok's phrase, has proven "delectably hospitable—practically porous."[5] As the fictional Nathan Zuckerman puts it to his Zionist brother in Philip Roth's *The Counterlife*, it could be that by "flourishing mundanely" in New Jersey, comfortably unconscious in everyday life of Judaism and things Jewish, he had "[made] Jewish history no less astonishing" than the Israelis.[6]

But "flourishing mundanely" as Americans must not be taken to mean turning entirely away from the nationalist concerns of one's forebears. Emblems of a tenacious diasporic imagination range from Golda Meir's success in raising over $50,000,000 for Israel's military struggle on her tour through the United States in 1948, to the more

recent "hesitancy," as British and Irish officials termed it, "of prominent Irish Americans to deplore the IRA's violence and efforts to raise
funds in the United States to buy weapons."[7] During one tense moment of the Solidarity struggle in Poland, the *New York Times* reported, "Several hundred Polish-Americans burned a Soviet flag in
mid-Manhattan yesterday. They sang the Polish national anthem and
some of them wept."[8] Indeed, assimilation notwithstanding, in at least
a limited way the Irish, Jewish, and Polish diaspora communities in the
United States have fulfilled precisely the roles assigned them a century
ago by nationalist theorists, as historians like Melvin Urofsky, Charles
Silberman, J. Bowyer Bell, and Donald Pienkos have documented.[9]

Among the most widely accepted interpretations of this lingering
sympathy with homeland causes is Herbert Gans's model of "symbolic
ethnicity." Awash in a relentlessly homogenizing mass culture, Gans
argues, third- and fourth-generation ethnics can "find their identity by
'affiliating' with an abstract collectivity which does not exist as an
interacting group. That collectivity . . . can be mythic or real, contemporary or historical." Such newly embraced identities are expressed
only intermittently, as most people "refrain from ethnic behavior that
requires an arduous or time-consuming commitment." Ethnic expression, adds sociologist Mary Waters, is largely a "leisure time" pursuit in
the case of white European ethnics.[10]

Hence distant homelands are especially attractive "identity symbols," in Gans' estimation, since they "cannot make arduous demands
on American ethnics." In this view twentieth-century gestures of ethnic nationalism respond to American alienation, to the post–New
Deal imperatives of interest-group politics, or to post–Civil Rights
imperatives of group mobilization. Such attachments are expressive or
instrumental in a purely American social context rather than in a
transnational one; such attachments are willfully invoked by the individual rather than evoked by the tenacity of transnational cultures
and the ebb and flow of international affairs.[11]

Gans does entertain the possibility that symbolic ethnicities may
emerge even among members of the migrating generation.[12] In general, however, this model obscures the extent to which *any* national
collectivity is in some sense fabricated—an "imagined community," in
Benedict Anderson's phrase. Those who fled the Famine in 1847 or
the Czar in 1881 experienced Old World authority and oppression
very differently from the American-born generations which succeeded
them, it is true. But inasmuch as national membership is articulated in
the imagery of Maccabean heroics, Gaelic chieftains, or the miracu-

lous seventeenth-century defense of Częstochowa, little distinguishes the symbolic attachments of nineteenth-century exiles from the symbolic attachments of their great-grandchildren a hundred years later. Nationalism requires a leap of imagination in either case.

The implicit dichotomy in Gans's scheme between identifications which are symbolic and those which are presumably more authentic, and his attention to the functions of ethnicity and ethnic attachments in a strictly American milieu, discount the longstanding engagement of ethnic groups with political communities which are transnational. Notions of symbolic ethnicity and ethnic revival are largely ahistorical in that they seek to explain the politicized understandings of national origin among American-born generations of unmeltable ethnics without any reference at all to nationalist interpretations of group life among the migrants themselves. Indeed, the intermittence which Gans has observed in ethnic expression often replicates the intermittent tides of calm and crisis overseas: in the years of renewed fighting in Ulster after British troops arrived in 1969, for instance, an array of Irish nationalist organizations crystallized in the United States, including sixty-two chapters of the IRA.[13] It is at least in part within the longer history of diasporic nationalism that we might best interpret these recent developments.

This is not to paint a picture of second-, third-, and fourth-generation ethnic populations as hotbeds of nationalist insurrectionary thinking; nor is it to imply a strict equivalence in the meaning of national liberation from one generation to the next. Ben Hecht was asserting a distance from nationalist affairs common to the American-born of many groups when he wrote in 1945,

> if [a Jewish state] did come into being, however attractive that being was, I would look on it with foreign eyes. I could no more feel myself part of it than of any other country beyond the U.S.A. I wish for its existence, and recognize the great value it would have for all the Jews of the world. But when I contemplate a Jewish state I become something I have never been before—an exile.[14]

Yet neither was Hecht entirely alone when, in the course of the same essay, he paused to muse, "On reading what I have written, I find a curious use of two first person pronouns beginning to confuse the syntax. The writer is, apparently, uncertain whether he is I, the Jew, or We, the Americans."[15] What follows is a beginning in the explo-

ration of the complicated syntax of twentieth-century group life—
snapshots of the emigrants' special national sorrows as they have been
rearticulated in the twentieth century in an array of political and
cultural forms, from World War I era lobbying efforts to children's
school primers and Philip Roth's bestsellers.

Self-Determination and the Emigrants

In late 1918 Secretary of State Robert Lansing worried privately over
the ramifications of Woodrow Wilson's rather loose rhetoric of national rights. "The more I think about the president's declaration as to
the right of 'self-determination,' " he recorded in his diary, "the more
convinced I am of the danger of putting such ideas into the minds of
certain races. It is bound to be the basis of impossible demands on the
Peace Congress and create troubles in many lands. What effect will it
have on the Irish, the Indians, the Egyptians . . . The phrase is simply
loaded with dynamite."[16]

Lansing was half right. The rhetoric of the war, the world remapping
determined in the peace, and the years-long discussion of how to
rationalize international affairs in the postwar era brought nationalist
claimants and supplicants forward from every corner of the globe.[17]
Activists who turned up in Paris during the peace conference to press
the claims of their various homelands ranged from Chaim Weizmann
to Ho Chi Minh.

Lansing erred, however, in his self-flattering notion that independence was an American idea, or that it was within the power of
political elites like himself and Wilson to "[put] such ideas into the
minds of certain races." In the cases of Ireland, Poland, and Zion the
ideas had been current for some time, as we have seen. Earlier, Lansing
had proposed segregating Polish-Americans into an ethnic military
unit "so that they would feel their nationality and be inspired to fight
for the freedom of their country."[18] The Poles, however, did not need
the U.S. government to so "inspire" them.

With or without U.S. participation, the European war would have
aroused high passions among immigrant nationalists in all three
groups: the conflict involved Ireland's oppressor, all three of the partitioning powers in Poland, the hated Czar, and the Turkish empire,
which held the key to the future of Palestine. In the days before the
United States entered the war, immigrant "neutrality" was strained, to
say the very least. Poles were divided on the question of whom to
support in the war, in part because of their disparate Old World

experiences and in part because of conflicting interpretations of whose victory promised to benefit Poland the most, since the partitioning powers were not all fighting on the same side.[19]

The other groups, however, had less delicate decisions to make—at least until the United States intervened on the side of the Allies. "The Jews support Germany because Russia bathes in Jewish blood," announced the *Tageblatt* flatly. In his treatise on *The King, the Kaiser, and Irish Freedom* (1915), James K. McGuire was as succinct: "God bless Germany! God save Ireland!"[20] "The present war has distinctly proved that Germany has but very few friends in the world," observed the *Irische Blatter*, the official organ of The German Irish Society (Berlin) in 1917; "the Irish have, however, shown themselves to be such, both in their own country and in America." A Society reception in Berlin, which included a rendition of "The Wearin' of the Green," mirrored a United Irish Societies rally at the Cohan Theatre in New York, which included the anthem "Deutschland über Alles." Nationwide Irish-American demonstrations in support of Germany included a "Parade of England's Enemies" in Butte, Montana, on St. Patrick's Day, 1915: the Irish were joined by German- and Austrian-Americans, and the traditional cavalcade was rerouted through German and Austrian neighborhoods. Indeed, so outspoken were the Irish that in 1918, once the United States had entered the war and the government had become sensitive to any signs of sedition, the *Gaelic American*, the *Irish World*, the *Irish Press*, and the *Freeman's Journal* were banned from the public mails.[21]

The potential dilemma of conflicting loyalties in wartime was largely averted in the case of Polish and Jewish immigrants. Woodrow Wilson's perceived sympathy for the Polish cause went a long way in simplifying the matter for the Poles. Despite unfortunate and widely publicized remarks which Wilson the historian had made about the "meaner" sort of immigrants from Poland—possessing "neither skill nor energy nor any initiative of quick intelligence,"—by 1915 Wilson the politician was receiving mail from every corner of Polonia thanking him for his generous interest in Poland's fate. The President's crusade for Polish relief early in the war, the recognition and respect he accorded Polish leader Ignacy Paderewski, the influence he allowed Paderewski through adviser Edward M. House, and his "peace without victory" speech (1917) alluding to the necessity for a "united, independent, and autonomous Poland," all established his reputation as an indispensable ally in the Polish cause. Wilson's concern crystallized, of course, in the thirteenth of his famous Fourteen Points:

XIII. An independent Polish state should be erected which should include the territories inhabited by indisputably Polish populations, which should be assured a free and secure access to the sea, and whose political and economic independence and territorial integrity should be guaranteed by international covenant.[22]

Some Polish-Americans did hew to the line developed by leader Józef Piłsudski, who identified Russia as the nation's primary enemy and so favored the Central Powers. Nonetheless, nearly half (42,000) of the first 100,000 volunteers for American service were Polish immigrants and their children. Studies undertaken at the time and in the years since have placed over 200,000 Poles in American uniform during the war years; another 22,000, ineligible for U.S. service because they were not U.S. citizens, were funneled by the Military Commission into the ranks of a diasporic Polish force assembled in France. Polonia likewise purchased a heroic $150,000,000 in Liberty Bonds.[23]

The question of loyalties was similarly eased for Jewish immigrants when the Russian Revolution toppled the Czarist regime in February 1917. With the Czar suddenly removed from the equation, the Allies became more palatable. The Allies became even more attractive in the estimation of many East European Jews, moreover, when Great Britain issued its Balfour Declaration on the question of Palestine later that same year. "His Majesty's Government view with favour the establishment in Palestine of a national home for the Jewish people," ran the declaration, "and will use their best endeavors to facilitate the achievement of this object." The Allies' desire to break up the Turkish empire, too, was compatible with the Zionist aim of acquiring the empire's Palestinian province. (When Wilson dispatched a delegation to explore the possibility of a separate peace with Turkey in 1917, Zionists were able to dissuade the leader of the mission, Henry Morgenthau, from pursuing this inquiry.)[24]

Like the Poles, Jewish nationalists also linked military service in the war to the fulfillment of national aspirations in the peace. Some American Jews, for instance, were among the 40th Royal Fusiliers, a Jewish regiment under the British Army Command. Many were convinced, recalls Golda Meir, "that an effective Jewish claim could be made to the Land of Israel after the war only if the Jewish people played a significant and visible military role, *as Jews*, in the fighting." When David Ben-Gurion visited Milwaukee to recruit soldiers for the Jewish Legion in 1916, a young Golda Meyerson [later Meir] herself volunteered, only to be "crushed when I learned that girls were not being accepted."[25]

Approval of U.S. intervention on the side of the Allies proved far more difficult for dedicated Irish nationalists, just as the question of Irish loyalties proved highly nettlesome to non-Irish Americans—not least of all to Woodrow Wilson himself—throughout the war years. As Colonel House remarked, in the wake of the Easter Rebellion and England's brutal reprisals, the Irish Question was "almost as much of a political issue in America as in England." The Clan na Gael's official line as it was ultimately articulated consisted of support for American war aims, along with vigorous agitation for the inclusion of Irish independence among those aims. Since Irish-American loyalty contained a significant anti-British element, it struck many non-Irish Americans as falling short of complete loyalty. As Wilson himself wrote to Jeremiah O'Leary, a vociferous critic of his pro-British policies, "I would feel deeply mortified to have you or anybody like you vote for me. Since you have access to many disloyal Americans and I have not, I will ask you to convey this message to them."[26]

From the Easter Rebellion of 1916, to the Sinn Fein (republican) electoral victories in Ireland in 1918, to the fighting in Ireland and the establishment of the Free State in the early 1920s, Irish-American activity on behalf of an independent Ireland was feverish and varied. Documents found in the German Embassy in New York implicated Clan na Gael leaders John Devoy and Judge Daniel Cohalan in coordinating arms shipments from Germany for the Easter Rising itself. Far more public and broad-based activity, however, erupted in the wake of that failed rebellion.[27] Groups like the Knights of St. Patrick urged Wilson to appeal for clemency for the prisoners of Easter. Nora Connolly, the daughter of Irish martyr James Connolly, established an Irish Bazaar in New York to raise money for Irish relief. Under the appellation "The Easter Week Exiles Association" Connolly and others made the Eastern seaboard a second center for the Irish republican cause, coordinating groups like the Friends of Irish Freedom, issuing works like The Irish Rebellion of 1916 and Its Martyrs, and sponsoring lectures like Hannah Sheehy-Skeffington's "British Militarism as I Have Known It."[28] Cumann-na-mBan, an Irish women's organization, meanwhile, established a Defense of Ireland Fund to "enable the Irish people to defend their homes, their rights, their liberties, and their persons now menaced by a foreign government"—by which, as David Emmons wryly notes, they did not mean Germany.[29]

Passions among Irish-Americans further intensified once fighting had erupted in Ireland in what was to become known as the Anglo-Irish War. At a dinner sponsored by the American Association for the

Recognition of the Irish Republic, Harry Boland, a republican envoy to the United States, asserted that 5,000 Irish-Americans had pledged to take up arms with the Irish Republican Army. One Cumann-na-mBan spokeswoman set the figure at 100,000. The American Women's Pickets, claiming to represent "thousands of women of Irish birth or ancestry," cabled Lloyd George to protest the harsh treatment of Irish prisoners; the same organization also picketed the British Embassy in Washington and the Consul's office in New York. Writers like Thomas Mahony sketched out and publicized the many *Similarities Between the American and Irish Revolutions.* And when war for independence gave way to Irish civil war, a highly engaged—and now divided—Irish-America staged rallies across the United States both in favor and in repudiation of republican aims.[30]

Throughout this period Irish-American nationalist activity ranged from highly orchestrated political events (the Irish Race Conventions, "Self-Determination for Ireland Week," Eamon de Valera's fundraising tour), to truly spontaneous and sporadic public outbursts (as when a mob in Boston set upon and destroyed a British flag flying on Clarendon Street).[31] Such political displays were further accompanied by unending Irish-American pressure upon the White House and both houses of Congress. American politicians became the focus of massive letter-writing and petition campaigns on the part of groups like the Clan na Gael, the United Irish Societies, the Friends of Irish Freedom, the Irish Progressive League, the Ancient Order of Hibernians, the Friendly Sons of St. Patrick, and the American Association for the Recognition of the Irish Republic. The Ladies' Auxiliary of the AOH, for instance, sent a "mothers' mission" to Washington bearing a 600,000 signature petition protesting Irish men's unfair conscription into the "foreign" army of England.[32]

Congress responded, in December 1918, with a series of Foreign Affairs Committee hearings, at which more than sixty witnesses (almost all of them sympathetic Irish-American activists) aired their views on the Irish Question. The years-long flurry of congressional resolutions in response to this lobbying campaign culminated in the Senate's Borah Resolution, which requested a hearing at the Paris Peace Conference for an Irish delegation consisting of Eamon de Valera, Arthur Griffith, and Sir Horace Plunkett. A resolution ushered along by Irish-American politicians in the House, meanwhile, averred, "it is the earnest hope of the Congress of the United States of America that the peace conference, now sitting in Paris, in passing upon the rights of various peoples, will favorably consider the claims of Ireland to the right of self-determination."[33]

Irish-American concern for Wilsonian diplomacy reached a fevered pitch in the vigorous debate over the proposed League of Nations, and particularly its controversial Article X. "The Members of the League," ran this provision, "undertake to respect and preserve as against external aggression the territorial integrity and existing political independence of all Members of the League." Some, like the sympathetic George Creel, argued that this arrangement would grant the United States more leverage in the affairs of fellow-member England and its treatment of Ireland. Most, however, felt that not only did the "territorial integrity" clause of Article X seal Ireland's status in the British empire, but, indeed, it committed the United States to England's military "defense" in the case of an Irish rebellion. This latter estimation was expressed, again, in mass rallies across the country; it ultimately found its way into the Senate's Gerry Reservation, calling for the "prompt" admittance of an independent Ireland into the League of Nations.[34]

The Paris Peace Conference of 1919 itself well symbolizes the centrality of World War I era diplomacy to all three national movements and their respective diaspora communities. Irish-America sent a delegation to Paris in an attempt to obtain safe conducts for Eamon de Valera and other Irish officials. Colonel House's assistant, Stephan Bonsal, meanwhile, remarked on the veritable deluge of Polish claimants who turned up at the Paris conference: "They have come in ever-increasing numbers not only from Cracow and Chicago, where Poles thrive, but they have come from all the four corners of the earth." And the American Jewish Congress, too, sent representatives to Paris to monitor events, just as European Zionist leaders had sent delegates to plead the Zionist case.[35]

Not since Versailles have Irish, Polish, and Zionist national questions burned so fiercely all in the same context. But just as debates and activities surrounding the war focused and rearticulated the nationalist strains which had been so evident in late-nineteenth-century immigrant cultures, so have street demonstrations, fundraising campaigns, electoral trends, and myriad political occasions betokened the persistent—if modified—diasporic imagination of later generations.

Enduring nationalist concerns have been registered with some regularity in ethnic lobbies and in American electoral politics. Irish disaffection with Wilson and the Democrats as a result of the war, for instance, is well known. "It is evident," lamented Irish-American historian Charles Callan Tansill decades later, "that President Wilson had scant sympathy for the Irish patriots who were summarily executed by British firing squads for participation in the Easter Rebellion." In a chapter titled "President Wilson Favors the Principle of Self-Determination for Every People but the Irish," Tansill echoed Judge Edward Gavegan's popular postwar pamphlet, "Every Race Saved from Bondage Except the Irish."[36] Seventy years later, in 1992, an organization called the American Irish Political Education Committee (PEC) endorsed Bill Clinton because he "has spoken out against British injustice in Northern Ireland."[37]

Similar passions surfaced in Polonia after the 1976 presidential debate, in which Gerald Ford commented that Poland and other East European nations were "not dominated" by the Soviet Union. Only Jimmy Carter, the Democratic Party candidate, expressed as much public outrage as the many Polish-American organizations still keen on issues of the Fatherland. A Republican organization of East European ethnics in Denver pronounced Ford "unfit for the Presidency." The Polish American Political League estimated that the misstep would cost Ford up to one million votes in Chicago alone. Pickets appeared at a Polish-American press conference in that city bedecked in banners reading, "Mr. President! Poland Is Not Free!" Others greeted Walter Mondale at a Pulaski Parade in Buffalo with signs, "Ford Doesn't Know What Freedom Is—Jimmy Does." Recognizing the trouble he had caused himself, Ford immediately contacted Aloyisius Mazewski, the president of the PNA, to apologize.[38]

Beyond electoral politics, activity has ranged from sporadic street demonstrations—as when the National Association for Irish Freedom picketed the British consulate and BOAC offices in Manhattan, chanting "British troops must go!"; or when a Philadelphia crowd of 30,000 greeted Golda Meir in 1970 with banners reading "We Dig You, Golda,"—to financial assistance, weapon supply, and outright military aid. It was not without cause that David Ben-Gurion identified American Jewry as a "reservoir" of Zionist resources.[39] In the wake of the Six Day War (1967) Israel became "the religion of the American Jews," in Nathan Glazer's phrase. The crisis elicited a wide array of responses. Whatever else American Jews "may or may not have done about being Jewish," wrote Norman Podhoretz, in the wake of Arab-Israeli violence "they all gave their support to Israel. Those who had money to give gave it; those who had arguments to make made them; those who had votes to cast cast them."[40] The Anglo-Irish War, the post-1969 Ulster violence, Hitler's invasion of Poland, and the rise of Lech Wałęsa and Solidarity reverberated throughout Irish-America and Polonia in a similar manner. Describing the prospects for the Irish republicans, historian J. Bowyer Bell has written, "What was needed was vision, gall, and competence applied to need." What better place to find this than America, "the great mill that ground huddled masses into consumers and richly rewarded producers—even the immigrant Gaels"?[41]

The "vision, gall, and competence" of these diaspora communities have often been dispensed in the form of dollars. Financial contributions—among many middle-class Americans, ever the easiest answer to clarion calls for political action—may largely belong in that category of "symbolic" expressions which, in Gans's term, are not "arduous." But some of the fundraising efforts over the years on behalf of these beleaguered nations have been impressive. In 1939 members of the Polish Women's Alliance in Pittsburgh donated their wedding rings and other jewelry to raise money for the defense of Poland, while 9,000 Poles in New York pledged a day's pay every week for the duration of the war. So extraordinary were Polish-American contributions to the war effort that the War Department named one of its bombers "The Polish National Alliance."[42] Likewise, asserting that American Jews had it within their power to decide whether or not Palestinian Jews would be victorious in their struggle with the Mufti, Golda Meir raised $50,000,000 on a two-month tour of the U.S. in 1948; a second tour turned up another $150,000,000 for the combined relief of Palestinian and European Jews. As Charles Silberman remarks, American Jews became "more conditioned" over time to this kind of sacrifice: during the Six Day War American Jews contributed over $317 million; during the Yom Kippur War, $670 million.[43]

But the support of these diaspora communities took various forms. The nature of some Irish-American aid to Ireland's struggle, for instance, is nicely summed up in Bell's surmise that "the huge New York City Water Tunnel under construction from 1970 to 1975 probably required ten percent more dynamite than a careful engineer would have anticipated." Or again, when two Sinn Fein members were arrested in Buffalo, New York, transporting weapons out of the country, an Immigration and Naturalization Service official offered the observation that "these people were not leprechauns."[44]

Other, less furtive instances of military involvement include the enlistment of 550,000 Jewish and 900,000 Polish-Americans in the American armed services during World War II, many, no doubt, mobilized by the plight of their "compatriots." An American Committee for a Jewish Army, too, agitated for the establishment of a Jewish unit under the Allied Command.[45] Jewish American veterans likewise answered the call of the Palestinian Jews in the wake of the war. Four thousand Jewish war veterans marched on Washington in 1946 in support of Truman's proposal to admit 100,000 European refugees in Palestine, promising to raise two divisions if American forces were needed to implement the policy. And during Israel's war of independence, between one thousand and fifteen hundred Americans served in Mahal (the Hebrew acronym for "volunteers from outside the country"). A generation later, in the wake of the Six Day War, Jewish Americans from across the country volunteered for Israeli military service—over 2,000 in New York City alone.[46]

As in the days of the Fenians, of course, activism to the extent of military engagement or gun-running has been rather the exception than the rule in these ethnic communities; Mahal, as Urofsky notes, attracted only a "minuscule" proportion of American Jewry. But the distance separating a Mahal volunteer from the more ordinary American ethnic whose nationalist sympathies are borne by ballot or doled out in dollars may reflect a difference of degree, not of kind. As one man-in-the-street told a journalist who was investigating the Irish-American political organizations which had emerged in response to recent (1971) volleys in Northern Ireland, "Like the Jews, I have a moral responsibility to help my own."[47] Among the descendents of the early exiles from all three groups, the "moral responsibility to help" has often been defined politically, whether the help itself has taken the form of votes, lobbies, or occasional exports of hardware or military talent. "My own," meanwhile, has continued to encompass the broad realm of a distant nation and its transnational diaspora.

Nationalism and Ethnic Culture

These constructions of political and moral responsibility are not independent of culture. One particularly suggestive moment in the politico-cultural articulation of ethnicity as diasporic nationalism was John F. Kennedy's visit to Ireland in 1963—an event of transnational political significance, laden with diasporic emotive force. In contemporary accounts and in the President's own positioning of himself vis-à-vis Ireland, the rhetoric and imagery surrounding the visit rearticulated in its essentials the psychodrama of Irish exile which was so familiar in nineteenth-century emigrant culture.

Maurice Hennessy's popular treatment of Kennedy and Ireland fully replicates the teleology of James Jeffrey Roche's political hagiography of John Boyle O'Reilly. Like O'Reilly, the Kennedy of *I'll Come Back in the Spring* (1966) emerges, as if foreordained, from a long and heroic nationalist history. "John Kennedy's ancestors," the account opens, attained an Irish political reputation some nine centuries ago, "when Brian Boru, whose name was O'Kenedy, destroyed the power of the Norsemen at the Battle of Clontarf." The narrative goes on to link Kennedy's more immediate paternal ancestors to the uprising of 1798 and the Battle of Ross; his maternal ancestors, the "Geraldines," too, "achieved European renown for the fervor of their Irish patriotism."[48] It was this Irish nationalist pedigree which explained Kennedy's political greatness, in Hennessy's estimation; and it was his eternal bond to Ireland which made the President's "return" such a momentous occasion. Upon his visit to the city of Cork, "the famous bells of Shandon pealed out for him, and that sound in itself stirs the heart of many a returning exile."[49]

Hennessy's was not merely an idiosyncratic reading. In the manner it was portrayed in the press, in the many local rituals of Irish welcome, and in the rhetorical flights it inspired on the part of the President himself, Kennedy's visit to Ireland was steeped in nationalist symbolism. In Wexford, for instance, he was greeted by Irish schoolchildren singing about the valor of "The Boys of Wexford" who had risen up to break the "galling chain" of British rule in 1798. In a reciprocal gesture to Irish rebellion and heroism, Kennedy later laid wreaths at the graves of the leaders of the 1916 Easter Rebellion. In his Wexford speech itself, Kennedy quoted a post-Civil War tribute to the gallant Irish 69th of New York:

> War battered dogs we,
> gnawing a naked bone,
> fighting in every land and clime,
> for every cause but our own.[50]

In an address in Dublin, Kennedy presented the Irish Parliament with a flag of the Irish 69th, declaring that the regiment "bore a proud heritage and a special courage, given to those who had long fought for the cause of freedom." This commitment to freedom constituted the keynote of the ensuing address, in which Kennedy described the United States and Ireland as "divided by distance" but "united by history." Kennedy proved himself an adept student of Irish nationalist politics, making reference over the course of his brief address to Lord Edward Fitzgerald, Daniel O'Connell, Robert Emmet, Charles Stewart Parnell, James Joyce, William Butler Yeats, Henry Grattan, John Boyle O'Reilly, "The Boys of Wexford," and the Irish soldiers known as the Wild Geese, who fought in France under Patrick Sarsfield after the defeat of James II.

In both his Dublin and Wexford addresses Kennedy drew upon Ireland's traditions of rebellion not only to liken the United States and Ireland in political spirit, but also to predict the outcome of the Cold War. Pressing Ireland's nationalist history into the service of Cold War homily, Kennedy urged the people of the Iron Curtain countries never to forget "The Boys of Wexford." The "Irish experience," he asserted, had shown that it was possible for a people despite "a hundred years of foreign domination and religious persecution . . . to maintain their identity and faith." "[Those] who may believe that freedom may be on the run, or that one nation may be permanently subjugated and eventually wiped out, would do well to remember Ireland."[51] Here diasporic nationalism is assimilated into the American political mainstream in a mutually legitimating symbolic exchange: an American president's ethnic Irishness uniquely outfits him for the liberatory struggle of the Cold War era, just as current U.S. righteousness puts a stamp of endorsement upon Ireland's long, heroic battle with England.

Nor are such momentary crystallizations of diasporic thinking entirely isolated. As in the late nineteenth century, the diasporic imagination in the twentieth has been manifest in a broad array of cultural forms. The nationalist content of ethnic identity has descended in children's primers, including Stanisław Szwajkart's compendium of heroic nationalist episodes, *Polish History for Use in Polish Schools in America* (1906), and Helen Fine's Hebrew school textbook, *Behold, the Land!* (1968), self-consciously written to reach "children who did not experience the miracle of Israel's rebirth."[52] Nationalist sentiment has been popularized in mass-produced trinkets of ethnic kitsch: "Erin go braugh" [Ireland forever] refrigerator magnets, single-decade rosaries symbolizing the anti-Catholic repressions of the Penal era,[53] and "26 + 6 = 1" bumperstickers, which reclaim the six Ulster counties and proclaim Irish unity. Just as Elizabeth Gurley Flynn observed of her own girlhood at the turn of the century, nationalism continues to pervade plaintive and heroic family lore. "Where is the political programme of Polonia, as expressed on the banners in the Pulaski and other parades, hammered out?" asked Stefan Korbonski in 1963. "Mainly in the kitchen of the average Polish home."[54]

Even if the somewhat bounded literary life of the immigrant enclave has largely merged into an English-speaking and mass-mediated American market, literary nationalism of the sort engaged by O'Donovan Rossa and Stefan Barszczewski has not faded away. Significant ventures in Polonian publishing replicate the nineteenth-century editorial practice of repositioning Old World classics. Just as Barszczewski and Szwajkart re-presented the Polish romantic canon for a displaced Polish peasantry in the 1890s, so have the Copernicus Society and the PNA issued a new translation of Sienkiewicz's epic *Trilogy* for an assimilated Polish-American audience a century later.

In a pamphlet produced by the Copernicus Society in advance of the first installment, Edward Piszek outlined the political rationale for the literary undertaking. "Sienkiewicz's great work must be alive for us again," he wrote, "and not merely as a set of books but as an idea common to us all . . . It remains our most powerful weapon for awakening the ethnic consciousness of Polish youth born and brought up in many different cultures." Not coincidentally, the release of *With Fire and Sword* was slated for May 3, 1991, the two-hundredth anniversary of the Polish Constitution.[55]

The translator of this project sought overtly to bridge the distance between the Poland of his text and the sensibilities of a largely assimilated, English-speaking readership. Indeed, translator Jack Kuniczak and his promoters prefer the word "transposition" over "translation" to describe the undertaking.

"Transpositioning" a text ultimately takes place on several different levels. "What we have done," writes Piszek, "is to create a totally new Classic."[56] At the cosmetic level, transpositioning means helping out a (now) American readership by rendering difficult Polish names phonetically (Chmielnicki is rendered "Hmyelnitzky," for instance) to assure proper pronunciation. It also means updating and Americanizing Sienkiewicz's early-modern dialogue (the American vernacular interjection of disbelief—"No way!"—comes tumbling out of the mouth of a seventeenth-century Polish knight). At the cultural-historical level, transpositioning means actually *adding* background material to the text, where Sienkiewicz had comfortably assumed his readers' familiarity with Polish history. And at the political level, transpositioning means underscoring wherever possible the parallels between the besieged Poland of the seventeenth century and the besieged Poland of the reader's own twentieth century: negotiations between one faction of Polish nobles and the dreaded Ukrainian Cossack Chmielnicki, for instance, are characterized as "appeasement."

The energy and care which have gone into the production and the aggressive distribution of this transpositioned classic bespeak an enduring Polish tradition of literature-as-politics.[57] But if Sienkiewicz's work is to remain alive, in Piszek's phrase, "not merely as a set of books but as an idea common to us all," what precisely is that idea? Its first premise is summed up in a speech by "iron warrior" Stefan Tcharnyetzki: "Listen, the Commonwealth has known many disasters. It's been struck such blows that no other nation could survive even a fraction of them. But where are those who struck them? Who remembers them? Even the wild winds no longer blow their ashes through the Steppe. But the Commonwealth endures!"[58]

The second, ancillary premise to Polish endurance is the necessity for every Pole to set the special sorrows of the Polish nation above virtually every individual concern. "Think of your [own] pain as just one drop in a sea of suffering," says Prince Yaremi.

> Let your despair dissolve in that ocean of anguish that is about to drown our entire country. Listen to me. When our beloved Commonwealth faces such times as these, private tears become a selfish luxury. Anyone who wears a saber and calls himself a man will put aside his heartaches and run to save our Mother. And then he'll either find peace and forgetfulness in service and duty, or he'll die in a selfless cause, and that will earn him God's love and that eternal happiness that comes from a clear conscience.[59]

The sentiment is later codified: "no citizen may spill more tears over his own misfortunes than over the disasters that befall his nation."[60]

If, as Herbert Gans and others might argue, this vision of collective, oceanic anguish is a kind of salve to the atomized social life of post-industrial America, this "totally new classic" also bridges time and tradition in the history of Polish exile and diasporic nationalism. The "common idea" of Polish endurance and this politico-literary project of "awakening the ethnic consciousness of Polish youth born and brought up in many different cultures" meld with and supplement the ongoing political activities of groups like the Polish National Alliance on behalf of an ever vulnerable, frequently besieged Poland.

Nowhere in American literary life, however, is the diasporic imagination as active as in recent Jewish writing. This is in part because few ethnic groups have been as prolific on the American literary scene, and in part because, far more than the other independence movements, the triumph of Zionism has created a peculiar position for those who voluntarily remain in the "exile" of the Diaspora. Recent Jewish-American writings reverberate with Jewish Questions altered, certainly, but not fundamentally different from those taken up almost a century ago by Leon Kobrin, Jacob Gordin, or Abraham Cahan. These include autobiographical essays by Irena Klepfisz, Saul Bellow, Alan Dershowitz, and Letty Cottin Pogrebin; scholarly works by Paul Breines and Melvin Urofsky; works of fiction by Melanie Kaye/Kantrowitz and Philip Roth; and periodical projects like *Tikkun*.

The founding of Israel represented not only independence for an existing populace but also an invitation to a *potential* populace drawn from all corners of the Jewish Diaspora. What of those who have refused the invitation? On the one hand, they are presumed in some quarters to imperil the nation by holding aloof. "It is not pleasant to contemplate the wondrous perversity of over 99% of the major post-Holocaust remnant of the world's Jews choosing *not* to dwell in the Jewish state," writes Haim Chertok, an American emigrant to Israel; a danger exists that the national dream will dwindle to "a sort of extended, holyistic Jewish commune." In the words of Eliezer Livneh, in 1948 Aliyah—resettlement to Israel—became "the heart of Zionism and its acid test."[61]

And on the other hand, because of Israel's value as a haven during the many crises which could (and have) beset world Jewry, and because of its liberal immigration laws regarding all Jews—the Law of Return,[62]—voluntary "exiles" from around the world are also presumed in many quarters to enjoy a special relationship to the nation, replete with both obligations and privileges. Amid the tempest occasioned by the Pollard spy case, for instance, Israeli scholar Shlomo Avineri remarked of American Jewry, "you, in America, are no different from French, German, Polish, Soviet and Egyptian Jews. Your exile is different—comfortable, padded with success and renown. It is exile nonetheless." America, he concluded, "may not be your promised land."[63]

The Jewish-American sense of obligation and belonging to Israel has received its starkest expression from extremists like the late Rabbi Meir Kahane of the Jewish Defense League. "Exile," he wrote, "—even to the most temporarily beautiful of all lands—has always been a curse for the Jew. It remains so." Regardless of his or her present circumstances and citizenship, the Jew's ties to Israel remain ever "unbroken": "the Jewish people and the Land of Israel are involved in a dual relationship that is eternal."[64]

Gentler acknowledgments of the tie to Israel have ranged from

Haim Chertok's charming assertion that Zionism is "the only seaworthy dream afloat," to Morris Janowitz's certainty that the defense of Israel remains "the paramount task of the Jewish community" in the United States.[65] Letty Cottin Pogrebin avers that, "given virtually every country's record of treating us as surplus citizenry, the survival of Israel is vital to the survival of the Jews." In his suggestively titled study *We Are One! American Jewry and Israel*, Melvin Urofsky characterizes the relationship as *mishpachah*—family—with all the tenderness, irritation, resentment, contentiousness, and devotion implied by the word.[66] (David Vital had precisely this relationship in mind when he noted with some irony that Israel's controversial policies and embattled history have tended "to rob Jews of the Diaspora of their long sought for and so very recently acquired peace of mind." Family indeed.)[67]

One dimension of this family feeling, particularly as Israel has become the focus of so much heat in world political forums in recent years, has been an angry defensiveness among American Jews about perceived instances of unwarranted Israel-bashing.[68] A second, perhaps subtler dimension of this family feeling is the tendency among many American Jews themselves passionately to denounce Israeli policies. Alan Dershowitz has complained that with the onset of the *Intifada*, "numerous Jews with no history of prior identification with Israel or other Jewish causes suddenly decided to speak out against Israel *as Jews*." Philip Roth aptly notes, "Disillusionment is a way of caring for one's country too."[69] The very depth of Jewish-American disillusionment with Israel in many cases betrays the extent to which Israel is tacitly being embraced as "one's country."

Historian Paul Breines offers one such citizenly critique of Israeli policy in *Tough Jews*, his study of post-1967 images of a militarist Jewish masculinity (cleverly rendered as "Rambowitz"). Breines laments the morally paralyzing use of historic Jewish persecution to justify any and all Israeli policies in the occupied territories. "The Holocaust," he charges,

> precisely because of its imagery of Jewish victimization, enabled Jewish Americans (and Israelis) to embrace the consequences of the Israeli victory [in the Six Day War]: occupying the West Bank and the Gaza Strip, turning the Palestinians there into a subject people, and now suppressing the Palestinian uprising. The Holocaust made this acceptable to large numbers of American (and Israeli) Jews. . . . the more brutal Israeli policies become,

and the more Israelis speak of the country's self-brutalization as well, the more American Jews discuss, indeed, the more they need, the Holocaust.[70]

Although Breines describes himself as having grown up in "a home that was more interested in Henry Wallace's presidential campaign than in the founding of Israel,"[71] *Tough Jews* was clearly written within a diasporic moral and intellectual universe. Only the thin stroke of a parenthesis separates American from Israeli Jews in his discussion; and Breines frankly presents and analyzes his own "tough Jewish fantasies" throughout the critique. Indeed, in an explanatory note on his politically motivated decision to ignore extremists like Meir Kahane, Breines writes, "It is . . . the Kahane present in virtually all of us that really interests me."[72]

This "family" relationship with Israel, in all its ambiguity, is likewise depicted, critiqued, and embodied in works of fiction by Jewish American writers as diverse as Melanie Kaye/Kantrowitz and Philip Roth. Kaye/Kantrowitz's "In the Middle of the Barbecue She Brings up Israel," for instance, recounts an impassioned backyard debate over Israel among several American Jews representing various generations and diverse political outlooks. "I know you think Israel is a tiny brave miracle," says Nadine Greenbaum, a twenty-two year old, spike-haired college student who is currently studying Islam. "You know what it's doing, our Israel? . . . It's breaking the hands of kids for throwing rocks."[73]

During the passionate debate over "our Israel" which follows, someone insists that "The Jewish people will never give up Jerusalem," and a second chimes in, "We refuse to negotiate with terrorists." Here the narrator pauses to wonder, "What does he mean *we*? He lives in the Bronx."[74] Throughout Kaye/Kantrowitz's stories this conflict between those who see world Jewry as indivisible ("we refuse to negotiate") and those who do not ("what does he mean we?") constantly asserts *and* critiques the nationalist posture of the American Diaspora.

Zionism itself is the controlling metaphor of Philip Roth's *The Counterlife*, described by Letty Cottin Pogrebin as the "quintessential novel of Jewish-American identity conflict."[75] Indeed, the novel derives its title from the Zionist movement's normalizing logic: "a highly conscious desire to be divested of virtually everything that had come to seem . . . distinctively Jewish behavior." The establishment of a Jewish nation among the world's nations thus amounts to "the construction of a counterlife."[76]

Through his gallery of characters and the frankly polemic exchanges between them, Roth offers an impressive tableau of Jewish political and social consciousness. The novel reflects and explores various positions along the spectrum of Jewish political identity, from American assimilationism to the most vociferous Israeli Zionism, allowing each to comment upon the complex, late twentieth-century relationship between Zion and the Diaspora. As these polemics accumulate over the course of the novel, the issues of Jewish toughness and violence, anti-Semitism and the threat of anti-Semitic violence, the Diaspora's dependence upon Israel as a haven, and Israel's dependence upon the Diaspora for security, all become entwined.

At the center of this mesh of rivaling political commentaries, however, and indeed central to the portion of the novel devoted to Judea, is the question of identity. The plot focuses upon the Zionist awakening of the narrator's brother, Henry Zuckerman, and the narrator's attempt to come to terms with this inexplicable departure from the habits of a lifetime. The narrator visits him in Israel in an effort to discover just how and why Henry, "a Jew whose history of intimidation by anti-Semitism was simply non-existent," had suddenly become a Zionist firebrand.[77]

Zuckerman's visit to Israel becomes the occasion for unceasing and varied polemics on the Jewish Question. But bounded by Nathan's stolid assimilationism on the one hand and Henry's ethnic revivalism on the other, and refracted, moreover, through Nathan's own consciousness, broad political comment ultimately serves the highly individualized question of psychology and private "anti-myths." For Roth, in other words, the political is primarily personal: Zionism is less a political program than, as Zuckerman puts it, a mode of "self-analysis."[78]

The primacy of psychology is made plain when, in a dizzying whirl of self-reflexivity, Nathan Zuckerman's account of Henry's *aliyah* turns out to be but a manuscript novel-within-the-novel—a fiction, moreover, which is angrily refuted by the *real* Henry. Railing at this fictive turn by which his older brother has depicted him as being "under the tutelage of some political hothead" in Israel, Henry remarks, "Another dream of domination, fastening upon me another obsession from which *he* was the one who could never be rescued." The earlier passages—the trip to Israel, the rantings of (Kahanite) Mordecai Lippman, the Zionist and anti-Zionist banter—are but the fevered dreams of Nathan Zuckerman himself; they reveal a fully obsessive concern for Zionism, Israel, and all manner of Jewish Questions on the part of this ostensibly "normalized" American Jew. "The poor bastard," in Henry's words, "had Jew on the brain."[79]

For Roth, as for many other writers who in one way or another "have Jew on the brain," Israel remains at or near the center of that constellation of questions which comprise the ever problematic Jewish-American identity. His most recent work, *Operation Shylock*, takes the theme of the nationalistic nature of Jewish ethnic identity even further. In this flight of feverish ethnic angst, the plot revolves around the figure of a Philip Roth double (nicknamed "Moishe Pipik" by the "real" Roth) who has appeared in Jerusalem, and, in the guise of the famous novelist, has begun to preach a new political credo of anti-Zionism known as "Diasporism." Israel, his argument runs, is bad for the Jews. A militarized and perpetually embattled state is the last thing in the world the Jews ever needed; Israel is endangering Jewish lives and corrupting the Jewish soul. Pipik proposes to lead the Jews out of Israel, and back to the ghettoes of Europe. "*Last* year in Jerusalem! Next year in Warsaw! Next year in Bucharest! Next year in Vilna and Cracow."[80]

The central reference points for the novel's convoluted plot are the Pollard spy case and the Israeli trial of John Demjanjuk as Treblinka's Ivan the Terrible. On the one hand, Pipik feels that Israel threatens to turn world Jewry into a mass of Jonathan Pollards—spies for a (in his view) vicious regime. Pollard becomes in this vision a victim of the Jewish state, and Israel is now "deforming and disfiguring Jews as only our anti-Semitic enemies once had the power to do."[81] "What the Dreyfus case was to Herzl," Pipik explains, "the Pollard case is to me."[82]

On the other hand, the action of the novel unfolds in Israel, against the backdrop of the trial of John Demjanjuk. This trial becomes the occasion for competing commentary on the centrality of both the Holocaust and Zionism in the construction of late-twentieth-century Jewish identity. Much of the commentary plays on the tender distinction between Israeli *justice*—the Jewish state will hold Ivan the Terrible accountable for his crimes against the Jews—and Israeli *justification*—the enormity of the Holocaust (embodied by Demjanjuk) overshadows, and so excuses, the Israeli response to the *Intifada*.

Operation Shylock is perhaps the supreme expression of the diasporic imagination in the late twentieth century. "Diasporism" takes as its unspoken premise not only the centrality of the Jewish state to Jewish existence, but a Zionism so triumphant that it has transformed (disfigured, in Pipik's estimation) Jewish life everywhere. Pipik's program of Diasporism is the most extreme articulation of the point, but the entire novel revolves on this axis. The novel, subtitled "a confession," ends with a flurry of complex political exchanges between the "real" Philip Roth and a (fictional?) Israeli official. Roth himself turns out to be, in the words of that official, "no less ideologically committed than your fellow patriot Jonathan Pollard."[83]

Like the "transpositioned" chivalry and liberationist axioms of Henryk Sienkiewicz, these works rearticulate ethnic identity as a brand of national belonging which entails an internal geography of national center and a diasporic periphery, deeply embedded nationalist mythologies and codes of enduring obligation—or, in the case of a Breines or a Roth, enduring ensnarement. As one of Kaye/Kantrowitz's characters asks, "What does Jewish mean now anyway except fussing for holidays and arms for Israel?"[84]

Several ambiguities have tended to cloud the issue of ethnic nationalism in American social thought. Not least of all is the fact that, despite the venom typically carried in the charge, "dual loyalty" has occasionally been deemed legitimate. Polish nationalism won accolades from no less an arbiter of American legitimacy than Harry Truman's Attorney General, for instance, who applauded Poles as an "advance guard" for American anti-Communism.[85] But more fundamentally, the principle of diasporic nationalism fails to fit neatly within the prevailing categories of pluralism and assimilationism: churches, ethnic lodges, foods, folk arts, languages, and group histories may all be plural, but the unyielding assimilationist code of American political life is expressed and ritually repeated in the pledge (singular) of allegiance (also singular). Reigning assumptions regarding the political imperative of "Americanism" on the one hand and the apolitical, chiefly cultural nature of "ethnic identity" on the other tend to obscure the nuances of the diasporic imagination—a sensibility which is embedded in culture yet has political overtones and consequences; a spirit which lays claim to America as home while remaining engaged in the struggles and the ideals of a distant homeland.

Indeed, if the assimilationist and nationalist traditions in ethnic politics did stand in opposition to one another, then the ascendance of Kennedy to the presidency would seem the zenith of the assimilationist. Insofar as his heritage raised questions about Kennedy's fitness for the post at all, it was generally his relationship to Rome, not Dublin, which caused concern.[86] But Kennedy's much-trumpeted "return" to Ireland in 1963 illustrates the salience of nationalist themes and idioms even in the case of one so Americanized as an American head of state.

If diasporic nationalism has sometimes informed ethnic American-ism, so have the idioms of nationalist subcultures and the moods of the American mainstream often blended together. Popular epics like James Michener's *Poland*, Leon Uris's *Trinity* and *Exodus*, television dramas like *A Woman Named Golda*, and Hollywood extravaganzas like *Cast a Giant Shadow* mark the extent to which the tributaries of ethnic nationalism have flowed into the broader currents of American pop-ular culture. "Liberty" serves as a kind of national mantra; and "lovers of liberty"—whether Polish, Irish, or Zionist—become metaphors for a grandly conceived American tradition. The mass market "Rambow-itz" paperbacks and the transpositioned chivalric sentiments of Sien-kiewicz's *With Fire and Sword*, too, may play into prevailing patterns of "remasculinization" (Susan Jeffords' term) in post-Vietnam American culture. Sienkiewicz's sexualized portrait of knights going "to battle as if to a wedding" is as suggestive in the era of Robert Bly's *Iron John* as it was in the era of Teddy Roosevelt's "Strenuous Life."[87]

In its focus upon questions of political identity—the ways in which migrants and their descendents have positioned themselves within the vying Old and New World myths of national collectivity—this study has raised more questions than it can hope to answer about the com-plexities of "identificational assimilation."[88] Some proposals for fur-ther study are in order. In particular, a revised view of nationalism and its salience in immigrant and ethnic cultures raises a number of ques-tions regarding gender, race, and assimilation.

First, as the masculinist rituals discussed in chapter 4 suggest, where identity is cast in the politicized terms of nationalist tradition, na-tional rights, and struggles for state power, the avenues of assimilation are implicitly and irrevocably gendered. Men and women have tradi-tionally held very different positions in relationship to matters of state—a fact which in itself suggests an important gender differential in the processes of identificational assimilation.

But further, these nationalist cultures guided men toward New World civic life while they ushered women away from it. While the soldiering ideal was articulated in terms of its benefit to the Old Country ("Let this war be for us a school for the future!"), military ideals nonetheless drew immigrant men into American affairs and encouraged them to see themselves as participants in American civic life. By contrast, the nationalist ideal of the feminine, articulated in figures like the Spartan mother and the culture-keeper, was highly insular. As culture-keeper, it was the nationalist mother's holiest obligation to protect herself and her family from the many menacing agents of "denationalization." This differential warrants further study, as it bears on many aspects of immigrant social life both within and without the home.[89]

And second, as the imperialism debates analyzed in Chapter 5 suggest, where identification is cast in the politicized terms of nationalist tradition, national rights, and state power, the avenues of assimilation are implicitly and irrevocably racialized. Against a backdrop of Chinese Exclusion, anti-Japanese agitation, Jim Crowism, an imperialist mission of civilization in Asia and the Americas, and a racialized rhetoric of immigration restriction, the prospect of "becoming American" was intimately related to conceptions of the nation's racial character, many of whose categories were fluid and in motion—"Anglo-Saxon," "Celt," "Slav," "Hebrew," "Caucasian." The categories of race and nation vied for salience in the early decades of the twentieth century, as the immigrants redefined themselves in a New World setting at the same time that their adopted country redefined itself vis-à-vis the weaker and stronger nations of the world. This racialized dimension of "becoming American" touches the very core issues of American politics and culture in the Progressive Era and begs for further examination.

But evident are the tenacity of nationalism in immigrant life, and the enduring transnational linkages between the politics of the homeland and the culture of the diaspora. Ethnic expressions such as the election of Bobby Sands as posthumous Grand Marshall of New York's St. Patrick's Day parade draw upon longstanding Old World political traditions, and they often emerge in response to international affairs. Such expressions reflect a transnational ethos which is distinct from, although not altogether independent of, specifically American politics of ethnic mobilization. A 1983 St. Patrick's Day parade banner identifying Ireland as "England's Vietnam"[90] is perhaps the perfect twentieth-century analogue to an earlier generation's identification of the Philippines as *America's Ireland*: the fundamental point of reference is now clearly the New World and not the Old, yet nationalist definitions of justice and nationalist propensities for analogy persist.

It may be no coincidence that the so-called "roots phenomenon" among these groups in the 1970s flourished against an international backdrop of Ulster violence, Arab-Israeli conflict, and escalating Polish civil strife. Engagement in matters of the homeland for these and other groups may not be a symbolic token but a very engine of resilient ethnic identification. The embedded nationalist strains of ethnic culture, in other words, may usefully be explored as one of the *causes*, not the effects, of late-twentieth-century ethnic revivalism during a period of mounting crisis in the homelands overseas. And the children, grandchildren, and great-grandchildren of Europe's exiles, pilgrims, and wanderers may usefully be viewed as members—distant, no question, but members nonetheless—of the transnational communities which their forebears created through myriad acts of migration and memory.

Glossary of Names

Barszczewski, Stefan (1870–1937). PNA and Polish Falcon activist; editor of *Zgoda* (1897–1901) and *Sokol* (1890–1901); author of five-act drama, *Cuba Libre!* (1899), in which the Spanish-Cuban-American War serves as a rehearsal for Poland's war of independence. Returned to Poland 1901.

Barzyński, Wincenty (1838–1899). Left Poland after the failed 1863 uprising; leader of Resurrectionist Order in Texas (1866–1874) and Chicago (1874–1899) and leading voice in Polish religionist camp; co-founder of Polish Roman Catholic Union.

Boucicault, Dion (1820–1890). Irish playwright whose productions remained among the most popular in Irish-America throughout the second half of the nineteenth century. Best known in Irish-America for *Arrah na Pogue, Shaun the Post*, and the *Shaughraun*, which treat nationalist themes rather playfully; and *Robert Emmet*, in which depiction of Irish martyrdom is serious indeed.

Brodowski, Zbigniew (1852–1901). Polish National Alliance activist; editor of *Zgoda* (1885–1889); author of popular play, *Związkowiec* [A Member of the Alliance] (c.1898); served as Chicago Parks Commissioner and U.S. Consul in Breslau.

Cahan, Abraham (1860–1951). Journalist, novelist, long-time editor of the *Forverts*. Author of *Yekl*, and other fiction dealing with questions of Jewish identity. Held aloof from Zionism but pressed the Jewish Question within the socialist movement, and so was to this extent sympathetic with Jewish nationalism.

Chmielinska, Stefania (1866–1939). Nationalist leader in Chicago; co-founder of the Polish Women's Alliance. Pressed for women's inclusion in Polonia's political activities.

Conway, Katherine (1853–1927). American-born novelist and journalist; author of *Lalor's Maples* (1901), a novel of Irish-American manners; succeeded James Jeffrey Roche as *Pilot* editor after several years on the staff.

Dangiel, Stanisław (1873–1938). Active in Polish National Catholic Church; editor of *Straż* (1900–1912) and frequent contributor of essays and poems; served as that journal's publisher 1906–1912.

Desmond, Humphrey (1858–1932). American-born editor of the Milwaukee *Catholic Citizen*, ever-sensitive to the Irish Question; author of *The A.P.A. Movement* (1912) and *Why God Loves the Irish* (1918).

Dunne, Finley Peter (1867–1936). Chicago journalist; creator of wagphilosopher Mr. Dooley; denounced by middle-class Irish-Americans for his "demeaning" dialect portraits of the immigrants, yet engaged via Mr. Dooley in the debate over the tactics and tenor of Irish nationalism in America.

Feygenbaum, Benjamin (1860–1923). Active in the Socialist Labor Party; labor theorist and frequent contributor to the *Abend blatt* and *Naye tzayt*; one of the leading voices of the cosmopolitanist position; denounced every stripe of Jewish nationalism.

Finerty, John (1846–1908). Irish nationalist leader in Chicago; active in Clan na Gael; editor of the *Chicago Citizen*; author of *Warpath and Bivouac*, a treatment of the Indian wars in the West.

Flynn, Elizabeth Gurley (1890–1964). The "rebel girl" of the IWW; her autobiography, *The Rebel Girl* (1955), includes recollections of growing up in an Irish nationalist household during the Spanish-Cuban-American and Phillipine-American wars.

Ford, Patrick (1837–1913). Irish nationalist leader in New York; editor of the *Irish World and Industrial Liberator*; author of *The Criminal History of the British Empire* (1881); active in the Land League and in American labor politics.

Gieryk, Teodor (1837–1878). Liberal religionist leader in early Polonia; among the founders of the Polish Roman Catholic Union.

Giller, Agaton (1831–1887). Veteran (and historian) of the Polish uprising of 1863; exiled in Switzerland after its defeat, where he organized and coordinated an international independence movement; his essay "On the Organization of the Poles in America" (1879) became the organizational blueprint for the Polish National Alliance.

Gordin, Jacob (1853–1909). Popular Yiddish short-story writer and dramatist; author of *Siberia, God, Man, and Devil, Mirele Efros*, and *Kapitan Dreyfus*; among the staunchest cosmopolitanist voices in Yiddish literature in the period; credited with bringing European realism to the Yiddish stage, and so sparking the "golden epoch" of Yiddish theater.

Guiney, Louise Imigen (1861–1920). American-born novelist, essay writer, and poet, whose work reflected a romantic interest in Ireland and the Irish Question; author of *Robert Emmet: A Survey of His Rebellion and His Romance* (1904); in addition to her own literary work, she translated the Irish poetry of James Clarence Mangan.

Hodur, Francis (1866–1953). Founder of the schismatic Polish Roman Catholic Church in Pennsylvania, based on proto-nationalist principles of ethnic control of local church property and vernacular-language services; excommunicated by the Catholic Church, 1898; publisher of *Straż* (1897–1906) and frequent contributor.

Kobrin, Leon (1873–1946). Yiddish short story writer and novelist; author of *Yankel Boyle*, "Anna's Ma-nishtane," "What Is He?" and other works exploring the eternal nature of Jewish identity; aligned with the socialists of the *Forverts*, though very sympathetic to Jewish nationalism.

Krantz, Philip [Jacob Rombro] (1858–1922). Yiddish activist in the Socialist Labor Party and editor of the *Abend blatt*; staunch cosmopolitanist voice within the Yiddish left; author of *Are the Jews a Nation?* (1903).

Kruszka, Michael (1860–1918). Polish leader in Milwaukee, editor of *Kuryer Polski* (1888–1900), who had been jailed in Poland for opposing *Kulturkampf* (1870); entered U.S. politics as Wisconsin Assemblyman (1890); tried to remain independent of PNA-PRCU warfare, although leaned ever more heavily toward the nationalist position over the course of the 1890s.

Liessen, Abraham [Abraham Wald] (1872–1938). Yiddish poet, ardent Jewish nationalist; believed in an identity of spirit between Macabbean heroes and modern, secular heroes of the labor movement, as evidenced in poems like "The Eternal Jew," "From the Dark Past," "A Martyr's Blood," and "In Battle"; *Forverts* contributor credited with bringing nationalism to life in the Yiddish radical press.

Miłkowski, Zygmunt [also known as T. T. Jeż] (1824–1915). Veteran of the Polish uprising of 1863, active (along with Agaton Giller) in organizing an international Polish insurgency from exile in Switzerland; popular novelist; traveled throughout the United States at the turn of the century to raise money for the National Fund and to survey the strength of Polish nationalism there; published his findings as *A Report from Travels in the Polish Colonies of North America* (1903).

Neuman, Kazimierz (1843–1907). Polish religionist leader and essayist; editor of *Dziennik Chicagoski* (1896–1902).

O'Reilly, John Boyle (1844–1890). Irish nationalist poet, former Fenian conspirator imprisoned in Australia; escaped to the United States (1869); longtime editor of the Boston *Pilot*; author of the novel *Moondyne Joe*; his life provided the material for James Jeffrey Roche's nationalist hagiography, *John Boyle O'Reilly* (1891).

Powderly, Terence (1849–1924). Knights of Labor leader and Clan na Gael activist in Pennsylvania; his memoir, *The Path I Trod*, recounts the close connection between labor and nationalist organizations in that region.

Roche, James Jeffrey (1847–1908). Irish nationalist poet, novelist, essayist, historian; editor of the Boston *Pilot* (1890–1904); outspoken critic of both British and American imperialism; author of *Songs and Satires* (1887), *John Boyle O'Reilly* (1891), *Her Majesty the King* (1899), and *The Sorrows of Sap'ed* (1904).

Rosenfeld, Morris (1862–1923). Best known and most beloved of the Yiddish labor poets; an early convert to Zionism around the time of the first Zionist congresses; works such as "Diaspora March," "Jerusalem," and "The Little Chanukah Candles" overtly hew to Jewish nationalist themes, although anti-Zionist critics wanted to peg him primarily as a "sweatshop" poet.

Rossa, Jeremiah O'Donovan (1831–1915). Fenian activist and dynamiter; memoirist; author of *Rossa's Recollections*, a literary attempt to marshal his personal history in the service of stirring the latent Irish nationalism of the American-born Irish.

Samolinska, Teofila (1848–1913). Nationalist, proto-feminist Polish organizer and writer; among the earliest and best-known poets in Polonia; known as "the Mother of the Polish National Alliance"; she was in close contact with the exiles in Europe, and it was on her insistence that Agaton Giller produced his essay "On Organizing the Poles in America"; founded the Central Association of Polish Women in Chicago (1887), a forerunner of the Polish Women's Alliance.

Sarasohn, Khasriel (1835–1905). Orthodox leader in New York; publisher of the *Yiddishes tageblatt* (1885–1905); highly supportive of the Zionist movement as it emerged behind Theodor Herzl, despite its secular cast.

Siemiradzki, Tomasz (1850–1939). Polish nationalist historian; arrived in the United States in 1896 and embarked on a speaking tour financed by the Polish National Alliance to publicize the Polish cause; author of *The Post-Partition History of Poland* (c.1899); succeeded Stefan Barszczewski as editor of *Zgoda* (1901–1912).

Szwajkart, Stanisław (1857–1918). Polish Roman Catholic Union activist, educator, and writer; editor of *Dziennik Chicagoski* (1890–1892, 1902–1907); frequent contributor on literary, historical, and political matters; author of *A History of Poland for Use in Polish Schools in America* (1906).

Winchevsky, Morris (1856–1932). Yiddish socialist poet, essayist, contributor (later editor) of the *Forverts*; like Rosenfeld, best known for his socialist poems and sketches, for which he had become famous in London in the 1880s, yet deeply drawn to Jewish nationalism.

Zeifert, Moishe (1851–1922). Yiddish novelist and dramatist, drawn to Jewish nationalist themes; author of *The Heroes of Israel* (1893) and *Kuba* (c.1898), a horrific depiction of Spanish rule steeped in the popular nationalist ethos of Spain-as-Inquisition-Country.

Zhitlowsky, Chaim (1865–1943). Yiddish socialist; cultural theorist and chief spokesperson for "Yiddishism," a brand of nationalism rooted in the immutability of Jewish identity and the galvanizing power of the Yiddish language; author of *Socialism and the National Question* (1908).

Zolotkoff, Leon (1866–1938). Chicago Zionist leader; organizer of the Western Zion Alliance; Secretary of the Knights of Zion; frequent contributor to *Der nayer geyst* on matters of both Zionist and American politics; sympathetic to socialism as a means of alleviating *some* social ills, but skeptical about any movement which failed to take up the Jewish Question directly.

Zychlynski, Casimir (1859–1927). Polish Falcon and Polish National Alliance official in Chicago; strong advocate of physical training and the importance of military readiness among Polish-American men for the coming war of Polish independence.

Notes

1. Introduction

1. Agaton Giller, "List o organizacyi Polaków w Ameryce" [1879] in Stanisław Osada, *Historia Związku Narodowego Polskiego i rozwój ruchu narodowego polskiego w Ameryce* (Chicago: Zgoda, 1905), p. 105.

2. The extent to which American scholars have tended to favor Lazarus' tempest-tost, huddled masses at the expense of the immigrant-as-exile is cast in bold relief when one compares American immigration historiography to European emigration historiography. By contrast, European scholars begin to sound rather like Agaton Giller. In his 1971 study *Ireland since the Famine*, for instance, F. S. L. Lyons offers the following commentary on the Famine migration: "It was not just that within the shores of Ireland the old bitterness of an oppressed peasantry against an alien and often ruthless landlord class was reinforced by resentment towards a government which . . . had shown itself . . . manifestly inadequate . . . to contain the crisis. . . . It was rather that this hatred, this bitterness, this resentment were carried overseas, and especially to America, by nearly four million Irish men, women and children who left their homeland." The political consequences of this exodus, Lyons continues, were plain to be seen: "The Irish question became and remained an international question." F. S. L. Lyons, *Ireland since the Famine* (n.l.: Collins-Fontana, 1971), p. 16.

Compare also Andrzej Pilch, *Emigracja z ziem polskich w czasach nowożytnych i najnowszych* (Warsaw: Państwowe Wydawnictwo Naukowe, 1984), p. 14; Florian Stasik, *Polska emigracja zarobkowa w Stanach Zjednoczonych Ameryki 1865–1914* (Warsaw: Państwowe Wydawnictwo Naukowe, 1985), pp. 189–258; Florian Stasik, *Polska emigracja polityczna w Stanach Zjednoczonych Ameryki 1831–1864* (Warsaw: Państwowe Wydawnictwo Naukowe, 1973); S. M. Dubnow, *History of the Jews in Russia and Poland: From the Earliest Times to the Present Day* (Philadelphia: The Jewish Publication Society of America, 1918), II, pp. 372–377.

3. Eva Hoffman, *Lost in Translation* (New York: Penguin Books, 1989), p. 132.

4. Ibid., p. 86.

5. See for example, Mona Harrington, "Loyalties: Dual and Divided," in Stephan Thernstrom, ed., *The Harvard Encyclopedia of American Ethnic Groups* (Cambridge, Mass.: Harvard University Press, 1980), pp. 676–686. A notable exception to this approach is David Noel Doyle, *Irish Americans, Native Rights, and National Empires* (New York: Arno, 1976).

6. Osada, *Historia Z.N.P.*, p. 467.

7. Boston *Pilot*, June 25, 1898, p. 4.

8. Elizabeth Gurley Flynn, *The Rebel Girl: An Autobiography* (New York: International Publishers, 1955), pp. 34–35.

9. *Kuryer Polski*, May 2, 1899, p. 2.

10. This international dimension of ethnic identity has been most fully developed in the literature on Jewish Americans. See Marshall Sklare, *America's Jews* (New York: Random House, 1971), pp. 216–222; Charles Silberman, *A Certain People: American Jews and Their Lives Today* (New York: Summit Books, 1985), chapter 5.

11. Robert Orsi, *The Madonna of 115th Street: Faith and Community in Italian Harlem, 1880–1950* (New Haven: Yale University Press, 1985). See also John Bukowczyk, *And My Children Did Not Know Me: A History of Polish-Americans* (Bloomington: Indiana University Press, 1987); Kerby Miller, *Emigrants and Exiles: Ireland and the Irish Exodus to North America* (New York: Oxford University Press, 1985); and Ewa Morawska, *For Bread With Butter: Lifeworlds of East Central European Immigrants in Johnstown, Pennsylvania, 1890–1940* (Cambridge: Cambridge University Press, 1985).

12. Miller, *Emigrants and Exiles*, pp. 102–130.

13. David Hollinger, "Historians and the Discourse of Intellectuals," collected in John Higham and Paul Conkin, eds., *New Directions in American Intellectual History* (Baltimore: Johns Hopkins University Press, 1979), pp. 42–45.

14. Mary Poovey, *Uneven Developments: The Ideological Work of Gender in Mid-Victorian England* (Chicago: University of Chicago Press, 1988).

15. For a formulation of nationalism as dependent on the imagination, see Benedict Anderson, *Imagined Communities: Reflections on the Origin and Spread of Nationalism* (London: Verso, 1983). Arnold Eisen, *Galut: Modern Jewish Reflection on Homelessness and Homecoming* (Bloomington: Indiana University Press, 1986), chapter 2, likewise addresses the deep (biblical) history of Jewish nationalism in terms of "Imagining Home."

16. For a review of the class arguments regarding nationalism, see esp. James Blaut, *The National Question: Decolonising the Theory of Nationalism* (London: Zed Books, 1987). For nationalist hegemony specifically in the context of immigration, see Kerby Miller, "Class, Culture, and Immigrant Group Identity in the United States: The Case of Irish-American Ethnicity,"

in Virginia Yans-McLaughlin, ed., *Immigration Reconsidered: History, Sociology, and Politics* (New York: Oxford, 1990), pp. 96–129.

17. Brook Thomas, *The New Historicism and Other Old Fashioned Topics* (Princeton: Princeton University Press, 1991), p. xv.

18. According to the U.S. Secretary of Labor's statistics, for instance, Polish re-emigration stood at 18,392 in 1920; 42,207 in 1921; and 31,004 in 1922. By contrast, Melvin Urofsky notes that, throughout the 1950s, American emigration to the newly established Jewish state "rarely rose over 200 or 300 a year . . ." Andrzej Brożek, *Polish Americans, 1854–1939* (Warsaw: Interpress, 1985), p. 234; Melvin I. Urofsky, *We Are One! American Jewry and Israel* (Garden City, N.Y.: Anchor/Doubleday, 1978), pp. 272, 265–277.

19. Brożek, *Polish Americans*, p. 234.

20. Cited in Urofsky, *We Are One!*, p. 270. Elsewhere Sklare concluded that "Commitment to Jewish [religious] life has no effect on sharing a pro-Israel position." On the question of whether American Jews should help Israel, 90% answered in the affirmative, regardless of their commitment to other aspects of Jewish life. Marshall Sklare and Benjamin Ringer, "A Study of Jewish Attitudes Toward the State of Israel," in Marshall Sklare, ed., *The Jews: Social Patterns of an American Ethnic Group* (New York: Free Press, 1958), p. 442.

21. James Jeffrey Roche, *John Boyle O'Reilly: His Life, Poems, and Speeches* (New York: Cassell Publishing, 1891), p. 416.

1. Exiles, Pilgrims, Wanderers

1. Cited in Kerby Miller, *Emigrants and Exiles: Ireland and the Irish Exodus to North America* (New York: Oxford University Press, 1985), p. 104. For Miller's full discussion of the "culture of exile," see pp. 102–130. See also Mary Helen Thuente, "The Folklore of Irish Nationalism," in Thomas Hachey and Lawrence McCaffrey, eds., *Perspectives on Irish Nationalism* (Lexington: University Press of Kentucky), p. 49.

2. Patrick Ford, *Criminal History of the British Empire* (New York: Irish World, 1881), p. 54. On Maud Gonne's N.Y. reception, see the *Irish World*, Jan. 8, 1898, p. 8. *Official Ritual and Manual of the Ladies' Auxiliary of the Ancient Order of Hibernians in America* [1895] (n.l.: Adelia Christy, 1916), p. 4. Boyle O'Reilly's St. Patrick's Day address cited in James Jeffrey Roche, *John Boyle O'Reilly: His Life, Poems, and Speeches* (New York: Cassell, 1891), p. 415. Nor was this exile motif reserved for public pronouncements. David M. Emmons, *The Butte Irish: Class and Ethnicity in an American Mining Town, 1875–1925* (Urbana: University of Illinois Press, 1989), cites these lines in the private diary of Edward Boyce: "There came to the beach a poor exile of Erine"; or again, "But Saxon bonds bind me, Erin, and I must sail from thee" p. 298.

3. Adam Mickiewicz, *Book of the Polish Pilgrims*, in George Rapall Noyes,

ed., *Poems by Adam Mickiewicz* (New York: Polish Institute for Arts and Sciences, 1944), p. 380.

4. Richard Gottheil, *The Aims of Zionism*, excerpted in Arthur Hertzberg, *The Zionist Idea* (New York: Atheneum, 1971), p. 498.

5. S. M. Dubnow, *History of the Jews in Russia and Poland: From the Earliest Times to the Present Day* (Philadelphia: The Jewish Publication Society of America, 1918), II, pp. 372–377.

6. Roche, *John Boyle O'Reilly*, p. 263. Davitt cited in Lawrence J. McCaffrey, *The Irish Diaspora in America* (Washington D.C.: The Catholic University of America Press, 1976), p. 130.

7. Stanisław Osada, *Historia Związku Narodowego Polskiego i rozwój ruchu narodowego polskiego w Ameryce* (Chicago: Zgoda, 1905), p. 105.

8. Emma Lazarus, *An Epistle to the Hebrews*, [1882–1883] (New York: Jewish Historical Society, 1987), p. 42. For a later variation on this same theme, see *Yiddishes tageblatt*, Jan. 26, 1898, p. 8.

9. James M. Blaut, Jr., *The National Question: Decolonising the Theory of Nationalism* (London: Zed Books, 1987), pp. 8–54.

10. Organized in Vilna in 1897, the Bund brought together elements of labor radicalism and Jewish nationalism.

11. For his general taxonomy of nationalist situations, see Blaut, *The National Question*, p. 13. Benedict Anderson, *Imagined Communities: Reflections on the Origin and Spread of Nationalism* (London: Verso, 1983), esp. pp. 41–49, similarly stresses the importance of state power and dynamic struggle, although Anderson is generally more concerned with the linguistic roots of nationalism and the degrees of privilege or marginality which inevitably stem from the establishment of "official" or "state" languages.

These works differ from the more traditional formulations of Hans Kohn and Louis Snyder primarily in their emphasis on nationalism as a dynamic relationship between opposing forces. For Kohn, nationalism is a matter of a group's "corporate will"—its "loyalty" or sense of mutual "attachment." In his framework political struggle does not constitute nationalism itself but is only one of its more common effects. See *Nationalism: Its Meaning and History* (New York: D. Van Nostrand, 1965), esp. pp. 9–11. Louis Snyder, too, sees political struggle as only one of many possible elements of nationalism rather than as its defining characteristic. See *The New Nationalism* (Ithaca, N.Y.: Cornell University Press, 1968), pp. 2–13.

12. Morris Rosenfeld, "Jerusalem," in *Shriften fun Morris Rosenfeld* (New York: Die internatzionale bibliotek, 1910), I, p. 96.

13. Moishe Zeifert, *Kuba: Oder die Shpanishe inkvizitzye fun dem nayntznten yorhundert* ([c.1898] n.l., n.p., n.d.). *Pilot*, Sept. 24, 1898, p. 4.

14. Michael Davitt, *Within the Pale: The True Story of Anti-Semitic Persecution in Russia* (New York: A. S. Barnes, 1903), p. 86.

15. Blaut, *The National Question*, esp. pp. 57–141.

16. For concise reviews of the recent trends in the scholarship on ethnicity,

see Felix M. Padilla, *Latino Ethnic Consciousness: The Case of Mexican Americans and Puerto Ricans in Chicago* (Notre Dame, Ind.: Notre Dame University Press, 1985), pp. 138–167; and Paul R. Spickard, *Mixed Blood: Intermarriage and Ethnic Identity in Twentieth-Century America* (Madison: University of Wisconsin Press, 1989), pp. 9–17. For a summary of the work on "emergent" ethnicity, see William Yancy et al, "Emergent Ethnicity: A Review and Reformulation," *American Sociological Review*, 41 (June 1976), pp. 391–403.

17. Agaton Giller, "List o organizacyi Polaków w Ameryce," in Osada, *Historia Z.N.P.*, p. 103.

18. Liah Greenfeld, *Nationalism: Five Roads to Modernity* (Cambridge, Mass.: Harvard University Press, 1992), p. 13; Eric Hobsbawm, *Nations and Nationalism since 1780: Programme, Myth, Reality* (Cambridge: Cambridge University Press, 1990), p. 46.

19. Cited in Thomas N. Brown, "The Origins and Character of Irish-American Nationalism," in Lawrence McCaffrey, ed., *Irish Nationalism and the American Contribution* (New York: Arno Press, 1976), p. 333.

20. Victor Greene, *For God and Country: The Rise of Polish and Lithuanian Ethnic Consciousness in America, 1860–1910* (Madison: University of Wisconsin Press, 1975), pp. 3–4. Specifically, Greene departs from Giller's central thesis that the social contrast between Pole and "other" in America lay at the heart of the process of "ethnicization." Rather, ethnic consciousness was generated from *inside* the group, as contending factions vied for the loyalties of a group whose aims and interests were a matter of some controversy. For Greene, internal debate over "group objectives" was more important in heightening ethnic consciousness. (*For God and Country*, pp. 30–43.) Giller's proposed link between ethnicization and politicization is still instructive, regardless of how ethnicization took place in a given instance.

21. Brian Mitchell, "Immigrants in Utopia: The Early Irish Community of Lowell, Massachusetts 1821–1861" (Ph.D. diss., University of Rochester, 1980), pp. 6–43; Irving Howe, *World of Our Fathers* (New York: Touchstone, 1976), pp. 183–190; Michael Weisser, *A Brotherhood of Memory: Jewish Landsmanshaftn in the New World* (Ithaca: Cornell University Press, 1989), esp. pp. 14–23; Florian Stasik, *Polska emigracja zarobkowa w Stanach Zjednoczonych Ameryki, 1865–1914* (Warsaw: Państwowe Wydawnictwo Naukowe, 1985), pp. 196–197; Andrzej Brożek, "The National Consciousness of the Polish Ethnic Group in the United States, 1854–1939: A Proposed Model," *Acta Poloniae Historica*, 37 (1978), pp. 97–99.

22. Assimilationist arguments, which had sounded fully anti-Semitic against the Russian backdrop of May Laws and pogroms, gained wide currency among the Yiddish proletariat after migration to the United States. See Kalmon Marmor, *Jacob Gordin* (New York: Yiddisher Kultur Farband, 1953), pp. 30–41; Isaiah Trunk, "The Cultural Dimension of the American Jewish Labor Movement," *YIVO Annual of Jewish Social Science*, 16 (1976), pp. 358–362.

23. Miller, *Emigrants and Exiles*, p. 93. Miller gives considerable attention to the sense of "distinctness" attending Irish language and culture in pre-famine Ireland, and the Anglicization program of the National Schools. See esp. pp. 69–79; Thomas Brown, *Irish-American Nationalism, 1870–1890* (Philadelphia: Lippincott, 1966), pp. 13–14; Andrzej Brożek, "The National Consciousness of the Polish Ethnic Group," pp. 106–107; Donald Pienkos, *PNA: A Centennial History of the Polish National Alliance of North America* (Boulder, CO: East European Monographs, 1984), pp. 43–44.

24. Miller, *Emigrants and Exiles*, pp. 124–130; Walter Laqueur, *History of Zionism* (New York: Holt, Rinehart and Winston, 1972), pp. 416–425. The issue of respectability is central to Brown, *Irish-American Nationalism*.

25. Cynthia Enloe, *Bananas, Beaches, and Bases: Making Feminist Sense of International Politics* (Berkeley: University of California Press, 1989), pp. 1, 44, 54, 42–64. See also George Mosse, *Nationalism and Sexuality: Respectability and Abnormal Sexuality in Modern Europe* (New York: Howard Fertig, 1985), pp. 23–47, 90–114.

26. *American Jewess*, Oct. 1897, p. 20.

27. Susan Weidman Schneider, *Jewish and Female: Choices and Changes in Our Lives Today* (New York: Touchstone, 1984) p. 106. On the force of Irish inheritance practices in shaping the gender ratio of the emigration, see Hasia Diner, *Erin's Daughters in America: Irish Immigrant Women in the Nineteenth Century* (Baltimore: Johns Hopkins University Press, 1983), pp. 7–16, 34–42, and Miller, *Emigrants and Exiles*, pp. 352, 403–409.

28. *American Jewess*, March 1898, p. 296.

29. Inasmuch as it is an attempt to defend Puerto Rican nationalism from its critics on the left, James Blaut's *National Question* deals from beginning to end with this question of whether nationalism in and of itself advances the cause of either the right or the left. See esp. pp. 83–87 on nationalism and fascism, and pp. 97–100 on nationalism and neo-Marxism.

A related debate has taken shape in the historiography of Irish-American nationalism. Thomas Brown argues that Irish nationalism in the United States primarily served the bourgeois aspirations of the Irish emigrant. Respect for Ireland, the argument ran, would translate into respect and enhanced opportunity for the Irish abroad, and ultimately provide an entrée into the American middle class. Eric Foner has countered with an analysis of the Land League of the 1870s, finding that Irish nationalism served to enhance worker consciousness and labor radicalism. If nationalism hastened assimilation at all, he argues, it hastened assimilation into the politicized American working class, not into Brown's staid and "respectable" middle class. See Brown, *Irish-American Nationalism*, pp. 24, 46, 133–140; and Eric Foner, "Class, Ethnicity, and Radicalism in the Gilded Age: The Land League and Irish-America," *Marxist Perspectives*, 1:2 (Summer 1978), pp. 42–47. Both accounts suffer from their underlying assumption that nationalism *nec-*

essarily bolstered either the right or the left. Contrast Emmons, *The Butte Irish*, pp. 292–300.

30. Brown, *Irish American Nationalism*, p. 35.

31. The following overview relies most heavily here upon J. C. Beckett, *The Making of Modern Ireland 1603–1923* (London: Faber and Faber, 1966); Mary Daly, *Social and Economic History of Ireland since 1800* (Dublin: The Educational Company of Ireland, 1981); T. A. Jackson, *Ireland Her Own: An Outline History of the Irish Struggle* (New York: International Publishers, 1970); Robert Kee, *The Green Flag*, I and II (London: Penguin, 1972); F. S. L. Lyons, *Ireland since the Famine* (n.l.: Collins-Fontana, 1971); Miller, *Emigrants and Exiles*.

32. Beckett, *Making of Modern Ireland*, pp. 122–161; Jackson, *Ireland Her Own*, pp. 36–53, 76–90; Kee, *The Green Flag*, I, pp. 9–20; Miller, *Emigrants and Exiles*, pp. 21–25.

33. Beckett, *Making of Modern Ireland*, pp. 176–179, 257–258, 206–245; Jackson, *Ireland Her Own*, pp. 102–113; Kee, *The Green Flag*, I, pp. 24–27, 28–38; Miller, *Emigrants and Exiles*, pp. 60–66.

34. For a point-by-point discussion of the eight articles of the Act of Union, see Beckett, *The Making of Modern Ireland*, pp. 280–283. On the oligarchic aspects of the Union, see Jackson, *Ireland Her Own*, pp. 187–190, 205–209.

These patterns of response to the Union took some time to emerge. In 1800, for instance, many Catholics viewed English power as a useful shield against the narrow prejudices of the local Protestant aristocracy; and for many others, parliamentary arrangements themselves were too remote to be of immediate concern one way or the other. For similar reasons, Irish Protestants warmed considerably to the idea of Union when the specter of Catholic Emancipation loomed on the horizon.

35. Kee, *The Green Flag*, I, p. 36. On the uses of the past by nationalist thinkers and activists, see also Mary Helen Thuente, "The Folklore of Irish Nationalism," in Hatchy and McCaffrey, *Perspectives on Irish Nationalism*, pp. 42–60.

36. John Asa Beadles, "The Syracuse Irish, 1812–1928: Immigration, Catholicism, Socio-Economic Status, Politics, and Irish Nationalism" (Ph.D. diss., Syracuse University, 1974), pp. 228–229, 221–275; David Brundage, "Irish Land and American Workers: Class and Ethnicity in Denver, Colorado" in Dirk Hoerder, ed., *Struggle a Hard Battle: Essays on Working-Class Immigrants* (Dekalb: Northern Illinois University Press, 1986); Dennis Clark, *Hibernia America: The Irish and Regional Cultures* (New York: Greenwood Press, 1986); John F. Delury, "Irish Nationalism in the Sacramento Region," *Eire/Ireland*, 13:1 (Spring 1978), pp. 7–14; Emmons, *The Butte Irish*, chapter 9; Michael Funchion, *Chicago's Irish Nationalists, 1881–1890* (New York: Arno, 1978); Oscar Handlin, *Boston's Immigrants, 1790–1865: A Study in*

Acculturation (Cambridge, Mass.: Harvard University Press, 1941); Timothy Meagher, "'The Lord Is Not Dead': Cultural and Social Change among the Irish in Worcester, Massachusetts" (Ph.D. diss., Brown University, 1981); Timothy Meagher, ed., *From Paddy to Studs: Irish-American Communities in the Turn of the Century Era, 1880 to 1920* (New York: Greenwood Press, 1986).

37. Miller, *Emigrants and Exiles*, pp. 110–121; R. F. Foster, *Modern Ireland, 1600–1972* (New York: Penguin, 1988), p. 351. On the American wake, see Thomas Gallagher, *Paddy's Lament: Ireland 1846–1847, Prelude to Hatred* (New York: Harcourt Brace Jovanovich, 1982), pp. 121–125.

38. Kee, *The Green Flag*, I., pp. 179–186; Beckett, *The Making of Modern Ireland*, pp. 295–305; Jackson, *Ireland Her Own*, pp. 210–216. On the peasantry's skepticism regarding this "victory," see also Brown, *Irish-American Nationalism*, p. 6.

39. Fixing the precise numbers for these Repeal meetings has proved impossible for historians. See Kee, *The Green Flag*, I, pp. 204–208 and Jackson, *Ireland Her Own*, pp. 233–234. Although accounts vary, the oft cited ballpark figures for the largest rallies are 300,000 at Tuam, 500,000 at Cork, and 750,000 at Tara. Pinpoint accuracy aside, one might conclude, with John Devoy, that the monster meetings were "among the greatest popular demonstrations in history." *Recollections of an Irish Rebel* (Shannon: Irish University Press, 1969), p. 3.

40. Handlin, *Boston's Immigrants*, pp. 137–138, 152–153; Francis Robert Walsh, "'The Boston Pilot': A Newspaper for the Irish Immigrant" (Ph.D. diss., Boston University, 1968), pp. 83–84; Miller, *Emigrants and Exiles*, p. 248.

41. Jeremiah O'Donovan Rossa, *Rossa's Recollections, 1838–1898* (Mariner's Harbor, N.Y.: O'Donovan Rossa, 1898), p. 262. Michael Funchion, ed., *Irish American Voluntary Organizations* (Westport, Conn.: Greenwood Press, 1983), pp. 52, 50–61.

42. Brown, "Origins and Character of Irish-American Nationalism," p. 334.

43. *Catholic Citizen*, Dec. 11, 1897, p. 1.

44. On the dialectical relations among the Repeal Movement, Young Ireland, the Fenians, and the Home Rule Movement, see Kee, *The Green Flag*, I, pp. 243–256, and II, pp. 3–14, 45–51, 55–67; Lyons, *Ireland since the Famine*, pp. 104–177.

45. Lyons, *Ireland since the Famine*, pp. 141–177; Kee, *The Green Flag*, II, pp. 55–79.

46. Lyons, *Ireland since the Famine*, pp. 164–168; Kee, *The Green Flag*, II, pp. 72–79; Brown, *Irish-American Nationalism*, pp. 85–98; McCaffrey, *The Irish Diaspora in America*, pp. 125–133; Foster, *Modern Ireland*, pp. 400–415; Funchion, *Irish American Voluntary Organizations*, pp. 74–79; Funchion, *Chicago's Irish Nationalists*, p. 28; James S. Donnelly, Jr., "The Land Question in Nationalist Politics," in Hatchy and McCaffrey, eds., *Perspectives on Irish*

Nationalism; Margaret Ward, *Unmanageable Revolutionaries: Women and Irish Nationalism* (London: Pluto Press, 1983), pp. 9–12.

47. Funchion, *Irish American Voluntary Organizations*, pp. 189–200.

48. Brown, *Irish-American Nationalism*, pp. 117–129; Lyons, *Ireland since the Famine*, pp. 166–167; Miller, *Emigrants and Exiles*, pp. 442–444, 538–540.

49. Brundage, "Irish Land and American Workers," in Hoerder, ed., *Struggle a Hard Battle*, pp. 55–64; Foner, "Class, Ethnicity, and Radicalism," pp. 20–30; Funchion, *Chicago's Irish Nationalists*, pp. 37–38. On Henry George's connection to Patrick Ford and the *Irish World*, see Edward J. Rose, "Henry George: America's Apostle to the Irish," in *Eire/Ireland*, 3:4 (Winter 1968), pp. 7–16, and James Paul Rodechko, *Patrick Ford and His Search for America: A Case Study of Irish-American Journalism* (New York: Arno, 1976), pp. 75–79. This affinity between nationalist and labor politics, though more widely articulated in 1878 and after, was by no means new. See, for example, Daniel J. Walkowitz, *Worker City, Company Town: Iron and Cotton-Worker Protest in Troy and Cohoes, New York, 1855–84* (Urbana: University of Illinois Press, 1978), pp. 160–170; Donald L. Miller and Richard E. Sharpless, *The Kingdom of Coal: Work, Enterprise, and Ethnic Communities in the Mine Fields* (Philadelphia: University of Pennsylvania Press, 1985), pp. 154–170 on the Molly McGuires and the link between the AOH and radical labor earlier in the decade.

50. Henry George, *The Land Question* [1881] (New York: Robert Schalkenbach Foundation, 1935), p. 21.

51. Ford's increasing concern with American labor and with the social or economic aspects of Irish liberation is reflected by his paper's name-change in 1878, from the *Irish World* to the *Irish World and American Industrial Liberator*. Funchion, *Irish American Voluntary Organizations*, pp. 212–218. The "radical" phase of Ford's career is summarized in Rodechko, *Patrick Ford and His Search for America*, pp. 58–90. Foner, "Class, Ethnicity, and Radicalism in the Gilded Age," p. 23, reprints information from the *World* on the financial contributions to Ford's Land League for the period Jan. 1, 1880 to Sept. 13, 1881.

52. Terence Powderly, *The Path I Trod* (New York: Columbia University Press, 1940), pp. 179, 182, 175–187. Foner, "Class, Ethnicity, and Radicalism in the Gilded Age," pp. 25–26; Paul Buhle, "The Knights of Labor in Rhode Island," *Radical History*, 17 (Spring 1978), pp. 56–57.

53. See E. Rumpf and A. C. Hepburn, *Nationalism and Socialism in Twentieth-Century Ireland* (Liverpool: Liverpool University Press, 1977).

54. Funchion, *Irish American Voluntary Organizations*, pp. 193–200; Brown, *Irish-American Nationalism*, pp. 133–134, 153–173.

55. Funchion, *Irish American Voluntary Organizations*, p. 194; Brown, *Irish-American Nationalism*, p. 155.

56. Brown, *Irish-American Nationalism*, pp. 164–182; Beckett, *The Making*

of Modern Ireland, pp. 394–404; Kee, *The Green Flag,* II, pp. 109–125; Lyons, *Ireland since the Famine,* pp. 195–201.

57. *Catholic Citizen,* Jan. 9, 1897, p. 4.

58. Until relatively recently 1891 was widely accepted as a closing date for nineteenth-century nationalism. See, for example, Brown, *Irish-American Nationalism* and Funchion, *Chicago's Irish Nationalists.* Timothy Meagher was among the first to point out just how vital nationalism actually remained in the 1890s, if perhaps sublimated to the cultural rather than the overtly political arena. See his "'The Lord Is Not Dead,'" esp. pp. 545–596. See also Foster, *Modern Ireland,* pp. 431–460.

59. Kee, *The Green Flag,* I, p. 145.

60. For instance, accounts of Irish-America's Emmet Day Celebrations and St. Patrick's Day festivities in the *Irish World,* March 12, 1898, p. 1, and March 26, 1898, p. 1, include notes on Clan na Gael and AOH festivities in San Francisco; Hartford and New Haven; Wilmington; Washington, D.C.; Atlanta and Augusta; Bloomington, Chicago, and Peoria; Evansville, Indianapolis, and Muncie; Boston, Lowell, and Worcester; Baltimore; St. Paul; Kansas City and Sedalia; Somersworth, New Hampshire; Jersey City and Newark; Brooklyn, New York, and Syracuse; Akron and Columbus; Chester, Philadelphia, Pittsburgh, Pittston, and Scranton; Pawtucket, Rhode Island; Roanoke and Williamsburg; and Wheeling, West Virginia. The *World's* coverage was by no means exhaustive, but this partial list does convey the geographical breadth of the movement during its "dead years."

61. *Official Constitution of the Ladies' Auxiliary, Ancient Order of Hibernians of America* [1895] (Syracuse: Catholic Sun Publishers, 1914), p. 6.

62. *Irish World,* Feb. 5, 1898, p. 7; Sean Cronin, "Nation Building and the Irish Language Revival Movement," *Eire/Ireland,* 13:1 (Spring 1978), pp. 7–14; Kohn, *Nationalism: Its Meaning and History,* pp. 146–149; Foster, *Modern Ireland,* pp. 446–456.

63. *Irish World,* Jan. 1, 1898, p. 1; April 2, 1898, p. 2; April 30, 1898, p. 9; *Catholic Citizen,* May 29, 1897, p. 5; Oct. 16, 1897, p. 5; Nov. 6, 1897, p. 4.

64. Boston *Pilot,* May 20, 1899, p. 4. Miller, *Emigrants and Exiles,* p. 541; John Higham, *Strangers in the Land: Patterns of American Nativism, 1860–1925* (New York: Atheneum, 1978), pp. 80–87; Barbara Miller Solomon, *Ancestors and Immigrants: A Changing New England Tradition* (Chicago: University of Chicago Press, 1956), pp. 59–81.

65. *Irish World,* Jan. 29, 1898, p. 1.

66. Rossa, *Rossa's Recollections,* p. 106; *Catholic Citizen,* June 3, 1899, p. 1.

67. *Irish World,* March 12, 1898, p. 4.

68. *Dziennik Chicagoski,* Feb. 3, 1898, p. 4; Oct. 4, 1900, p. 4.

69. Brożek, "The National Consciousness of the Polish Ethnic Group in the United States"; Greene, *For God and Country;* Stanisław Osada, *Jak się kształtowała polska dusza wychodźtwa w Ameryce* (Pittsburgh: Pittsburgher Press, 1930); Casimir Stec, "The National Orientation of the Poles in the

United States, 1608–1935" (M.A. Thesis, Marquette University, 1946).

Helena Brodowska, *Chłopi o sobie i Polsce* (Warsaw: Ludowa Spółdzielnia Wydawnicza, 1984), pp. 12–38, posits a higher level of peasant national consciousness in the premigration period. Problematically, however, Brodowska relies heavily upon *post*migration sources in making this argument.

70. Finerty's address was carried in *Zgoda*, Nov. 12, 1896, p. 1.

71. Norman Davies, *God's Playground: A History of Poland* (New York: Columbia University Press, 1982), I, pp. 511–546; O. Halecki, *A History of Poland* (New York: David McKay Co., 1961), pp. 202–217.

72. Halecki, *A History of Poland*, pp. 206–208; Davies, *God's Playground*, I, pp. 538–541, II, pp. 267–274; Emanuel Halicz, "Kościuszko and the Historical Vicissitudes of the Kościuszko Tradition," in *Polish National Liberation Struggles and the Genesis of the Modern Nation* (n.l.: Odense University Press, 1982), pp. 28–29, 18–38; Jerzy Kozłowski, "Emigracja okresu schyłkowego Rzeczypospolitej szlacheckiej i porozbiorowa (do 1864 r.)," in Andrzej Pilch, ed., *Emigracja z ziem polskich w czasach nowożytnych i najnowszych, XVIII–XXw* (Warsaw: Państwowe Wydawnictwo Naukowe, 1984), pp. 65–80.

73. Dąbrowski's "Appeal to the Poles" is collected in both Polish and English in Jerzy Zubrzycki, *Soldiers and Peasants* (London: Orbis Books, 1988), pp. 101–103. See also pp. 17–21.

74. Davies, *God's Playground*, pp. 331–332; Halecki, *A History of Poland*, pp. 233–234; Michelet quoted in Jerzy Lerski, *A Polish Chapter in Jacksonian America: The United States and the Polish Exiles of 1831* (Madison: University of Wisconsin Press, 1958), p. 8 (emphasis in original).

75. Davies, *God's Playground*, II, pp. 351–364; Halecki, *A History of Poland*, pp. 238–241; Richard Blanke, *Prussian Poland in the German Empire (1871–1900)* (New York: Columbia University Press, 1981), pp. 8–9.

76. *Zgoda* women's supplement, Sept. 27, 1900, p. 1; *Zgoda*, Oct. 27, 1898, p. 4; William Galush, "Purity and Power: Chicago Polonian Feminists, 1880–1914," *Polish American Studies*, 47:1 (Spring 1990), pp. 5–24. See also *Dziennik Chicagoski*, Jan. 13, 1899, p. 2, on the theme of Polish women as the bulwark against *Kulturkampf*.

77. The burgeoning literature of Polish Messianism ranged from poetry and drama across the disciplines of philosophy, theology, and political theory. For overviews of Polish messianism, see esp. Andrzej Walicki, *Philosophy and Romantic Nationalism: The Case of Poland* (Oxford: Clarendon Press, 1982); Czesław Miłosz, *The History of Polish Literature* (Berkeley: University of California Press, 1969), pp. 200–201; Donald Pirie, "The Agony in the Garden: Polish Romanticism," in Roy Porter and Mikulas Teich, eds., *Romanticism in National Context* (Cambridge: Cambridge University Press, 1988), pp. 329–332.

78. Noyes, *Poems by Adam Mickiewicz*, p. 414.

79. *Zgoda*, Nov. 26, 1896; Jan. 6, 1898, p. 1; March 3, 1898, p. 8; Stasik, *Emigracja zarobkowa*, p. 207. Tomasz Siemiradzki, *Porozbiorowe dzieje Polski*

(Chicago: Zgoda, 1906), II, pp. 83–86 is a good example of the romanticized, didactic uses of the Mickiewicz biography. ("Defending with enthusiasm the causes of the innocent, the peasants, and the workers, he did not disseminate class hatreds. Always and everywhere he strove to build, not destroy." [p. 86]) Siemiradzki had originally come to the United States on a popular lecture tour sponsored by the Polish National Alliance in 1896. See Pienkos, *PNA*, pp. 396–397.

80. Davies, *God's Playground*, II, p. 45.

81. Adam Bromke, *Poland's Politics: Idealism vs. Realism* (Cambridge, Mass.: Harvard University Press, 1967), pp. 10–14; Halecki, *A History of Poland*, pp. 252–262; Miłosz, *The History of Polish Literature*, pp. 283–289; Joseph A. Wytrwal, *America's Polish Heritage: A Social History of Poles in America* (Detroit: Endurance Press, 1961), pp. 177–180.

82. Andrzej Brożek, "Ruchy migracyjne z ziem polskich pod panowaniem pruskim w latach 1850–1918," and Jerzy Kozłowski, "Emigracja okresu schyłkowego," both in Pilch, *Emigracja z ziem polskich*, pp. 81–83, 115, 181–183; Pienkos, *PNA*, pp. 22–23, 367–405.

83. Mieczysław Haiman, *Zjednoczenie Polskie Rzymsko-Katolickie, 1873–1948* (Chicago: ZPRK [Polish Roman Catholic Union], 1948), p. 25, 29; Wacław Kruszka, *Historja polska w Ameryce od czasów najdawniejszych aż do najnowszych*, [1905] (Pittsburgh: Sokoł Polski, 1978), II, pp. 151–157; Alexander Janta, "Two Documents on Polish-American Ethnic History," *The Polish Review*, 19:2 (1974), pp. 3–19.

84. Haiman, *Zjednoczenie P.R.K.*, pp. 29–34, 32; Kruszka, *Historja Polska w Ameryce*, II, pp. 161–164; Pienkos, *PNA*, pp. 50–51; Andrzej Brożek, *Polish Americans, 1854–1939* (Warsaw: Interpress, 1977), pp. 219–220.

85. Kruszka, *Historja Polska w Ameryce*, II, pp. 161–169; Pienkos, *PNA*, pp. 50–51; Haiman, *Zjednoczenie P.R.K.*, pp. 40–41, 57–63; Greene, *For God and Country*, p. 87.

86. Osada, *Historia Z.N.P.*, p. 105; Haiman, *Zjednoczenie P.R.K.*, p. 59.

87. Giller, "List o organizacyi Polaków w Ameryce," in Osada, *Historia Z.N.P.*, pp. 98, 102. For a political profile of Giller, see *Zgoda*, April 23, 1896, p. 4.

88. Osada, *Historia Z.N.P.*, pp. 97–108.

89. The figures for 1901 are 30,355 for the PNA, to 10,943 for the PRCU. Brożek, *Polish Americans*, pp. 217, 220. On the founders and founding of the PNA, see Pienkos, *PNA*, pp. 46–66, and Appendix C (pp. 367–405).

90. Letter to *Gazeta Katolicka* from Franciszek Ksawery, in Osada, *Historia Z.N.P.*, p. 142. *Zgoda*, Nov. 24, 1898, p. 1; Kruszka, *Historja polska w Ameryce*, II, pp. 173–187, 185, 774.

On the differing perspectives and the political competition of the PNA and PRCU, see also Pienkos, *PNA*, pp. 69–84; Haiman, *Zjednoczenie P.R.K.*, pp. 61, 57–63; Brożek, *Polish Americans*, pp. 60–67; Greene, *For God and Country*, pp. 66–99.

91. The terms "religionist" and "secularist" (as opposed to Victor Greene's "religionist" and "nationalist") derive from William Galush, "Purity and Power: Chicago Polonian Feminists, 1880–1914," *Polish American Studies*, 47:1 (Spring 1990), p. 17.

92. Kruszka, *Historja Polska w Ameryce*, II, pp. 161, 177–181, 193; Haiman, *Zjednoczenie P.R.K*, pp. 36, 143–144; Wytrwal, *America's Polish Heritage*, pp. 168, 175, 148–190; Henryk Sienkiewicz, *Listy z podróży do Ameryki* [1879] (Warsaw: Państwowy Instytut Wydawniczy, 1978), p. 370.

93. Pienkos, *PNA*, p. 84–86; Krzysztof Groniowski, "Polonia amerykańska a narodowa demokracja (1893–1914)," *Kwartalnik Historyczny*, 79:1 (1972), esp. pp. 24–34; Stasik, *Polska emigracja zarobkowa*, pp. 232–235.

94. Donald Pienkos, *One Hundred Years Young: A History of the Polish Falcons of America, 1887–1987* (Boulder: East European Monographs, 1987), pp. 10, 37, 24–51; Zygmunt Miłkowski, *Opowiadanie z wędrówki po koloniach polskich w Ameryce północnej* (Paris: Goniec Polski, 1903), p. 265.

95. An outline of the principles of the National Democratic Party appeared in *Zgoda*, July 1, 1897, p. 6. Of the eight general points, five regard cultural issues of national consciousness, religious liberty, preservation of the language, national education, and an oppositional press.

96. *Zgoda*, Dec. 9, 1897, p. 5; Jan Marcinkiewicz et al, *Historia w poezji: Antologia polskiej poezji historycznej i patriotycznej* (n.l.: Instytut Wydawniczy, 1965), p. 272.

97. *Zgoda*, Feb. 4, 1897, p. 1; May 13, 1897, p. 8; Feb. 24, 1898, p. 1; June 16, 1898, p. 8. Stasik, *Polska emigracja zarobkowa*, pp. 205–206; Haiman, *Zjednoczenie P.R.K.*, pp. 107–114; Wytrwal, *America's Polish Heritage*, p. 215.

98. Greene, *For God and Country*, pp. 10–13, 28, 66–142; Brożek, *Polish Americans*, pp. 217, 220, 211–225. A census in *Zgoda*, May 18, 1899, p. 6, for example, notes PNA-affiliates in Arkansas, California, Colorado, Connecticut, Delaware, Illinois, Indiana, Maryland, Massachusetts, Michigan, Minnesota, Missouri, Nebraska, New Jersey, New York, Ohio, Oregon, Pennsylvania, Rhode Island, Texas, Washington, and Wisconsin.

99. Miłkowski, *Opowiadanie z wędrówki*, pp. 92, 96–102, 138, 144, 259–266.

100. *Naród Polski*, Sept. 19, 1900, p. 1; Oct. 3, 1900, p. 4; Haiman, *Zjednoczenie P.R.K.*, p. 184.

101. Lazarus, *An Epistle to the Hebrews*, p. 39.

102. Peter Viernik, "Iz di tzion-bevegung a fortshrit?" *Der nayer geyst*, May, 1898, pp. 483–486; Philip Krantz, *Vos heyst a natzion? Zaynen di yidn a natzion?* (New York: International Publishers, 1903); Jacob Gordin, "Natzionalizmus un assimilatzion," in *Ale shriften* (New York: Hebrew Publishing Co., 1910), IV, pp. 267–284.

103. Calvin Goldscheider and Alan Zuckerman, *The Transformation of the Jews* (Chicago: University of Chicago Press, 1984), pp. 116–135; Laqueur, *A History of Zionism*, pp. 63–69; David Vital, *The Origins of Zionism* (London:

Oxford University Press, 1975), pp. 312–315; Salo W. Baron, *The Russian Jews Under Tsars and Soviets* (New York: Schocken, 1964), pp. 124–131, 136–151; Moses Rischin, *The Promised City: New York's Jews, 1870–1914* (Cambridge, Mass.: Harvard University Press, 1962), pp. 38–47; Melvin Urofsky, *American Zionism from Herzl to the Holocaust* (Garden City: Anchor Press, 1975), pp. 8–13.

104. Vital, *The Origins of Zionism*, p. 183.

105. Ibid., pp. 119, 116–122, 126–132, and 49–186; Dubnow, *History of the Jews in Russia and Poland*, II, pp. 309–335; Laqueur, *A History of Zionism*, pp. 40–78; Hertzberg, *The Zionist Idea*, pp. 40–45, 168–198; Baron, *The Russian Jew Under Tsars and Soviets*, pp. 144–146; Urofsky, *American Zionism*, pp. 11–18.

106. Vital, *The Origins of Zionism*, p. 246; Laqueur, *A History of Zionism*, p. 87.

107. Theodore Herzl, *The Jewish State* [1896] (New York: Dover Publications, 1988), p. 157.

108. Ibid., p. 76, 81–82, 87; Vital, *The Origins of Zionism*, pp. 272–280; Urofsky, *American Zionism*, p. 24.

109. Vital, *The Origins of Zionism*, pp. 267–308; Laqueur, *A History of Zionism*, pp. 94–95, 98–102.

110. On the make-up and proceedings of the first Congress, see esp. Vital, *The Origins of Zionism*, pp. 354–370.

111. *Yiddishes tageblatt*, Sept. 22, 1898, p. 8; April 6, 1899, p. 4. Urofsky, *American Zionism*, p. 18.

112. *The Aim of Zionism* is excerpted in Hertzberg, *The Zionist Idea*, p. 500. Urofsky, *American Zionism*, pp. 80–85; Yonathan Shapiro, *Leadership of the American Zionist Organization, 1897–1930* (Urbana: University of Illinois Press, 1971), pp. 24–26, 29–36; Howe, *The World of Our Fathers*, p. 205.

113. A second rival to the FAZ arose within two years. The United Zionists adopted a scheme of organization similar to the Knights' federation of *landsmanshaften*, and likewise geared their arguments toward the more traditional sensibilities of the Yiddish immigrants. Shapiro, *Leadership of the American Zionist Organization*, pp. 27–29; Urofsky, *American Zionism*, pp. 92–94; Henry Feingold, *Zion in America* (New York: Twayne Publishers, 1974), p. 201; Michael N. Dobkowski, ed., *Jewish American Voluntary Organizations* (New York: Greenwood Press, 1986), pp. 532–534.

114. Cyrus Adler, ed., *Jewish American Yearbook 5661* [1900] (Philadelphia: Jewish Publication Society of America, 1900), pp. 170, 169–183; *Yiddishes Tageblatt*, Feb. 11, 1898, p. 8; April 2, 1898, p. 7; Marnin Feinstein, *American Zionism, 1884–1904* (New York: Herzl Press, 1965), pp. 124–134, 195–197.

Urofsky, *American Zionism*, p. 83, sets the FAZ figure at 10,000 based on a contemporary *New York Times* article; in 1902 Leon Zolotkoff set the membership of the Knights of Zion at 2,249. *The Maccabean*, June 1902, p. 339.

115. Ben Halpern, "The Americanization of Zionism, 1880–1930," *American Jewish History*, 69:1 (Sept. 1979), p. 18.

116. Leon Zolotkoff, "Tsionizmus," *Der nayer geyst*, Feb. 1898, pp. 306, 308.

117. Herzl, *The Jewish State*, pp. 116, 118–122.

118. *Abend blatt*, May 29, 1899, p. 2; May 30, 1899, p. 2. Laqueur, *A History of Zionism*, pp. 416–425; David Vital, *Zionism, the Formative Years* (London: Oxford University Press, 1982), pp. 70–74; Arthur Liebman, *Jews and the Left*, (New York: John Wiley and Sons, 1979), pp. 114–115.

119. Goldscheider and Zuckerman, *The Transformation of the Jews*, pp. 122–126; Ronald Sanders, *Shores of Refuge: A Hundred Years of Jewish Emigration* (New York: Schocken, 1988), pp. 20–26; Baron, *The Russian Jew under Tsars and Soviets*, pp. 138–139; Vital, *The Origins of Zionism*, p. 56.

120. Kalmon Marmor, *Jacob Gordin* (New York: Yiddisher Kultur Farlag, 1953), pp. 36–41.

121. Sanders, *Shores of Refuge*, p. 23; Ronald Sanders, *The Downtown Jews: Portraits of an Immigrant Generation* (New York: Dover Publications, 1969), pp. 14–15; Abraham Cahan, *Bleter fun mayn leben* (New York: Forverts Association, 1926), I, pp. 501, 500–505.

122. Cahan, *Bleter*, I, pp. 500–501.

123. Herzl, *The Jewish State*, p. 92.

124. Goldscheider and Zuckerman, *The Transformation of the Jews*, pp. 129–133; Baron, *The Russian Jew under Tsars and Soviets*, pp. 140–144; Vital, *The Origins of Zionism*, pp. 311–315; Vital, *Zionism, the Formative Years*, pp. 172–175; Sanders, *The Downtown Jews*, pp. 330–334; Milton Doroshkin, *Yiddish in America: Social and Cultural Foundations* (Rutherford, N.J.: Fairleigh Dickinson University Press, 1969), pp. 161–163; Liebman, *Jews and the Left*, pp. 111–127.

125. Will Herberg, "The Jewish Labor Movement in the United States," in *American Jewish Yearbook*, 53 (Philadelphia: American Jewish Publication Society, 1952), pp. 8, 12; Howe, *World of Our Fathers*, pp. 108–110.

126. Cahan, *Bleter*, III, p. 158. The entire episode at the Brussels Congress runs from pp. 158–174.

127. Ibid., pp. 159–165.

128. Ibid., pp. 168–170.

129. Dobkowski, *Jewish American Voluntary Organizations*, pp. 305–309.

130. *Abend blatt*, March 24, 1900, p. 7.

131. Sanders, *The Downtown Jews*, pp. 98, 109–110.

132. Moishe Baranov, "Di eybige frage," *Di naye tsayt*, Oct., 1898, pp. 39, 42; Chaim Zhitlovsky, *Der sotzializm un di natzionale frage* (New York: A. M. Evalenko, 1908).

133. Philip Krantz, "Ken a yiddisher sotzialist zayn a yiddisher patriot?" *Di naye tsayt*, Oct. 1898, p. 45.

134. Howe, *The World of Our Fathers*, pp. 289–295; Feingold, *Zion in*

America, p. 203; Trunk, "The Cultural Dimension of the American Jewish Labor Movement," pp. 347–357; Leon Kobrin, *Mein fuftzik yor in Amerike* (New York: YKUF, 1966), pp. 115–132, 191–200; Hillel Rogoff, *Der geyst fun "Forverts"* (New York: Forverts, 1954), pp. 41–46.

2. Plaintive Song, Heroic Story

1. Finley Peter Dunne, *Mr. Dooley in the Hearts of His Countrymen* (Boston: Small, Maynard, 1899), p. 92.

2. Cited in James Jeffrey Roche, *John Boyle O'Reilly: His Life, Poems, and Speeches* (New York: Cassell Publishing, 1891), pp. 226, 315. A similar fusion of sport and militarism, of course, was central to the philosophy of the Polish Falcons, whose motto was "Salute to the Fatherland, talons to the enemy!" See Donald Pienkos, *One Hundred Years Young: A History of the Polish Falcons of America, 1887–1987* (Boulder, CO: East European Monographs, 1987); and Stanisław Osada, *Sokołstwo polskie: jego dzieje, ideologja, i posłannictwo* (Pittsburgh: Sokoł Polski, 1929), pp. 7–15.

3. *Zgoda*, Jan. 9, 1896, p. 2 and Jan. 2, 1896, p. 8; *Irish World*, April 29, 1899, p. 7; Florian Stasik, *Polska emigracja zarobkowa w Stanach Zjednoczonych Ameryki, 1865–1914* (Warsaw: Państwowe Wydawnictwo Naukowe, 1973), p. 213; *Irish-American*, Feb. 14, 1898, p. 5; Joseph Wytrwal, *America's Polish Heritage: A Social History of Poles in America* (Detroit: Endurance Press, 1961), pp. 157, 197.

4. George Lipsitz, *Time Passages: Collective Memory and American Popular Culture* (Minneapolis: University of Minnesota Press, 1990), p. 6.

5. Victor Greene, *American Immigrant Leaders, 1800–1910: Marginality and Identity* (Baltimore: Johns Hopkins University Press, 1987), pp. 91–92.

6. Henryk Sienkiewicz, *Listy z podróży do Ameryki* [c.1879] (Warsaw: Państwowy Instytut Wydawniczy, 1979) pp. 375–384, 402–404; Carl Wittke, *The Irish in America* (Baton Rouge: Louisiana State University Press, 1956), pp. 213, 202–215; James Paul Rodechko, *Patrick Ford and His Search for America: A Case Study in Irish-American Journalism, 1870–1913* (New York: Arno, 1976), pp. 46–50; Roger Lane, "James Jeffrey Roche and the Boston *Pilot*," *New England Quarterly*, 33 (1960), p. 341; *Yiddishes tageblatt*, Sept. 12, 1898, p. 8; Irving Howe, *World of Our Fathers* (New York: Harcourt Brace Jovanovich, 1976), pp. 522, 518–551; Nagiel cited in Wacław Kruszka, *Historja Polska w Ameryce* (Pittsburgh: Sokoł Polski, 1978), II, pp. 215, 213–216; Stanisław Osada, *Prasa i publicystyka Polska w Ameryce* (Pittsburgh: Pittsburczanin, 1930), p. 13.

The following discussion of the immigrant press has also relied upon Abraham Cahan, *Bleter fun mayn leben* (New York: Forverts Association, 1926), III, chapter 13, and IV, chapters 9 and 10; Milton Doroshkin, *Yiddish in America: Social and Cultural Foundations* (Rutherford, NJ: Fairleigh Dickinson University Press, 1969); Hutchins Hapgood, *The Spirit of the Ghetto* [1902]

(New York: Schocken, 1965), pp. 176–198; Leon Kobrin, *Mayne fuftzik yor in Amerike* (New York: YKUF, 1966); Jan Kowalik, *The Polish Press in America* (San Francisco: R & E Research Associates, 1978); Anthony Kuzniewski, *Faith and Fatherland: The Polish Church War in Wisconsin, 1896–1918* (South Bend: Notre Dame University Press, 1980); Edmund Olszyk, "The Polish Press in America" (Milwaukee: Marquette University Press, 1940); Moses Rischin, *The Promised City: New York's Jews, 1870–1914* (Cambridge, Mass.: Harvard University Press, 1962), pp. 117–130; Hillel Rogoff, *Der geyst fun "Forverts"* (New York: Forverts, 1954); Ronald Sanders, *The Downtown Jews: Portraits of an Immigrant Generation* (New York: Dover, 1969); Robert Francis Walsh, "The Boston *Pilot*: A Newspaper for the Irish Immigrant, 1829–1908" (Ph.D. diss, Boston University, 1968).

7. Olszyk, *The Polish Press in America*, pp. 31–32.

8. Roche, *John Boyle O'Reilly*, p. 206; *Yiddishes tageblatt*, Feb. 1, 1899, p. 2.

9. Roche, *John Boyle O'Reilly*, p. 224.

10. *Catholic Citizen*, Dec 10, 1898, p. 4. On Ford's quest for "respectability," see Rodechko, *Patrick Ford and the Search for America*, pp. 91–121.

11. *Yiddishes tageblatt*, Feb. 24, 1898, p. 8; Rogoff, *Der geyst fun "Forverts"*, p. 44.

12. Osada, *Prasa i publicystyka polska*, pp. 26, 52; Olszyk, *The Polish Press in America*, pp. 56–57.

13. *Kuryer Polski*, Dec. 22, 1898, p. 2.

14. *Dziennik Chicagoski*, May 3, 1899, pp. 5–9.

15. *Catholic Citizen*, March 12, 1898, p. 2; Oct. 30, 1897, p. 2. The "Men of '48" series ran from January to May, 1899, typically on p. 4.

16. *Kuryer Polski*, Nov. 29, 1898, p. 2. *Zgoda*, Jan. 7, 1897, p. 4; Aug. 6, 1896, p. 1; April 21, 1898, p. 4.

17. *Yiddishes tageblatt*, Jan. 18, 1898, p. 8 [English].

18. Ibid., Jan. 16, 1898, pp. 4–5.

19. Ibid., Feb. 2, 1898, p. 8; Feb. 3, 1898, p. 8; Feb. 15, 1898, p. 8; Nov. 24–27, 1898, p. 8; March 1, 1899, p. 8.

20. *Irish World*, Jan. 1, 1898, p. 4; April 9, 1898, p. 1.

21. *Catholic Citizen*, July 29, 1899, p. 3.

22. *Dziennik Chicagoski*, Feb. 7, 1899, p. 2; *Irish World*, March 5, 1898, p. 4.

23. *Yiddishes tageblatt*, Aug. 1, 1898, p. 8; *Irish World*, April 9, 1898, p. 5; May 21, 1898, p. 1; June 11, 1898, p. 1.

24. *Zgoda* women's edition, Sept. 27, 1900, p. 1. On the controversy surrounding the formation of the Women's Alliance, see Jadwiga Karlowiczowna, *Historia Związku Polek w Ameryce: Przyczynki do poznania duszy wychodźstwa polskiego w Stanach Zjednoczonych Ameryki północnej* (Chicago: Związek Polek w Ameryce, 1938), pp. 1–9, 25–31; and *Kuryer Polski*, March 6, 1899, p. 2.

25. *Catholic Citizen*, Nov. 13, 1897, p. 2; *Irish World*, April 2, 1898, p. 1.

Margaret Ward, *Unmanageable Revolutionaries: Women and Irish Nationalism* (London: Pluto Press, 1983), pp. 42–45.

26. *Dziennik Chicagoski*, Sept. 22, 1900, p. 2.

27. *Straż*, Aug. 11, 1900, p. 4; *Irish American*, Jan. 31, 1898, p. 4.

28. *Irish World*, Feb. 5, 1898, p. 7.

29. *Yiddishes tageblatt*, Feb. 17, 1898, p. 8.

30. For full coverage of the Second Basle Congress, for example, see the *Yiddishes tageblatt*, Sept. 16-Oct.6, 1898, p. 8.

31. For the classic formulation of the immigrant journal as an agent of assimilation, see Robert Park, *The Immigrant Press and Its Control* (New York: Harper and Bros., 1922), pp. 49–88; Mordecai Soltes, *The Yiddish Press: An Americanizing Agency* (New York: Teachers' College, 1925).

32. Benedict Anderson, *Imagined Communities: Reflections on the Origin and Spread of Nationalism* (London: Verso, 1983), pp. 30, 61–65. Anderson's observations refer to the concurrent emergence of "print capitalism" and national consciousness long before the advent of the journals under consideration here, and he remains most interested in broadest theoretical questions regarding the cultural roots of nationalist consciousness in the eighteenth century. Nonetheless, his comments do fruitfully point up the ways in which newspapers construct worlds along national lines, and in so doing construct readers as members of nations.

33. *Abend blatt*, Nov. 27, 1899, p. 4. On the significance of "civilization" in this formulation, see Chapter 5.

34. "Vos tut zikh mit die Dreyfus-geshikhte?" *Abend blatt*, Jan. 14, 1898, p. 4.

35. *Abend blatt*, Sept. 8, 1897, p. 1; Nov. 16, 1897, p. 1; Nov. 17, 1897, p. 1; Nov. 19, 1897, p. 1; Dec. 6, 1897, p. 1; Dec. 8, 1897, p. 1; Jan. 14, 1898, p. 1; Jan. 24, 1898, p. 1; Jan. 25, 1898, p. 1; Jan. 31, 1898, p. 1; Feb. 16, 1898, p. 1. On the coverage of Dreyfus in the Yiddish press in general, and its impact on the Lower East Side, see Moses Rischin, ed., *Grandma Never Lived in America: The New Journalism of Abraham Cahan* (Bloomington: Indiana University Press, 1985), pp. 36–42.

36. *Abend blatt*, Sept. 11, 1899, p. 4; Sept. 19, 1899, p. 4; Sept. 26–27, 1899, p. 4; Jan. 14, 1898, p. 4; Feb. 3, 1898, p. 4; June 21, 1898, p. 4; March 28, 1899, p. 2.

37. In the spring of 1900, the editors acknowledged this tacit policy, and instituted columns entitled "Jewish News" and "Jewish Letters" from abroad. It may have been too late, however: the *Abend blatt's* stance on the Dreyfus affair may have been the turning point in its decline, as the *Forverts*—always more eager to appeal to its readership's *Yiddishkayt* directly—gained in popularity. See Doroshkin, *Yiddish in America*, pp. 114–117.

38. "Popular religion" here refers, most simply, to religion as it was understood and practiced not by theologians but by broad masses of "the people." In the present context this includes not only those aspects of established

religion as they filtered down from the Rabbinate or the Roman Catholic hierarchy, but also local or regional variations (cults of the saints, for instance), and mass-circulated religious expressions such as prescriptive literature on Jewish ceremonies or standardized sermons for Catholic priests. It includes as well the pieties of the immigrant press itself.

As Peter W. Williams has convincingly argued, a more fitting term for this level of cosmology and devotion in immigrant and ethnic enclave communities might be "clerico-popular": popular in that it is the religion of the people, departing in significant ways from Rome, for instance, in its retention of certain folk elements; yet "clerical" in the sense that enclave culture may allow for a great deal of influence on the part of the parish priest or the rabbi. See *Popular Religion in America: Symbolic Change and the Modernization Process in Historical Perspective* (Urbana: University of Illinois Press, 1980), pp. 3–5, 75, 232.

39. Williams, *Popular Religion in America*, p. 13.

40. *Catholic Citizen*, Feb. 20, 1897, p. 2; Stanisław Osada, *Historia Związku Narodowego Polskiego i rozwój ruchu narodowego polskiego w Ameryce* (Chicago: Zgoda, 1905), p. 142.

41. Mark Zborowski and Elizabeth Herzog, *Life Is with People: The Culture of the Shtetl* (New York: Schocken Books, 1952), pp. 164–165.

42. John Boyle O'Reilly, "The Priests of Ireland," *Irish World*, April 2, 1898, p. 11; Roche, *John Boyle O'Reilly*, pp. 471–474; Wittke, *The Irish in America*, pp. 89–90, 96.

43. *"Hear O Israel": The History of American Jewish Preaching, 1654–1970* (Tuscaloosa: University of Alabama Press, 1989), pp. 94–101; Kuzniewski, *Faith and Fatherland*, pp. 13, 7–51.

44. Morris Rosenfeld, *Shriften* (New York: Literarisher Farlog, 1910), I, p. 132.

45. Clifford Stevens, *The One Year Book of Saints* (Huntington, IN: Our Sunday Visitor, 1989), pp. 23, 40, 48, 57, 84, 94, 144, 167, 259, 274, 306, 321, 326, 335, 336, 364.

46. *Irish-American*, March 18, 1899, p. 1.

47. *Irish World*, March 19, 1898, p. 1.

48. John Talbot Smith, *The Chaplain's Sermons* (New York: Wm. H. Young and Co., 1896), pp. 69–70, 75, 76.

49. Ibid., p. 76.

50. Robert Ellis Thompson, "The Spirit of the Irish Nation," *Irish World*, March 12, 1898, p. 4.

51. Emmet Larkin, "The Irish Political Tradition," in Thomas Hachey and Lawrence McCaffrey, eds., *Perspectives on Irish Nationalism* (Lexington: University Press of Kentucky, 1989), p. 103; Andrew M. Greely, *The Irish Americans: The Rise to Money and Power* (New York: Warner Books, 1981), p. 178. Kerby Miller has argued that this fusion of politics and religion as a "sacred cause" was "the central element of the Catholic bourgeoisie's hege-

monic culture." See his "Class, Culture, and the Immigrant Group Identity in the United States: The Case of Irish-American Ethnicity," in Virginia Yans-McLaughlin, ed., *Immigration Reconsidered: History, Sociology, and Politics* (New York: Oxford University Press, 1990), pp. 100–106.

52. William Thomas and Florian Znaniecki [Eli Zaretsky, ed.], *The Polish Peasant in Europe and America* (Urbana: University of Illinois Press, 1984), pp. 234–235.

53. William Wolkovich, *Lithuanian Pioneer Priest of New England* (Waterbury, CT, 1974), p. 29. Sienkiewicz, *Listy z podróży*, p. 388; Henryk Sienkiewicz, "Za chlebem," in *Wybór nowel i opowiadań* (Warsaw: Zakład Narodowy im. Ossolińskich, 1979), p. 199.

54. Zbigniew Wierzbicki, "Polska schizma i Kościół Narodowy w Stanach Zjednoczonych," in Edmund Mokrzycki et al, eds., *O społeczeństwie i teorii społecznej: Księga poświęcona pamięci Stanisława Ossowskiego* (Warsaw: Państwowe Wydawnictwo Naukowe, 1985), pp. 569–572; Stephen Wlodarski, *Origin and Growth of the Polish National Catholic Church* (Scranton: Polish National Catholic Church, 1974), pp. 52–53, 66, 73, 180–181. On the Chicago and Buffalo precedents, see pp. 16–19, and Hieronim Kubiak, *Polski Narodowy Kościół Katolicki w Stanach Zjednoczonych Ameryki w latach 1897–1965: jego społeczne uwarunkowania i społeczne funkcje* (Warsaw: Zakład Narodowy im. Ossolińskich, 1970), pp. 102–105.

55. "Konstytucja Kościoła Polsko-Katolickiego," *Straż*, May 28, 1898, p. 1. Stasik, *Polska emigracja zarobkowa*, pp. 237–241. On the activist clerical tradition which Hodur came out of in his native Galicia, see Wlodarski, *Origins and Growth of the PNCC*, pp. 40–42. See also the tribute to "Ks. Stojałowski" in *Straż*, May 14, 1898, p. 3. For a sample of Hodur's thoughts on Bismarck and *Kulturkampf*, see "Bismark, wróg Polaków—nie żyje" in *Straż*, Aug. 6, 1898, p. 3. For a good sample of Polish ambivalence on the point of Ireland's being both oppressed and oppressor, see "Niesummieność Irlandczyków," in *Kuryer Polski*, Dec. 17, 1898, p. 4.

56. Wlodarski, *Origins and Growth of the PNCC*, pp. 224, 214–225; Kubiak, *Polski N.K.K.*, pp. 143–147.

57. Wlodarski, *Origins and Growth of the PNCC*, p. 76. Kubiak, *Polski N.K.K.*, pp. 134–135 provides figures on the growth of the church culled from the U.S. *Census of Religious Bodies*. For the base year of 1906, Kubiak cites 15,473 members in 24 churches.

58. Daniel Buczek, "Polish-Americans and the Roman Catholic Church," *Polish Review*, 21:3, p. 57; Kuzniewski, *Faith and Fatherland*, p. 45; Brożek, *Polish Americans*, pp. 97–110; Robert Lord et al, *History of the Archdiocese of Boston* (New York: Sheed and Ward, 1944), III, p. 230.

59. "Wielki Tydzień," *Dziennik Chicagoski*, March 29, 1899, p. 2. *Zgoda*, April 7, 1898, p. 1 made a similar point without calling on Mickiewicz.

60. The Feast of the Assumption, August 15, celebrates the Virgin Mary's ascent to heaven after her death. See Helen Laura Bilda, "The Influence of

Częstochowa on Polish Nationalism," (M.A. thesis, St. Johns University, 1948), pp. 122–139; *Our Lady of Częstochowa Parish 90th Anniversary* (South Boston, MA., pamphlet, 1983) in the author's possession; Williams, *Popular Religion in America*, p. 76.

61. *Zgoda* periodically listed and updated the roll of PNA locals. See, for instance, Jan. 26, 1899, p. 6, and May 18, 1899, p. 6.

62. Kruszka, *Historja polska w Ameryce*, II, pp. 149–150.

63. Israel Cohen, *The Zionist Movement* (New York: Zionist Organization of America, 1946), p. 20.

64. David Vital, *The Origins of Zionism* (London: Oxford, 1975), pp. 5, 3–10; Zborowski and Herzog, *Life Is with People*, pp. 381–405; Hayyim Schauss, *The Jewish Festivals: History and Observance* (New York: Schocken Books, 1938). Susan Weidman Schneider, *Jewish and Female: Choices and Changes in Our Lives Today* (New York: Touchstone, 1984), pp. 84–117 offers an excellent discussion of the masculinized heroism embedded in the Jewish religious calendar.

65. G. Selikowitz, *Der yiddisher-amerikaner redner* (New York: Hebrew Publishing Co., 1907), pp. 34–35.

66. "Speech for a Bar Mitzvah," in ibid., pp. 3–4; 67, 69.

67. Ibid., p. 10, 37.

68. *Yiddishes tageblatt*, Feb. 21, 1899, p. 8; "Tzionizmus un yudentum," Feb. 26, 1899, p. 4. On the biblical basis of modern Zionist thought, see Arnold M. Eisen, *Galut: Modern Jewish Reflection on Homelessness and Homecoming* (Bloomington: Indiana University Press, 1986).

69. *Yiddishes tageblatt*, March 7, 1898, p. 8.

70. "Mah Nishtane," literally "how does it differ?" refers to the ceremonial questions of the Passover seder.

71. *Yiddishes tageblatt*, April 20, 1899, p. 8; see also "Pesach und tzionizmus," April 6, 1898, p. 2.

72. *Yiddishes tageblatt*, March 12, 1899, p. 12; June 4, 1899, p. 4. See also A. Manenbaum, "Undzer macht," in *Yiddishes tageblatt*, Feb. 23, 1899, p. 4.

73. *Abend blatt*, March 8, 1898, p. 4.

74. Morris Winchevsky, "Mein natzionale ani-mamin," *Gezamlte verk* (New York: Frayhayt Publishing, 1927), VII, p. 224.

75. Among the nationalist discussants in the immigrant press who also produced works of Old or New World history were Abraham Cahan (*Forverts*), Humphrey Desmond (*Catholic Citizen*), Władysław Dyniewicz (*Gazeta Polska*), John Finerty (*Chicago Citizen*), Patrick Ford (*Irish World*), Philip Krantz (*Abend blatt*), Stanisław Osada (*Dziennik Milwaucki*), James Jeffrey Roche (Boston *Pilot*), Tomasz Siemiradzki (*Zgoda*), Stanisław Szwajkart (*Dziennik Chicagoski*), and Karol Wachtl (*Naród Polski*).

76. Tomasz Siemiradzki, *Porozbiorowe dzieje Polski* (Chicago: Zgoda, 1906), p. 20. Siemiradzki traveled throughout Polonia in the late 1890s, delivering lectures on Polish history and popularizing the obligations of nationality.

77. *Catholic Citizen*, May 22, 1897, p. 1.

78. *Zgoda*, Dec. 9, 1897, p. 1.

79. The Constitution of the Third of May, furtively written and passed by the Polish Sejm in defiance of Russian hegemony in 1791, epitomized to later generations the progressive potential of the Polish nation, the Poles' unity as a people, and their spirit of rebellion. "Freed from the shameful coercion of foreign orders," ran the preamble, "and valuing national independence and freedom over life itself . . . we pass the following statute."

80. *Dziennik Chicagoski*, Feb. 12, 1898, p. 4; Feb. 26, 1898, p. 2; *Zgoda*, Jan. 5, 1899, p. 6; Dec. 9, 1897, p. 5; Oct. 29, 1896, p. 8; Sept. 2, 1897, p. 3; *Straż*, March 12, 1898, p. 2; Michael Funchion, *Irish American Voluntary Organizations* (Westport, CT: Greenwood Press, 1983), p. 198.

81. *Catholic Citizen*, June 19, 1897, p. 4; *Kuryer Polski*, March 7, 1899, p. 2.

82. *Yiddishes tageblatt*, Feb. 24, 1898, p. 8. There are a few traces of Jewish nationalist display: the *Maccabean*, Nov., 1901, p. 85 notes a "Zionist Mass Meeting" in Baltimore, whose program, like the Irish and Polish national programs, included lectures and song; and Mary Ryan discovered "a band of young Jewish men" marching behind the banner of the Empire Hussars in New York City. "The American Parade: Representations of the Nineteenth-Century Social Order," in Lynn Hunt, ed., *The New Cultural History* (Berkeley: University of California Press, 1989), p. 143. Clearly, however, such festivities neither achieved the scale nor took on the significance in the Jewish community that they did in Irish-America and Polonia.

83. On the Yom Kippur Ball, see Sanders, *The Downtown Jews*, pp. 99–100.

84. *Irish World*, Feb. 12, 1898, p. 8.

This account is based on the myriad of reports and notices about holidays that appeared in the immigrant press in the years 1896–1900. An indispensable part of the ritual on these national occasions, evidently, was the public announcement of local patriotic activity: the press at holiday times typically brimmed not only with advance advertisements of local celebrations (often complete with point-by-point schedules of events), but also with detailed descriptions written up afterwards and submitted by local PNA or Clan na Gael secretaries. Most useful on this score are *Zgoda* and the *Irish World*. Virtually all of the journals, however, offered some account of festivities at the immediate local or regional level. See also Stasik, *Polska emigracja zarobkowa*, pp. 197–215, 255; Kruszka, *Historja polska w Ameryce*, II, pp. 194, 203–205.

85. *Irish World*, Jan. 15, 1898, p. 1; April 16, 1898, p. 2; Kruszka, *Historja polska w Ameryce*, II, pp. 203–204.

86. *Irish World*, Jan. 15, 1898, p. 1; *Zgoda*, May 13, 1897, p. 3; Feb. 6, 1896, p. 3.

87. *Irish World*, Jan. 15, 1898, p. 1; *Zgoda*, Dec. 24, 1896, p. 2; Dec. 16, 1897, p. 3; Feb 17, 1898, p. 2; *Irish-American*, March 7, 1898, p. 4.

88. *Irish World*, March 12, 1898, p. 1; *Dziennik Chicagoski*, Jan. 21 and 23, 1899, p. 4.

89. *Zgoda*, Oct. 29, 1896, p. 8; *Dziennik Chicagoski*, Jan. 21, 1899, p. 4; Jan. 23, 1899, p. 4; *Irish World*, March 26, 1898, p. 1.

90. For lyrics see Antoni Małłek, *Ziarno: zbiór pieśni narodowych na cztery męskie głosy* (Chicago: Author, 1890); Jan Marcinkiewicz et al, eds., *Historia w poezji: Antologia polskiej poezji historycznej i patriotycznej* (Warsaw: Instytut Wydawniczy, 1965). See also Wittke, *The Irish in America*, pp. 241–245.

91. *Zgoda*, May 21, 1896, p. 5. In Polish the rhythmic and forceful couplet runs, "Boże daj, Boże daj/ By nam wrócić wolny kraj!"

92. *Irish World*, Jan. 22, 1898, p. 4; Feb. 5, 1898, p. 7.

93. Susan G. Davis, *Parades and Power: Street Theatre in Nineteenth-Century Philadelphia* (Berkeley: University of California Press, 1986), pp. 47, 33–48.

94. *Irish World*, May 28, 1898, pp. 1, 8; June 4, 1898, p. 1; June 11, 1898, p. 8; *Kuryer Polski*, Jan. 26, 1899, p. 2; *Catholic Citizen*, July 15, 1899, p. 1. Likewise at a '98 celebration at the St. Louis fairgrounds, "After adopting resolutions reiterating the principles promulgated and fought for by the Irish people of a hundred years ago, resolutions were wired to President McKinley, Vice President Hobart, and Speaker Reed protesting against any Anglo-American alliance and the use of the term Anglo-Saxon." *Catholic Citizen*, June 11, 1898, p. 4.

95. *Zgoda*, Dec. 10, 1896, p. 2–3; Feb. 13, 1896, p. 2; Timothy Meagher, "'The Lord Is Not Dead': Cultural and Social Change Among the Irish in Worcester, Massachusetts" (Ph.D. diss., Brown University, 1982), p. 609.

96. *Zgoda*, Feb. 10, 1898, p. 3; Dec. 24, 1896, p. 2; David Emmons, *The Butte Irish: Class and Ethnicity in an American Mining Town, 1875–1925* (Urbana: University of Illinois Press, 1989), p. 312; Mary Ryan, "The American Parade," in Hunt, *New Cultural History*, pp. 147–151. This is not to say that these gendered rituals were experienced as constraining by the women involved, or were necessarily points of contention within these communities. On the contrary, similar rituals of the woman-as-icon were enacted even in Ladies' Auxiliary meetings when no men were present. *Official Ritual and Manual of the Ladies' Auxiliary of the Ancient Order of Hibernians in America* (n.l.: Adelia Christy, 1916), pp. 22, 34. Women's organizations such as the Daughters of the United Irishmen (New York) or the Irish Women's '98 Club (Chicago) were also active in planning many nationalist events. *Catholic Citizen*, Sept. 10, 1898, p. 1; *Irish World*, April 16, 1898, p. 2.

97. *Zgoda*, Feb. 6, 1896, p. 3; Feb. 13, 1896, p. 2. On the various social divisions within Polish-America—the friction they created and the various attempts at their management—see esp. John Bukowczyk, *And My Children Did Not Know Me: A History of Polish-America* (Bloomington: Indiana University Press, 1987), pp. 34–51.

98. *Catholic Citizen*, Dec. 12, 1896, p. 4; *Zgoda*, Dec. 22, 1898, p. 6; May 20, 1897, p. 3; May 12, 1898, p. 1.

99. Davis, *Parades and Power*, pp. 47, 170; William V. Shannon, *The American Irish: A Political and Social Portrait* (New York: Collier, 1963), pp. 75–76; Finley Peter Dunne, "St. Patrick's Day," in Charles Fanning, ed., *Mr. Dooley and the Chicago Irish: The Autobiography of a Nineteenth-Century Ethnic Group* (Washington, D.C.: Catholic University Press of America, 1976), p. 289; *Catholic Citizen*, July 24, 1897, p. 1; Aug. 21, 1897, p. 8.

100. *Zgoda*, May 6, 1897, p. 8.

101. *Zgoda*, Sept. 8, 1898, p. 6. This was part of an essay contest sponsored by the Education Department of the PNA on the question of "The Significance of National Celebrations for the Polish Emigration in America." See *Zgoda*, Aug. 25, 1898, p. 6; Sept. 1, 1898, p. 2; Sept. 8, 1898, p. 6; Sept. 15, 1898, p. 6.

102. Quoted in Thomas N. Brown, "The Origins and Character of Irish-American Nationalism," in Lawrence McCaffrey, ed., *Irish Nationalism and the American Contribution* (New York: Arno, 1976), p. 330.

103. *Catholic Citizen*, Oct. 8, 1898, p. 5; *Zgoda*, Feb. 6, 1896, p. 3.

104. Stephen Crane, *Maggie: A Girl of the Streets* [1893] (New York: Bantam Books, 1986), p. 24.

105. Matthew J. Strumski, "The Beginnings of the Polish American Theatre," *Polish American Studies*, 4 (Jan.-June 1947), p. 36.

106. Kruszka, *Historja polska w Ameryce*, II, pp. 150–151, 175, 186, 245, 252, 786; Strumski, "Beginnings of the Polish American Theatre," pp. 33–36; Arthur Leonard Waldo, "Polish-American Theatre," in Maxine Schwartz Seller, ed., *Ethnic Theatre in the United States* (Westport, CT: Greenwood Press, 1983), pp. 389–406; Frank Renkiewicz, *The Poles in America, 1608–1972: A Chronology and Fact Book* (Dobbs Ferry, NY: Oceana Publications, 1973), pp. 60–61; Wlodarski, *Origins and Growth of the PNCC*, p. 45; *Zgoda*, Dec. 23, 1897, p. 5 and Dec. 30, 1897, p. 4; Emil Orzechowski, *Teatr Polonijny w Stanach Zjednoczonych* (Warsaw: Zakład Narodowy im. Ossolińskich, 1989), esp. pp. 9–81.

107. *November Night* depicts Warsaw on the eve of the November Rising; *Varsovienne* refers to a popular song about the women of that city during the battle; Joachim Lelewel (1786–1861) was a historian and political activist, numbered among the "pilgrims" in France after the Rising was put down.

108. Czesław Miłosz, *The History of Polish Literature* (Berkeley: University of California Press, 1969), pp. 340–342, 351–358, 365–369; Leon Schiller cited p. 354. Marian Stepien and Aleksander Wilkon, eds., *Historia literatury polskiej w zarysie* (Warsaw: Państwowe Wydawnictwo Naukowe, 1988), II, pp. 61–74.

109. Orzechowski, *Teatr Polonijny*, p. 53.

110. Miłosz, *History of Polish Literature*, p. 353.

111. *Zgoda*, Nov. 26, 1896, p. 3; May 6, 1897, p. 1; Dec. 23, 1897, p. 5; Dec. 30, 1897, p. 4; Renkiewicz, *The Poles in America*, p. 60; Waldo, "Polish-American Theatre," p. 390; Strumski, "The Beginnings of Polish American Theatre," pp. 33–34.

112. Strumski, "The Beginnings of Polish American Theatre," pp. 35–36.

113. *Zgoda*, Feb. 11, 1897, p. 8. According to this write-up, *Związkowiec* was to play in New York, South Bend, and Grand Rapids in addition to its opening in Chicago.

114. Strumski, "The Beginnings of Polish American Theatre," p. 36.

115. Mari Kathleen Fielder, "Chauncey Olcott: Irish-American Mother-Love, Romance, and Nationalism," *Eire/Ireland*, 22:2 (Summer 1987), p. 6; Emmons, *The Butte Irish*, pp. 114–117; *Catholic Citizen*, Dec. 18, 1897, p. 4; John Talbot Smith, *The Parish Theatre: A Brief Account of Its Rise, Its Present Condition, and Its Prospects* (New York: Longmans, Green, 1917), pp. 80–81; Roche, *John Boyle O'Reilly*, p. 129.

116. *Catholic Citizen*, Jan. 29, 1899, p. 8.

117. Maureen Murphy, "Irish-American Theatre," in Seller, *Ethnic Theatre*, pp. 228–229.

There is, of course, some irony in Synge's *Playboy* being the most notorious target of this agitation for stage respectability: Synge was a member of the Irish League, and a close colleague of Lady Gregory and William Butler Yeats. Irish-America's hostile reception of Synge's national drama as "anti-Irish" stems from the age-old problem of Irish national life—the problem of defining the national community. Heavily Catholic Irish-America held a very different view of the Irish nation and the Irish peasant from that presented by the Anglo-Irish Synge.

118. *Irish World*, March 26, 1898, p. 8; April 23, 1898, p. 2; April 15, 1899, p. 2. The *Irish World* routinely ran theater and entertainment notices from around the country. On *Ireland as It Is*, see James Malcolm Nelson, "From Rory and Paddy to Boucicault's Myles, Shaun and Conn: The Irishman on the London Stage, 1830–1860," *Eire/Ireland*, 13:3 (Fall 1978). On Irish-American theater and its content, see Wittke, *The Irish in America*, pp. 253–263; George Potter, *To the Golden Door* (New York: Macmillan, 1960), pp. 608–612; Murphy, "Irish-American Theatre"; Richard Moody, *Ned Harrigan: From Corlear's Hook to Herald Square* (Chicago: Nelson-Hall, 1980), p. 158.

119. *Irish World*, April 2, 1898, p. 2; April 23, 1898, p. 2; Smith, *The Parish Theatre*, pp. 11–12, 67–68.

120. See David Krause's introduction to *The Dolmen Boucicault* (n.l.: Dolmen Press, 1964), p. 33–36; and F. Theodore Cloak's introduction to *Robert Emmet* in *Forbidden Fruit and Other Plays* (Princeton: Princeton University Press, 1940), p. 263. Augustine Filon quoted in Andrew Parkin, ed., *Selected Plays of Dion Boucicault* (Washington, D.C.: Catholic University of America Press, 1987), p. 15. For general assessments of Boucicault as a nationalist playwright, see Murphy, "Irish-American Theatre," pp. 222–224; Stephen M. Watt, "Boucicault and Whitbread: The Dublin Stage at the End of the Nineteenth Century," *Eire/Ireland*, 18:3 (Fall 1983).

121. *Arrah-na-Pogue*, in Boucicault, *The Dolmen Boucicault*, p. 150; *The Shaughraun*, in ibid., p. 176.

122. Co-founder of the United Irish Society (1791) and secretary of the Dublin branch.

123. *Irish World*, June 11, 1898, p. 8; *Catholic Citizen*, May 22, 1897, p. 2; Boucicault, *The Dolmen Boucicault*, pp. 171–172.

124. *Robert Emmet*, in Cloak, ed., *Forbidden Fruit and Other Plays*, pp. 302–303.

125. Rischin, *The Promised City*, p. 133.

126. Lulla Adler Rosenfeld, *The Yiddish Theatre and Jacob P. Adler* (New York: Shapolsky Publishers, 1977), pp. 225, 257. B. Gorin, *Die geshikhte fun yidishn teater* (New York: Yiddisher Farlag far Literatur un Visenshaft, 1923), II, pp. 256–282 contains an excellent index of the Yiddish repertoire.

127. Gorin, *Die geshikhte fun yiddishn teatre*, I., pp. 19–63, II, p. 115; David Lifson, *The Yiddish Theatre in America* (New York: Thomas Yoseloff, 1965), pp. 20–21; David Lifson, "Yiddish Theatre," in Seller, *Ethnic Theatre*, pp. 550–552.

128. Gorin, *Die geshikhte fun yiddishn teater*, II, pp. 32, 257, 267, 276; *Yiddishes tageblatt*, March 15, 1899, p. 4.

129. Lifson, "Yiddish Theatre," pp. 553–555; Lifson, *Yiddish Theatre in America*, pp. 37–39, 51–52; Gorin, *Die geshikhte fun yiddishn teater*, II, pp. 32–33, 41–42, 73–87.

130. Rosenfeld, *The Yiddish Theatre and Jacob Adler*, p. 261; Kalmon Marmor, *Jacob Gordin* (New York: Yiddisher Kultur Farband, 1953), pp. 57–58.

131. Jacob Gordin, *Yokel der oper'n macher*, in *Jacob Gordin's Eyn-akters* (New York: Tog, 1917), pp. 184, 185.

132. Marmor, *Jacob Gordin*, pp. 61–79; Gorin, *Die geshikhte fun yiddishn teater*, II, pp. 107–126; Lifson, *The Yiddish Theatre in America*, pp. 78–83; Lifson, "Yiddish Theatre," pp. 562–564; Hapgood, *The Spirit of the Ghetto*, pp. 136–149.

133. See Yul Entin, "Leon Kobrin der dramaturg," in Leon Kobrin, *Dramatishe shriften* (New York: Leon Kobrin's Bukh Komitet, 1952), p. xiii. Kalmon Marmor dates the Golden Epoch from 1898, when *Mirele Efros* became the first Yiddish play to capture both the intelligentsia and the mass audience. Marmor, *Jacob Gordin*, pp. 100–109.

134. *Abend blatt*, March 24, 1900, p. 5 and March 31, 1900, p. 8. See also, "Vi men shraybt a drama far der yiddisher bihne," in the *Abend blatt*, Dec. 30, 1899, p. 2; Rogoff, *Der geyst fun "Forverts"*, pp. 100–106.

135. Marmor, *Jacob Gordin*, p. 106; Jacob Gordin, *Jacob Gordin's Dramen* (New York: Farlag fun dem "soyrkel fun Jacob Gordin's fraynd," n.d.), II, pp. 3–6; Howe, *World of Our Fathers*, pp. 494–495.

136. Gordin, *Eyn-akters*, p. 176.

137. Sydney Stahl Weinberg, *World of Our Mothers: The Lives of Jewish Immigrant Women* (New York: Schocken, 1988), p. 116; Gordin, *Eyn-akters*, p. 165.

138. See esp. Zangwill's "Afterword" in Israel Zangwill, *The Melting-Pot* (New York: Macmillan, 1914), pp. 199–216.

139. "Natzionalizm un asimilatzion," in Jacob Gordin, *Ale Shriften* (New York: Hebrew Publishing Co, 1910), IV, pp. 272, 278. (*Kvass* is a fermented Russian drink made of rye; *kugel* is an east European Jewish dessert.)

140. Lipsitz, *Time Passages*, pp. 12–20.

141. See for example, Edward Kantrowicz, *Polish-American Politics in Chicago, 1888–1940* (Chicago: University of Chicago Press, 1975).

142. David Steven Cohen, ed., *America the Dream of My Life: Selections from the Federal Writers' Project's New Jersey Ethnic Survey* (New Brunswick, NJ: Rutgers University Press, 1990), pp. 83, 106.

143. Teofila Samolinska, "Józefowi Ignacemu Kraszewskiemu od Polek z Ameryki," in Osada, *Historia Z.N.P.*, pp. 88–92.

3. Pillars of Fire

1. Cited in Adam Czerniawski, "The Polish Poet as Custodian of the Nation's Conscience," *Polish Review*, 24:4 (1979), p. 5.

2. Ernest Renan's "What Is a Nation?" appears in Homi K. Bhabha, *Nation and Narration* (London: Routledge, 1990), pp. 8–22, and his central propositions are outlined in Hans Kohn, *Nationalism: Its Meaning and History* (New York: D. Van Nostrand, 1965), pp. 135–140. For immigrant views, see Antoni Malecki, "Poezja Mickiewicza a naród," *Zgoda*, June 16, 1898, p. 3, and Philip Krantz, "Di natzionale frage," *Naye tzayt*, March 1899, pp. 16–19.

3. Nahum Sokolow, *History of Zionism, 1600–1918* (London: Longman, Green, 1919), I, pp. 273–280; David Aberbach, *Bialik* (New York: Grove Press, 1988); David Cairns and Shaun Richards, *Writing Ireland: Colonialism, Nationalism, and Culture* (Manchester: Manchester University Press, 1988); Czesław Miłosz, *The History of Polish Literature* (Berkeley: University of California Press, 1969); Roy Porter and Mikulas Teich, eds., *Romanticism in National Context* (Cambridge: Cambridge University Press, 1988).

4. Roger Chartier, "Texts, Printing, Readings," in Lynn Hunt, ed., *The New Cultural History* (Berkeley: University of California Press, 1989), pp. 154–175.

5. Mary Poovey, *Uneven Developments: The Ideological Work of Gender in Mid-Victorian England* (Chicago: University of Chicago Press, 1988), pp. 2, 1–23.

6. Miłosz, *History of Polish Literature*, pp. 296–297; Seamus Deane, "Introduction" to Terry Eagleton et al, *Nationalism, Colonialism, and Literature* (Minneapolis: University of Minnesota Press, 1990); Poovey, *Uneven Developments*, pp. 109–110, 89–125.

7. "Printzipiele kritik," in *Nayer geyst*, Feb. 1898, pp. 293–297. See also *Nayer geyst*, Jan. 1898, pp. 242–245.

8. Aberbach, *Bialik*, p. 17.

9. Irving Howe and Eliezer Greenberg, A *Treasury of Yiddish Stories* [1953] (New York: Penguin, 1990), pp. 30, 32.

10. Mendele Mokher Sforim [Sholem Jacob Abramovich], "Notes for My Literary Biography," in Lucy Dawidowicz, ed., *The Golden Tradition: Jewish Life and Thought in Eastern Europe* (New York: Holt, Rinehart and Winston, 1967), p. 277.

11. "The *Shabbes-Goy*," in I. L. Peretz, *Selected Stories*, Irving Howe and Eliezer Greenberg, eds. (New York: Schocken, 1974), p. 49; Sholom Aleichem, "On Account of a Hat," in Howe and Greenberg, eds., A *Treasury of Yiddish Stories*, p. 116; Sholom Aleichem, "Dos meserl" [The Pocketknife], *Ale verk fun Sholom Aleichem* (New York: Sholom Aleichem's Folksfond Oysgabe, 1925), VII, p. 15.

12. A *golem* is a creature with no soul; a *shabbes-goy* (literally "sabbath-gentile") is a Christian hired to do routine tasks which are forbidden to Jews on the Sabbath, such as lighting candles.

13. Sholom Aleichem, "Di royte yidlekh," in *Ale verk*, XXVIII, pp. 7–67, 66–67; I. L. Peretz, "The Golem," in Howe and Greenberg, A *Treasury of Yiddish Stories*, pp. 245–246; "The *Shabbes-Goy*," in Peretz, *Selected Stories*, pp. 49–57.

14. "Three Gifts" [trans. Aaron Kramer], in Peretz, *Selected Stories*, pp. 41–48.

15. Howe and Greenberg, A *Treasury of Yiddish Stories*, p. 34.

16. *Yente*: a female busybody; *schlimazl*: a victim of perpetual misfortune, a ne'er do well; *Chelmer*: a resident of Chelm, a Russian town characterized in Yiddish folk convention by the stupidity of its inhabitants. The presentation of characters as faceless "types" survived, although to quite different effect, in the works of later Jewish writers like Anzia Yezierska and Franz Kafka.

17. Nor is language unimportant here. One critic has noted the Irish nationalist's "ludicrous necessity" of forging a literature of opposition in the language of the oppressor. The difficulty was mirrored by the circumstance of the Yiddish cosmopolitanist, who renounced the centrality of "Jewish" concerns in a language spoken only by Jews.

18. Jacob Gordin, "Natzionalizmus un asimilatzion," in *Ale shriften* (New York: Hebrew Publishing, 1910), IV, pp. 281, 267–284.

19. Jacob Gordin, "Vos zingt der yid?" (c.1897), in *Ertzeylungen* (New York: Der internatzionale bibliotek, 1908), pp. 116–121. (The Kol Nidre is the prayer of atonement.) Gordin employs the same theme in the sketch "Kol shofar" ["The Voice of the Ram's Horn"], pp. 85–88.

20. Gordin, "In tales un tfilin: a fakt," in *Ertzeylungen*, pp. 93–95.

21. Gordin, "Natsionalizmus un asimilatsion," *Ale shriften*, IV, p. 272. See also "Di blinde nakht," which pivots on the universalizing injunction to "Love your neighbor as yourself," yet attributes the historic appearance of

Lasalle, Heine, Mendelsohn, or Marx to "the spirit of the Jewish people." Gordin, *Ertzeylungen*, pp. 96–99.

22. Leon Kobrin, "Yankel Boyle" [1898], in *Gezamelte shriften* (New York: Hebrew Publishing, 1910), pp. 20, 59.

23. Abraham Cahan, *Yekl, the Imported Bridegroom, and Other Stories* (New York: Dover Publications, 1970), pp. 70, 44. "Yekl" appeared in 1893 in Yiddish, 1895 in English.

24. Upon her first glimpse of the Americanized Yekl, Gitl remarked that he looked "like a *poritz* [nobleman]"; and later, confronted with her own mirror image wearing a department store hat, she saw herself as "quite a *panenke* [noblewoman]." Likewise, when Mamie Fein swept through Gitl's apartment for the first time, "apparently dressed for some occasion of state," Gitl commented sarcastically, "She looks like a veritable *panenke* . . . Was she born here?" Cahan, *Yekl*, pp. 35, 36, 40, 52.

25. Ibid., pp. 30–31.

26. Ibid., pp. 3, 5, 6.

27. Cited in Bernard G. Richards, "Abraham Cahan Cast in a New Role," in Cahan, *Yekl*, p. vii.

28. Susan Kress, "Women and Marriage in Abraham Cahan's Fiction," *Studies in American Jewish Literature*, 3 (1983), pp. 26–39. In addition to *Yekl*, Kress discusses at some length "The Imported Bridegroom" (1898), "The Apostate of Chego-Chegg" (1899), "The Daughter of Reb Avrom Leib" (1900), "A Ghetto Wedding" (1898), and *The Rise of David Levinsky* (1917).

29. Cahan, *Yekl*, p. 30.

30. Ibid., p. 89.

31. The only positive obligations of ritual (as opposed to the negative "Thou shalt nots") that are binding for women are preparing bread, lighting the Sabbath candles, and obeying "laws of family purity."

32. Paula Hyman, "The Other Half: Women in the Jewish Tradition," in Elizabeth Koltun, ed., *The Jewish Woman: New Perspectives* (New York: Schocken, 1976), pp. 105–113, 109; Saul Berman, "The Status of Women in Halakhic Judaism," in Koltun, *Jewish Woman*, pp. 114–128, 116; Anne Gold-feld, "Women as Sources of Torah in the Rabbinic Tradition," in Koltun, *Jewish Woman*, p. 258; A. Cohen, *Everyman's Talmud* (New York: Schocken, 1975), pp. 159–161; Adin Steinsaltz, *The Essential Talmud* (New York: Bantam, 1976), pp. 137–144.

33. Cahan, *Yekl*, pp. 65, 83. Gitl's transformation is not entirely painless. Mrs. Kavarsky's help in Americanizing her appearance entails as much violence as a hairstyling scene possibly could: Gitl uttered "a painful hiss each time there came a violent tug at the comb; for, indeed, Mrs. Kavarsky plied her weapon . . . with a bloodthirsty air, as if inflicting punishment" (67). Overall, however, Mrs. Kavarsky is a kind of personified Aggadah, laying out the practical considerations of keeping the family of Israel together in perilous times. Significantly, her homilies on the importance of Gitl's Americaniza-

tion are aimed at preserving the Jewish family, not escaping from it (pp. 65–69).

After his "discovery" by William Dean Howells and the English-speaking mainstream, Cahan increasingly directed his energies toward a wider "American" audience (earning him, ironically, the nickname "Yekl" among his Jewish colleague-competitors). He did not abandon Yiddishist argument altogether, however. His novella *Neshomah yeseroh* [Transcendent Spirit], which ran in the *Forverts* in 1900–1901, explored the possibility of infusing socialism with the "second soul" of the Jewish Sabbath. And *The White Terror and the Red* (1905) harked back to the 1880s and the dilemmas faced by Jewish socialists in the age of the "revolutionary" wave of pogroms in Russia. See Jules Chametzky, *From the Ghetto: The Fiction of Abraham Cahan* (Amherst: University of Massachusetts Press, 1977), pp. 107–110; 114–123.

34. Irving Howe, *The World of Our Fathers* (New York: Harcourt Brace Jovanovich, 1976), pp. 494–495.

35. Mendele Makher Sforim, "Notes for My Literary Biography," in Dawidowicz, ed., *The Golden Tradition*, p. 280. Likewise, Yiddish literary history itself has always been defined as a patrilineal descent from the "grandfathers" and "fathers" of the late nineteenth century to the "young ones" [*di yunge*] of the early twentieth century. On the patriarchal tradition in Yiddish literature, see also Norma Fain Pratt, "Anna Margolin's *Lider*: A Study in Women's History, Autobiography, and Poetry," *Studies in American Jewish Literature*, 3 (1983), pp. 11–25; Norma Fain Pratt, "Culture and Radical Politics: Yiddish Women Writers, 1890–1940," *American Jewish History*, 70:1 (Sept. 1980), pp. 68–90.

36. Bernard Gorin, "Yom Kippur," *Abend blatt*, Sept. 12, 1899, p. 2; Sept. 13, 1899, pp. 2, 5; Leon Kobrin, "Jenny's Kol Nidre," *Gezamlte shriften*, pp. 197–209; "Anna's Ma-nishtane," in the *Abend blatt*, March 25, 1899, p. 6 and *Gezamlte shriften*, pp. 675–679; "Borekh dayen emes," *Gezamlte shriften*, pp. 197–209; "Ver iz shuldig?" *Gezamlte shriften*, pp. 87–101.

37. Leon Kobrin, "Vos iz er?" The version collected in *Gezamelte shriften*, pp. 614–620, dated 1897, has a male narrator. The version which Kobrin quoted and discussed years later in *Mayn fuftzik yohr in Amerike* (New York: YKUF, 1966), pp. 191–200 (also dated 1897), and a somewhat shorter variation which ran in the *Abend blatt*, May 18, 1899, p. 2, both have a female narrator and bear the subtitle "oys a togbukh fun a muter a sotzialistke."

38. Nikolai Chernyshevsky was a Russian revolutionary and novelist, author of *What Is to Be Done?* It was fashionable for a time among Jewish freethinkers to name their children after such non-Jewish political figures.

39. On the controversy surrounding "Vos iz er" and on Kobrin's second sketch, "Yo, vos iz er," see Kobrin, *Mayn fuftzik yohr in Amerike*, pp. 191–200, 196.

40. For contrasting responses to Kobrin's politics, see Moishe Baranov, "Leon Kobrin's ershter bukh," in the *Abend blatt*, Sept. 27, 1898, p. 4; Jacob

Gordin, "Eynige kritishe bamerkungen vegen herr Libin un herr Kobrin," *Ale shriften*, III, p. 167; Kobrin, *Mayn fuftzik yohr in Amerike*, p. 194.

41. Kobrin, *Mayn fuftzik yohr in Amerike*, p. 116; Morris Rosenfeld, "Di Hanukkah likhtlakh," *Shriften* (New York: Literarisher Farlag, 1910), I, pp. 132–134.

42. Isaac Hurvitch cited in Kobrin, *Mayn fuftzik yohr in Amerike*, p. 121. On Liessen, his work, and his place in Yiddish literature, see also pp. 115–132; Hillel Rogoff, *Der geyst fun "Forverts"* (New York: Forverts, 1954), pp. 47–53; Hutchins Hapgood, *The Spirit of the Ghetto* [1902] (New York: Schocken, 1965), pp. 113–117; and Hannah and Joseph Mlotek, "Abraham Liessen, der dichter fun kidesh-hashem," in *Forverts*, Dec. 2, 1988, p. 18.

43. "My people." The problem in translation here lies not in the lack of a strict English equivalent. Rather, it lies in bridging the gap in time and consciousness to a moment when one might address "my people" with ease and intimacy—qualities which are betrayed by the stilted, unnatural ring of the English words from the vantage point of the late twentieth century.

44. Abraham Liessen, "Nokh a bletl, mayn folk" [1894], *Lider un poemen* (New York: Forverts Association, 1938), III, p. 15.

45. Abraham Liessen, "Martirer-blut" (1895) and "In shtreyt" (1896) in *Lider un poemen*, III, pp. 272–275, 278–279.

46. Liessen, "Fun fintztern over" (1897), *Lider un poemen*, III, p. 21.

47. Liessen, "Der eybiker yid" [1894] *Forverts*, Feb. 20, 1898, p. 2; also in Liessen, *Lider un poemen*, III, p. 12, and Kobrin, *Mayn fuftzik yohr in Amerike*, p. 116.

48. In poems such as "The Jewish Book of Records," "The Eternal Spark," and "Historical Bundles" Rosenfeld echoed the theme of the individual subsumed by group identity, and the historical-yet-transhistorical basis of that nexus. "Yiddisher pinkus," "Der eybiger funk," "Di historishe pekhlakh," *Shriften*, II, pp. 78–79, 98–99, 121–124.

49. Charles Madison, *Yiddish Literature: Its Scope and Major Writers* (New York: Frederick Ungar, 1968), pp. 159, 159–162. *Maccabean*, Oct. 1901, pp. 50–51. On Rosenfeld's place in American Yiddish literature, see Howe, *The World of Our Fathers*, pp. 420–424; Ronald Sanders, *The Downtown Jews: A Portrait of an Immigrant Generation* (New York: Dover, 1969), pp. 134–143; Hapgood, *The Spirit of the Ghetto*, pp. 108–112; Kalmon Marmor, *Der onhoib fun der yiddisher literatur in Amerike (1870–1890)* (New York: Yiddishe Kultur Farband, 1944), pp. 68–80. For the debate on the left concerning Rosenfeld's nationalism, see "A blondzhener poet," *Der nayer geyst*, Nov. 1897, pp. 106, 107, 103–107; "A blondzhene kritik," *Nayer geyst*, Dec. 1897, pp. 168–171; "Printzipiele kritik," *Nayer geyst*, Jan. 1898, pp. 242–245 and Feb. 1898, pp. 293–297.

50. Morris Rosenfeld, "Napoleon un Herzl," in *Oysgeklibene shriften* (Buenos Aires: Ateneo Literario, 1965), pp. 138–140; Madison, *Yiddish Literature*, p. 162. For collected samples of his nationalistic poetry, see also Morris Rosen-

feld, *Songs from the Ghetto* (Boston: Small, Maynard, 1900), which contains English translations, and *Shriften*, I, pp. 96–193; II, pp. 73–132; IV, pp. 70–120.

51. Budyanov, "A blondzhener poet," *Nayer geyst*, Nov. 1897, p. 107.

52. Forty-nine days after the second day of Passover, during which there are no festivities.

53. Rosenfeld, "Di Hanukkah likhtlakh," "Judas Maccabeus," *Shriften*, I, pp. 132–134, II, pp. 96–97.

54. Rosenfeld, "Der shoyfer," "Goles," "Jerusalem," *Shriften*, IV, p. 89; II, pp. 84–85; I, pp. 96–97.

55. Rosenfeld, "A galut marsh," *Shriften*, I, pp. 100–101.

56. Hapgood, *The Spirit of the Ghetto*, pp. 105–108; "Mete midbar ha-aharonim" [The Last Dead of the Wilderness] cited in Aberbach, *Bialik*, p. 97; Rosenfeld, "Di Hanukkah likhtlakh," *Shriften*, I, p. 134.

57. Theodore Herzl, *The Jewish State* (New York: Dover, 1988), p. 146.

58. Kobrin, *Mayn fuftzik yohr in Amerike*, pp. 194, 200. Moishe Baranov, "Leon Kobrin's ershter bukh," in the *Abend blatt*, Sept. 27, 1898, p. 4.

59. Cited in Lucy Dawidowicz, "The World of East European Jewry," in *The Golden Tradition*, pp. 66–67; Chaim Zhitlovsky, *Yidn un Yiddishkayt* (New York: Chaim Zhitlovsky Farlag-Komitet, 1939), pp. 11–17.

60. Maria Rodziewiczówna, *Pożary i zgliszcza: powieść na tle powstania styczniowego* [1894] (Warsaw: Ludowa Spółdzielnia Wydawnicza, 1990), p. 48.

61. "Mowa ojczysta," *Zgoda*, July 22, 1897, p. 4.

62. *Kuryer Polski*, Oct. 31, 1898, p. 2; Monica M. Gardener, "Introduction" to Henryk Sienkiewicz [C. J. Hogarth, trans.], *Quo Vadis?* [1896] (New York: E.P. Dutton, 1941), p. viii; Mieczyslaw Giergielewicz, *Henryk Sienkiewicz* (New York: Twayne, 1968), p. 39; Henryk Sienkiewicz, "Latarnik," in *Wybór nowel i opowiadań* (Warsaw: Zakład Narodowy im. Ossolińskich, 1986), pp. 314–332.

63. *Kuryer Lwówski's* detailed account of the Warsaw ceremony ran in *Zgoda*, Jan. 19, 1899, p. 1. It was in this spirit, ultimately, that members of the Polish underground during World War II took their aliases from the heroes of Sienkiewicz's novels. See Miłosz, *History of Polish Literature*, p. 313.

64. Stanisław Osada, *Literatura polska i polsko-amerykańska dla ludu polskiego w Ameryce* (Chicago: Wl. Dyniewicz, 1910). See also Stanisław Osada, *Prasa i publicystyka polska w Ameryce* (Pittsburgh: Pittsburgher Press, 1930), p. 14.

65. *Zgoda*, Dec. 1, 1898, p. 8. Titles included, for example, *Peasant Heroes: A Novel of Kościuszko's Times, Orphans: A Contemporary Picture of the Last Uprising*, and *Moments of Blood: A Historical Novel of the Cossack Wars in the Ukraine*. Prices ranged from ten to sixty cents. For a similar inventory of the publications distributed by A. A. Paryski, see *Ameryka*, Aug. 7, 1897.

66. Józef Ignacy Kraszewski, *Dziecię starego miasta* [1863] (Warsaw: Zakład Narodowy im. Ossolińskich, 1988), p. xcii. *Kuryer Polski* serialized *The Teu-*

tonic Knights throughout 1898; *With Fire and Sword* was serialized in nickel pamphlets by Polish-American Publishing in 1896 [*Zgoda*, Jan. 2, 1896, p. 4]. Anna Lewicka's "Dzielny chłopiec," *Dziennik Chicagoski*, Feb. 12, 1898, p. 3. "Jak kowal umie, tak Ojczyźnie służy," *Dziennik Chicagoski*, Feb. 25, 1899, p. 3. "Hymn nowej Polski," *Zgoda*, April 14, 1898, p. 6. Jozef Szujski, "Pod Twoją obroną," *Dziennik Chicagoski*, Jan. 8, 1898, p. 3. The untitled piece quoted here appeared in *Zgoda*, Feb. 25, 1897, p. 6.

Other popularizations in this vein in the 1890s included Józef Kraszewski's *Tułacze*, about the Confederation of Bar and the Kościuszko Rising (*Zgoda*, Spring, 1897); "Krakowiak śląski," a protest against Germanization (*Zgoda*, Oct. 14, 1897); "About Kościuszko," an elegy (*Zgoda*, May 27, 1897, p. 3); Marya Rodziewiczówna's *Pożary i Zgliszcza*, set against the backdrop of the rising of 1863 (published by *Zgoda* in 1894 and released as a companion volume to Tomasz Siemiradzki's *Porozbiorowe dzieje Polski* six years later); "Bartek Nowak," a story of 1863 (*Kuryer Polski*, Aug. 19, 26, Sept. 2, 1898); "Razem z życiem," a tale of 1863 (*Dziennik Chicagoski*, March 11, 1899, p. 2); Szczęsny Rogala's *Dzielny chłopiec*, a novel of 1863 (*Zgoda*, throughout 1896); Mieczysław Sleczkowski's *Ksiądz Mackiewicz, bojownik za wiarę i wolność*, a tale of 1863 (*Zgoda*, Sept., 1896); Kornel Ujejski's "Pogrzeb Kościuszki," on Kościuszko's death (*Dziennik Chicagoski*, Feb. 12, 1898, p. 2); Henryk Sienkiewicz's *Potop*, on the seventeenth-century invasion of Poland by Swedes and their miraculous repulsion (*Ameryka*, 1897).

67. J. C. O'Connell, *The Irish in the Revolution and the Civil War, Revised and Enlarged Embracing the Spanish-American and Philippine Wars and Every Walk of Life* (Washington, D.C.: Trades Unionist Press, 1903), p. 41. One wonders, too, how Jewish readers positioned themselves in relation to this tale of religious persecution when, in the spring of 1899, the *Forverts* serialized a Yiddish translation of *Quo Vadis?*

68. *The Pharoah* (*Zgoda*, throughout 1898); see also *Kuryer Polski*, Sept 13, 1898, p. 2. "Maraton" (*Zgoda*, Oct. 21, 1897, p. 6); "Powstaniec Grecki" (*Zgoda*, 1896). *Ksiądz Placydy* and *Opatrzność Boska czuwa*, on the Moors and on the Catholics in England, were distributed by *Gazeta Katolicka* for thirty cents and ten cents, respectively [*Zgoda*, Dec. 1, 1898, p. 8]. See also *Wielki rok*, on the Napoleonic Wars (*Zgoda*, serialized 1896); *Piekielna zemsta*, also on the Napoleonic wars (*Kuryer Polski*, serialized 1899).

69. "Testament mój," in *Zgoda*, Jan. 5, 1899, p. 7; *Ameryka*, April, 1899, p. 1. See also Słowacki's "O Polsko," *Straż*, Dec. 3, 1898 p. 2; Mickiewicz's "Pieśń Zołnierza," *Dziennik Chicagoski*, Jan. 7, 1899, p. 2 and *Zgoda*, March 10, 1898, p. 6; "Do Matki Polki," *Zgoda*, Jan. 20, 1898, p. 5; Seweryna Duchinska's "Idźmy dalej!" *Zgoda*, Jan. 13, 1898, p. 2.

70. *Kordjan* introduced in *Zgoda*, Jan. 5, 1899, p. 1, serialized thereafter; see also the biographical sketch of Slowacki in *Dziennik Chicagoski*, April 1, 1899, p. 2.

Of the longer works, "Grażyna," "Dziady," and *Konrad Wallenrod* were excerpted in *Zgoda*, Jan. 6, 1898, pp. 1–10; *Pan Tadeusz*, in *Zgoda*, May 5, 1898, p. 6; and *Anhelli*, Słowacki's mythic treatment of Siberian deportees, ran in *Zgoda* in 1897. *Konrad Wallenrod* was offered in a popular edition by *Straż* as a gift for initiating a subscription [*Straż*, Aug. 27, 1898, p. 3]; and *Gazeta Katolicka* Bookstore advertised a complete edition of Mickiewicz's works, at the rate of $1.25 for four volumes [*Zgoda*, March 3, 1898, p. 8]. This catalogue is by no means exhaustive; but it begins to convey the extent to which the Polish classics were made accessible to the Polish-American reading public.

71. Miłosz, *The History of Polish Literature*, p. 201.

72. Donald Pirie, "The Agony in the Garden," in Porter and Teich, *Romanticism in National Context*, p. 331. For critical and biographical information on Mickiewicz, I have relied most heavily upon Miłosz, *The History of Polish Literature*, pp. 208–232.

73. Adam Mickiewicz, *The Books of the Polish Nation from the Beginning of the World to the Martyrdom of the Polish Nation* [1832], in George Rapall Noyes, trans. and ed., *Poems by Adam Mickiewicz* (New York: Polish Institute for the Arts and Sciences, 1944), pp. 378–380. *The Books of the Polish Pilgrims and Polish Nation* were also excerpted in *Dziennik Chicagoski*, Jan. 17, 1899, p. 2 and *Zgoda*, Nov. 26, 1896, p. 1.

74. *Dziennik Chicagoski*, June 24, 1898, p. 2; Miłosz, *History of Polish Literature*, p. 239.

75. "The Pilgrim's Litany," in Noyes, *Poems by Adam Mickiewicz*, pp. 414–415.

76. *Zgoda*, Oct. 22, 1896, pp. 4–5; Oct. 29, 1896, p. 4. Stanisław Osada lamented in 1910 that more Polish-Americans were not familiar with Konopnicka. *Literatura polska i polsko-amerykańska*, p. 301. In the late 1890s, however, she was among the most frequently reprinted Old World poets in the Polish-American press. Indeed, Konopnicka was a kind of patron saint to the fledgling Polish Women's Alliance at the turn of the century. See, for example, *Głos Polek*, July 1902, p. 6; Nov. 1902, p. 3.

77. "Tam, w moim kraju," in Maria Konopnicka, *Poezje* (Warsaw: Czytelnik, 1977), pp. 90–91. See also "Trzeci Maj," pp. 200–204. *Zgoda*, Feb. 2, 1899, p. 2, also carried a poem Konopnicka wrote in honor of Mickiewicz. On Konopnicka's career see Miłosz, *The History of Polish Literature*, pp. 318–320; Stepien and Wilkon, *Historia literatury polskiej*, I, pp. 342–345.

78. Maria Konopnicka, "Chłopskie serce," *Poezje*, pp. 38–40; *Zgoda*, Oct. 29, 1896, p. 4.

79. Konopnicka, "O wrześniu," "Budujmy miłej ojczyźnie dom," "Chodziły tu Niemce," *Poezje*, pp. 77–79, 198–200, 209–211; "Dola Stacha," *Kuryer Polski*, Oct. 8, 1898, p. 4.

80. *Zgoda*, May 19, 1898, p. 4; April 14, 1898, p. 6. Sienkiewicz originally conceived *After Bread* as a sermon for his fellow Poles, a political melodrama aimed at deterring further emigration. While the title has provided a useful

shorthand for the material pursuits of the immigrants in America, the novella itself testifies more to the crisis within Poland and the literary attempt to rescue it. Giergielewicz, *Henryk Sienkiewicz*, p. 67; Sienkiewicz, *Za chlebem*, in *Wybór nowel i opowiadań*, pp. 196–269.

81. *Zgoda*, Oct. 21, 1897, p. 6. On the role of the printer in imposing or enforcing certain meanings above others, see Roger Chartier, "Texts, Printing, Readings," in Hunt, *The New Cultural History*, p. 157.

82. *Dziennik Chicagoski*, Jan. 3, 1898, p. 2. X. Paweł Smolikowski, "Stosunek A. Mickiewicza do Zmartwychwstańców" serialized March 19, 1898, pp. 2–3; March 26, 1898, p. 2; April 1, 1898, p. 2. For an extensive treatment of Mickiewicz, see *Dziennik Chicagoski*, June 25, 1898 ("Na dzień obchodu setnej rocznicy urodzin Adama Mickiewicza").

83. Stanisław Szwajkart, "Cześć Mickiewicza dla Najśw. Panny" (after Józef Tretiak), *Dziennik Chicagoski*, June 4, 1898, p. 2. See also *Dziennik Chicagoski*, Jan. 6, 1899, p. 2.

84. *Zgoda*, June 16, 1898, p. 3.

85. *Ruch Literacki* [The Literary Movement], cited in Wacław Kruszka, *Historja polska w Ameryce* (Pittsburgh: Sokoł Polski, 1978), II, p. 234.

86. "Gwiazdka," in *Zgoda*, Dec. 23, 1897, p. 1.

87. *Zgoda*, March 4, 1897, p. 6; *Dziennik Chicagoski*, Nov. 10, 1900, p. 2; Jan. 8, 1898, p. 3. For a third factional variation, see also Jerzy Mirski, "Trzeci Maj," *Słońce*, April 28, 1898, p. 1. Mirski was the editor of *Słońce*, and a leader of the Polish Union, a splinter of the PNA which sought a compromise position between secularist and religionist stances.

88. M. Skalkowski, "Dalej bracia!" in *Straż*, March 19, 1898, p. 1.

89. "Do rodaków," in Arthur Leonard Waldo, *Teofila Samolinska, matka Związku Narodowego Polskiego w Ameryce* (Chicago: Author, 1980), p. 20; Kruszka, *Historja polska w Ameryce*, II, p. 235.

90. *Dziennik Chicagoski*, April 21, 1899, p. 2; *Straż*, April 23, 1898, p. 2; Nov. 6, 1897, p. 1.

91. *Zgoda*, May 13, 1897, p. 6.

92. "Ile?" in *Zgoda*, Jan. 21, 1897, p. 6.

93. "Ostatnia koszula!" *Straż*, Dec. 31, 1897, p. 1; "Oto 'patryoci,'" *Straż*, Oct. 15, 1898, p. 1. See also "Ugoda!" *Straż*, Nov. 19, 1898, p. 1. On Hodur's novel, see Kruszka, *Historja polska w Ameryce*, II, p. 786.

94. Franciszek Hodur, "Hymn dla członków narodowego kościoła," *Straż*, Aug. 27, 1898, p. 1.

95. Franciszek Hodur, "Kiedy my zmartwychwstaniemy?" in *Straż*, April 14, 1900, p. 1.

96. Zbigniew Brodowski, "Odkrycie Ameryki: Historyczne opowiadanie wędrownego ptaka, który także Ameryki nie odkrył. Przekład z niemieckiego," *Zgoda*, Aug. 4, 1898, p. 4. The American Indian analogy was not without precedent in Polish nationalist literature. In Adam Mickiewicz's "Potato" (1819) the Columbus expedition gives rise to a lively debate among the saints

in Heaven: will the benefits that the New World will yield to Europe's hungry and oppressed peoples outweigh the the certain slaughter of the Indians? Henryk Sienkiewicz's highly sympathetic "Sachem" also revolves around the destruction of an Indian village in Texas (not coincidentally) by German settlers. Czeslaw Miłosz, *The History of Polish Literature*, p. 210; Henryk Sienkiewicz, *Wybór nowel i opowiadań*, pp. 410–419.

97. Osada, *Literatura polska i polsko-amerykańska*, p. 299.

98. Charles J. Kickham, *Knocknagow: or, the Homes of Tipperary* (Dublin: James Duffy, c.1930), p. 584. On Kickham as a political figure, see R. F. Foster, *Modern Ireland: 1600–1972* (New York: Penguin, 1988), pp. 359, 375, 390–392.

99. Jeremiah O'Donovan Rossa, *Rossa's Recollections: 1838–1898* (Mariner's Harbor, NY: O'Donovan Rossa, 1898), p. 107.

100. Foster, *Modern Ireland*, pp. 358–359.

101. *Irish-American*, Aug. 16, 1897, p. 5; Jan. 31, 1898, p. 7; March 14, 1898, p. 1; April 4, 1898, p. 1.

102. On the discourse and contortions of Ascendancy nationalism, see Cairns and Richards, *Writing Ireland*, pp. 22–41, 28; Tom Dunne, "Haunted by History: Irish Romantic Writing, 1800–1850," in Porter and Teich, *Romanticism in National Context*.

103. John Boyle O'Reilly, "The Priests of Ireland," in James Jeffrey Roche, *John Boyle O'Reilly: His Life, Poems and Speeches* (New York: Cassell Publishing, 1891), p. 474.

104. Tom Dunne, "Haunted by History," in Porter and Teich, *Romanticism in National Context*, p. 69.

105. Seamus Deane in Eagleton et al, *Nationalism, Colonialism, and Literature*, p. 10; F. S. L. Lyons, *Culture and Anarchy in Ireland, 1890–1939* (New York: Oxford University Press, 1979), pp. 27–55; Foster, *Modern Ireland*, 446–456.

106. Charles Fanning, *The Exiles of Erin: Nineteenth-Century Irish-American Fiction* (South Bend: Notre Dame University Press, 1987), pp. 14–15. John Boyle O'Reilly, *Moondyne Joe* (Boston: Pilot Publishing, 1879); Peter McCorry, *The Irish Widow's Son: Or, the Pikemen of '98* (Boston: Patrick Donahoe, 1869); Robert Grant, John Boyle O'Reilly, Fred J. Stimson, and John T. Wheelwright, *The King's Men: A Tale of To-Morrow* (New York: Charles Scribner and Sons, 1885), also serialized in the *Boston Globe*, beginning August, 1884.

107. William McDermott [Walter Lecky], *Pere Monnier's Ward*, excerpted in Fanning, *The Exiles of Erin*, pp. 223–230.

108. Finley Peter Dunne, *Mr. Dooley in the Hearts of His Countrymen* (Boston: Small, Maynard, 1899), pp. 204–205. On the nationalist content of Dunne's work and Dunne's relationship with the movement's leadership, see esp. Charles Fanning, *Finley Peter Dunne and Mr. Dooley: The Chicago Years* (Lexington: University Press of Kentucky, 1978), pp. 141–172; and Charles

Fanning, ed., Mr. *Dooley and the Chicago Irish: The Autobiography of a Nineteenth-Century Ethnic Group* (Washington, D.C.: Catholic University of America Press, 1976), pp. 256–299.

109. Katherine Conway, *Lalor's Maples* (Boston: Pilot Publishing, 1901), pp. 12, 36. Conway also wrote some national poems. See "A Vigil Song for Erin: 1881," collected in Katherine Conway, *The Color of Life* (Boston: Thomas Flynn, 1927), p. 76.

110. Conway, *Lalor's Maples*, p. 112.

111. Louise Imogen Guiney, *Robert Emmet: a Survey of His Rebellion and of His Romance* (London: David Nutt, 1904), p. 103.

112. E.M. Tenison cited in Alice Brown and Robert Haven Schauffler, *Louise Imogen Guiney: An Appreciation* (London: Macmillan, 1923), p. 12.

113. In addition to touching upon Irish issues in her own poetry, Guiney produced a study of Gaelic poet Charles Mangan. On her work on Mangan and its place in her own view of Irish affairs, see E. M. Tenison, *Louise Imogen Guiney: Her Life and Works, 1861–1920* (London: Macmillan, 1923), pp. 172–186.

114. The second Earl of Tyrone; led the Irish at the battle of Yellow Ford, 1598.

115. Louise Imogen Guiney, *The Martyr's Idyl* (Boston: Houghton Mifflin, 1899), pp. 44–47.

116. Louise Imogen Guiney, *Patrins* (Boston: Copeland and Day, 1897), pp. 154, 157, 165–166.

117. John Brennan, *Erin Mor: The Story of Irish Republicanism* (San Francisco: P. M. Diers, 1892), p. 126.

118. Ibid., p. 82.

119. Ibid., p. v.

120. Ibid., pp. 16–24, 245–246.

121. Ibid., pp. 271–272.

122. James Jeffrey Roche, "The Lament of the Scotch-Irish Exile," in *The V-A-S-E and Other Bric-a-Brac* (Boston: Richard G. Badger, 1900), p. 79.

123. James Jeffrey Roche, *Her Majesty the King: A Romance of the Harem* (Boston: Richard G. Badger, 1899), p. 148.

124. Ibid., pp. 113–114.

125. Roche, *The V-A-S-E*, pp. 96–97.

126. *Catholic Citizen*, Dec. 24, 1898, p. 2; Thomas B. O'Grady, "James Jeffrey Roche: A Proper Bostonian Irishman," paper presented at the American Conference on Irish Studies, New England Regional Meeting, October 1988, p. 13; Roche, *The V-A-S-E*, pp. 96–97.

127. Roche, *John Boyle O'Reilly*, p. 8.

128. Ibid., pp. 1–2.

129. Ibid., pp. 2–4.

130. Cairns and Richards, *Writing Ireland*, pp. 49, 42–57.

131. *Her Majesty the King* is the tale of a princess disguised as a prince for

the sake of dynastic perpetuity, who turns out in the end to have been a prince all along. (His mother had presented him as a girl in order to save him "from the contamination of a wicked world.") The truth is finally known when the youth "proved his manhood on the field [of battle]." Roche, *Her Majesty the King*, pp. 156–160.

132. Roche, *John Boyle O'Reilly*, p. 227. Roche concurred, identifying O'Reilly's essay as "one of the best [answers] ever given to the arguments of the woman suffragists."

133. Ibid., pp. ix, 75.

134. Ibid., p. 174.

135. Ibid., pp. 50–51, 55, 61.

136. Ibid., p. 53.

137. Rossa, *Rossa's Recollections*, pp. vi–vii. *Rossa's Recollections* were serialized in *United Irishman* from January 1896 to May 1898, then published in a single volume in the summer of 1898.

138. Ibid., p. 220.

139. Ibid., p. 105. "The Kerry Eagle," pp. 40–41; "The Battle of Ross," pp. 42–47.

140. Rossa, *Rossa's Recollections*, p. 115.

141. Ibid., pp. 76–77.

142. Ibid., pp. 55, 61–63, 64, 72, 75.

143. Dunne, *Mr. Dooley in the Hearts of His Countrymen*, p. 204; Fanning, *Finley Peter Dunne and Mr. Dooley*, p. 149; William Butler Yeats, *The Autobiography of William Butler Yeats* (New York: Collier, 1965), p. 176.

144. McKinley's war message in Thomas G. Paterson, ed., *Major Problems in U.S. Foreign Policy: Documents and Essays* (Lexington, Mass.: D.C. Heath, 1978), I, p. 263.

145. Albert J. Beveridge, "The March of the Flag," [1898, 1900] in Daniel J. Boorstin, ed., *An American Primer* (New York: Mentor, 1966), pp. 644–653; and Paterson, *Major Problems in American Foreign Policy*, I, pp. 269–272.

4. Cuba Libre!

1. *Yiddishes tageblatt*, April 1, 1898, p. 1.

2. Philip S. Foner, *The Spanish-Cuban-American War and the Birth of American Imperialism* (New York: Monthly Review Press, 1972), I, chapters 1–4. Gomez cited p. 21.

3. See for example Charles S. Campbell, *The Transformation of American Foreign Relations, 1865–1900* (New York: Harper and Row, 1976), pp. 239–278; Lewis L. Gould, *The Spanish-American War and President McKinley* (Lawrence: University Press of Kansas, 1980); Gerald F. Linderman, *The Mirror of War: American Society and the Spanish-American War* (Ann Arbor: University of Michigan Press, 1974), pp. 9–59; Ernest R. May, *Imperial Democracy: The Emergence of America as a Great Power* (New York: Harper and Row, 1961).

4. Foner, *The Spanish-Cuban-American War*, I, pp. xxx, 270. For similar assessments, see Ray Ginger, *Age of Excess: The United States from 1877 to 1914* (New York: Macmillan Publishing, 1975), pp. 202–213; Walter La-Feber, *The New Empire: An Interpretation of American Expansion, 1860–1898* (Ithaca: Cornell University Press, 1963); William Appleman Williams, *The Tragedy of American Diplomacy* (New York: Dell Publishing, 1959).

5. Thomas Bell, *Out of This Furnace* [1941] (Pittsburgh: University of Pittsburgh Press, 1976), p. 103.

6. Richard Hofstadter, "Manifest Destiny and the Philippines," in Daniel Aaron, ed., *America in Crisis* (New York: Knopf, 1952), pp. 172–200; Richard Hofstadter, "Cuba, the Philippines, and Manifest Destiny," in *The Paranoid Style in American Politics and Other Essays* [1951] (Chicago: University of Chicago Press, 1979), pp. 145–187.

7. May, *Imperial Democracy*, pp. 23–24, 133–147; Hofstadter, "Cuba, the Philippines, and Manifest Destiny," p. 146; Foner, *The Spanish-Cuban-American War*, p. 169; Philip Foner, *History of the Labor Movement in the United States. Vol. II: From the Founding of the A.F. of L. to the Emergence of American Imperialism* (New York: International Publishers, 1955), p. 416.

8. James De Mille, "Song of the Irish Legion," cited in Paul Jones, *The Irish Brigade* (Washington, D.C.: Robert Luce, 1969), frontispiece.

9. Jones, *The Irish Brigade*, pp. 100–101.

10. Jacob Gordin, "Milkhome silueten," *Ertzeylungen* (New York: International Library, 1909), pp. 74–77.

11. Chief among the issues at the heart of this ongoing dispute were trade unionism and Americanization. For thumbnail sketches of these issues, the stakes involved, and the development of the factional battle, see Norma Fain Pratt, *Morris Hillquit: A Political History of an American Jewish Socialist* (Westport, CT: Greenwood Press, 1979), pp. 25–35; Moses Rischin, *The Promised City: New York's Jews, 1870–1914* (Cambridge, Mass.: Harvard University Press, 1962), pp. 175–190; Irving Howe, *The World of Our Fathers* (New York: Harcourt Brace Jovanovich, 1976), pp. 522–524.

12. Milton Doroshkin, *Yiddish in America: Social and Cultural Foundations* (Rutherford: Fairleigh Dickinson University Press, 1969), pp. 114–115; *Yiddishes tageblatt*, April 24, 1898, p. 4; *Forverts*, Dec. 5, 1897, p. 2. Morris Winchevsky's poem to "Sweet Daniel" bid farewell to the De Leon faction [*Forverts*, Jan. 9, 1898, p. 3.]: "Good-bye! Go ahead, ever hale, ever hearty,/ Not heeding what malice may say or may do./ And give my regards to your glorious old Party,/ I trust she will pardon my being a Jew."

13. New York *Times*, May 1, 1898, p. 9; Foner, *History of the Labor Movement in the U.S.*, II, p. 416.

14. Kajetan Kozmian (1771–1856), ultraconservative poet, senator, and wealthy landowner who extolled the redemptive national virtues of the Polish nobility; Jan Tarnowski (1488–1561), soldier and tactician, author of an influential *Outline of Military Method*.

15. *Zgoda*, April 9, 1896, p. 4; *Catholic Citizen*, March 5, 1898, p. 4; *Yiddishes tageblatt*, March 11, 1898, p. 1.

16. *Pilot*, April 16, 1898, p. 4.

17. *Yiddishes tageblatt*, April 12, 1898, p. 4.

18. *Zgoda*, Dec. 17, 1896, p. 1. The PNA pledge was made at an observance of the January Rising in Chicago, reported in *Zgoda*, Feb. 4, 1897, p. 2.

19. Stanisław Osada, *Historia związku narodowego polskiego i rozwój ruchu narodowego polskiego w Ameryce* (Chicago: Zgoda, 1905), p. 467.

20. *Catholic Citizen*, May 28, 1898, p. 1; April 30, 1898, p. 8; *Pilot*, May 21, 1898, p. 6; *Zgoda*, Aug. 20, 1896, p. 2; Moses Rischin, ed., *Grandma Never Lived in America: The New Journalism of Abraham Cahan* (Bloomington: Indiana University Press, 1985), p. 8.

21. *Irish World*, May 28, 1898, p. 4.

22. *Catholic Citizen*, Dec. 12, 1896, p. 4; April 23, 1898, p. 4; David Emmons, *The Butte Irish: Class and Ethnicity in an American Mining Town, 1875–1925* (Urbana: University of Illinois Press, 1989) p. 313.

23. *Forverts*, Feb. 26, 1898, p. 1; April 22, 1898, p. 4; May 8, 1898, p. 4. Cahan was not an editor of the *Forverts* in this period, but his contributions were frequently signed. The *Forverts* also gave socialist doctrine a pro-war twist, arguing that the island would be better off as a U.S. state than as a colony under the feudal lords of Spain: capitalist tutelage under the U.S. would serve as a necessary stage in preparation for Cuban socialism.

24. *Der nayer geyst*, May, 1898, pp. 482, 483.

25. *Irish World*, April 23, 1898, p. 4.

26. Ibid., p. 8.

27. A double entendre: Haggadah here refers, broadly, to a point of Talmudic law, a high principle in opposition to crass material concerns. Significantly, haggadah also refers to the liberationist narratives, songs, and prayers pertaining to Exodus which are read during the Passover seder.

28. *Der nayer geyst*, April, 1898, pp. 425–427. The next month "Politicus" denounced the "patriotic mouth-heroes, the jingoes," who had led the United States into an ill-advised war for the benefit, ultimately, of the sugar trusts. *Der nayer geyst*, May, 1898, pp. 486–488. See also Philip Krantz, "Di kubaner frage," in *Naye tzayt*, May, 1898, pp. 7–12, and June, 1898, pp. 8–13.

29. *Dziennik Chicagoski*, April 19, 1898, p. 2.

30. Cited in *Zgoda*, April 28, 1898, p. 4.

31. See esp. *Abend blatt*, Feb. 20, 1898, p. 4; March 1, 1898, p. 4; March 9, 1898, p. 4; April 14, 1898, p. 4; April 17, 1898, p. 4; April 17, 1898, p. 4; April 19, 1898, p. 4; April 24, 1898, p. 4; May 3, 1898, p. 4; May 7, 1898, p. 4.

32. *Dziennik Chicagoski*, Feb 19, 1898, p. 1; March 1, 1898, p. 1; March 9, 1898, p. 1; June 2, 1898, p. 2.

33. *Irish World*, May 7, 1898, p. 4.

34. *Yiddishes tageblatt*, April 28, 1898, p. 8.

35. Ibid., March 4, 1898, p. 1; March 13, 1898, p. 1; May 16, 1898, p. 8; April 24, 1898, p. 4; April 4, 1898, p. 4.

36. Ibid., March 21, 1898, p. 1; March 1, 1898, p. 4; July 14, 1898, p. 1; March 6, 1898, p. 1; April 12, 1898, p. 4; March 13, 1898, p. 1.

37. *American Jewess*, March, 1898, pp. 296–297; Rabbi Max Heller cited in Jeanne Abrams, "'Remembering the *Maine*': The Jewish Attitude Toward the Spanish-American War as Reflected in the *American Israelite*," *American Jewish History*, 76:4 (June 1987), p. 439; *Forverts*, June 19, 1898, p. 2; Rischin, *The Promised City*, p. 159.

38. Rischin, *Grandma Never Lived in America*, pp. 7–9. See also Abraham Cahan, *Bleter fun mein leben* (New York: Forverts Association, 1926), IV, pp. 132–144.

39. *New York Times*, May 1, 1898, p. 3.

40. Moishe Zeifert, *Kuba: Oder, di shpanishe inkvizitzion fun 19-ten yohrhundert* [c.1898] (n.l.: n.p. , n.d.), pp. 2, 3.

41. "Cuba Libre," in *Yiddishes tageblatt*, April 28, 1898, p. 8.

42. *Abend blatt*, March 24, 1900, p. 5; Bernard Gorin, *Geshikhte fun yiddishn teater* (New York: Max N. Meizel, 1923), II, p. 259.

43. May, *Imperial Democracy*, pp. 73; V. Edmund McDevitt, *The First California's Chaplain* (Fresno: Academy Library Guild, 1956), pp. 59, 142–143; *Pilot*, April, 16, 1898, p. 4; June 25, 1898, p. 4.

44. *Catholic Citizen*, March 12, 1898, p. 1. On Catholic defensiveness during this period, see esp. David Noel Doyle, *Irish Americans, Native Rights and National Empires* (New York: Arno, 1976), pp. 165–209.

45. *Pilot*, April 23, 1898, p. 4; March 5, 1898, p. 4; June 25, 1898, p. 4; *Dziennik Chicagoski*, March 3, 1898, p. 2.

46. *Catholic Citizen*, Feb. 19, 1898, p. 2.

47. Ibid., Feb. 26, 1898, p. 4.

48. Ibid., March 12, 1898, p. 4.

49. *Pilot*, April 30, 1898, p. 8; *Polak w Ameryce* cited in *Dziennik Chicagoski*, April 29, 1898, p. 2.

50. *Catholic Citizen*, June 11, 1898, p. 4. The *Merrimac* was sunk in the mouth of Santiago Harbor, bottling-in the Spanish fleet.

51. Cited in an untitled history of the Hebrew Veterans of the War with Spain, in the file on that organization held at the Jewish War Veterans' Archive and Museum, Washington, D.C. The *Harper's* piece by Twain is a prime example of the attitude which war volunteers and community leaders countered by forming an organization of Jewish Veterans. Although in essence a *defense* of the Jews, the Twain piece uncritically absorbs and retains many elements of late-nineteenth-century anti-Semitism. See Charles Neider, ed., *The Complete Essays of Mark Twain* (Garden City, N.Y.: Doubleday, 1963), pp. 235–250.

52. *Yiddishes tageblatt*, April 24, 1898, pp. 4, 8; March 16, 1898, p. 4.

53. Ibid., Feb. 18, 1898, p. 4; April 19, 1898, p. 4; April 21, 1898, p. 2.

54. Ibid., May 2, 1899, p. 8 [English].

55. *Pilot*, April 30, 1898, p. 8.

56. *Dziennik Chicagoski*, April 27, 1898, p. 4; Donald Pienkos, *One Hundred Years Young: A History of the Polish Falcons of America, 1887–1987* (Boulder: East European Monographs, 1987), p. 46.

57. *Zgoda*, June 23, 1898, p. 1.

58. A synopsis of *Cuba Libre* appears in *Dziennik Chicagoski*, May 1 and 2, 1899, p. 4.

59. *Yiddishes tageblatt*, May 15, 1898, p. 4; May 19, 1899, p. 8; *Zgoda*, July 14, 1898, p. 1; *Pilot*, April 30, 1898, p. 4; *Catholic Citizen*, April 30, 1898, p. 2; May 21, 1898, p. 2; Aug 13, 1898, p. 4.

60. George L. Mosse, *Nationalism and Sexuality: Respectability and Abnormal Sexuality in Modern Europe* (New York: Howard Fertig, 1985), p. 114; San Francisco *Chronicle*, May 4, 1898, p. 9.

61. Margaret Randolph Higonnet et al, eds., *Behind the Lines: Gender and the Two World Wars* (New Haven: Yale University Press, 1987), p. 4.

62. Jean Bethke Elshtain, *Women and War* (New York: Basic Books, 1987); Cynthia Enloe, *Does Khaki Become You? The Militarization of Women's Lives* (London: Pandora, 1983), pp. xxxiii, 6–17; Peter Gabriel Filene, *Him/Her/Self: Sex Roles in Modern America* (New York: New American Library, 1974), pp. 94–115; Susan Gubar, "'This Is My Rifle, This Is My Gun': World War II and the Blitz on Women," in Higonnet, *Behind the Lines*, pp. 227–259; Mosse, *Nationalism and Sexuality*, pp. 23–47, 90–114.

63. C. B. Botsford, "The Test of War," in Sidney A. Withersbee, *Spanish-American War Songs* (Detroit: Sidney A. Witherbee, 1898), p. 181; *Ladies' Home Journal* cited in Filene, *Him/Her/Self*, p. 96.

64. Chicago *Tribune*, April 26, 1898, p. 3.

65. Stefan Barszczewski, *Cuba Libre! Melodramat w 5-ciu odsłonach* (Chicago: n.p. , 1899), pp. 20–21.

66. Enloe, *Does Khaki Become You?*, p. 7.

67. *San Francisco Chronicle*, May 24, 1898, p. 3.

68. *Chicago Daily News*, April 27, 1898, p. 3; *San Francisco Chronicle*, May 24, 1898, p. 3.

69. *New York Times*, May 25, 1898, p. 3; *Pittsburgh Post*, April 28, 1898, p. 2; *San Francisco Examiner*, May 24, 1898, p. 4; Paul Fussell, *The Great War and Modern Memory* (New York: Oxford University Press, 1975), pp. 21–22. On the importance of female spectatorship in constituting male valor, see Amy Kaplan, "Romancing the Empire: The Embodiment of American Masculinity in the Popular Historical Novel of the 1890s," *American Literary History*, 3 (Dec. 1990), pp. 659, 675–681.

70. Foner, *The Spanish-Cuban-American War*, I, p. 169; Joyce Milton, *The Yellow Kids: Foreign Correspondents in the Heyday of Yellow Journalism* (New York: Harper, 1989), pp. 82, 141–142, 196–202.

71. Milton, *The Yellow Kids*, p. 202; Linderman, *The Mirror of War*, p. 131; Kaplan, "Romancing the Empire," pp. 666, 674. For an example of the contemporary treatment of Cisneros as fair damsel, see George Clarke Musgrave, *Under Three Flags in Cuba: A Personal Account of the Cuban Insurrection and Spanish-American War* (Boston: Little, Brown, 1899), pp. 92–108. Musgrave describes Cisneros as having "a white face, young, pure, and beautiful"—in sharp contrast to the "negresses" who inhabit the adjoining cells [p. 93].

72. Lester A. Bushnell, "Our Little Sister Cuba," in Witherbee, *Spanish-American War Songs*, pp. 123–124.

73. Michael Hunt, *Ideology and U.S. Foreign Policy* (New Haven: Yale University Press, 1987), pp. 58–68; White cited in Foner, *The Spanish-Cuban-American War*, I, p. 239.

74. "Wojenko" quoted (in this translation) in Norman Davies, *God's Playground: A History of Poland* (New York: Columbia University Press, 1982), II, p. 273.

75. James Jeffrey Roche, *John Boyle O'Reilly: His Life, Poems, and Speeches* (New York: Cassell Publishing, 1891), p. 227.

76. Susan Jeffords, *The Remasculinization of America: Gender and the Vietnam War* (Bloomington: Indiana University Press, 1989), p. xv.

77. Mieczysław Haiman, *Zjednoczenie Polskie Rzymsko-Katolickie w Ameryce, 1873–1948* (Chicago: Polish Roman Catholic Union, 1948), pp. 171–172.

78. *Yiddishes tageblatt*, May 16, 1898, p. 4.

79. *Irish World*, April 30, 1898, p. 8.

80. *Abend blatt*, May 6, 1898, p. 4.

81. *Kuryer Polski*, March 22, 1899, p. 2.

82. *Irish World*, June 18, 1898, p. 8.

83. *Forverts*, April 13, 1898, p. 2.

84. *San Francisco Chronicle*, April 25, 1898, p. 7; Enloe, *Does Khaki Become You?*, pp. 106, 92–116; Elshtain, *Women and War*, pp. 182–184.

85. *Irish World*, June 11, 1898, p. 1.

86. *Zgoda*, May 26, 1898, p. 1; *Yiddishes tageblatt*, March 13, 1898, p. 8; March 14, 1898, p. 8.

87. *Catholic Citizen*, May 28, 1898, p. 7.

88. *Yiddishes tageblatt*, May 3, 1898, p. 8; *Catholic Citizen*, April 30, 1898, p. 7; *Polak w Ameryce* cited in *Dziennik Chicagoski*, April 29, 1898, p. 2; *Irish World*, May 7, 1898, p. 8; *Chicago Tribune*, April 26, 1898, p. 3; *Milwaukee Sentinel*, April 29, 1898, p. 3.

89. Doyle, *Irish Americans, Native Rights and National Empires*, pp. 184–185; McDevitt, *First California's Chaplain*, p. 60; Office of the Adjutant General, *War with Spain, Volunteer Muster Rolls*, National Archives, Washington, D.C. Record Group 94, Boxes 9–10 (1st California), 37–38 (7th Illinois), 80 (9th Massachusetts), 139–140 (69th New York). According to the muster-in rolls, the 9th Massachusetts carried roughly 150 foreign-born Irish (Company

"J" is missing from the file); the 7th Illinois carried over 260 (Company "J" is also missing from this file). Significantly, despite the presence of the celebrated 69th in New York, other regiments from that city also attracted a fair number of foreign-born Irish volunteers. The 22nd New York Volunteer Infantry (Boxes 134–135), for instance, carried about as many foreign-born Irish as the "Irish" regiment in California.

90. *Zgoda*, April 28, 1898, p. 4; *Milwaukee Sentinel*, April 23, 1898, p. 3; *Milwaukee Journal* April 22, 1898, p. 1. Office of the Adjutant General, *War with Spain, Volunteer Muster Rolls*, 1st Wisconsin Volunteer Infantry, National Archives Record Group 94, Box 242. The figure is based upon the regiment's muster-in roll, although the muster roll of June 30 (which does not give place of birth) indicates that the company had increased to 105 members.

91. On Jewish participation, see Cyrus Adler, ed., *The American Jewish Yearbook, 5661* [Sept. 1900-Sept. 1901] (Philadelphia: Jewish Publication Society of America, 1901), pp. 529–622. Heaviest Jewish participation was in the New York State 8th, 9th, 12th, 14th, 22nd, 47th, 65th, 71st, 201st, and 202nd Volunteer Infantries.

92. *Rocky Mountain News*, May 1, 1898, p. 9. The enlistment scrolls in the mining area of Gilpin County, Colorado, were headed up by the Captain of the local Emmet Guards. *Rocky Mountain News*, May 5, 1898, p. 2.

93. *Boston Globe*, May 3, 1898, p. 7; *New York Times*, May 27, 1898, p. 2.

94. *Milwaukee Sentinel*, April 28, 1898, p. 3; April 29, 1898, p. 3; *Milwaukee Journal*, April 28, 1898, p. 3; *Pittsburgh Post*, April 28, 1898, p. 2. Polish names and births likewise dot the muster rolls of many regiments from the industrial cities of the Midwest and Northeast. See, for instance, Adjutant General's Office, *War with Spain, Volunteer Muster Rolls*, 7th Illinois Volunteer Infantry, National Archives Record Group 94, Boxes 37–38; Paul Rever, *Cleveland in the War with Spain* (Cleveland: n.p., 1900), pp. 282–285.

95. Virgil Carrington Jones, *Roosevelt's Rough Riders* (Garden City: Doubleday, 1971), p. 341; Theodore Roosevelt, *The Rough Riders* (New York: New American Library, 1961), pp. 36–37; Ralph Keithley, *Bucky O'Neill: He Stayed With 'Em While He Lasted* (Caldwell, ID: Caxton Printers, 1949), p. 15.

96. On the efforts of national figures like William Lyman (Irish National League) and John Finerty (United Irish Societies) to assemble an Irish Brigade, see the *Catholic Citizen*, April 30, 1898, p. 1; May 6, 1898, p. 1; May 14, 1898, p. 1; *Boston Globe*, April 25, 1898, p. 3; April 26, 1898, p. 7; *San Francisco Chronicle*, April 30, 1898, p. 4.

97. *Yiddishes tageblatt*, Feb. 24, 1898, p. 1; *New York Times*, April 26, 1898, p. 2; May 1, 1898, p. 3; *Boston Globe*, May 3, 1898, p. 7; *Providence Journal*, May 3, 1898, p. 3; *Forverts*, Feb. 26, 1898, p. 1.

98. *Dziennik Chicagoski*, April 27, 1898, p. 4; April 29, 1898, p. 2.

99. *San Francisco Chronicle*, April 30, 1898, p. 9; Rhode Island Governor,

Rhode Island in the War with Spain (Providence: E. L. Freeman and Sons, 1900), p. 29.

100. *Irish World*, April 30, 1898, p. 8; May 7, 1898, p. 8; May 14, 1898, pp. 1–2; May 21, 1898, pp. 8, 10; May 28, 1898, p. 2; June 4, 1898, p. 2; June 11, 1898, p. 10; June 18, 1898, p. 10; June 25, 1898, p. 2; *Chicago Tribune*, April 26, 1898, p. 3; *Boston Globe*, May 3, 1898, p. 7.

101. *Irish World*, May 21, 1898, p. 10.

102. *Boston Globe*, April 26, 1898, p. 12.

103. Ibid., May 4, 1898, pp. 2,4; May 5, p. 7.

104. *Irish World*, June 11, 1898, p. 3; *Boston Evening Transcript*, May 4, 1898, p. 3.

105. *Chicago Tribune*, April 27, 1898, p. 3; *Irish World*, May 7, 1898, p. 8. The *Tribune* set attendance at 4,000, the *World* at 10,000.

106. *Irish World*, June 4, 1898, p. 8; *New York Times*, May 27, 1898, p. 2; *Zgoda*, May 26, 1898, p. 1; Józef Nowalski, "Listy żołnierza" (I), *Zgoda*, June 2, 1898, p. 1.

107. *New York Times*, May 20, 1898, p. 4; *Irish World*, June 4, 1898, p. 8. New York State Historian, *New York and the War with Spain: History of the Empire State Regiments* (Albany: Argus Printers, 1903), p. 132.

108. *Irish World*, June 4, 1898, p. 8; *New York Times*, May 25, 1898, p. 3. Contemporary accounts of New York and Chicago festivities contrast sharply with those of parallel celebrations for the 1st California Volunteers in San Francisco. An orator in an Oakland church did insist that "the cause of Cuba and of Ireland were one and the same"; and an area St. Patrick's Day celebration in 1899 did feature skirmish drills by "The First Regiment League," led by a veteran of the 1st California. *San Francisco Examiner*, May 7, 1898, p. 4; March 18, 1899, p. 14. Overall, however, Ireland and Irish symbols receive far less attention in Bay Area accounts than in cities of the Midwest and East.

109. *Milwaukee Journal*, April 29, 1898, p. 1.

110. *Dziennik Chicagoski*, April 30, 1898, p. 2; *Zgoda*, May 12, 1898, p. 1; *Milwaukee Journal*, April 29, 1898, p. 1.

111. The First *Aliyah*, or wave, was the initial migration of Jews from eastern Europe to Palestine (then the Ottoman Empire) in the wake of the crises of 1881–82.

112. Files on Mayer Benjamin Dodek and Morris Mendelsohn, Jewish War Veterans Museum and Archive, Washington, D.C.

113. *San Francisco Examiner*, Feb. 6, 1899, p. 1; Feb. 7, 1899, p. 1; McDevitt, *First California's Chaplain*, pp. 119–120.

114. The letter was printed—by the request of the writer—in *Kuryer Polski*, Aug. 17, 1898, p. 2. Kruszka's decision to publish the piece was highly controversial. See *Kuryer Polski*, Aug. 23, 1898, p. 1; Aug. 25, 1898, p. 2.

115. *New York Times*, May 22, 1898, p. 5; June 15, 1898, p. 2; June 16, 1898, p. 4; Nowalski, "Listy żołnierza" (II), *Zgoda*, June 16, 1898, p. 4 and (III), *Zgoda*, June 23, 1898, p. 1; John Bowe, *With the Thirteenth Minnesota*

(Minneapolis: A.B. Farnham, 1905), p. 105; *Abend blatt*, June 23, 1898, p. 2; New York State Historian, *New York and the War with Spain*, pp. 139–144; McDevitt, *First California's Chaplain*, p. 62; Gould, *The Spanish-American War and President McKinley*, pp. 91–94. Colonel Duffy of the Irish 69th decried these conditions in a well-publicized letter which, significantly, an officer of the Friendly Sons of St. Patrick hailed as "one of the most manly letters" he had ever read; "there was no kick or grumble" [*New York Times*, June 15, 1898, p. 2].

116. *Kuryer Polski*, Aug. 25, 1898, p. 1; Sept 5, 1898, p. 1; *Dziennik Chicagoski*, June 4, 1898, p. 4; Nowalski, "Listy żołnierza" (I), *Zgoda*, June 2, 1898, p. 1. Office of the Adjutant General, *War with Spain*, *Volunteer Muster Rolls*, Company K, 1st Wisconsin Volunteer Infantry, (Muster roll of August 31, 1898), National Archives Record Group 94, Box 242.

117. Nowalski, "Listy żołnierza" (VIII), *Zgoda*, July 28, 1898, p. 4; and (IX), *Zgoda*, Aug. 4, 1898, p. 1.

118. *New York Times*, Dec. 18, 1898, p. 3; Feb. 1, 1899, p. 1.

119. Nowalski, "Listy żołnierza" (VI), *Zgoda*, July 14, 1898, p. 1.

120. Nowalski, "Listy żołnierza" (III and IV), *Zgoda*, June 23, 1898, p. 1; June 30, 1898, p. 1.

121. Although Poland itself was relatively quiet as the spirit of revolution spread across Europe in 1848, Poles did participate in significant numbers in political uprisings elsewhere. The most celebrated of the Polish forces of '48 were the Polish Legion formed by Adam Mickiewicz which fought in Lombardy and Genoa; and the force assembled by Józef Bem which fought in Hungary. Which battles of '48 Dzialynski took part in is not clear from any of the letters.

122. Nowalski, "Listy żołnierza" (II, V, X), *Zgoda*, June 16, 1898, p. 4; July 7, 1898, p. 1; Aug. 11, 1898, p. 4. The troops' meeting with Dzialynski is also mentioned in a letter from Tadeusz Wild to *Dziennik Chicagoski*, June 2, 1898, p. 4.

123. Nowalski, "Listy żołnierza" (III), *Zgoda*, June 23, 1898, p. 1.

124. Bowe, *With the Thirteenth Minnesota*, pp. 94, 133–134.

125. The site of rebel victories during the rising of 1798.

126. *New York Times*, Jan. 31, 1899, pp. 1–2. An account of preliminary plans for the reception appeared Jan. 11, 1899, p. 3.

127. *Kuryer Polski*, Sept. 6, 1898, p. 1.

128. *Kuryer Polski*, Sept. 8, 1898, p. 1; Sept. 10, 1898, p. 1.

129. *San Francisco Examiner*, Aug. 27, 1899, *passim*.

130. *San Francisco Examiner*, Aug. 26, 1899, p. 3.

131. *Yiddishes tageblatt*, May 4, 1898, p. 7; May 11, 1898, p. 4; Jan. 16, 1899, p. 4; Gorin, *Die geshikhte fun yidishn teater*, II, p. 262.

132. "Der yiddisher soldat in kampf gegen Shpanien," *Yiddishes tageblatt*, May 8, 1898, p. 5. See also "The Hebrew Soldier," *Yiddishes tageblatt*, May 13, 1898, p. 8.

133. J. C. O'Connell, *The Irish in the Revolution and the Civil War, Revised and Enlarged Embracing the Spanish-American and Philippine Wars and Every Walk of Life* (Washington, D.C.: Trades Unionist Press, 1903), pp. 35–37, 55–57.

134. A. E. Hirschowitz, *Jewish Patriotism and Its Martyrs in the Spanish-American War, 1898* (New York: A. Sheinkopf, n.d.), pp. 6, 8.

135. Stefan Barszczewski, "Pod Santiago," in *Czerwony mesyasz* (Warsaw: Gebethner and Wolff, 1913), p. 183.

136. Article III granted the United States "the right to intervene for the preservation of Cuban independence, the maintenance of a government adequate for the protection of life, property, and individual liberty, and for discharging the obligations with respect to Cuba imposed by the Treaty of Paris." Article VII guaranteed that Cuba would "sell or lease to the United States lands necessary for coaling or naval stations, at certain specified points, to be agreed upon with the president of the United States."

137. O'Connell, *The Irish in the Revolution and the Civil War*, p. 108.

138. *Straż*, March 1, 1902, p. 7. This was an assessment shared by many black Americans, who were further attracted by the racial climate of the island, as compared with that in Progressive-Era America. See Willard Gatewood, *Black Americans and "the White Man's Burden," 1898–1903* (Urbana: University of Illinois Press, 1975).

139. *Abend blatt*, July 20, 1898, p. 4; June 5, 1898, p. 2.

140. *Dziennik Chicagoski*, Jan. 3, 1899, p. 1.

141. Ibid., Aug. 27, 1900, p. 1.

142. *Zgoda*, July 28, 1898, p. 1.

143. *Pilot*, Nov. 19, 1898, p. 4; Dec. 3, 1898, p. 4.

144. Ibid., Dec. 31, 1898, p. 4.

5. Windows on Imperialism

1. *Catholic Citizen*, May 21, 1898, p. 4; June 18, 1898, p. 4.

2. Finley Peter Dunne, "On the Philippines," in *Mr. Dooley in Peace and in War* (Boston: Small, Maynard, 1899), pp. 43, 44.

3. Walter LaFeber, *The New Empire: An Interpretation of American Expansion, 1860–1898* (Ithaca: Cornell University Press, 1963), pp. 110, 203–209; Gavan Daws, *Shoal of Time: A History of the Hawaiian Islands* (Honolulu: University Press of Hawaii, 1968), pp. 278, 264–280; Charles Campbell, *The Transformation of American Foreign Relations, 1865–1900* (New York: Harper and Row, 1976), pp. 186–193.

4. Cited in E. Berkeley Tompkins, *Anti-Imperialism in the United States: The Great Debate, 1890–1920* (Philadelphia: University of Pennsylvania Press, 1970), p. 105.

5. Tompkins, *Anti-Imperialism in the United States*, pp. 95–119; LaFeber, *The New Empire*, pp. 362–370, 408–411.

6. Tompkins, *Anti-Imperialism in the United States*, pp. 161–182; Campbell, *The Transformation of American Foreign Relations*, pp. 302–308; Daniel Schirmer, *Republic or Empire: American Resistance to the Philippine War* (Cambridge: Schenkman Publishing, 1972), pp. 105–120.

7. V. Edmund McDevitt, *The First California's Chaplain* (Fresno: Academy Library Guild, 1956), pp. 142, 146; New York *Herald*, Oct. 30, 1899, p. 7; *New York Times*, Oct. 30, 1899, p. 3.

8. *Yiddishes tageblatt*, Jan. 24, 1899, p. 7; Jan. 19, 1899, p. 7; Feb 12, 1899, p. 4; May 12, 1899, p. 4; May 19, 1899, p. 4.

9. *Catholic Citizen*, Feb. 11, 1899, p. 4; *Kuryer Polski*, April 22, 1899, p. 4.

10. *Zgoda*, April 13, 1899, p. 8; *Yiddishes tageblatt*, Feb. 7, 1899, p. 1.

11. Cited in Stuart Creighton Miller, *"Benevolent Assimilation": The American Conquest of the Philippines, 1899–1903* (New Haven: Yale University Press, 1982), frontispiece, p. 52.

12. *Kuryer Polski*, March 27, 1899, p. 2; May 2, 1899, p. 2; *Yiddishes tageblatt*, Jan. 16, 1899, p. 4.

13. Elizabeth Gurley Flynn, *The Rebel Girl: An Autobiography* (New York: International Publishers, 1973), p. 35.

14. *Yiddishes tageblatt*, May 3, 1898, p. 1.

15. *Pilot*, Feb. 11, 1899, p. 4; Flynn, *Rebel Girl*, p. 35.

16. Milton Gordon, *Assimilation in American Life: The Role of Race, Religion, and National Origins* (New York: Oxford University Press, 1964), p. 71.

17. *Catholic Citizen*, Dec. 10, 1898, p. 4.

18. *Catholic Citizen*, Dec. 11, 1897, p. 4; March 26, 1898, p. 4.

19. *Catholic Citizen*, July 30, 1898, p. 4.

20. *Catholic Citizen*, Aug. 6, 1898, p. 4; Aug. 27, 1898, p. 4. David Noel Doyle has rather dubiously commented that Desmond "had a brilliant mind and owned the largest private library in Milwaukee. The views of lesser folk cannot have been more liberal." David Noel Doyle, *Irish Americans, Native Rights and National Empires* (New York: Arno, 1976), p. 290. But given the scientific cast of nineteenth-century racialism—or, conversely, the racialist cast of nineteenth-century science—it was largely because of his erudition, not in spite of it, that Desmond thought as he did about the relationship between "civilized Caucasians" and "barbarian dominions." On the period's scientific racialism, see esp. Thomas F. Gossett, *Race: The History of an Idea in America* (New York: Schocken, 1965); Richard Hofstadter, *Social Darwinism in American Thought* (Philadelphia: University of Pennsylvania Press, 1944); Thomas G. Dyer, *Theodore Roosevelt and the Idea of Race* (Baton Rouge: Louisiana State University Press, 1980).

21. *Pilot*, Nov. 19, 1898, p. 4. See also *Yiddishes tageblatt*, May 10, 1898, p. 1; *Abend blatt*, May 7, 1898, p. 2; July 21, 1898, p. 2; *Zgoda*, Aug. 25, 1898, p. 4.

22. *Kuryer Polski*, June 9, 1899, p. 2.

23. *Pilot*, July 30, 1898, p. 4.

24. Dale Knobel, *Paddy and the Republic: Ethnicity and Nationality in Antebellum America* (Middletown, CT: Wesleyan University Press, 1986), p. 179.

25. John Finerty, *Warpath and Bivouac: or, the Conquest of the Sioux* [1890] (Norman: University of Oklahoma Press, 1961), p. 70.

26. James Jeffrey Roche, *The V-A-S-E and other Bric-a-Brac* (Boston: Richard G. Badger, 1900), pp. 59–60.

27. Alfred P. Schultz, *Race or Mongrel* (Boston: L.C. Page, 1908), p. 276; Dyer, *Theodore Roosevelt and the Idea of Race*, pp. 143–167; Robert Singerman, "The Jew as Racial Alien: The Genetic Component of American Anti-Semitism," in David A. Gerber, ed., *Anti-Semitism in American History* (Urbana: University of Illinois Press, 1987), pp. 103–128. Adams quoted in Robert Beisner, *Twelve Against Empire: The Anti-Imperialists, 1898–1900* (Chicago: University of Chicago Press, 1968), p. 109; English commentator quoted in F. S. L. Lyons, *Culture and Anarchy in Ireland, 1890–1939* (New York: Oxford, 1979) p. 12.

28. Schultz, *Race or Mongrel*, pp. 259, 261, p. 43.

29. Emma Lazarus, *An Epistle to the Hebrews* [1900] (New York: Jewish Historical Society, 1987), pp. 9, 20.

30. Morris Winchevsky, "Mayn natsionale ani-mamin," *Gezamlte verk* (New York: Frayhayt Publishing Association, 1927), VII, pp. 221, 222.

31. Stanisław Osada, *Historia związku narodowego polskiego i rozwój ruchu narodowego polskiego w Ameryce* (Chicago: Zgoda, 1905), p. 101.

32. Schultz, *Race or Mongrel?*, p. 131.

33. John Brennan, *Erin Mor: The Story of Irish Republicanism* (San Francisco: P. M. Diers, 1892), pp. 35, 263.

34. *Irish World*, May 7, 1898, p. 1.

35. Ibid., May 21, 1898, p. 1. On the racial dimensions of turn-of-the-century diplomacy, see esp. Stuart Anderson, *Race and Rapprochement: Anglo-Saxonism and Anglo-American Relations, 1895–1904* (Rutherford, N.J.: Fairleigh Dickinson University Press, 1981). Anglo-Saxonism often merged with (or fell under the rubric of) a second body of racialist thought, "Teutonism." See esp. Reginald Horsman, *Race and Manifest Destiny: The Origins of American Racial Anglo-Saxonism* (Cambridge, Mass.: Harvard University Press, 1981), pp. 27–29, 62–77. In the political rhetoric of the 1890s, however, "Anglo-Saxon" was the dominant classification.

36. Gender was integral to the rhetoric. "There ought to be a coming together of Americans of all races and antecedents," wrote one Irish nationalist, "in opposition to the Anglicized set who would *emasculate the virility of American nationality* and reduce it to a British colony" [*Irish World*, March 5, 1898, p. 4, emphasis added.]

37. *Pilot*, June 25, 1898, p. 4.

38. *Irish World*, May 28, 1898, p. 1, 8; June 4, 1898, p. 1; *Catholic Citizen*, Jan. 21, 1899, p. 1; July 15, 1899, p. 1. (Finerty quoted June 4, 1898, p. 1.) At one such anti-alliance rally in New York, reported the *Irish World*, "Green

flags, green lights, green floats, and green banners were everywhere. But there were also little green flags bearing the harp of Erin, the lone star of the Cuban Republic, and the stars and stripes. Englishmen were not in evidence." (May 28, 1898, p. 1.) Also outspoken and consistent in their opposition to the alliance were Irish leaders like Michael Davitt, and the Irish within the labor movement of the United States. One poet, for instance, applauded the stand of Knights of Labor on the issue: "Oh, gallant Knights of Labor,/ Undaunted Sons of Toil,/ Who scorn to aid Britannia/ To pillage and despoil." See *Irish World*, Feb. 5, 1898, p. 5; March 26, 1898, pp. 1, 8; June 11, 1898, p. 1.

39. Dunne, "On the Anglo-Saxon," in *Mr. Dooley in Peace and in War*, p. 56; *Pilot*, Oct. 22, 1898, p. 4; July 8, 1899, p. 4.

40. *Pilot*, Feb. 12, 1898, p. 4.

41. *Irish World*, May 28, 1898, p. 1; June 11, 1898, p. 2.

42. Ibid., March 19, 1898, p. 4; April 30, 1898, p. 4.

43. *Pilot*, March 25, 1899, p. 1. My understanding of this dynamic of simultaneous recognition and erasure in Anglo-Saxonism derives in part from Joan Scott's discussion of the more recent, but analogous, position of "the universal figure" of the white male in American historiography. See Joan Scott, "History and Difference," in Jill K. Conway, Susan C. Bourque, and Joan W. Scott, eds., *Learning About Women: Gender, Politics, and Power* (Ann Arbor: University of Michigan Press, 1987), p. 98.

44. *Pilot*, Jan. 29, 1898, p. 1; *Irish World*, July 9, 1898, p. 1.

45. *Irish World*, Feb. 26, 1898, p. 4; April 23, 1898, p. 4.

46. *Pilot*, Feb. 4, 1899, p. 4.

47. Cited in Hofstadter, *Social Darwinism in American Thought*, p. 154. See also LaFeber, *The New Empire*, pp. 72–80.

48. Miller, *"Benevolent Assimilation"*, p. 132; Dyer, *Theodore Roosevelt and the Idea of Race*, pp. 140, 141. For the breadth of racial consensus among white imperialists and anti-imperialists, see esp. Christopher Lasch, "The Anti-Imperialist as Racist," in Thomas G. Paterson, ed., *American Imperialism and Anti-Imperialism* (New York: Crowell, 1973), pp. 110–117, and Richard E. Welch, Jr., "Twelve Anti-Imperialists and Imperialists Compared: Racism and Economic Expansion," in Paterson, *American Imperialism and Anti-Imperialism*, pp. 118–125.

49. "The March of the Flag," in Daniel J. Boorstin, ed., *An American Primer* (New York: Mentor, 1966), p. 647.

50. Marshall Everett, *Exciting Experiences in Our Wars with Spain and the Filipinos* (Chicago: Book Publishers Union, 1899), p. 383.

51. Hunt, *Ideology and U.S. Foreign Policy*, pp. 82–89; Robert W. Rydell, *All the World's a Fair: Visions of Empire at American International Expositions, 1876–1916* (Chicago: University of Chicago Press, 1984), esp. pp. 136–151.

52. Beveridge cited in Richard E. Welch, Jr., *Response to Imperialism: The United States and the Philippine-American War, 1899–1902* (Chapel Hill: University of North Carolina Press, 1979) p. 101. Compare Roche's description

of O'Reilly in Roche, *John Boyle O'Reilly*, pp. 104–105. On the nationalist aesthetics of male beauty, see esp. George Mosse, *Nationalism and Sexuality: Respectability and Abnormal Sexuality in Modern Europe* (New York: Howard Fertig, 1985), and Paul Breines, *Tough Jews: Political Fantasies and the Moral Dilemma of American Jewry* (New York: Basic Books, 1990).

53. *Catholic Citizen*, May 13, 1899, p. 1; Sept. 2, 1899, p. 6. The *Pilot* ran a regular feature on the Irish soldiers called "The Fighting Race in the Present War."

54. *Pilot*, May 21, 1898, p. 4.

55. Ibid., June 25, 1898, p. 4.

56. Ibid., April 22, 1899, p. 4. The astonishing willingness of the oppressed to serve in the causes of the oppressor was a running theme in Roche's writing. In this connection the Irish themselves were the objects of his sharpest invective. On the unfolding crisis in the Transvaal, for instance, he wrote, "There are Irishmen, God forgive them! serving today in the ranks of England against the Boers; . . . no true Irishman wishes to honor them with a monument, though all will rejoice when they qualify for it by dying as soon as possible." (*Pilot*, Nov. 18, 1899, p. 4.)

57. *Irish World*, April 2, 1898, p. 5 (emphasis added).

58. James Jeffrey Roche, *John Boyle O'Reilly: His Life, Poems, and Speeches* (New York: Cassell Publishing, 1891), pp. 142, 184–185, 341. On the *Pilot* tradition on questions of race, see also Francis Robert Walsh, "The 'Boston Pilot': A Newspaper For the Irish Immigrant, 1829–1908," (Ph.D. diss., Boston University, 1968).

59. *Yiddishes tageblatt*, Jan. 19, 1899, p. 7; Jan. 20, 1899, p. 7; Jan. 24, 1899, p. 7.

60. Lyons, *Culture and Anarchy*, pp. 5, 11; Norman Davies, *God's Playground: A History of Poland* (New York: Columbia University Press, 1982), II, pp. 124–126; *Kuryer Polski*, March 7, 1899, p. 2.

61. *Pilot*, March 18, 1899, p. 4.

62. Ibid., April 8, 1899, p. 4.

63. James Jeffrey Roche, *The Sorrows of Sap'ed: A Problem Story of the East* (New York: Harper and Bros., 1904), pp. 42–48. Like *Her Majesty the King*, *Sorrows* also contains a number of anti-imperialist one-liners as false epigrams at the head of chapters. For instance, the following lines are attributed to *The Lives of Bacalli:* "Mice are unfit for self government. That is why a cat may look at a king without blushing" [p. 89.].

64. *Straż*, April 13, 1900, p. 1; Feb. 10, 1900, p. 2.

65. *Dziennik Chicagoski*, April 7, 1899, p. 2; April 10, 1899, p. 1; April 20, 1899, p. 2. This latter piece, on the violence involved in extending the "blessings of civilization," credited an article in the *Chicago Chronicle*.

66. David A. Gerber, "Cutting Out Shylock: Elite Anti-Semitism and the Quest for Moral Order in the Mid-Nineteenth-Century American Marketplace," in Gerber, *Anti-Semitism in American History*, pp. 201–232; John

Higham, *Send These to Me: Immigrants in Urban America* (Baltimore: Johns Hopkins University Press, 1984), pp. 95–116; John Higham, *Strangers in the Land: Patterns of American Nativism, 1860–1925* (New Brunswick: Rutgers University Press, 1963), pp. 92–94. Shylock imagery was indeed rife in the United States in the 1890s, as many Populists had seized upon the Jew-as-urban-oligarch to explain the economic plight of both farmers and workers. See, for example, Ignatius Donnelly's apocalyptic *Caesar's Column* (1890).

67. *Abend blatt*, Feb. 21, 1899, p. 4.

68. *Nayer geyst*, July 1898, p. 612. Among the older generation of Yiddish immigrants, card-playing and gambling were in common usage as symbols of the degenerative influences of American culture and of Jewish youth's falling away.

69. *Naye tzayt*, May 1899, pp. 1–4.

70. *Yiddishes tageblatt*, Jan. 23, 1899, p. 4.

71. Numbers, 16.

72. *Yiddishes tageblatt*, Jan. 8, 1899, p. 4; Feb. 6, 1899, p. 4.

73. *Yiddishes tageblatt*, Feb. 23, 1899, p. 4.

74. *Yiddishes tageblatt*, Jan. 1, 1899, p. 8 [English]; May 8, 1898, p. 4; Jeanne Abrams, "Remembering the *Maine*: The Jewish Attitude toward the Spanish-American War as Reflected in the *American Israelite*," *American Jewish History*, 76:4 (June 1987), p. 453.

75. *Abend blatt*, Nov. 15, 1898, p. 4.

76. *Naye tzayt*, March 1899, pp. 8–9; April 1899, pp. 1–7, 2, 3. On the nativist strains in the anti-imperialist arguments of American labor, see Welch, *Response to Imperialism*, pp,84–88. On labor and the earlier movement for Chinese Exclusion, see Alexander Saxton, *The Indispensable Enemy: Labor and the Anti-Chinese Movement in California* (Berkeley: University of California Press, 1971).

77. For Feygenbaum's most extended treatment of the subject (and his gloss of Karl Kautsky), see "Enderungen in Amerike durkh di eroberung fun di filipinen," in *Naye tzayt*, March 1899, pp. 1–9; April 1899, pp. 6–7; *Abend blatt*, Feb. 6, 1899, p. 4. Patrick Goode, ed., *Karl Kautsky: Selected Political Writings* (London: Macmillan, 1983), pp. 74–96, esp. pp. 89–92.

78. *Yiddishes tageblatt*, Jan. 17, 1898, p. 5; Jan 18, 1898, p. 5.

79. *Abend blatt*, May 7, 1898, p. 2; July 21, 1898, p. 2.

80. Ibid., March 31, 1900, p. 9.

81. *Yiddishes tageblatt*, May 10, 1898, p. 1; March 6, 1899, p. 4.

82. *Abend blatt*, Feb. 16, 1899, p. 4.

83. *Dziennik Chicagoski*, Jan. 23, 1899, p. 2; *Zgoda*, May 5, 1898, p. 4. Indeed, although *Zgoda* was far more sympathetic to the Filipino cause, the journal's racial commentary was similar to that of the *Tageblatt*. Early on Aguinaldo was identified as "an only superficially civilized Tagal" and a "savage dictator" (*Zgoda*, Aug. 25, 1898, p. 4). Once the struggle for independence had begun, however, the journal cited a report by General King,

who estimated that the Filipinos "stand far higher than Cubans in point of education." King's assessment, noted the editor, may give pause "to those impassioned adherents of empire who see in the Filipinos only savage, bloodthirsty mutineers" (*Zgoda*, June 29, 1899, p. 8).

84. *Irish-American*, March 4, 1899, p. 4.

85. *Dziennik Chicagoski*, Oct. 3, 1900, p. 1; Oct. 4, 1900, p. 1; Aug. 24, 1900, p. 1.

86. *Abend blatt*, March 6, 1899, p. 2.

87. *Irish World*, June 26, 1897, pp. 4, 5. On Ford's anti-imperialism, see also James Paul Rodechko, *Patrick Ford and His Search for America: A Case Study in Irish-American Journalism* (New York: Arno, 1976), pp. 177–179.

88. *Zgoda*, April 7, 1898, p. 4.

89. *Kuryer Polski*, Sept. 7, 1898, p. 2.

90. *Abend blatt*, Feb. 25, 1899, p. 2.

91. One inevitable shadow of this kind of commentary-by-parallel was a keen concern for the implications of Asian and Pacific struggles for the various Old World powers. The Irish tended to favor any policy which collided with perceived British interests, and identified Russia as "our firmest and sincerest friend in the day when we needed friends" (*Irish World*, May 7, 1898, p. 4); Jewish commentators, on the contrary, argued that only the United States and England together could thwart Russian designs in Asia (*Naye tzayt*, Feb. 1899, p. 47); and Polish commentators kept an anxious eye on both Russia and Germany.

The use of parallels for polemical purposes (the Philippines-as-Ireland, China-as-Poland) was ever subject to adjustment in view of the actual presence and interests of Germany, Russia, and England in the Pacific basin. Hence many Irish writers winced at the prospect of Hawaiian annexation, but ultimately excused it on the grounds that U.S. expansionism would keep the islands out of England's domain (see for example, *Irish World*, March 12, 1898, p. 1; *Pilot*, Feb. 5, 1898, p. 6; July 16, 1898, p. 4). *Kuryer Polski* advanced a similar argument for the Philippines, adding Russia and Germany to the list of villainous powers which stood to gain by any restraint on the part of the United States (July 5, 1899, p. 2). Significantly, when *Kuryer Polski* was in its anti-imperialist phase, it noted that German consul Muenster had been the first to congratulate the United States on the "profitable" terms of the Treaty of Paris (Nov. 29, 1898, p. 1). Once hostilities had erupted in Manila, however, and after the journal had adopted an expansionist position, it loudly announced in a page-one headline, "Germany Helps the Insurgents" (Feb. 8, 1899, p. 1). The following year the *Irish World* greeted the signing of the Hay-Pauncefote Treaty regarding a Nicaraguan canal with the headline, "U.S. Surrender to England" (Feb. 17, 1900, p. 1).

92. Stephen Wlodarski, *Origin and Growth of the Polish National Catholic Church* (Scranton: PNCC, 1973), pp. 78, 190.

93. *Pilot*, Oct. 20, 1900, p. 1; May 13, 1899, p. 4.

94. *Zgoda*, Feb. 23, 1899, p. 1.

95. Ibid., March 2, 1899, p. 8.

96. *Dziennik Chicagoski*, Nov. 3, 1900, p. 4; Jan. 6, 1899, p. 1; Jan. 11, 1899, p. 2.

97. *Irish World*, Feb. 11, 1899, p. 4; Nov. 3, 1900, p. 4.

98. *Abend blatt*, Feb. 7, 1899, p. 4; Feb. 8, 1899, p. 4; Feb. 11, 1899, p. 2.

99. *Naye tzayt*, March 1899, p. 17.

100. *Forverts*, Nov. 8, 1899, p. 4.

101. For a sample of the rivalrous in-fighting between the two wings of the Yiddish left, see the *Forverts*, May 3, 1899, p. 2.

102. See for example *Yiddishes tageblatt*, April 28, 1899, p. 1; May 2, 1899, p. 1. On Otis's "sublime optimism," see Miller, *"Benevolent Assimilation"*, pp. 69–102; Schirmer, *Republic or Empire*, pp. 151, 172, 184.

103. *Zgoda*, Feb. 16, 1899, p. 8; Feb. 23, 1899, p. 8; March 30, 1899, p. 8; April 6, 1899, p. 8; June 8, 1899, p. 8; *Dziennik Chicagoski*, Feb. 14, 1899, p. 2; March 18, 1899, p. 1; Feb. 16, 1899, p. 1; *Forverts*, Feb. 12, 1899, p. 1; March 12, 1899, p. 1; March 26, 1899, p. 1; May 1, 1899, p. 4; May 5, 1899, p. 1.

104. *Pilot*, April 8, 1899, p. 4; May 20, 1899, p. 4; July 8, 1899, p. 4.

105. *Zgoda*, March 9, 1899, p. 8; June 22, 1899, p. 8.

106. *Irish World*, April 20, 1901, p. 4; Feb. 2, 1901, p. 4.

107. Ibid., June 23, 1900, p. 4.

108. Ibid., Dec. 28, 1901, p. 4.

109. Ibid., May 3, 1902, pp. 1,4; May 10, 1904, p. 4. On General Smith, the atrocities alleged under his command, and the controversy in the United States, see Miller, *"Benevolent Assimilation"*, pp. 94–95, 227–238; Daniel Schirmer, *Republic or Empire*, pp. 232–240.

110. *Pilot*, Oct. 1, 1898, p. 4.

111. David Emmons, *The Butte Irish: Class and Ethnicity in an American Mining Town, 1875–1925* (Urbana: University of Illinois Press, 1989), p. 331; *Irish World*, April 22, 1899, p. 10.

112. *Congressional Record*, Feb. 6, 1899, p. 1493. On "patriotism," "Americanism," and the dangers of dissent in this period, see Welch, *Response to Imperialism*, pp. 43–57.

113. *Pilot*, Feb. 11, 1899, p. 4.

114. Stanisław Osada, *Historia Z.N.P.* , p. 490.

115. *Zgoda*, Aug. 11, 1898, p. 1.

116. *Pilot*, June 25, 1898, p. 4; Aug.26, 1899, p. 4.

117. James McGurrin, *Bourke Cockran: A Free Lance in American Politics* (New York: Charles Scribner's Sons, 1948), pp. 210, 189–212; *Catholic Citizen*, Jan. 28, 1899, p. 1.

118. *Dziennik Chicagoski*, April 7, 1899, p. 2. "The starry flag must be a sign of freedom," Michael Kruszka similarly commented, "not annexation and violence" (*Kuryer Polski*, Dec. 6, 1898, p. 2).

119. *Irish World*, Feb. 19, 1898, p. 5; *Pilot*, Aug. 26, 1899, p. 4.

120. *Straż*, April 7, 1900, p. 1.

121. *Pilot*, July 30, 1898, p. 4.

122. *Dziennik Chicagoski*, Feb. 27, 1899, p. 1.

123. *Irish World*, Feb. 18, 1899, p. 4.

124. Commented Adams in his *Autobiography*, "I believe in the equality of men before the law; but social equality, whether for man or child, is altogether another thing." Beisner, *Twelve Against Empire*, p. 109; Miller, *"Benevolent Assimilation,"* p. 120.

125. Schirmer, *Republic or Empire*, p. 17.

126. *Pilot*, Nov. 26, 1898, p. 1. Doyle, *Irish Americans, Native Rights, and National Empires*, pp. 268–269; Tompkins, *Anti-Imperialism in the United States*, pp. 127–128.

127. *Abend blatt*, Sept. 6, 1899, p. 4. For instances of immigrant support of the League, see the *Pilot*, Aug. 18, 1900, p. 1; Oct. 27, 1900, p. 1; *Irish World*, Aug. 19, 1899, p. 1; Aug. 26, 1899, p. 1; *Catholic Citizen*, Jan. 21, 1899, p. 8; *Kuryer Polski*, Nov. 21, 1898, p. 1; Jan. 10, 1899, p. 1; *Dziennik Chicagoski*, Oct. 19, 1900, p. 2; Oct. 20, 1900, p. 2; Oct. 27, 1900, p. 6; Nov. 2, 1900, p. 2.

128. Carl I. Meyerhuber, "U.S. Imperialism and Ethnic Journalism: The New Manifest Destiny as Reflected in Boston's Irish-American Press, 1890–1900," *Eire/Ireland*, 9:4 (1974), pp. 22, 27.

129. *Pilot*, Feb. 4, 1899, p. 4; Dec. 24, 1898, p. 4. Although it was not a conspicuous issue in the Yiddish press, Jewish anti-imperialists may have been made similarly uneasy by the prominence in the movement of William Jennings Bryan, who had freely traded on the image of the Jew-as-Shylock in his 1896 assaults on "Rothschild" and the gold standard. Higham, *Strangers in the Land*, pp. 92–94; Higham, *Send These to Me*, pp. 110–111, 95–116; Henry Feingold, *Zion in America* (New York: Twayne, 1974), p. 146; Nathaniel Weyl, *The Jew in American Politics* (New Rochelle, NY: Arlington House, 1968), pp. 68–72.

130. *Abend blatt*, Nov. 30, 1899, p. 4.

131. Winslow cited in Schirmer, *Republic or Empire*, p. 18.

132. *Irish World*, Nov. 19, 1898, p. 4; Feb. 17, 1900, p. 4.

133. Quoted in Miller, *"Benevolent Assimilation"*, pp. 140–141; Beisner, *Twelve Against Empire*, p. 192.

134. Quoted in Tompkins, *Anti-Imperialism in the United States*, p. 234.

135. Paul Kleppner, *The Cross of Culture: A Social Analysis of Midwestern Politics, 1850–1900* (New York: The Free Press, 1970), esp. pp. 316–368.

136. *Kuryer Polski*, Oct. 22, 1900, p. 2; Nov. 2, 1900, p. 2; Oct. 13, 1900, p. 4; Nov. 3, 1900, p. 2; Zygmunt Miłkowski, *Opowiadanie z wędrówki po koloniach polskich w Ameryce północnej* (Paris: Goniec Polski, 1903), pp. 199–201. Among the Polish journals to come out for McKinley were *Kuryer Polski*, *Dziennik Narodowy*, *Polak w Ameryce*, *Echo*, *Gazeta Polska*, *Kuryer Tygodniowy*, *Gazeta Wisconsinska*, *Kuryer Nowoyorski*, *Wielkopolanin*, and *Goniec Polski*.

137. *Catholic Citizen*, May 27, 1899, p. 1; Doyle, *Irish Americans, Native Rights and National Empires*, pp. 270–271.

138. *Irish World*, April 28, 1900, p. 4; Oct. 20, 1900, p. 5. Elsewhere Ford explained that "The Keynote of President McKinley's Policy Is Subservience to England" (April 22, 1899, p. 10). Nor was Ford alone in this Celto-centric view of the stakes of the election. The Democratic Party in Iowa installed a platform plank denouncing the "British cabal" in control of the McKinley Administration (*Irish World*, Aug. 26, 1899, p. 4).

139. *Dziennik Chicagoski*, Nov. 5, 1900, p. 1; *Kuryer Polski*, Nov. 7, 1900, p. 2.

140. Tompkins, *Anti-Imperialism in the United States*, pp. 235, 214–235; Schirmer, *Republic or Empire*, pp. 220–221.

141. *Pilot*, Nov. 10, 1900, p. 1.

142. *Irish World*, Nov. 17, 1900, p. 1.

143. Quoted in Doyle, *Irish Americans, Native Rights and National Empires*, p. 271.

144. *Irish World*, June 23, 1900, p. 4; Emmons, *The Butte Irish*, p. 331.

145. Flynn, *The Rebel Girl*, p. 35; *Catholic Citizen*, March 25, 1899, p. 1; *New York Times*, May 2, 1899, p. 3.

146. Letter originally published in *Gazeta Pittsburghska*, reprinted in *Kuryer Polski*, May 8, 1899, p. 2.

Conclusion

1. *With Fire and Sword, The Deluge,* and *Pan Wolodyjowski*, Henryk Sienkiewicz's chivalric romance of seventeenth-century Poland's travails and triumphs. The Trilogy was written, in Sienkiewicz's own words, "to uplift the hearts of my countrymen."

2. Stefan Korbonski, *Warsaw in Exile* (New York: Frederick A. Praeger, 1966), p. 64.

3. *New York Times*, March 17, 1982, p. B3.

4. Ibid., Jan. 26, 1948, p. 11.

5. Haim Chertok, *Stealing Home: Israel Bound and Rebound* (New York: Fordham University Press, 1988), p. 9.

6. Philip Roth, *The Counterlife* (New York: Penguin Books, 1988), p. 165.

7. Golda Meir, *My Life* (New York: G.P. Putnam's Sons, 1975), p. 214; *New York Times*, March 17, 1977, p. A9.

8. *New York Times*, Aug. 24, 1980, p. 22. The *Times*, of course, has had no particular stake in perpetuating diasporic outlooks or in popularizing nationalist appeals, which is why I have drawn upon that journal here rather than upon specifically ethnic journals like the *Forverts* or the *Irish Echo*. As we move into the twentieth century, we are looking at traces of the diasporic imagination which survive despite the more pervasive current of Americanization. Reliance upon ethnic journals would magnify those traces considerably.

9. Melvin I. Urofsky, *We Are One! American Jewry and Israel* (Garden City, NY: Anchor/Doubleday, 1978); Charles Silberman, *A Certain People: American Jews and Their Lives Today* (New York: Summit Books, 1985); J. Bowyer Bell, *The Secret Army: The IRA, 1916–1979* (Cambridge: MIT Press, 1980); J. Bowyer Bell, *The Gun in Politics: An Analysis of Irish Political Conflict, 1916–1986* (New Brunswick, NJ: Transaction Publishers, 1987); Donald Pienkos, *For Your Freedom Through Ours: Polish-American Efforts on Poland's Behalf, 1863–1991* (Boulder, CO: East European Monographs, 1991).

10. Herbert J. Gans, "Symbolic Ethnicity: The Future of Ethnic Groups and Cultures in America," *Ethnic and Racial Studies*, 2:1 (Jan. 1979), p. 8; Mary C. Waters, *Ethnic Options: Choosing Identities in America* (Berkeley: University of California Press, 1990), pp. 1–15, 164. For a useful discussion of the "symbolic ethnicity" model and some alternatives, see J. Milton Yinger, "Toward a Theory of Assimilation and Dissimilation," *Ethnic and Racial Studies* 4:3 (July 1981), pp. 249–264.

11. Gans, "Symbolic Ethnicity," pp. 8–10. This interpretation has been challenged by writers on the Jewish experience. On the Six Day War as energizing Jewish identification, see Silberman, *A Certain People*, pp. 159–220; Marshall Sklare, *America's Jews* (New York: Random House, 1971), pp. 216–222.

12. Gans, "Symbolic Ethnicity," p. 13.

13. The *New York Times*, Dec. 2, 1971, pp. 49, 84, catalogued the groups in the New York area. The list features the National Association for Irish Freedom, the American Committee for Ulster Justice, the Irish Republican Clubs of the United States, and Noraid. Waters, *Ethnic Options*, pp. 83–84, does note the influence of the Solidarity movement in heightening the salience of ethnic Polishness in the United States; and in an exchange on the possible conflict between "Irish" and "American" identifications, one of her informants cited U.S. anti-terrorist intervention against the IRA as his worst-case scenario: "Although I do not like the IRA, I guess somehow I do identify with the IRA" [pp. 55–56]. In general, however, Waters eschews historical explanations of the link between national histories and American ethnic identities.

14. Ben Hecht, *A Guide for the Bedevilled* (Garden City, NY: Garden City Publishing Co., 1945), p. 273.

15. Ibid., p. 43.

16. Cited in John B. Duff, "The Versailles Treaty and the Irish-Americans," *Journal of American History*, 55:3 (December, 1968), p. 586. See also Alan J. Ward, *Ireland and Anglo-American Relations, 1899–1921* (London: Weidenfeld and Nicolson, 1969), pp. 170–171.

17. Nor, ultimately, were colonized peoples and active nationalists the only ones whose passions were stirred by the Wilsonian promise of self-determination for small nations. After a visit to Ireland, George Creel, of Wilson's information agency, turned his considerable skills as a propagandist

to the Irish Question and the answer implicit in Wilson's rhetoric. George Creel, *Ireland's Fight for Freedom: Setting Forth the High Lights of Irish History* (New York: Harper and Brothers, 1919).

18. Louis Gerson, *Woodrow Wilson and the Rebirth of Poland, 1914–920: A Study in the Influence on American Foreign Policy of Minority Groups of Foreign Origin* (Hamden, CT: Archon Books, 1972), p. 77.

19. This basic division was added to the many other criss-crossing factionalisms in Polish-America: the continuing rivalries among religionists and secularists; emergent tensions between supporters of Ignacy Paderewski and of Józef Piłsudski for the leadership of the newly envisioned independent Poland; and the attendant conflict among monarchists, socialists, and liberals. Gerson, *Woodrow Wilson and the Rebirth of Poland*, pp. 46–54.

20. *Yiddishes tageblatt* cited in Melvin Urofsky, *American Zionism from Herzl to the Holocaust* (Garden City, NY: Anchor, 1975), p. 187; Ronald Sanders, *The Downtown Jews: Portraits of an Immigrant Generation* (New York: Dover, 1969), p. 429; James K. McGuire, *The King, the Kaiser, and Irish Freedom* (New York: Devin-Adair, 1915), p. 285. McGuire also put forth one of the sharpest articulations of the persistent ideology of "exile" in Irish-America: "The true Irish exiles, transplanted to lands of freedom, long to see Ireland a free nation . . . Make of Eire a mere West British dependency and you have destroyed the soul and spirit of the movement which has been inspired by the love and faith of the emigrants" (pp. 126–129).

21. David Emmons, *The Butte Irish: Class and Ethnicity in an American Mining Town, 1875–1925* (Urbana: University of Illinois Press, 1989), pp. 347–348; T. St. John Gaffney, *Breaking the Silence* (New York: Horace Liveright, 1930), pp. 190–195; Francis Carroll, *American Opinion and the Irish Question, 1910–1923* (Dublin: Gill and Macmillan, 1978), pp. 66–67, 103, 107.

22. Collected in Thomas G. Paterson, ed., *Major Problems in American Foreign Policy* (Lexington, MA: D.C. Heath, 1978), II, p. 65. On Wilson and the Polish cause, see esp. Gerson, *Woodrow Wilson and the Rebirth of Poland*, pp. 55–85. Woodrow Wilson, *A History of the American People*, cited p. 55; Wilson's "peace without victory" speech, p. 71. For a summary of the same argument, see Louis Gerson, "The Poles," in Joseph O'Grady, ed., *The Immigrant's Influence on Wilson's Peace Policies* (Lexington: University Press of Kentucky, 1967), pp. 272–286.

23. Donald Pienkos, *PNA: A Centennial History of the Polish National Alliance of the United States of North America* (Boulder: East European Monographs, 1984), pp. 111–113, 99–118; Donald Pienkos, *One Hundred Years Young: A History of the Polish Falcons of America, 1887–1987* (Boulder: East European Monographs, 1987), pp. 95–100; Joseph T. Hapak, "The Polish Military Commission, 1917–1919" *Polish American Studies*, 38:2 (Fall, 1981), pp. 26–38; Joseph T. Hapak, "Selective Service and Polish Army Recruitment During World War One," *American Ethnic History*, 10:4 (Summer

1991), pp. 53, 55; John Bukowczyk, *And My Children Did Not Know Me: A History of Polish-Americans* (Bloomington: Indiana University Press, 1987), p. 49.

Some native Americans were not entirely comfortable with the reactionary shades of that faction in Polonian politics which did favor the Allies, notwithstanding the Poles' evident "loyalty." Reporting from a Polish-American convention in Detroit in 1918, for example, John Dewey noted the political power of Polish nationalist culture and lamented where it seemed to be leading many Polish-Americans. "Ignorance" combined with an "emotional knowledge of the past glories of historic Poland," he warned, made Poles "readier material" for subjection to monarchistic nationalism. Cited in Louis Gerson, *Woodrow Wilson and the Rebirth of Poland*, p. 91. Gerson has reprinted Dewey's entire report from the Detroit convention in an Appendix.

24. Morton Tenzer, "The Jews," in O'Grady, *Immigrant's Influence*, pp. 294, 299. On the vicissitudes of Yiddish opinion, see Urofsky, *American Zionism*, pp. 183–230; Henry Feingold, *Zion in America* (New York: Twayne, 1974), pp. 248–257. The Balfour Declaration is reprinted in Paul R. Mendes-Flohr and Jehuda Reinharz, eds., *The Jew in the Modern World* (New York: Oxford University Press, 1980), p. 458.

25. Meir, *My Life*, pp. 56–57; File on Benjamin Bronstein, Jewish War Veterans' Archives, Washington, D.C.

26. Carroll, *American Opinion and the Irish Question*, pp. 97–98, 106, 184; William M. Leary, Jr., "Woodrow Wilson, Irish Americans, and the Election of 1916," *Journal of American History*, 54:1 (June, 1967), p. 64.

27. Carroll, *American Opinion and the Irish Question*, p. 61; Charles Callan Tansill, *America and the Fight for Irish Freedom, 1866–1922* (New York: Devin-Adair, 1957), p. 196.

28. Carroll, *American Opinion and the Irish Question*, pp. 71, 85–86; Leary, "Woodrow Wilson, Irish Americans, and the Election of 1916," p. 59. Among the principal objectives of the Friends of Irish Freedom was "To maintain America's position as the champion of human freedom, by preserving American ideals of liberty," and "To uphold the right of the Republic of Ireland to international recognition, and to inform the American people to the end that the Government of the United States, applying American principles, shall accord full official recognition to the elected Government of the Republic of Ireland." Friends of Irish Freedom, *Constitution and State, Local and Branch By-Laws of the Friends of Irish Freedom* (New York: Diarmuid Lynch, 1920), p. 7.

29. Emmons, *The Butte Irish*, p. 346.

30. *New York Times*, Dec. 27, 1921, p. 3; Carroll, *American Opinion and the Irish Question*, pp. 63–69; Thomas H. Mahony, *Similarities Between the American and Irish Revolutions* (New York: Friendly Sons of St. Patrick, 1921). Among the "similarities" which Mahony noted was a marked reliance upon guerrilla tactics in both revolutions. Mahony endorsed IRA tactics by citing

Woodrow Wilson's own description of the American colonists' taste for terror: "they could make every wayside covert a sort of ambush, every narrow bridge a trap in which to catch [the British] at disadvantage." [p. 13, citing Wilson's *History of the American People*.]

31. Carroll, *American Opinion and the Irish Question*, pp. 51–53, 126, 149–151; Kerby Miller, *Emigrants and Exiles: Ireland and the Irish Exodus to North America* (New York: Oxford, 1975), pp. 542–543; *New York Times*, March 28, 1921, p. 1.

32. Joseph O'Grady, "The Irish," in O'Grady, ed., *Immigrant's Influence*, pp. 56–84; Carroll, *American Opinion and the Irish Question*, p. 114.

33. Carroll, *American Opinion and the Irish Question*, pp. 124–125, 137; Ward, *Ireland and Anglo-American Relations*, pp. 170–171, 176; Tansell, *America and the Fight for Irish Freedom*, p. 306.

34. Article X is reprinted in Paterson, *Major Problems in American Foreign Policy*, II, p. 66. George Creel, *Rebel at Large: Recollections of 50 Crowded Years* (New York: G.P. Putnam's Sons, 1947), pp. 218–222; George Creel, *The War, the World and Wilson* (New York: Harper and Brothers, 1920), pp. 315–317, 331; Carroll, *American Opinion and the Irish Question*, p. 147–148. For descriptions of anti-League rallies in Irish-America, see for example, *New York Times*, Jan. 6, 1919, p. 6; March 17, 1919, p. 2.

35. Carroll, *American Opinion and the Irish Question*, p. 131; Bonsal cited in Gerson, *Woodrow Wilson and the Rebirth of Poland*, p. 124; Tenzer, "The Jews," in O'Grady, *Immigrant's Influence*, pp. 309–317; Chaim Weizmann, *Trial and Error* (New York: Harper and Bros., 1949), pp. 243–245. Jews ultimately found two distinct gains in Wilson's peace policies: Versailles seemed at once to lay the foundation for the (re)building of a Jewish Palestine and to secure minority rights for Jews in Europe.

36. Tansill, *America and the Fight for Irish Freedom*, p. 215; Carroll, *American Opinion and the Irish Question*, p. 143.

37. Hoping to capitalize upon Irish-American disillusionment with Wilson's wartime policies, one Republican politician asked an Irish assembly in Springfield, Massachusetts, "What did England get from the war?" The answer: "Everything in sight as usual." J. Joseph Huthmacher, *Massachusetts People and Politics, 1919–1933* (Cambridge, Mass.: Harvard University Press, 1959), pp. 37, 23–26, 30–31. In his study of Wilson's reelection in 1916, William Leary, Jr. argues that the *perception* of Irish abandonment of the Democratic party exceeded the reality. "Even the most vociferous of the Irish-American newspapers," he notes, "was unable to work up any enthusiasm for [Charles Evans Hughes]." While the disaffection was very real, Leary argues, it did not override economics and Hughes' own weaknesses in determining electoral behavior: "Wilson did not receive [Irish-Americans'] vocal support, but he did receive their votes." Leary, "Woodrow Wilson, Irish-Americans, and the Election of 1916," pp. 71, 72. The PEC ad ran in the *New York Times*, Nov. 1, 1992, p. E17.

38. *New York Times*, October 9, 1976, p. 1; Oct. 10, 1976, p. 42; Oct. 11, 1976, p. 52; *Chicago Tribune*, Oct. 9, 1976, pp. 1, 2; Bukowczyk, *And My Children Did Not Know Me*, pp. 132–133.

In its convergence with generalized American animosity against the Soviet Union, Polish nationalism represents perhaps a special case for the extent of its "assimilation" into American politics. Few themes in American political life have approached the pitch of anti-Communism as it was enunciated and practiced by both Polonian activists and American officials for the better part of this century. As early as 1919 many State Department officials had identified Poland as a useful buffer against newly revolutionized Russia—a view which blended exceptionally well with the variations of Polish messianism which had characterized nationalist expression since the romantic era of Mickiewicz.

39. *New York Times*, Aug. 11, 1971, p. 3; Aug. 15, 1971, p. 10; Meir, *My Life*, pp. 388–389.

40. Norman Podhoretz, *Breaking Ranks: A Political Memoir* (New York: Harper and Row, 1979), p. 335; Norman Podhoretz, "Now, Instant Zionism," *New York Times Magazine*, Feb. 3, 1974. This theme is central to Silberman, *A Certain People*.

41. Bell, *The Gun in Politics*, p. 32.

42. *New York Times*, April 3, 1939, p. 6; Sept. 10, 1939, p. 31; Sept. 14, 1939, p. 23; Pienkos, *PNA*, p. 152; Pienkos, *One Hundred Years Young*, p. 140.

43. Meir, *My Life*, pp. 214, 235; Melvin I. Urofsky, *We Are One! American Jewry and Israel* (Garden City, NY: Anchor/ Doubleday, 1978), p. 183; Silberman, *A Certain People*, pp. 185, 197.

44. Bell, *Secret Army*, p. 438; *Buffalo Evening News*, Feb. 5, 1982, p. B4.

45. Bukowczyk, *And My Children Did Not Know Me*, p. 96; Jewish Welfare Board statistics, cited in the text of "Perspectives on Patriotism," Jewish War Veterans Museum, Washington, D.C. Donald Pienkos notes that efforts to raise a Polish regiment "failed miserably" during World War II, in part because of Polonian enmity toward both Hitler and Stalin, and in part because the low percentage of foreign-born, military-age Polish men was quite low in comparison to the World War I era. Polonian participation in the war was forbidden until the United States itself entered the war. Pienkos, *PNA*, pp. 158–161; Pienkos, *One Hundred Years Young*, pp. 137–142, 140.

On the American Committee for a Jewish Army, see Urofsky, *We Are One!*, pp. 75–81. The Committee's close connections to Israel's Irgun Zvai Le'umi (National Military Organization) was a matter of some concern to many Zionists, who, even when they supported the organization of a Jewish unit in principle, resented Irgun's presumption in broadly agitating and organizing on behalf of "the Jews." See, for example, the ambivalent editorials in *The Reconstructionist*, Jan. 23, 1942, p. 5; Feb. 6, 1942, pp. 5–6. Urofsky concludes that Irgun accomplished little in this venture beyond factionalizing America's Zionist community, though it had "tapped a vein of eagerness in American Jewry."

46. Urofsky, *We Are One!*, pp. 180–183; Meir, *My Life*, p. 360; Alan M. Dershowitz, *Chutzpah* (Boston: Little, Brown, 1991), p. 80. The American Veterans of Israel continue each year to commemorate the eighty American and Canadian soldiers who died in Israel's War of Independence. For program notes on several of these memorial services at West Point, see the file on Harry Aizenstat at the Jewish War Veterans' Archives, Washington, D.C. One such sheet, from the ceremony of May 4, 1986, contains the roll of the dead, in English and Yiddish.

47. *New York Times*, Dec. 2, 1971, pp. 49, 84.

48. Maurice N. Hennessy, *I'll Come Back in the Springtime: John F. Kennedy and the Irish* (New York: Ives, Washburn, 1966), pp. 1, 6–7.

49. Hennessy, *I'll Come Back in the Spring*, p. 68.

50. *New York Times*, June 28, 1963 pp. 1, 3; June 29, 1963, pp. 1,3.

51. Ibid.

52. Stanisław Szwajkart, *Dzieje Polski dla użytku szkół polskich w Ameryce* (Chicago: Spółka Nakładowa Wydawnictwa Polskiego, 1906); Helen Fine, *Behold, the Land!* (New York: Union of American Hebrew Congregations, 1968, 1977), p. v.

53. A small, linear chain consisting of a finger ring, ten rosary beads, and a cross. Its peculiar design was meant to conceal its religious significance at a time when English law proscribed the practice of Catholicism in Ireland.

54. Korbonski, *Warsaw in Exile*, p. 70.

55. Edward J. Piszek, "Polish Literature in America: Publishing the New Translation of 'The Trilogy' of Henryk Sienkiewicz" (Warrington, PA: The Copernicus Society of America, 1990), pp. 3, 14.

56. Ibid., p. 7.

57. As, indeed, does the response in some quarters: having generated significant opposition by his unorthodox treatment of this national literary treasure, Kuniczak was subjected to "a short-lived campaign of personal abuse," including a death-threat. Ibid., pp. 10–11.

58. Henryk Sienkiewicz, *With Fire and Sword* (New York: Copernicus Society of America with Hippocrene Books, 1991), p. 209.

59. Ibid., p. 348.

60. Ibid., p. 356.

61. Chertok, *Stealing Home*, pp. 8, 64–65. On the ambiguous position of American Zionists once the state had been established, see esp. Melvin I. Urofsky, "A Cause in Search of Itself: American Zionism After the State" in Nathan M. Kaganoff, ed., *Solidarity and Kinship: Essays on American Zionism* (Waltham, Mass.: American Jewish Historical Society, 1980), pp. 101–113, 107. In response to a charge of Zionist fanaticism, one Zionist in Philip Roth's *Counterlife* rails, "What is fanatical is the Jew who never learns! The Jew oblivious to the Jewish state and the Jewish land and the survival of the Jewish people! *That* is the fanatic—fanatically ignorant, fanatically self-deluded, fanatically full of shame!" Roth, *The Counterlife*, pp. 114–115.

NOTES TO PAGES 235-237

62. The law grants Israeli citizenship to any Jew who immigrates.

63. Cited in Dershowitz, Chutzpah, p. 7.

64. Meir Kahane, *Time to Go Home* (Los Angeles: Nash Publishing, 1972), pp. 100–101, 260, 279; Meir Kahane, *Our Challenge* (Radnor, PA: Chilton Book, 1974), p. 113; Meir Kahane, *Uncomfortable Questions for Comfortable Jews* (Secaucus, NJ: Lyle Stuart, 1987), p. 324.

65. Chertok, *Stealing Home*, p. 64; Janowitz cited in Saul Bellow, *To Jerusalem and Back: A Personal Account* (New York: The Viking Press, 1976), p. 166.

66. "There are relatively few Jews," Pogrebin ventures, "who do not identify as Zionists." Letty Cottin Pogrebin, *Deborah, Golda, and Me: Being Female and Jewish in America* (New York: Crown Publishers, 1991), pp. 213, 155; Urofsky, *We Are One!*, p. 392. "We Are One" is the slogan of the United Jewish Appeal.

67. David Vital, *The Future of the Jews: A People at the Crossroads?* (Cambridge, Mass.: Harvard University Press, 1990), p. 136.

68. "In this disorderly century," laments Saul Bellow, "refugees have fled from many countries. In India, in Africa, in Europe, millions of human beings have been put to flight, transported, enslaved, stampeded over the borders, left to starve, but only the case of the Palestinians is held permanently open." Bellow, *To Jerusalem and Back*, p. 135.

69. Dershowitz, *Chutzpah*, pp. 234–235; Roth, *The Counterlife*, p. 180.

70. Paul Breines, *Tough Jews: Political Fantasies and the Moral Dilemma of American Jewry* (New York: Basic Books, 1990), p. 73. Breines recently reiterated this position in a rejoinder to Alan Dershowitz's *Chutzpah*. Citing Dershowitz's claims that the world owes Israel ("which was built on the ashes of Auschwitz") a "special understanding," Breines declared, "*Chutzpah*'s real chutzpah . . . [is] its use of Auschwitz to provide an impregnable moral basis for Israel's brutalization of Palestinians." *Washington Post* "Book World," May 19, 1991, p. 11.

Like Breines, Irena Klepfisz, an American immigrant born in Poland during the war, decries this political calculus and worries over its moral ramifications for both the Jewish state and the state of Judaism: "I was always taught: never use Holocaust terminology to describe other situations; *never* in relation to Israel's own actions. Never, that is, unless you want to support Israel, justify its policies; then always bring up the Holocaust, point to what we have endured, claim that we will never again endure it." Irena Klepfisz, *Dreams of an Insomniac: Jewish Feminist Essays, Speeches and Diatribes* (Portland: The Eighth Mountain Press, 1990), pp. 129–131.

71. Breines, *Tough Jews*, p. 19.

72. Ibid., p. xiv.

73. Melanie Kaye/Kantrowitz, *My Jewish Face and Other Stories* (San Francisco: Spinster-Aunt Lute, 1990), p. 228.

74. Kaye/Kantrowitz, *My Jewish Face*, 231.

75. Pogrebin, *Deborah, Golda, and Me*, p. 147.

76. Roth, *The Counterlife*, pp. 166–167.

77. Ibid., p. 125.

78. Ibid., pp. 124–125.

79. Ibid., pp. 259, 260.

80. Philip Roth, *Operation Shylock: A Confession* (New York: Simon and Schuster, 1993), p. 158.

81. Ibid., p. 81.

82. Ibid., p. 193.

83. Ibid., p. 388.

84. Kaye/Kantrowitz, *My Jewish Face*, p. 172.

85. Korbonski, *Warsaw in Exile*, pp. 34–35.

86. Lawrence Fuchs, *The American Kaleidoscope: Race, Ethnicity, and the Civic Culture* (Hanover: Wesleyan University Press, 1990), p. 35; William V. Shannon, *The American Irish: A Political and Social Portrait* (New York: Collier, 1963), pp. 406–413.

87. Sienkiewicz, *With Fire and Sword*, p. 1006; Susan Jeffords, *The Remasculinization of America: Gender and the Vietnam War* (Bloomington: Indiana University Press, 1989). For a slightly earlier version of the "Rambowitz" genre, see Harold U. Ribalow, *Fighting Heroes of Israel* (New York: Signet, 1967). J. Bowyer Bell has likewise discovered a significant subgenre of IRA thrillers whose characters, in Bell's own unfortunate terminology, fall generally into the categories "hard men," "soft men," and "good girls." Bell, *The Gun in Politics*, pp. 330–335.

88. As defined by Milton Gordon: the sense of group membership or peoplehood as it shifts from the culture of origin to the new host culture. See *Assimilation in American Life: The Role of Race, Religion, and National Origins,* (New York: Oxford, 1964), pp. 70–71.

89. I am especially indebted to Lee Kolm and Gail Bederman for their articulation of this tacit gender differential in the prospect of assimilation.

90. *New York Times*, March 18, 1983, p. B2.

Index